Faiths on Display

Faiths on Display

Religion, Tourism, and the Chinese State

Edited by
Tim Oakes and Donald S. Sutton

ROWMAN & LITTLEFIELD PUBLISHERS, INC.
Lanham • Boulder • New York • Toronto • Plymouth, UK

Published by Rowman & Littlefield Publishers, Inc.
A wholly owned subsidiary of The Rowman & Littlefield Publishing Group, Inc.
4501 Forbes Boulevard, Suite 200, Lanham, Maryland 20706
http://www.rowmanlittlefield.com

Estover Road, Plymouth PL6 7PY, United Kingdom

British Library Cataloguing in Publication Information Available

Library of Congress Cataloging-in-Publication Data

Faiths on display : religion, tourism, and the Chinese state / edited by Tim Oakes and
Donald S. Sutton.
   p. cm.
 Includes bibliographical references and index.
 ISBN 978-1-4422-0506-2 (cloth : alk. paper) — ISBN 978-1-4422-0508-6 (electronic)
 1. China—Religion—20th century. 2. China—Religion—21st century. 3. China—
Religious life and customs. 4. Religion and state—China. 5. Tourism—China. 6.
Tourism—Religious aspects. I. Oakes, Tim. II. Sutton, Donald S.
 BL1803.F35 2010
 203'.5095109051—dc22

2010023686

Contents

Figures

Introduction

Tim Oakes and Donald S. Sutton

The hotel lobby is the inverted image of the house of God.

—Siegfried Kracauer, *The Mass Ornament*, 1927

Siegfried Kracauer is probably not the first writer to suggest an affinity be-tween tourism and secular modernity. But the profanity he saw in the hotel lobby prefigured in some ways an important theme in tourism studies: viewing "the tourist" as a metaphor for "the modern" and seeing in tourism a particu-larly clear lens for viewing "the modern condition" (MacCannell 1989, 1992; Oakes 1998; Wang 2000; Dong 2006). The equation of the hotel lobby with secularism marks one version of interpreting tourism as an inherently modern phenomenon. Kracauer viewed the hotel lobby as the same kind of nonplace that Marc Augé has found in airport terminals and other spaces of transit and consumption (1995). Kracauer's hotel lobby was what Henri Lefebvre would call an "absolute space" of pure individualism, a temple of rational standard-ization, of guaranteed anonymity in the crowd (1991). A space of business, transaction, and most of all a commodified space, Kracauer's hotel lobby was the polar opposite of sacred space.

We begin this book with the premise that the modern binary epitomized by Kracauer's epigram is of little use for appreciating the transformations of spiritual and leisure travel practices, and the ways these practices intersect each other in China today. The accounts collected in this volume make clear that the spaces of touristic and spiritual practice cannot be so neatly distin-guished from one another, and that therefore the conceptual categories by which someone like Siegfried Kracauer came to separate "secularism" from "religion" no longer stand up to empirical scrutiny, if they ever did. Indeed, one of our central arguments in this volume is that such categories of Western epistemology merely confuse and misguide our understanding of such complex human phenomena as faith and travel. If anything, the polarizing of tourism and religion marks a specific moment in the history of Euro-American thought, a moment epitomized by Kracauer's Frankfurt, but one that leaves us ill-prepared for analyzing the kinds of social transformations occurring in a place like China today. How for instance do we grasp, conceptually, what has been happening in a place like Dazhai?

Dazhai, of course, was that model of rural development, revolutionary spirit, and collective power celebrated during the Cultural Revolution. A poor brigade in the hardscrabble hills of eastern Shanxi, Dazhai's transformation into a landscape of abundance proselytized the virtues of the peasant's low-tech stubborn determination to conquer nature. Dazhai's Chen Yonggui was the embodiment of Mao's "foolish old man who moved the mountain." Along with brigade leader Guo Fengliang, Chen became a household name throughout China, while "Learn From Dazhai!" posters and slogans were pasted and painted on walls from Hainan to Heilongjiang. Red Guards streamed in. Barracks were built. And a site of political pilgrimage was born (Zweig 1989; Sun and Xiong 1990).

It turned out, however, that Dazhai's spirit of self-reliance was a sham. The People's Liberation Army (PLA) was behind much of the "miraculous" infrastructural and agricultural improvements that were said to have been achieved solely by the peasants. In the early years of the post-Mao reforms, Dazhai became the disgraced poster child of Mao's leftist excesses. But Guo Fengliang wasn't finished, and in 1991, she formed the Dazhai Economic Development Company and gambled that Dazhai's name recognition would trump the ambivalent historical memory it conjured (Xinhuanet 2002). Her bet paid off. By 2002, Dazhai had set up twelve businesses with combined assets worth more than $10 billion. Peasants stopped farming and became entrepreneurs, factory workers, and tour guides. Dazhai became a brand name. Tourists streamed in. Hotels were built. By 2002, three hundred thousand tourists were arriving each year and spending nearly $750,000 annually. Then, Dazhai raised private investment funds to build a large Buddhist temple atop Tiger Head Hill, the very hill tamed in an earlier day by Chen Yonggui (with the clandestine help of the PLA). More tourists streamed in. Souvenir amulets were sold alongside statues of Mao. Dazhai was transformed once again, from a sacred site of revolutionary faith to one presumably of religious faith.

But the story of Dazhai's transformation is in fact much more complicated than this simple trajectory of political to religious pilgrimage suggests. Because in some ways, things haven't changed that much for Dazhai. And in some ways, the secular and spiritual qualities of Dazhai's transformations might be seen as different versions of the same process. It is tourism and pilgrimage, we think, that sheds a particularly bright light on our understanding of why this might be so.

In a recent article published in *South Wind View* (*Nanfengchuang*) and excerpted on the Chinese news media blog Danwei.org, Li Xiangping wrote about how the people of Dazhai saw no contradiction between worship of Mao Zedong and worship of Sakyamuni (Martinsen 2007). While some tourists apparently viewed Dazhai's turn to religion as indicative of China's crisis of faith in the post-Mao vacuum of consumption and commercialism, Li found instead a lively traffic in what he termed "spiritual smuggling" (*jingshen zousi*), a stealthy spiritual vitality that continues to flow under the cover of secular materialism. As a monk at the temple told Li, "There's no fundamental conflict between worshiping Mao Zedong and belief in Sakyamuni. Chairman Mao is Buddha, and Buddha is Chairman Mao. Mao Zedong was a leader; Sakyamuni is the embrace of the universe, the everlasting spirit." This comparison, Li notes however, may not be quite accurate. For the people of Dazhai, it is not Sakyamuni but the God of Wealth that people now see in Mao. One man told Li that "without Chairman Mao, there'd be no Dazhai today. Chairman Mao is the God of Wealth for the people of Dazhai." A woman who ran a hotel said, "Chairman Mao is our account-book."

Li observed that at Dazhai's souvenir shops, Mao statues stood alongside images of Guanyin. "Many of the Mao statues have 'Great One, Protect Me' (*weiren hushen*) written on them and seem like they've made Mao Zedong's image into an amulet. More curiously, written on the boxes for those Mao statues is the line, 'A blessed divine manifestation' (*kaiguang xianling*). A shopkeeper told me, 'After Pule Temple was built, Chairman Mao's statues no longer needed to be taken to other places to be blessed. Pule Temple itself could bless the Mao statues.'" Li concluded that "political faith does not have a simple antagonistic relationship with the accumulation of folk, religious, and personal faith. When political faith ruled, private, scattered faith naturally had no choice or expression, but now that political faith no longer rules men's hearts, private faith has sprouted, providing choice and free expression."

While the transformation of Dazhai is fascinating enough on its own terms—laying bare as it does the religious qualities of Mao's status in China today, the sacredness of China's revolutionary heritage, and the faith that underlies Chinese nationalism—we find the example of Dazhai indicative also of a broader set of problems that we set out to tackle in this volume. First among these is the problem of categories: tourist, pilgrim, secular, spiritual, and a host of others, the meanings of which tend to depend upon being contrasted with some "other" category. Are Dazhai's visitors pilgrims or tourists? Do they come for leisure and entertainment? Or do they come for inspiration and blessings? Rather than answering these kinds of questions, or providing definitions to clarify the analytic distinctions in these terms, we seek to explore in this volume the ways that places like Dazhai render impossible the neat separation of these categories of knowledge and the behaviors presumed to be associated with them. Are Dazhai's visitors pilgrims or tourists? The answer depends on the actual sites of behavior and the social contexts within which visitors act and interact. The chapters of this volume all strive to reveal in various ways how the social contexts within which tourist and religious practices occur render it impossible to speak of "the tourist" as a stable social category conveniently separated from other aspects of daily life (such as "the spiritual").

Second is the problem of the state and its role in brokering both tourism development and religious revival in China today. The story of Dazhai reveals how the state has not only played midwife to the social changes taking place, but has also sought, however fitfully, to *control* those changes—mobilizing Buddhism, for example, as an instrument in its campaign to promote "harmonious society" and a "spiritual socialist civilization." The story of Dazhai has been dictated precisely by the state in an effort to authorize the *meaning* of social transformation. The Chinese state, in other words, seeks not only to be the ultimate guide for economic development, but also the authority for Chinese culture. And in these twin endeavors, tourism plays a central role.

Like many of the chapters in this volume, the story of Dazhai also reveals, however, that state control is never total. Even in Dazhai a lively underground economy of "spiritual smuggling" thrives. As Li's account notes, faith in China has largely been privatized, and this deliberately blurs its supposed separation from the world of commerce and materialism. Yet, as Chau (2006) has observed in Shanxi, and as Dean has noted (2001), religious practice has also become for many communities the central vehicle for reenacting collective forms of governance. There has been an explosion of spaces, beliefs, and practices that now lie beyond the reach of the state. Tourism, we believe, is one of the most important producers of these multiple private and collective spaces within which practices of faith now occur in China, and tourism is central to our understanding of the ways the state continues to try and maintain its cultural authority as the country undergoes massive economic and social transformation.

Third is the problem of "revival" itself. As the thirty-year experiment with Maoist socialism fades into history and "traditional" practices emerge—including rituals of worship and other religious activities—what exactly is being revived, what is being recycled, and what is being invented anew? Is Dazhai's turn to religion a genuine expression of faith? Is it merely an instrumental extension of the money-generating Dazhai brand? After all, even Dazhai's celebration of Maoist socialism was, it turns out, an act of profoundly bad faith. And yet, the God of Wealth that Mao has become today could hardly be called a fake. And the devotion with which people continue to worship him is as genuine as any faith could be. Again, we argue in this volume that tourism illuminates these issues in China today with particular clarity.

Given the importance we place on the social contexts within which tourism and religion occur, and the ways those contexts shape the relationships and experiences with place for tourists and religious travelers alike, we provide in the remainder of this introduction a brief outline of tourism development and religious revival in China. Our goal is to provide a coherent historical and political-economic setting for the chapters that follow, as well as articulate the links between the Chinese social context and the epistemological arguments laid out in the preceding paragraphs.

MOBILITY AND GOVERNANCE IN CHINA

Mobility has long been an important sphere of social regulation for the Chinese state. While mobility in pre-twentieth-century China was certainly very limited, there were well-established patterns and traditions of mobility with which the state was always intimately concerned. One of these was pilgrimage (Naquin and Yu 1992). As Brian Dott's chapter in this volume makes clear, pilgrimages to sacred sites in China were an ongoing focus of the imperial state's governance concerns. Not only was it important for the state to maintain some control over the cash that pilgrims were prepared to spend in order to entreat the gods, but it was also crucial for the state to maintain its authority as the central arbiter of relations between the earthly realm and the heavens. Another important form of pre-twentieth-century mobility was the sojourning of a great variety of tradesmen and merchants. So-called native-place associations (*huiguan*), generally associated with the sojourners' local god at home, played a key governance role in the management of urban sojourners who congregated in China's commercial centers (Ho 1966; Belsky 2005; Rowe 1989; Goodman 1995). These associations reinforced the principle that one always belonged to the place of one's ancestral home, and that was where one lived legally, normally subject to the *baojia* mutual responsibility system.

In contemporary China, it is the so-called *hukou* system of household registration that ties citizenship rights and entitlements to local residence. Yet while hukou provides a mechanism for the management of labor migrants streaming into China's cities and fueling its export manufacturing model of development and modernization, the presence of millions of rural migrants has brought with it a great deal of public anxiety over the "quality" (*suzhi*) of China's population. In this context, the state has turned to a growing middle-class (*zhongchang jieji* or *zhongchang jiechen*) of educated, mobile consumers as exemplary self-governing citizen-subjects (Tomba 2009). "The tourist," then, emerges as the mobile version of this exemplary middle-class subject, an ideal model of "quality" mobility in China today. Leisure is not simply an industry with enormous revenue-generating power in China today, but also enjoys prominence as the symbolic apogee of the advanced and "civilized" consuming citizen. Leisure travelers serve as exemplars for their rural hosts to emulate—raising the "quality" of the rural population by, for example, insisting on clean toilets and attentive service—and they demonstrate "healthy" forms of consumption by, for example, purchasing song and dance performances rather than gambling (Nyíri 2009, 157). Being modern citizens, tourists are expected to consume in specific ways that reinforce state-sanctioned narratives of history, culture, national identity, and so on. When religious spaces are opened for tourism, therefore, the experience is meant to be thoroughly secular.

This link between tourism and exemplary modern behavior has a specific history in China and, in particular, China's encounter with the colonial modernity of the West. As Madeleine Yue Dong has pointed out, travel and mobility were identified by the early twentieth-century editors of Shanghai's *China Traveler* magazine as emblems of a cosmopolitan civility lacking in traditional China (2006). Leisure travel, the editors argued, was not a Chinese habit, and this in comparison to the mobile desires of Westerners served as a measure of China's lack of modernity. The Chinese were said to prefer to simply stay home, "drink and play mahjong to kill time," whereas Germans, for example, loved music, liked to go outdoors, and traveled to faraway places (205). Implicit in this criticism was the idea that tourism represented a healthy form of consumption associated with strong nations and self-disciplined citizens. Modern people used their leisure time to experience the world and improve themselves, rather than whiling away the time in teahouses or participating in the superstitious activities of popular religion.

Tourism is thus a field of governance in China, part of a strategy of social and cultural regulation that promises the state some purchase on managing the inherent instability and chaos of a consumer-oriented market economy. Given the elevation of the tourist to model status in China today, it is important for the state not only to ensure that tourist behavior is indeed exemplary, but also to control the contexts within which tourist consumption occurs. This involves comprehensive "development" of tourist sites, standardized management of the tourist experience, and authority in the production of places, cultures, ethnicities, landscapes, and stories consumed by tourists (Nyíri 2006).

But tourists can never be relied upon to enact the exemplary behavior that is expected of them. Instead of consuming religious sites by buying some souvenirs, or snapping some pictures within the prayer hall where photography is prohibited by temple officiants, tourists might actually pray at these sites, request blessings, and redeem vows. Tourists may visit rural villages to gamble, pay for sex, and otherwise engage in behavior that is of decidedly "low quality" from the state's perspective. Indeed, throughout China they do all of these things. This has been a surprisingly hard lesson for the state to learn. In a more abstract sense, it has also been a hard lesson for the tourism industry as well as tourism studies scholarship. Conventional theory in tourism studies has been dominated by the premise of "the tourist" as a particular kind of person with a distinct and identifiable set of typical motivations and ways of experiencing tourism. The tourist, we have been told, seeks authenticity to compensate for his alienated workaday life (MacCannell 1989). Or the tourist seeks out and gazes upon otherness as she constructs her self-identity in a world of difference (Urry 2002). Not only do these approaches mask the ethnocentric and gendered assumptions underlying conventional Anglophone social theory, as pointed out now by numerous critics, but they reify abstract constructions that cannot hold up to the empirical messiness of the social world (Kaplan 1996; Winter 2009; Franklin and Crang 2001).

In this volume, then, we proceed from the premise that a typology of tourist motivations or behaviors cannot be relied upon to draw clear distinctions between the realms of tourism and religion. To put it more provocatively, there is no such thing as "the tourist." There is, rather, an infinite array of social contexts within which people engage in tourism. In China, these contexts have much to do with the state's efforts to develop and modernize both rural and urban regions, as well as guide the consuming desires of its increasingly affluent and mobile population.

RELIGION, PILGRIMAGE, AND TOURISM IN CHINA

Underlying Kracauer's epigram is an anxiety over the rise of instrumental rationality and secularism as capitalist modernity works its disenchantment on the world. Along with the neat conceptual separation of the spiritual and the profane, the religious and the secular, came a melancholy belief that the former world of spirit and faith was being eclipsed by the latter world of reason and science. Yet religion itself must be viewed as a modern category that has been constituted through the rise of secularism (Asad 1993). Ashiwa (2009, 48) has applied this perspective to China, arguing that "religion in China has to be viewed as a thread of the fabric of modernity, the design of which began to take distinctive and visible form around the end of the nineteenth century." The formation of the modern state is so closely involved with religion in China that modern religion and the modern state may be said to have constructed each other.

The revival of religion since the Cultural Revolution, as China has rapidly modernized its economy, argues against the facile confrontation of religion with modernity. Government figures put the number of people who consider themselves religious at 100 million; yet one-third of 4,500 people surveyed by Shanghai's East China Normal University described themselves as religious (Yardley 2007), which might be extrapolated to as many as 300 million people for the whole of China. This includes not only isolated believers but communities of the faithful practicing public rituals of territorial identification.

In China and beyond, the belief that religion and modernity represent antithetical poles of the spiritual and the secular can no longer stand after the briefest glance at the social movements and political conflicts of the early twenty-first century. And if "being modern" fundamentally means being mobile, as John Urry has suggested, it is important to recognize that a great deal of that mobility occurs for religious or spiritual reasons (1995). Indeed, as Timothy and Olsen have noted (2006, 3), there has been a rise in religious pilgrimage and religious tourism worldwide. It was estimated in the early 1990s that over 200 million people annually engage in international, national, or regional pilgrimage journeys—a figure that is probably too low (Kaelber 2006, 58).

There has also long been an affinity between the practices of pilgrimage and those of tourism. As Timothy and Olsen comment, "Religion has played a key role in the development of leisure over the centuries and has influenced how people utilize their leisure time" (1). This is seen not only in the role that pilgrimage has played as a precursor to leisure travel, but also in the establishment of spaces and times in daily life devoted to rest, reflection, and removal from the cares of the instrumental world. Indeed, even the so-called founder of modern tourism, Thomas Cook, was a lay clergyman and spiritual traveler. Cook was a preacher in the working-class religious revival movement of the 1830s and 1840s when he came upon the idea of organized excursions to both bring people from the cities to the rural revival sites, and to create a kind of "traveling pleasurability" among believers along the way (Franklin 2004, 292). Tourism has since been likened to a kind of modern pilgrimage (Graburn 1989). And it has become common to observe the extent to which religious sites, sacred architecture, pilgrimage paths, and the lure of the metaphysical are all now commodified for tourists.

Historically, religious pilgrimage generated wealth in the areas pilgrims visited (Timothy and Olsen 2006, 10), for like tourists, religious pilgrims were free spenders; and as with modern tourism, locals felt ambivalent as they balanced the impact of their new visitors with the economic benefits gained (Baedcharoen 2000; Robinson and Boniface 1999). One could even argue, as Digance does, that medieval pilgrimage was the first example of mass tourism as we know it today (2006). Pilgrimages were offered to the wealthy in the form of a package tour, and by the end of the Middle Ages, pilgrimage had become quite commercialized. Pilgrim hostels were a major industry, as was the production, marketing, and trade in pilgrim badges (Kaelber 2006). Kaelber also notes that medieval pilgrimage was not immune from the commodification and criticism commonly thought to characterize later forms of secular travel. "Moreover, in religious travel, ludic elements and political issues sometimes intermingled with religious ones" (50). As noted above, this was certainly true for Thomas Cook as well. Kaelber documents that for those who could not afford to travel to faraway places, makeshift spiritual theme parks were available. Guidebook authors claimed that armchair pilgrimages were just as spiritually effective. And wealthy penitents could even hire professional pilgrim-travelers to carry out a proxy pilgrimage for them.

Thus, the contrast between the categories of traditional religious pilgrim and modern secular mass tourist is overdrawn. Where there are differences, we prefer to imagine a continuum from pilgrim to tourist (see Eade and Sallnow 1991)—from one ideal-typical polarity to the other. Seen thus, there is admittedly a tendency to relate differently to the site and a different sense of place. Tourists often move vast distances from urban centers to what is often a peripheral place; for pilgrims, by contrast, the sacred site serves as the regional center toward which they travel (Digance 2003, 30). The tourist expects to visit once, spending a few hours in its vicinity, while the pilgrim comes regularly and tarries for a while to make proper contact with the numinous (Digance 2003, citing Rinschede 1988). So the tourist sees each new site in comparison with a range of analogous regional, nationwide, and even overseas attractions, while the pilgrim has a narrower frame of comparison but a longer temporal perspective, and a deeper commitment to the site's power and sanctity.

Beyond these broad distinctions, the experiences overlap considerably. People came on pilgrimage during one of the few times of the year that they were free from work, and not unlike tourists, must have enjoyed the experience as entertainment (Naquin and Yü 1992). Women on pilgrimage were freer than at other times to socialize with each other and escape patriarchal supervision. At places like Mount Tai and Mount Emei, pilgrims were not blind to the beauty of the sites, and pilgrimages often included sightseeing and the purchases of local trinkets. At such remarkable sites perhaps known only by hearsay, pilgrims could "define identities that transcend local particularisms, class and status" (Sangren 1987, 190) and "come to realize the difference between themselves and the world" (Siegel 1969, 282, cited by San-gren 1987, 191). This is no different than tourism, which brings people into contact with the exotic other, and puts the self in a sharp light at the end of a journey of discovery. As Oakes's chapter in this volume argues, both kinds of ritualistic behavior flourish at boundaries between heaven and earth, center and periphery, my group and their group; marking such boundaries, playing with them and traversing them, is perhaps, as Seligman et al. argue (2008, 93–97), the way of all rituals. For tourists too such places make them aware of their nature as both Han and Chinese, belonging to the most advanced yet most culturally despoiled parts of China. As Sangren (1987, 196) also argues, "It is only through contrast with encompassing unity that awareness of more particular dimensions of identity is achieved," and this seems to work equally well for Han Chinese pilgrims and Han Chinese tourists.

Moreover, the categories of pilgrim and tourist are converging. Pilgrims are becoming more like tourists in what they see and do. Official restrictions at many World Heritage parks have transformed their temporal relationship to the site. Though improved roads make visits easier for local worshipers it is often impractical to stay overnight. As a result their experience in recent annual visits is often as cursory as that of the tourists who arrive by coach and leave two hours later. In terms of space and distance, the old sense of a local community with its protective deities has given way to wider concerns. Even if they have never left the region of their birth, pilgrims in China cannot but be conscious of the impinging party-state and its modernizing economy, since the familiar and local have been thoroughly transformed in relationship with the regional and national. Pilgrims who rub shoulders with tourists know they are all part of the same interdependent global economy and seem often to share a similar aesthetic, merging the sacred with natural beauty (cf. Bremer 2004, 150–51). The tendency for tourists to become more like pilgrims is also apparent in a number of our chapters. Tourists may be spiritual seek-ers. Arriving at a temple, wondering what they should do, they see pilgrims lighting incense and kowtowing to the images. It is not unusual that they too make efforts to copy the ritual themselves, as the appropriate thing to do at a temple. These tourists are at least half pilgrims, just as modern-day pilgrims more and more resemble them.

As Yu Luo Rioux's chapter in this volume shows, all sorts of travel "types" happen together, not simply within the same site, but often within the same individuals. Officials traveling to sacred revolutionary sites like Jinggangshan may be simultaneously engaging in a "secular pilgrimage" to a shrine of the nation-state, having a pleasurable leisure travel experience, and sometimes even asking for blessings for career advancement from Mao Zedong's spirit. Dott's chapter demonstrates something similar going on at Mount Tai. In Ken

and religion in state efforts to foster tourism development in Xishuangbanna. And yet, all of these chapters also demonstrate how the local contexts of tourism development yield different outcomes. They do not, in other words, confirm the assumption of a powerful state pulling the levers of tourism and religion to bolster its nation-building project.

Tourism, then, should be viewed as a major front in the state's efforts to maintain its paramount authority over the realms of cultural production and national identity construction. This is a significant conclusion for our purposes because it suggests that tourism can serve as a medium of cultural control within a broader social context in which the state appears to have relinquished much of that control to nonstate social actors. That relinquishment is nowhere better illustrated than in the realm of popular religion. As suggested in Dean's chapter, despite the central state's reluctance, locally organized religious temple building and festivals have seen unprecedented expansion since the 1990s (Chau 2006), particularly in Fujian communities where the role of overseas Chinese pilgrim-tourist returnees is well documented (Tan 2006). By looking at religion and tourism in China together, we gain an important perspective on the state's struggles, dilemmas, and negotiations to maintain authority during a time of profound social transformation.

RELIGION AND STATE AUTHORITY IN CHINA

Dazhai is a contemporary example of what we might call a super-symbol—not a nonplace like Kracauer's hotel lobby but one overflowing with irreconcilable meanings. Dazhai powerfully conveys a place, but no longer a single interpretation—it is a symbol appropriated for such diverse purposes that it has broken free from particular ideology or social interest. There are traditional examples of such super-symbols, for example the deity Tianhou (Mazu) as described by James L. Watson (1985); she was a local protector of Fujian sailors who drew the worship of land-dwellers of all classes and eventually of Chinese everywhere. Mazu became popular before her cult was standardized by the state; Dazhai was invented by the state, popularized, and eventually unmoored from original Maoist meanings. Symbols, and especially super-symbols, draw strong feelings, attract groups of like-minded constituents, and are therefore sources of power. The state cannot afford to ignore them. In the case of officially recognized cults in late imperial times, as analyzed by Prasenjit Duara (1988), it tried to superscribe and subordinate them by enforcing its interpretation and its ritual calendar and form.[1] As this volume often illustrates, most gods' cults and sites of historic significance have the status of super-symbols. Official attempts to standardize interpretations continue but are always incomplete and sometimes nominal, even in the case of heroic sites from the most glorious chapters of party history. Co-opting and subsuming such symbols are, then, imperfect means of control, and tend to be followed by continual negotiation. A key theme of the reform period is the continuing state effort to co-opt and subsume religious activities, as well as (more obviously) to control and supervise them administratively and by law. The Chinese state has a long history of positioning itself as a legitimate authority over religious matters (Potter 2003). As noted earlier, Talal Asad has argued that the modern state created an administrative space for religion. In the Chinese case, however, administrative control of religious activity cannot be explained simply as an outcome of modern state formation, but has instead been a much longer-term project of governance and cultural authority in China (Brook 2009).

What we would emphasize is that the state's attitude toward religion in imperial times had nothing to do with any presumed division of function with "secular" activities or powers, because imperial governments were themselves "religious" entities: the emperor was, after all, the Son of Heaven—humankind's sole authorized mediator with Heaven—in which capacity he performed regular seasonal rituals to assure good harvests and harmony in the world "under Heaven" (*tianxia*), and to atone or give thanks in response to Heaven's acts. The state left room for religious entities such as lineage temples, which echoed the ideology of the state, and local gods too, provided that they assisted in maintaining harmony in society and did not challenge the state's authority; it distinguished between unapproved gods and standardized gods on whom titles and particular ritual forms and times were bestowed by the emperor's Board of Ritual. These gods were co-opted to assist in the maintenance of local order. Indeed the imperial metaphor as a whole, long a staple of popular thinking, was corralled by Ming emperors as a parallel source of stable authority. The first Ming emperor understood the City God, in each walled city, as a partner to the magistrate, appointed to rule the living, exercising authority over the region's dead souls; and the local god, in a less successful effort, was supposed to represent imperial authority down to the village level. In the newly conquered territories of Tibet and in Mongolia the emperors of the mid and late Qing sponsored Tibetan Buddhism as personal patrons, as if to center the empire on themselves. However ideologically appropriate, such policies of toleration reflected loose and indirect control.

These policies of co-option placed the emperor, as worshiper of Heaven and enfeoffer of the gods, atop the religious system, with his officials assisting him. Religion—that is to say approved, orthodox religion—was a means of ruling other believers. Such policies assumed the supremacy of Heaven and the existence of the gods. Twentieth-century governments abandoned these ideas. When leaders attached themselves to a religion (Chiang Kai-shek to Christianity, Jiang Zemin to Buddhism) it was as individuals. This fitted with modern, originally Western, notions of "religion" as a separate sphere of the individual in which freedom of belief is supposed to be guaranteed by the state (Asad 1993).

Patronage within a cosmic order headed by the supreme leader was incompatible with modern secular notions, yet the state still commands people's minds and emotions with the legitimating force of nationalism, which a number of analysts compare with or equate to religion (Sutton and Kang 2009, 195). The one-party state tries to monopolize the institutions that mobilize nationalistic sentiment and to standardize the interpretation of the supersymbols that figure in our chapters: the water city of Wuzhen (Svensson), the temples of Xishuangbanna (McCarthy), the medieval city of Songpan (Sutton and Kang), Naxi culture (McKhann), and the goddess Mazu (Dean). It teaches nationalism in its schools and permits its public expression. Nationalism can at times threaten the state (as student nationalism confronted the Nanjing government in the 1930s), but it is intended to support it, much as co-opted gods and the imperial metaphor did in the past. During the prosperous reform period since 1978, it usually has. Our chapters show that nationalism is a theme of tourist sites of all kinds, whether religion is their principal focus or not. The gods and churches are sponsored and in principle subsumed within the party-state—much as approved gods and religious institutions in imperial times were subsumed ideologically within the imperial metaphor and bureaucratically within the official system; religious officers are expected to declare their patriotism; temples often display patriotic slogans. The gods are presented as an aspect of national culture, not as a source of power and reassurance or local cohesion. Ethnic groups present their culture to tourists not in defiant assertion of difference but as illustrations of the all-encompassing nature of the People's Republic, with its fifty-six nationalities (Han and the fifty-five minorities) proclaimed to be living in harmony.

In the reform period, the Chinese state has officially recognized five faiths within China that meet its definition of "religion" (*zongjiao*). These are Buddhism, Daoism, Islam, Catholicism, and Protestantism. They meet the criteria of "having such attributes as a logical system of thought oriented to the afterlife that is contained in scriptures, specially trained clergy, and fixed sites for religious activities (temples, churches, etc.) managed by clergy" (Ashiwa 2009, 58). Freedom of belief in these officially sanctioned faiths is constitutionally protected in China. They are closely regulated and supervised, and held responsible for the behavior of their subordinate officers and followers; those worshiping groups that don't fit the state model of a religion go underground and risk suppression and the destruction of unauthorized religious buildings.

Dealing with popular religious expression is altogether more complicated. Tolerance is rationalized in the evolutionary framework: education will eventually make people turn away from religion, but in a relaxation of ideological principles it is permitted for the time being. So local officials monitor or turn a blind eye to vigorous expressions of territorial or lineage ritual practice in select places such as northern Shaanxi (Chau 2006) and Fujian (Dean 1998; Tan 2006). In justifying their tolerance they may also suggest that religion serves as a source of stability and harmony, a position that fits with the Hu Jintao/Wen Jiabao social policy since 2002. But their main concern is to repackage religion and display it to tourists, emphasizing the spectacular and the picturesque. As demonstrated in the chapters by Oakes, and Sutton and Kang, local officials market what might be called religion as "folk customs" and "local culture," selecting portions suited for display in onstage or offstage performance, and augmenting them with artistic elements from other provinces as taught in the schools for popular arts.

"Religion" is also officially distinguished from "superstition" (*mixin*), "feudal superstition" (*fengjian mixin*), and "popular belief" (*minjian xinyang*). Beyond the five sanctioned religions lies a vast and highly varied world of popular religion that is seemingly expanding unchecked. Chau (2009, 211) has noted the irony of the present situation by observing that while state control over the five recognized religions remains firm, its grip on popular religion has loosened significantly, largely because local officials derive no benefit from cracking down on what could easily be defined as superstitions (219). Yet there have been exemplary campaigns, if not particularly effective ones, like Beijing's against the God of Wealth (McCarthy 2004).

"Popular belief" occupies a gray zone between (legal) religion and (illegal) superstition, with many gods and deities worshiped in specific locales, usually at fixed sites, but without a "logical system" of thought and scripture. "However," Ashiwa (2009, 59) notes, "activities involving popular beliefs that are acknowledged as having 'historical' and 'cultural' value are permitted so long as they are defined as 'cultural' rather than 'religious.'" This approach is demonstrated clearly in many of the chapters in this volume. McKhann for instance illustrates this approach in his analysis of dongba's transformation from religion to culture, as does Oakes in his chapter's discussion of the tiaoshen ritual's transformation into a heritage product called dixi. As suggested in both Svensson's and Makley's chapters, state planners like to envisage temples as museums, and priests as their caretakers, serving the needs of the tourist industry. Reframing religious sites as tourism destinations allows the local state to reconfigure a local popular belief with questionable "superstitious" attributes as a "local custom" with cultural and historical value. There remains a great deal of uncertainty, however, in the outcome of these arrangements, as a number of this volume's chapters also demonstrate. The local state tends to view temples from a rent-seeking perspective and to promote them as part of its local development policy. "Temples are like enterprises that generate prosperity for the local economy (especially if they are regional pilgrimage centers) and income for the local state. It is thus in the interest of the local state to protect local temples as it would local enterprises" (Chau 2009, 220; McCarthy 2004). Yet official decisions about the actual rebuilding of temples and monasteries and their fencing off and financial management have often aroused local dissatisfaction (Rack 2005, 106–7), and as several of our chapters show, there remain significant tensions between state and religious actors over how local faiths are expressed by their own practitioners and how they are displayed to tourists.

Does the state regard "religious revival" as a potential threat to its authority and stability? Folk customs may be ignored but the state does not tolerate independent organizations, of any kind. While the "indigenous" religions of Daoism and popular Buddhism are typically viewed as less threatening than Christianity, Islam, or Tibetan Buddhism, tourism may be deployed as a vehicle for state control. This, for instance, would be the case when Buddhist or Bön monasteries in Tibet and Islamic shrines in Xinjiang are opened for tourism. This seems entirely consistent with other state efforts to maintain its cultural and political authority in religious matters away from the frontier regions. As Dott points out in his chapter, the state reserves the right to appoint the abbot of the main Bixia Temple on Mount Tai. It claims sole authority to appoint Muslim imams. It seeks to govern the belief in salvation by faith and the Resurrection among Chinese Christians. It bars Catholics from hearing mass performed by unsanctioned priests, and usurps the right of the Vatican to appoint bishops in China. It even claims sole authority in matters of reincarnation. As Tibetan Autonomous Region party secretary Zhang Qingli stated in 2008, "The Central Party Committee is the real Buddha for Tibetans" (quoted in Yardley 2008).

Clearly, then, there is more to the modern Chinese state's relationship with religion than simply relegating belief to the private space of the individual. Those faiths viewed as potentially threatening (Islam, Christianity, Tibetan Buddhism) are closely supervised by local and provincial authorities as well as state-level laws. In such cases, state-promoted tourism development may run counter to the desires of many in the local religious community. Those faiths viewed as less threatening (popular Buddhism, Daoism, Confucianism) are circumscribed by the same laws, but the state may act as patron. Thus, the state sponsored an International Buddhism Forum in 2006, and in April 2007 threw a *Daodejing* festival in Xi'an, promoting Daoism as an indigenous faith (Kwok 2007), and in recent years it has promoted Confucius Institutes worldwide as a form of soft power. There have also been conferences celebrating many local deities, such as Dayu and Linshui furen, the latter appealing to patriotic sentiments in the guise of Taiwan regionalism. In such events, tourism plays a more complicated role in constituting the state's religious authority. Certainly events like the Daodejing festival are major tourist promotions that seek to explicitly blur the distinction between tourist and pilgrim, but they seek to do so on the state's terms. Meanwhile, as the chapters by McCarthy, Svensson, and Sutton and Kang demonstrate, religious agents often remain ambivalent about these state-sponsored commercial events.

As in imperial times, central and local authorities are not necessarily in agreement on all aspects of religious policy, though local and central officials use the same language. In principle, the center permits freedom of belief, bans certain religious practices, presents religion as an aspect of regional and national cultural history, and suggests that religion can actively help to promote an orderly and harmonious society. Meanwhile local authorities have to deal with the reality of religious revival. The party's ideological buzzwords of "harmonious society" and "patriotic religion" are much in evidence in wall slogans, as rationalizations for tourism at religious sites. Despite the dubious standing of religion in Marxism, still the party's official creed, there are worse alternatives than religiously tinged pilgrimage. "Isn't it better for society to promote tourist pilgrimages to Wutai Mountain than sex tourism to Zhuhai?" Brahm (2007) asks rhetorically. "As for an economic model for its tourism, should China choose Kathmandu or Bangkok?" Yet the center's notions of combating superstition and furthering "spiritual civilization" may receive no more than lip service, especially if they conflict with realities on the ground. The "red tourism" of former revolutionary sites is another ideologically inspired goal at the level of the central government, but the actual popularity of such places will ultimately determine the attention paid by local officials. In short, despite the high-minded view of tourism envisioned in some central plans, at the local level religious tourism is promoted for essentially instrumental reasons.

There are two main areas where the local officials have been very willing to put faiths on display for instrumental reasons. First, the places where overseas investment can be attracted, initially near the special economic zones set up under Deng Xiaoping's reform policies near Taiwan, Hong Kong, and Macau, which grew markedly in the 1990s, have been places where religious revival is hard to separate from the influence of these *sanbao* returnees. The number of returnees is not few (perhaps as much as five times the number of non-Chinese international travelers) and in establishing local relationships they attend to local religion in their ancestral homes as well as business investments. The returning visitors, a few of whom become residents, supply much of the money for temple rebuilding. As Ken Dean's chapter shows, the Xinghua community has actively helped to reconstitute or reinvent practices dimly remembered from before the Maoist suppression. In these cases the returnees are themselves in a sense tourists, but as Dean emphasizes, they are the latest expression of a long-lived Southeast Asian transnational network. Local officials go along with the religious revival because the ritual economy is inseparable from the capital flows upon which their regions have come to depend.

A second area where religion flourishes with unambiguous local official approval in connection with tourism is in the minority nationality regions where the central government since the 1980s has encouraged commercial development and tourism has become an important source of local income and revenue. In the southwest especially, the cultures of the nationalities are a significant tourist attraction. Chinese and other tourists can enjoy visual and aural aspects of their religions on stage, and visit temples, mosques, and monasteries reconstructed with state help. Although religion is marketed as "local culture" and "folk customs," and the revival of minority religions is hindered by state educational and cultural policies, which mandate Chinese education from the beginning of primary school, a space is left for religion, and in places tourists acquire a sense of the local importance of religious expression even if they learn little of its content and accept the official line that religion is incompatible with modern development. Once again, officials are able to use the appeal of religion, even in a superficial form, for local economic purposes, and to present it as a proof of the rich texture of minority culture and as an inseparable part of the national fabric, as shown in the chapters by McKhann and McCarthy.

The instrumentalism of local officials can lead indirectly to the fostering of religion. The local state often promotes religious sites (Buddhist temples, specifically) with the explicit intent of attracting overseas Chinese pilgrims-tourists whose religious motives may prompt not only money donations to the temple but other forms of community investment. By associating temple rebuilding with these official fundraising activities, canny religious promoters find they can gain official protection and support. In some regions such promoters broaden temple activities into areas of public welfare, as they had done in late imperial times, and deal with problems that exceed the state's own resources. Writing about Shaanxi, Adam Chau (2006) describes how the Black Dragon King Temple acquired recognition by the provincial Daoist Association as an orthodox "religious" operation as a result of such public-spirited actions. Such concessions can lead to a rebalancing of local and state authority as local officials are obliged to cede financial power and moral influence to religious authorities. This tendency is exemplified clearly in the protracted battle over an important temple-academy that is a big tourist attraction: the Nanputuo Monastery in Xiamen studied by Yoshiko Ashiwa and David Wank (2009).

Religious promotion may lead to further unexpected results in tourism itself, because the state cannot rely on tourism to hew narrowly to the instrumental role laid out for it. Even tourists from China's big cities are not predictably "secular." As we have noted, there is a continuum of practices from tourism to pilgrimage, and some tourists become spontaneous pilgrims at temples or other religious sites. The problem lies in the magic of place: restoring religious sites makes possible the renewal of religious practices among locals, as well as their adoption by tourists. Hence the difficulty of expanding the institutional room for religion and simultaneously expecting to contain belief within a private space (Ashiwa 2009, 68). The contradiction is illustrated in unsuccessful Republican efforts in the 1930s to eradicate the Guangzhou City God cult yet modernize its temple (Poon 2008).

In such cases, as often illustrated in our chapters, locals not only take advantage of new opportunities for tourist income, but also discover ingenious and sometimes surprising ways to express religious faith and organize its expression. The state more often tolerates or ignores than tries to prevent, but there are too many different local relationships for us to hazard predictions of significant political consequences. Whereas in Taiwan in the 1980s, the growing democracy movement was intimately connected to the island's vigorous religious life, it is not clear that the mainland's religious revitalization will lead to similar results in the People's Republic of China (PRC). Echoing the work of Asad (1993) by arguing against the idea of an unresolvable contradiction between the state and religion, Ashiwa and Wank see religion and the modern state emerging in a gradual process of mutual construction. In this process tourism, we think, has its role to play, for it provides the local state with some purchase on managing the burgeoning realm of popular religion in China today.

CONCLUSION

Several themes emerge repeatedly from this brief overview of the social, economic, and political contexts in which faiths are being put on display in contemporary China. First among these is the overwhelming complexity of these contexts, a complexity that defies easy categorization into abstract or ideal types such as tourist, pilgrim, spiritual, secular, and so on. While these can be useful concepts for many kinds of analysis, the contributors of this volume are committed to making a case for the messiness of place. Real places not only disrupt ideal types, but also allow us to see phenomena occurring together that more abstract or generalized analyses might be content to keep separate. Second is the observation that the state continues to assert its authority over religious matters and that tourism is at times being promoted as a vehicle for this control. And yet—and this is the third theme—that control is never assured and must always be reasserted. One reason is that tourists don't always behave the way they're supposed to. But then, neither does anyone else! And this, again, is the advantage of examining places in their contextual richness. For in the chapters collected in this volume we see a range of responses as tourists, locals, pilgrims, and even state actors themselves all struggle over, resist, appropriate, and sometimes just ignore the roles that have been laid out for them.

Ultimately, then, this volume presents a case for tourism as a crucial framework within which to better understand both the "revival" of religion in contemporary China as well as the state's efforts to usurp, authorize, and narrate that revival for its own purposes. Indeed, tourism helps us appreciate the messiness of "the state" itself with its internal contradictions, complex variety of scales, and ability to transcend the dichotomies of modernity and tradition, secular and spiritual, tourist and pilgrim even as it tries to shore up the boundaries between these.

NOTE

1. This argument adapts Lee Hai-yan's 2009 discussion of the Yuanmingyuan.

REFERENCES

Asad, Talal. 1993. "Toward a Genealogy of the Concept of Religion." In *Genealogies of Religion: Discipline & Reasons of Power in Christianity and Islam*. Baltimore: Johns Hopkins University Press, 55–82.

Ashiwa, Yoshiko. 2009. "Positioning Religion in Modernity: State and Buddhism in China." In *Making Religion, Making the State: The Politics of Religion in Modern China*, ed. Y. Ashiwa and D. Wank. Stanford: Stanford University Press, 43–73.

Ashiwa, Yoshiko, and David L. Wank. 2009. *Making Religion, Making the State: The Politics of Religion in Modern China*. Stanford: Stanford University Press.

Augé, Marc. 1995. *Non-Places: Introduction to an Anthropology of Supermodernity*. London: Verso.

Baedcharoen, Isaree. 2000. "Impacts of Religious Tourism in Thailand." Master's thesis, Department of Tourism, University of Otago, Dunedin.

Barmé, Geremie R. 1996. *Shades of Mao: The Posthumous Cult of the Great Leader*. New York and London: M.E. Sharpe.

Barnes, Nicole E. 2008. "Constructing the Race and Revitalizing an Emasculated Nation: Traveling Intellectuals in China's Northwestern Borderlands." Paper presented at the Critical Han Studies Workshop, Stanford, 25–27 April.

Bellocq, Maylis. 2006. "The Cultural Heritage Industry in the PRC: What Memories Are Being Passed On? A Case Study of Tongli, a Protected Township in Jiangsu Province." *China Perspectives* 67: 22–32.

Belsky, Richard. 2005. *Localities at the Center: Native Place, Space, and Power in Late Imperial Beijing*. Cambridge, MA: Harvard University Asia Center.

Brahm, Laurence. 2007. "Buddhist Path to Harmony?" *South China Morning Post,* 30 January. columns.scmp.com/colart/blackcat/ZZZ38TNTEXE.html.

Bremer, Thomas S. 2004. *Blessed with Tourists: The Borderlands of Religion and Tourism in San Antonio*. Chapel Hill: University of North Carolina Press.

Brook, Timothy. 2009. "The Politics of Religion: Late-Imperial Origins of the Regulatory State." In *Making Religion, Making the State: The Politics of Religion in Modern China*, ed. Y. Ashiwa and D. Wank. Stanford: Stanford University Press, 22–42.

Chau, Adam Yuet. 2006. *Miraculous Response: Doing Popular Religion in Contemporary China*. Stanford: Stanford University Press.

———. 2009. "Expanding the Space of Popular Religion: Local Temple Activism and the Politics of Legitimation in Contemporary Rural China." In *Making Religion, Making the State: The Politics of Religion in Modern China*, ed. Y. Ashiwa and D. Wank. Stanford: Stanford University Press, 211–40.

Chipman, Elana. 2006. "Local Goddess or State Agent? Competing Visions of a Pilgrimage Site in Fujian." Paper presented at the Annual Meeting of the American Anthropological Association, San Jose, CA.

Dean, Kenneth. 1998. *Lord of the Three in One: The Spread of a Cult in Southeast China*. Princeton: Princeton University Press.

———. 2001. "China's Second Government: Regional Ritual Systems in Southeast China." In *Shehui, Minzu yu Wenhua Zhanyan Guoji Yantaohui Lunwenji*. Taipei: Centre for Chinese Studies, 77–109.

Digance, Justine. 2003. "Pilgrimage at Contested Sites." *Annals of Tourism Research* 30(1): 143–59.

———. 2006. "Religious and Secular Pilgrimage: Journeys Redolent with Meaning." In *Tourism, Religion and Spiritual Journeys*, ed. D. Timothy and D. Olsen. London and New York: Routledge.

Dong, Madeleine Yue. 2006. "Shanghai's *China Traveler*." In *Everyday Modernity in China*, ed. M. Y. Dong and J. Goldstein. Seattle: University of Washington Press, 195–226.

Duara, Prasenjit. 1988. "Superscribing Symbols: The Myth of Guandi, Chinese God of War." *Journal of Asian Studies* 47(4): 778–95.

Eade, John, and Michael J. Sallnow. 2000 [1991]. *Contesting the Sacred: The Anthropology of Christian Pilgrimage*. London and New York: Routledge.

Fisher, Gareth. 2008. "The Spiritual Land Rush: Merit and Morality in New Chinese Buddhist Temple Construction." *Journal of Asian Studies* 67: 143–70.

Franklin, Adrian. 2004. "Tourism as an Ordering: Towards a New Ontology of Tourism." *Tourist Studies* 4(3): 277–301.

Franklin, Adrian, and Mike Crang. 2001. "The Trouble with Tourism and Travel Theory?" *Tourist Studies* 1(1): 5–22.

Goodman, Bryna. 1995. *Native Place, City, and Nation: Regional Networks and Identities in Shanghai, 1853–1937*. Berkeley: University of California Press.

Graburn, Nelson. 1989. "Tourism: the Sacred Journey." In *Hosts and Guests: The Anthropology of Tourism*, ed. V. Smith. Philadelphia: University of Pennsylvania Press, 21–36.

Hevia, James. 2001. "World Heritage, National Culture, and the Restoration of Chengde." *positions: east asia cultures critique* 9(1): 219–43.

Ho, Ping-ti. 1966. "The Geographical Distribution of Hui-Kuan (Landsmannschaften) in Central and Upper Yangtze Provinces." *Tsing Hua Journal of Chinese Studies* 5(2): 120–52.

Kaelber, Lutz. 2006. "Paradigms of Travel: From Medieval Pilgrimage to the Postmodern Virtual Tour." In *Tourism, Religion, and Spiritual Journeys*, ed. D. Timothy and D. Olsen. London and New York: Routledge.

Kang, Xiaofei, and Donald S. Sutton. 2008. "Purity and Pollution: From Pilgrimage Center to World Heritage Park," In *(Im)permanence: Cultures In/Out of Time*, ed. Stephen Brockman and Judith Modell. University Park: Pennsylvania State University Press, 197–211.

Kaplan, Caren. 1996. *Questions of Travel: Postmodern Discourses of Displacement.* Durham, NC: Duke University Press.

Kracauer, Siegfried. 2005 [1927]. *The Mass Ornament: Weimar Essays*. Trans. Thomas Y. Levin. Cambridge, MA: Harvard University Press.

Kuah-Pierce, Khun Eng. 2006. "The Worship of Qingshui Zushi and Religious Revivalism in South China." In *Southern Fujian: The Reproduction of Traditions in Post-Mao China*, ed. C-b. Tan. Hong Kong: Chinese University Press, 121–44.

Kwok, Kristine. 2007. "Rebirth of Taoism Fills Spiritual Void in Rush to Consumerism." *South China Morning Post*, 30 April. china.scmp.com/chifeatures/ZZZ9-IDQU01F.html.

Lee, Hai-yan. 2009. "The Ruins of Yuanmingyuan: Or, How to Enjoy a National Wound." *Modern China* 35: 155–90.

Lefebvre, Henri. 1991 [1974]. *The Production of Space*. Trans. Donald Nicholson-Smith. Oxford: Blackwell.

MacCannell, Dean. 1989. *The Tourist: A New Theory of the Leisure Class*, 2nd ed. New York: Schocken.

———. 1992. *Empty Meeting Grounds*. New York and London: Routledge.

Martinsen, Joel. 2007. "The Dazhai Spirit Gets Religion." Danwei, October 8. www.danwei.org/magazines/dazhai_gets_religion_and_other.php.

McCarthy, Susan. 2004. "Gods of Wealth, Temples of Prosperity: Party-State Participation in the Minority Cultural Revival." *China: An International Journal* 2(1): 28–52.

Naquin, Susan, and Yü, Chün-fang. 1992. "Introduction: Pilgrimage in China." In *Pilgrims and Sacred Sites in China*. Berkeley: University of California Press.

National Tourism Administration. 2007. *China Tourism Yearbook 2006*. Beijing: National Tourism Administration Press.

Nyíri, Pál. 2006. *Scenic Spots: Chinese Tourism, the State, and Cultural Authority.* Seattle: University of Washington Press.

————. 2009. "Between Encouragement and Control: Tourism, Modernity, and Discipline in China." In *Asia on Tour: Exploring the Rise of Asian Tourism*, ed. T. Winter, P. Teo, and T. C. Chang. London and New York: Routledge, 153–69.

Oakes, Tim. 1998. *Tourism and Modernity in China.* New York and London: Routledge.

Poon, Shuk-wah. 2008. "Religion, Modernity, and Urban Space: The City God Temple in Republican Guangzhou." *Modern China* 34(2): 247–75.

Potter, Pitman B. 2003. "Belief in Control: Regulation of Religion in China." In *Religion in China Today*, ed. Daniel Overmyer. Cambridge: Cambridge University Press, 12–31.

Rack, Mary. 2005. *Ethnic Distinctions, Local Meanings: Negotiating Cultural Identities in China.* London: Pluto.

Rinschede, G. 1988. "The Pilgrimage Center of Fátima/Portugal." In *Pilgrimage in World Religions, Geographia Religionum*, ed. S. Bhardwaj and G. Rinschede. Berlin: Dietrich Reimer 4: 65–98.

Robinson, Mike, and Priscilla Boniface. 1999. *Tourism and Cultural Conflicts.* New Delhi: CABI.

Rowe, William T. 1989. *Hankow: Conflict and Community in a Chinese City.* Stanford: Stanford University Press.

Sangren, P. Steven. 1987. *History and Magical Power in a Chinese Community.* Stanford: Stanford University Press.

Seligman, Adam B., Robert P. Weller, Michael Puett, and Bennett Simon, eds. 2008. *Ritual and Its Consequences: An Essay on the Limits of Sincerity.* London and New York: Oxford University Press.

Shackley, Myra. 1999. "Managing the Cultural Impacts of Religious Tourism in the Himalayas, Tibet and Nepal." In *Tourism and Cultural Conflicts,* ed. M. Robinson and P. Boniface. New York: CABI.

Shepherd, Robert. 2006. "UNESCO and the Politics of Cultural Heritage in Tibet." *Journal of Contemporary Asia* 36(2): 243–57.

Siegel, James T. 1969. *The Rope of God.* Berkeley: University of California Press.

Sun, Qitai, and Xiong Zhiyong. 1990. *Dazhai Hongqide Shengqing yu zhuiluo.* Zhengzhou: Henan renmin chubanshe.

Sutton, Donald S., and Xiaofei Kang. 2009. "Recasting Religion and Ethnicity: Tourism and Socialism in Northern Sichuan, 1992–2005." In *Casting Faiths: The Construction of Religion in East and Southeast Asia*, ed. Thomas Dubois. New York: Palgrave Macmillan, 190–214.

Tan, Chee-Beng, ed. 2006. *Southern Fujian: Reproduction of Traditions in Post-Mao China.* Hong Kong: Chinese University Press.

Timothy, Dallen J., and Daniel H. Olsen. 2006. "Tourism and Religious Journeys." In *Tourism, Religion, and Spiritual Journeys*, ed. D. Timothy and D. Olsen. London and New York: Routledge.

Tomba, Luigi. 2009. "Of Quality, Harmony, and Community: Civilization and the Middle Class in Urban China." *positions: east asia cultures critique* 17(3): 591–616.

Turner, Victor, and Edith Turner. 1978. *Image and Pilgrimage in Christian Culture: Anthropological Perspectives*. New York: Columbia University Press.

Urry, John. 1995. *Consuming Places*. London and New York: Routledge.

———. 2002. *The Tourist Gaze*, 2nd ed. London: Sage.

Wang, Ning. 2000. *Tourism and Modernity: A Sociological Analysis*. London: Pergamon.

Watson, James. 1985. "Standardizing the Gods: The Promotion of T'ien Hou ('Empress of Heaven') Along the South China Coast, 960–1960." In *Popular Culture in Late Imperial China*, ed. D. Johnson, A. J. Nathan, and E. S. Rawski. Berkeley: University of California Press, 292–324.

Winter, Tim. 2009. "Asian Tourism and the Retreat of Anglo-Western Centrism in Tourism Theory." *Current Issues in Tourism* 12(1): 21–31.

Xinhuanet. 2002. "China's Model Village: From Political Symbol to Brand Name." 27 June. news.xinhuanet.com/english/2002–06/27/content_460077.htm.

Yang, Mayfair Mei-hui. 2008. *Chinese Religiosities: Afflictions of Modernity and State Formation*. Berkeley: University of California Press.

Yardley, Jim. 2007. "China: Survey Suggests Greater Religious Belief." *New York Times*, 8 February. www.nytimes.com/2007/02/08/world/asia/08briefs-chinareligion.html.

———. 2008. "China's Tough Line in Tibet Is Seen to Have Brought Only Resentment." *International Herald Tribune,* 17 March.

Zweig, David. 1989. *Agrarian Radicalism in China, 1968–1981*. Cambridge, MA: Harvard University Press.

Spirit Money

Tourism and Pilgrimage on the Sacred Slopes of Mount Tai

Brian R. Dott

Mount Tai (Taishan) is one of the most famous religious and tourism sites in China. Located in the center of the North China Plain about 450 kilometers south of Beijing, the first among the Five Marchmounts (*wuyue*), it was ascended by Confucius, has been the frequent site for rituals of legitimation and filial piety, is a place to interact with nature and a space covered with historic sites. Over the centuries beliefs centered on the mountain have shifted significantly. In recent years the government of the People's Republic of China has been actively promoting cultural and religious sites as both a means to earn tourism monies and as an expression of nationalist pride in China's past. The officially atheist government of the PRC is continually walking a fine line between preserving culture and actually encouraging religious practice at Mount Tai. Since the mid-1980s the government has been supporting both domestic and international tourism to the mountain. There are a number of new hotels both on the mountain and in the city of Tai'an at its base. On a mountain famous for the hardships that believers had to endure during the ascent as proof of their faith, a recently renovated gondola as well as two chair lifts carry visitors effortlessly to the top. While most of the recent state-endorsed literature about the mountain emphasizes its history and the natural scenery, much restoration is taking place in temples. While the majority of visitors would probably identify themselves as tourists, many still make offerings in the temples. Similarly many self-identified pilgrims engage in what many would regard as tourism. This evidence from Mount Tai thus forces us to dismantle artificial dichotomies such as tourist or pilgrim, sacred or secular, and economic development or preservation of culture. Most visitors to Mount Tai approach the mountain from multiple perspectives. Since 1949 the state has encouraged secular and what is now called "red" tourism at the mountain. More recently "green" tourism has also been marketed. In addition, although not directly promoted by the state, religious worship is an important draw as well. Like Jinggangshan, studied in chapter 3 by Yu Luo Rioux, Mount Tai is a popular destination because of these multiple factors. Individual visitors approach the mountain with differing levels of interest in each of these factors. While significant changes have occurred in the way people interact with Mount Tai since 1949, there are limits to how much change can be imposed from the top down. To be long-lasting, the changes must resonate with popular beliefs and desires. Mount Tai as a "red" tourist destination has not taken off because revolutionary sites do not resonate with the symbolic capital of the mountain.

BACKGROUND

Beliefs about Mount Tai are intimately connected with natural renewal, life, birth, and rejuvenation. In prehistoric times Mount Tai was almost certainly a focus for agricultural worship. The highest point (1,545 meters) in the North China Plain, Mount Tai was a recipient of prayers for rain. Such agricultural worship is often associated with fertility in general and Mount Tai came to be seen as the source of all life (*wanwu zhi shi*). The earliest references to Four and Five Marchmounts (*si yue*, *wu yue*) assign Mount Tai, the Eastern Marchmount (*Dongyue*), to the position of leader (*wuyue zhi zhang*). The mountain's position in the east associated it with the sunrise and the source of life (see Dott 2004, part 1). The sacred nature of the mountain itself means that rocks, trees, springs, and even man-made structures, such as temples and arches, on the mountain's slopes can absorb and manifest sacrality or be utilized in rituals. As the highest point in the region it was a natural site for prayers to Heaven, and served as an *axis mundi* (see Eliade 1959, 20–25, 35–37).

Mount Tai was an important site for imperial legitimation rituals at least since the earliest written historical works. The *Book of History*, for example, includes accounts of the sage-ruler Shun visiting Mount Tai as part of his duties (*Shang shu* 1991, 99–100). The *feng* and *shan* sacrifices (*fengshan si*) were important, rarely performed imperial legitimation rites at Mount Tai. Although purported to be of ancient origin, they were first performed by Qin Shihuangdi in 219 BCE. The list of other emperors who performed these rites is quite short: Han Wudi (r. 140–87 BCE) was the only emperor to perform the rites multiple times, Guangwu di of the Later Han dynasty performed them in 56 CE, Gaozong of the Tang dynasty performed them in 666, Xuanzong also of the Tang dynasty in 725, and Shenzong of the Northern Song dynasty in 1008.[1] No emperors during the Yuan or Ming dynasties personally visited the mountain, although they did send emissaries. During the Qing dynasty both the Kangxi (r. 1662–1722) and Qianlong (r. 1736–1795, d. 1799) emperors made multiple trips to the mountain, but both refused to perform the *feng* and *shan* sacrifices. They argued that since the rites were not actually ancient they were not as significant as had been claimed. Performance of the rites implied that the performer was announcing to Heaven and Earth that he had reached the epitome of rulership. Both the Kangxi and Qianlong emperors, however, viewed rulership as a continuous process that could hardly be said to have been accomplished. Despite this attitude, however, these two Manchu rulers did still use their trips to the mountain as means to project their imperial power. By visiting a key Han Chinese sacred site Kangxi sought to demonstrate to the Han elite that he both understood and honored Chinese culture. He needed to legitimate Manchu rule and recruit Han into the bureaucracy. Despite this need to project a positive image to the Han elite, Kangxi also found ways to emphasize his Manchu identity while on Mount Tai. By the time of his grandson's reign there was no longer any such need for broad legitimation of the dynasty. Instead Qianlong used the mountain in his project of imperial self-aggrandizement.[2]

By about 1500 the Goddess of Mount Tai (*Taishan niangniang*, or *Bixia Yuanjun*) had become the most popular deity at Mount Tai. The rise in popularity of this goddess parallels the increasing popularity of other female deities such as Guanyin, Mazu, and the Eternal Mother.[3] The main temple to this fertility goddess, the Bixia Temple (*Bixia ci*), just below the summit, was and still is the focal point of pilgrimages in honor of the goddess. This temple, being located on top of the mountain and thus close to Heaven was and still is seen as the most efficacious place to worship the goddess. From 1500 until the middle of the twentieth century on average about four hundred thousand people made the pilgrimage to Mount Tai annually (Dott 2004, 88; Pomeranz 1997, 182).[4] The vast majority of these pilgrims traveled from within about 350 kilometers of the mountain. The goddess was prayed to by women and men, most commonly for sons. She is almost always flanked by at least two assistant goddesses. The chief of these is the Goddess of Eyesight, her connection with Mount Tai most likely coming from the mountain's association with the source of light—the sun. All of the other assistants specialize in some aspect of pregnancy or infancy, including conception, delivery, nursing, measles, and smallpox. Many women on pilgrimage to the Bixia Temple view their prayers as a conversation with a community of goddesses. The close, personal connection worshipers feel with the Goddess of Mount Tai is seen in the popular form of address for her—Old Granny (*lao nainai*). Indeed, some of the female pilgrims refer to their prayers to the goddess as "chatting with Old Granny (*gen lao nainai tanyitan*)."[5]

In addition to mass pilgrimages by people from the lower strata of late imperial society, Mount Tai also attracted visitors from the elite. During the late imperial period, travel, including leisure travel, became more and more common among the elite.[6] Mount Tai was an important site to be visited. Officials journeying to or from the capital would often make a trip to the mountain. Literati were seeking a very different experience from the pilgrims visiting the goddess's temple. They sought to walk in Confucius's footsteps: according to the *Mencius* Confucius climbed Mount Tai and saw that the world was small (1970, 187).[7] A number of sites on the mountain take their names from stories about Confucius's ascent, and these were popular stops as the literati made their ascents. In the late sixteenth century a temple honoring Confucius was erected on the top of the mountain. Literati visitors also enjoyed viewing natural scenery and historic sites. While many of their actions seem like those of modern tourists, I argue elsewhere that these men often focused on moral self-renewal or self-cultivation through interactions with nature and reflections about history (Dott 2004, ch. 3; see also Wu 1990, 1992; and Dudbridge 1991). Thus, while for the most part they were not praying at the goddess's temple, they were nonetheless also pilgrims. The majority of contemporary visitors to Mount Tai fit into this literati mode of interacting with the mountain. They enjoy the scenery, examine the historic sites, recite poetry, and fasten locks in temples.

Communist leaders in charge of overseeing Mount Tai built upon changes begun during the Republican period (1911–1949). The primary instigators of these changes or reforms were well-educated elite, many working for the government, but others operating privately. They had two main motivations. The first was reduction, if not elimination, of what they saw as "superstitious" practices. Some of the most vocal members of the elite, during late imperial times as well as the Republican era, viewed popular religious practices, including pilgrimages, skeptically, seeing them as means for confidence tricksters and corrupt religionists to dupe money out of the naïve and unsuspecting masses.[8] This paternalistic attitude meshed nicely with the neo-Confucian education that most of these men had received. It was the duty of the better educated and more privileged to look out for the interests of those socially below them. These reformers shared the general belief among mid and late Qing elites that the Goddess of Mount Tai was illegitimate, and that female pilgrims engaged in unseemly behavior, as Kenneth Pomeranz has discussed in his article "Orthopraxy, Orthodoxy, and the Goddess(es) of Taishan" (2007). The other major goal of reshaping the symbolism of Mount Tai was to create a national icon around which the new nation could build images of strength and vitality. Both goals included downplaying religious and sacred aspects, and representing the mountain instead as a secular icon for the new, modern China. Early leaders in Communist China initially treated Mount Tai in ways very similar to their Republican predecessors. They sought to make what they viewed as a site for superstitious, feudal practices into secular space and a national symbol of the New China. In addition, the official Marxist belief that religion was a system for enslaving and deceiving the masses meant that religious practices on the mountain were in need of dismantling. Furthermore, Communist leaders sought to make the mountain a revolutionary pilgrimage site.

In promoting visits to Mount Tai the contemporary state is caught in a conundrum—attracted by the potential for tourism monies, yet reluctant to encourage what it traditionally condemned as superstitious practices. In addition, there are both internal and external pressures for religious freedom. Thus the state finds itself indirectly promoting religious practices that it has officially condemned. However, the religious practices on Mount Tai are perceived by the state as less dangerous than many others. This type of indigenous Chinese religion does not carry the perceived threat of dividing loyalties or charismatic living leaders, as Catholicism, Tibetan Lamaism, or Islam can. At Mount Tai, the state is directly in control of religious professionals; in 2006 the abbot at the main Bixia Temple was trained at the state-run, national Daoist seminary in Beijing (the *Baiyun guan*). The state can point to costly temple renovations and an increase in the number of resident monks and nuns as proof of religious tolerance. Since I first started visiting the mountain there has been a continuous series of temple renovations. This does not mean that the state is going out of its way to promote religious practice. Indeed, as will be shown in detail in the next section, in print and presentation the state primarily emphasizes secular aspects of the mountain.

There is, however, one group to which the government seems to actively promote Mount Tai's religious traditions. Overseas Chinese, especially Taiwanese, are specifically targeted for religious tourism. Many of the temples contain plaques listing donations for renovations that are filled, sometimes exclusively, with names of overseas Chinese, especially from Taiwan. On a visit in 2000 during the off-season the largest group by far that I saw worshiping at the main Bixia Temple was a religious society from Taizhong, Taiwan.

It is easy to characterize "the state" or "the party" under the PRC and individual officials as representing a single viewpoint and always acting in concert. This is far from the truth. In fact the motives of local officials often differ widely from those of national leaders. Unfortunately the nature of many of the sources related to Mount Tai make discerning motives quite difficult. I will return to this theme in the section on secularization below.

SEARCH FOR BLESSINGS

In contemporary times many worshipers still beseech the Goddess of Mount Tai and her assistants for a son. At Spring Festival and the birthdays of Bixia Yuanjun and Xiwangmu (the Queen Mother of the West), another popular goddess associated with Mount Tai, pilgrims dominate the path up the mountain.[9] At other times of the year those who ascend primarily for the purpose of praying in the goddess's main temple can come at any time, but are most numerous on the first and fifteenth of the lunar months. Recent changes in medical science, such as fertility drugs, have not stopped prayers to end infertility. Those who are fertile may request that their one child allowed by the state be a son. Thus, while changes in medicine and society have not ended the desire to pray for children, some interesting changes in emphasis have occurred. For example, girl votive dolls, once unknown, while not as numerous as boy ones, are now available. Related to this, a few pilgrims expressed their desire for a daughter rather than a son. Also, the Smallpox Goddess has not been worshiped on Mount Tai since the widespread use of the smallpox vaccine. In fact, her image is rarely found on the mountain. Another change is the primary motivation for pilgrimage to the goddess's main temple. In late imperial and Republican times the main purpose was to pray for sons. At least since the mid-1990s more pilgrims seem to be emphasizing prayers for general well-being (*bao ping'an*).

The state, through the Mount Tai Scenic and Historic Site Administrative Committee, controls who can sell things on the mountain and what they can sell. Some of the most popular items are incense, spirit money, images of Bixia Yuanjun, and votive figures of boys and girls. At the peak points of pilgrimage many worshipers travel in organized societies. These groups typically bring their offerings of incense and spirit money with them. Those who buy the incense and spirit money on site tend to be those whose primary motivation in coming to the mountain was not prayer. The sellers of these religious items, predominantly women, also act as religious instructors, teaching the ardent, and especially the reluctant, worshipers how to properly light the incense, kowtow, and phrase their prayers. While state-endorsed brochures, maps, signs, and picture books de-emphasize prayers and rituals on the mountain, many visitors who had not planned to pray end up doing so. For example, I have witnessed couples who somewhat reluctantly agreed to pray to the goddess and make an incense offering, laughing during the whole process, yet still following through with three full kowtows.

A new ritual that had become common in 2000 and even more popular since is fastening a lock to one of the bronze incense burners in the main Bixia Temple. This was done by couples who wanted to seal their relationships for

Figure 1.1. Worshipers near the base of the mountain on Bixia Yuanjun's birthday (Lunar calendar 3/15). Incense sellers' stock can be seen stacked along the right-hand edge of the photo. B. Dott photo, 1995.

life. In the past, when the vast majority of marriages were arranged, the two families involved, as well as a matchmaker, all worked to preserve a relationship. In contemporary China, when many matches are now made solely by the choice of the two individuals, some couples are searching for new ways to protect their union. While this ritual is new and not unique to Mount Tai, it would not resonate so strongly with modern youth unless there was some link with other beliefs and practices associated with the mountain. Bixia Yuanjun, as a fertility goddess, is intimately connected with conjugal relationships. Characteristics associated with Mount Tai expressed in the popular sayings (discussed below)—stable, steady, and significant—are also all desirable attributes for long and happy relationships. The locks and these sayings are examples of what Jun Jing calls "cultural invention" and Helen Siu refers to as "recycling rituals." Jing and Siu argue that the upsurge in popular religious practice in reform-era China is not simply a reemergence of pre-1949 practices, but adaptations of past practices to fit new social realities (Jing 1996, 175; Siu 1989).

In dismantling the black-and-white separation of modern tourism from pilgrimage, it is important to remember that there has always been an element of tourism in any historic pilgrimage. This is certainly true of modern pilgrimages to Mount Tai. After their prayers are completed many of the pilgrims spend time on top of the mountain in more mundane pursuits, such as visiting the very top of the mountain, watching the sunrise, looking at inscriptions, and taking photos. One pilgrimage group that I observed and spoke with on Bixia's birthday in 1995 spent a couple of hours praying, singing, and burning offerings at the incense oven located just below the main temple on top of the mountain. Due to the danger of fire, incense and spirit money can only be burned in this detached edifice. Since all prayers are carried by the smoke of the burning offerings, this incense oven is for many pilgrims the ultimate goal of their journey. Indeed this particular pilgrimage group did not enter the main temple proper until the following day, when their main activity was taking photos of one another in the main courtyard.

The tourist-like actions of these pilgrims touch upon the concept of "authenticity." Many commentators on modern religious practices, often when examining a culture different from their own, decry changes and the lack of "authenticity." For example, many visitors to Mount Tai have not had many opportunities to offer incense or pray at temples and therefore may do so "incorrectly" from the perspective of a seasoned practitioner. However, if both offerings are sincere does authenticity really matter? In 1995 the same pilgrimage group discussed above included a number of songs about Guanyin during their long session of prayers and offerings. While this could be seen as inauthentic worship, one could not help but be impressed by the sincerity, devotion, and piety of this group of women.

An additional recent change falls under the rubric of economic development and commercialization. In this context a widely perceived disparity between cultural preservation and economic development needs to be assessed. While recent building booms in China, especially in urban areas, have indeed resulted in the destruction of numerous temples, on Mount Tai development has actually led to much temple restoration. The Confucian Temple was repaired in 1994; in 2000 a Sanguan (three officials) Temple had been recently restored and opened; in 2002 the Lingying Palace (a subsidiary Bixia temple) reopened; in 2006 a Guandi Temple (God of War), closed since the 1960s, reopened and was undergoing repairs; and in 2010 work began to double the size of the Lingying Palace. While commercialization can impact the landscape or even the tone of a site, it does not automatically lead to a decrease in the piety of visitors. From 1994 through the summer of 2000 it was not possible for worshipers to pray to the goddess inside the main hall of the Bixia Temple. The doors to the hall contain latticework so worshipers could see the statues of Bixia and two of her assistant goddesses, but they had to pray on the porch outside the doors. In the summer of 2006, however, worshipers who made a donation of at least 100 yuan were allowed by the resident monks to pray inside the hall. While this gives the appearance of crass commercialization associated with the new market economy, such relationships between the wealthy and religious institutions are nearly universal. Certainly members of different social classes have always had distinct experiences on Mount Tai. In the past the wealthy were carried up the mountain in sedan chairs, ate better food, and lodged in better rooms.[10] Today the only difference is that the wealthy mostly take the gondola to the top, although sedan chairs became available again in the 1980s after being banned in the 1960s.

Viewing the sunrise from mountain tops is a common ritual in East Asia. While many of the recent publications about the mountain emphasize the natural beauty and professional photographers take tourist poses of visitors balancing the sun on the palms of their hands, it is difficult to dissociate the sunrise from spiritual renewal and reawakening. The sunsets viewed from the peak are equally stunning visually, but almost no one gathers on the western side of the summit to watch this daily natural phenomenon. Many late imperial literati writings take a similar stance. Indeed viewing the sunrise was the most common subject for poetry, which tended to focus on the natural beauty, though some authors referred to the metaphor of renewal. Many Republican-era writers took the same approach. For example, a geography text from 1936 notes that Mount Tai is the Eastern Marchmount, gives another ancient name for the mountain, then states that the sunrise can be viewed from the Sun Viewing Peak on clear days (*Benguo dili* 1936, 97). While many of the modern visitors may not be conscious of the religious aspects of viewing the sunrise, they are cognizant of the fact that the "Sun Viewing Peak" is located on the eastern edge of the summit and that one should watch the sun *rise* from there. Any line separating tourists from pilgrims on Mount Tai is exceedingly difficult to delineate. Instead of secular and sacred motivations being contradictory, visitors to the mountain seek varying levels of both.

SECULARIZATION

The first Communist monument was built on the mountain in 1946. In that year an obelisk was erected to honor the 708 martyrs who died during the liberation of Tai'an from the Nationalists. When the Nationalists retook the city shortly afterward one of their first acts was to destroy this Communist monument. After Liberation, the Communists reerected it in 1953. The Communists also decided to honor the warlord Feng Yuxiang for his resistance of Japanese occupation, building a tomb for him at the base of the mountain in 1952 (Yan 1993, 27, 75). In addition, the party buried two of its own members at the mountain's base. Fan Mingshu was born near Mount Tai in 1866 and died in 1947. He was active in the May Fourth Movement, and became a member of the party in 1946. His body was reburied on the mountain in 1950 (Yan 1993, 76). Qiu Huanwen was a native of Shandong who became a member of the Communist Party in 1931. His grave and memorial stele, much more modest in scale than those of Feng Yuxiang or Fan Mingshu, was put up in 1961 (*Qiu Huanwen* 1961). In these attempts to create revolutionary space out of what was officially seen as superstitious space, there is a strong parallel with the party's conversion of the so-called feudal, imperial space of Tiananmen Square into revolutionary space. During the 1950s and early 1960s while the party attempted to add this new revolutionary layer to the mountain, there was no active campaign to suppress religious practice. A number of restoration projects were completed during this time, including extensive repairs to the Bixia Temple in 1956 (Taishan fengjing 2001, 76–93). The government allowed pilgrimage to continue and the resident monks to remain, but did little to promote religious practice on Mount Tai during this period.

An interesting example of the interplay between traditional practices and these revolutionary sites can be seen in an adaptation of an earlier ritual at both of the Communist graves mentioned above. Again, we can see what Jing and Siu respectively label "invention" or "recycling" in the creation of new rituals (Jing 1996 and Siu 1989). A fertility ritual that is still practiced involves picking twigs from cypress trees and placing them behind one's ear or upon an altar. This ritual is based on a pun. Cypress twig (*baizhi*) is pronounced *baizi* in the local dialect, which is a homophone for one hundred, or many children. The placing of a cypress twig then represents a request for many children. Being green it can represent renewal, and being an evergreen, the cypress also represents long life. In the spring of 1995 I observed that both of the tombs of the Communist cadres were covered with cypress twigs. While it could be argued that revolutionary space has appropriated the earlier ritual, it would be just as easy to say that the original practice has reappropriated the revolutionary space. Rather than giving precedence to one over the other, a more complex synthesis makes a more compelling explanation. The twigs on the tombs could be seen as expressing gratitude for the renewal that these early Communists brought to China. While the tombs honor these men for their worldly contributions to creating a new China, the cypress twigs add religious intensity to their memory. A similar mingling of the sacred and secular can be seen in an event I witnessed in 1994. An older woman kowtowed and prayed before a bust of the warlord Feng Yuxiang in the Buddhist temple at the base of the mountain that he made into his headquarters during his fight to resist the Japanese. Such an act would not have been endorsed by Feng, who emphasized that he was a Christian, or by the Communists who placed the bust there not as a religious icon, but as a monument to Feng's populist political views and his ardent resistance of the Japanese. The sacrality of space on the mountain, due to its power as an *axis mundi*—surely the core of what the Communists were seeking to dismantle—continues to manifest itself, although often in new ways.

The mid-1960s through the late 1970s was a time of major change on Mount Tai. Throughout this period, especially during the height of the Red Guards during the Cultural Revolution, the party made a concerted effort to sever the Chinese people from their past traditions, because they were deemed "feudal" and oppressive. This philosophy often resulted in the destruction of temples, homes, gardens, and other buildings connected with historic sites. At the same time the government also severely restricted all visits to the mountain, especially any that could be viewed as religious pilgrimages. Religious worship of any kind was banned. In 1965 the government forced all the monks and nuns residing on Mount Tai to leave the temples and to enter secular life elsewhere. Red Guards destroyed numerous religious statues and damaged many of the temples. A portrait of Mao was placed on the Southern Heavenly Gate (Taishan fengjing 2001, 103). In 1967 plans were made to tear down and replace the Jade Emperor Temple at the extreme summit of Mount Tai with a fifteen-meter-tall statue of Mao. While the planners went so far as to build a model of the top of the mountain with the statue in place and send it to Beijing, the plans did not go any further (Taishan fengjing 2001, 100–101). It seems that without some major event, battle, or speech associated with Mao or other major Communist leaders and Mount Tai it was not possible to mold the mountain into a predominantly revolutionary site. Mount Tai, unlike Jing-gangshan, discussed in Rioux's chapter, does not draw "red tourists."

In 1994 the Tai'an Municipal Communist Party Committee and the Tai'an Municipal Government erected a large bust of the famous PLA soldier Lei Feng in a plaza adjacent to the train and long-distance bus stations. Thus, when visitors got their first glimpses of the mountain, they were also confronted with the bust personifying revolutionary self-sacrifice for the greater good of the whole society. Lei Feng died saving a fellow soldier. He became larger than life when he was used as an exemplum of selfless duty to the army, party, and country. A diary published under his name became mandatory reading for PLA soldiers in 1963. Subsequently Chairman Mao encouraged everyone, not just soldiers, to learn from Lei Feng (Spence 1990, 597–98). The writing beneath the bust at Mount Tai, in Mao's calligraphy, urged everyone to "Learn from Comrade Lei Feng's example." Admiration of Lei Feng was at its height during the Cultural Revolution, a time when all the temples on Mount Tai were closed to worshipers and when "superstitious practices" were violently condemned. The Lei Feng statue was part of the government suppression of religion through promotion of revolutionary heroes. The message of the state, however, did not seem to get to the visitors. They quickly passed this potentially "red" site as they sought the path up the mountain. The message of self-sacrifice for the betterment of society does not resonate with visitors to the mountain, in contrast to the spontaneous new rituals with the locks or the cypress twigs, which have become very popular. Indeed, between 2006 and 2010, officials removed the statue, replacing it with a rock garden. One informant acknowledged that the statue was deemed "inappropriate" (*bu heshi*).

In contrast, the top of the mountain is a good example of successful secularization. The ultimate peak is surrounded by a small temple to the Jade Emperor. In the courtyard is a stone balustrade surrounding the very top of the mountain. A stone inscribed with the phrase "Ultimate summit of Mount Tai"[11] and the mountain's height, 1,545 meters, has been erected inside the balustrade. Most of those who climb to this summit do not even enter the shrine building containing a statue of the Jade Emperor. Instead they pose for photos in front of the inscription as proof they made it to the top.

With Deng Xiaoping's launching of the "Four Modernizations" in the late 1970s came a relaxation in restrictions on religious practice. People were able once again to visit local temples and pilgrimage sites. In 1985 monks and nuns were allowed to return to temples on Mount Tai.[12] The market reforms of the early 1980s created the possibility of promoting tourism to the newly emerging Chinese middle class. On Mount Tai many of the temples and shrines were renovated, and, to make access easier, the gondola was completed in 1983 (Shandongsheng 1993, 156). Concurrent with internal market

Figure 1.2. Statue of the revolutionary hero Lei Feng erected adjacent to the train station by the Tai'an Municipal Communist Party Committee and the Tai'an Municipal Government in 1994. The text is in Chairman Mao's handwriting. B. Dott photo, 1995.

reforms, the government was actively pursuing its "Open Door Policy" to the rest of the world. To become a more active player on the world stage, the leaders of the People's Republic of China, in addition to trade and diplomacy, promoted China's cultural and historic past. In 1987 the United Nations Educational, Scientific and Cultural Organization (UNESCO) endorsed the Chinese government's application to make Mount Tai a "World Cultural and Natural Heritage Site." In applying for World Heritage Site classification for various places in China, the Chinese government was looking for sites of national significance that would project Chinese culture and history to the rest of the world. The other sites also approved in 1987, the first year any Chinese sites were adopted, were the Forbidden City, the Great Wall, Qin Shihuangdi's tomb with its terra-cotta army, the Mogao Caves at Dunhuang, and the Peking Man site (UNESCO 2007).

In print the government endorsed a secular and natural image of Mount Tai. For example, a brochure for the goddess's main temple describes it as "an important Daoist temple" but does not discuss Bixia Yuanjun or her assistant goddesses and fertility rituals. Instead, it goes on to describe the physical layout, significant architectural details, and the history of the temple (Chen 1992). The party-state, which officially condemns elitism and seeks to root out so-called feudal practices, dates the various parts of the complex by

imperial reign. A similar ignoring of religious practice can be seen in a book
published by the Mount Tai Scenic and Historic Site Administrative Committee, which focuses on the natural beauty and historic sites (Taishan fengjing
1993). This work contains 233 photographs of sites on the mountain, but
the only pictures that include people worshiping are several taken during a
reenactment of an imperial offering to the God of Mount Tai that took place
in the main temple at the base of the mountain. It has no pictures of anyone
praying to Bixia Yuanjun.

There are numerous books about the history of Mount Tai, which tend to
focus on emperors, poets, and famous literati, and downplay the popular religious worship on the mountain. When religion is addressed it is to detail the
size of temples, the dates of renovations, and unique architectural features.
Several recent publications that reproduce inscriptions on the mountain claim
to do so with the goals of preserving historic texts for posterity and important calligraphy for its aesthetic appeal. In addition, several Ming and Qing
period texts have been reprinted recently in punctuated editions. Print media
reproduce a predominantly male view of the mountain, focusing on what the
authors and officials see as most rational, practical, and perhaps profitable to
the local economy. In contrast, how to worship the goddesses is passed along
orally by the predominantly female incense sellers and pilgrimage society
leaders. Furthermore, the influence of the leader of the 1995 pilgrimage group
extended well beyond the length of the pilgrimage; she was actively consulted
in religious and healing matters back in her hometown throughout the year.[13]
Thus, despite government attempts to write over female religious practice on
the mountain, women continue to assert their own agency and beliefs.

The push to revolutionize and secularize Mount Tai can be seen dramatically in a shift of the busiest day on the mountain. Prior to 1949 the greatest
number of pilgrims climbing the sacred mountain peaked on the lunar new
year and the birthday of the Goddess of Mount Tai. By the 1990s, however,
the busiest day on the mountain had become May Day. In 1997, 120,000
people climbed the mountain on May Day (Shandong dianshitai 1998, episode 5).[14] Most of these visitors do not make offerings in the various temples,
but instead focus on historic sites, reading inscriptions, reciting poetry, and
watching the sunrise from the summit. In 1995 a student at Renmin University in Beijing, recounting his visit to Mount Tai on May Day, remarked upon
the beautiful scenery, his recitation of a famous poem by Du Fu about the
mountain, and on watching the sunrise.[15] From the party's perspective, this
has been a highly successful secularizing and revolutionizing of the sacred
space of Mount Tai. The activities are, at least on the surface, all secular, occurring on a day honored by Communist parties and labor groups around the
world. However, despite the large number of visitors on May Day, the state

has not succeeded in revolutionizing the mountain to the degree that its official publications imply. For example, most visitors travel to the mountain on May Day not to honor the world's workers, but because it is a national holiday and spring is a good time of the year to enjoy the natural scenery. There is no mass honoring of Mao, Sun Yat-sen, Lei Feng, or any other revolutionary on top of the mountain. Instead, everyone is focused on the sunrise, which, as noted earlier, emphasizes renewal. Some of the visitors on May Day make offerings in temples. While secularization has occurred, these visitors' primary motivation for visiting is best described as tourism, but not as revolutionary or red pilgrimage. Interestingly, the activities undertaken by many visitors to Mount Tai today, visiting historic sites, reading inscriptions, reciting poetry, and watching the sunrise, are exactly the same as those favored by late imperial literati. One of the largest changes on Mount Tai is the greater percentage of visitors who are literate.

Mount Tai has also developed into a green destination. The natural beauty of the mountain was emphasized by many literati visitors throughout the late imperial period. Natural scenery predominates in the numerous recently published books about Mount Tai. This includes a number of books that mostly consist of beautiful photographs of the scenery. Indeed, the Chinese application for Mount Tai as a World Heritage Site emphasized the natural landscape as much as its historic and cultural significance: "Mt. Taishan possesses outstanding general value of natural science and unique value of aesthetics and historical culture" (Taishan fengjing 1993, 4). The importance of maintaining the mountain's verdant covering is reflected in a bas-relief and inscription erected at the base of the mountain in 1998 that express a deep nostalgia for past collective endeavors while emphasizing the need to preserve the natural environment:

Inscription Commemorating the Creation of the Mount Tai Forest

Since ancient times Mount Tai was heavily forested. From the end of the Qing, [because of] the decaying government, prohibitions [protecting] mountain pines [became] lax. Chaotic warfare was frequent, resulting in disaster for the mountain's forests. . . .

In the 1950s the Forestry Center's staff and workers, and masses stationed at [Mount] Tai from all over [the country], lived in stone rooms, drank from mountain springs, and waded into ever narrower ravines. They were combed by the wind and washed by the rain. It was as if [they were] fighting a war of many years. [As a result] the mountain's trees [reached their] greatest level of greenery. The Forestry Center's staff and workers, eating in the wind and sleeping in the dew, meticulously cultivated all of the seedlings [they] planted. . . .This achievement of our day will benefit posterity. The virtue of this endeavor is on a par with [the grandeur] of Mount Tai [itself]. (Tai'anshi lühua 1998)

Figure 1.3. **"Inscription Commemorating the Creation of the Mount Tai Forest,"** **erected by the Tai'an Municipal Greening Committee near the base of the mountain in** **1998. B. Dott photo, 2000.**

Here we see the desire to preserve collective cooperation as a positive characteristic of the Chinese people under the Communists. According to Maria Hsia Chang, selflessness, hard work, dedication, and collectivism are all traits "which the Communist Party now claims as uniquely 'Communist sentiments and principles'" (Chang 2001, 183). The inscription implies that past corrupt regimes abused the environment. In contrast, workers under the direction of the new state respected the environment, preserving it for future generations. The fact that few visitors take much time examining this inscription, while they enjoy the trees themselves, reflects Mount Tai's draw as a "green" rather than a "red" destination.

During Republican and Communist eras there were concerted efforts to redefine Mount Tai as a national symbol. The last line of the tree-planting inscription above is a good example of this. Mount Tai as a symbol of continuity between past and present, the foundation of Chinese culture, and the communal strength of all the Chinese people recurs throughout the Communist period. While the use of Mount Tai to project Chinese nationalism first developed in the twentieth century, it would have been much more difficult to achieve if it had not built upon earlier beliefs about the mountain. Most of the illiterate pilgrims during the late imperial period probably did not see the mountain as a broad cultural symbol, but they did see it as an important symbol of strength and endurance, particularly in association with its connections to life and death. Literati and emperors from that time definitely saw the mountain as an important symbol for a broader geographical area. The Kangxi emperor wrote a fascinating essay in which he demonstrated that the roots of Mount Tai's dragon veins (a *fengshui* term) originated in the Changbai Mountains in Manchuria (Kangxi 1969). Thus, as part of his campaign to legitimate Manchu rule in the eyes of the Han elite, he linked Mount Tai, a symbol for all of the former Ming territory, to his homeland. If Mount Tai originated in Manchuria, then surely so could the Son of Heaven. Qianlong, Kangxi's grandson, used his own inscriptions on Mount Tai to incorporate it into his imperial collection.[16] He too saw Mount Tai as much more than one mountain—it represented the core of his empire. Literati from the late imperial era also perceived Mount Tai as more than a regional pilgrimage site. Han Chinese elite from all over the empire journeyed to the mountain. They focused on it as the leader of the Five Marchmounts—the ancient demarcators of Chinese territory. They also associated it with the sage Confucius, the most important individual in their social-philosophic and education systems, and, to some, even a deity.

Various authors and officials during the Republican period found in the mountain a symbol for the whole nation. An excellent example of this can be found in a 1934 text:

> Mount Tai! The leader of the Five Marchmounts Mount Tai! Since the beginning has been a symbol (*xiangzheng*) of our China. Nation (*guo*) is an [abstract] concept; it needs something concrete to represent it. [If] this thing is not a river then it is a mountain, for example, Germany's Rhine or Japan's Mount Fuji. Our China uses both a river and a mountain as metaphors for national territory (*guo tu*). The river, I contend, is the Yellow River. The mountain, I contend, is Mount Tai. The Yellow River flows through the birthplace of the Chinese people (*zhonghua minzu*); it is also the place of origin of the world's ancient culture. China's Five Marchmounts originally marked the four extremes of early China's national borders (*guojing*). [Since] Mount Tai is the leader of the Five Marchmounts, Mount Tai can represent our China. (Lao Taipo 1934, 17)

The anonymous author of this short text lays out the logic of using Mount Tai as a national symbol quite well. While using the mountain to represent the abstract concept of a nation-state is necessarily new, it could not have been successful if the mountain had not already acquired layers of significance and fame over the preceding centuries.

Several popular sayings that refer to Mount Tai provide the basis for many of the ways in which Mount Tai has been used symbolically in the post-1949 period. These popular sayings draw upon Mount Tai's position as the leader of the

Five Marchmounts and its physical domination of the North China Plain, using Mount Tai as a symbol for Chinese national identity. "As significant as Mount Tai" (*zhong ru Taishan*) derives from a letter by Sima Qian found in the *Hanshu* in which he proclaimed that a person's death could be as significant as Mount Tai or as insignificant as a feather (Ban Gu 1962, 9.2732). Since 1949 the state has utilized this metaphor as a means of promoting Mount Tai as a symbol for the entire nation. For example, a 1998 documentary informs the viewers, "The foundation stones for the Monument to the People's Heroes come from the mountain veins of Mount Tai, epitomizing the phrase 'As significant as Mount Tai'" (Shandong dianshitai 1998, episode 1). The documentary continues, "The foundation stones for the Great Hall of the People are Mount Tai stones, epitomizing the phrase 'Steady as Mount Tai (*wen ru Taishan*).'" Both of these important revolutionary sites were built in the 1950s in the former imperial space of Tiananmen Square. The origins of a third phrase, "Stable Country and Peaceful People (*guo tai min an*)," may have nothing to do with Mount Tai, but in recent years many people have connected it with the mountain. In 1989 the phrase was engraved on the top of the mountain, directly linking it to the solid rock of this sacred site (Yang and Xue 1997, 47). One source even argues that the name of the city Tai'an derives from the saying (Taian Investment 2007). These metaphors utilize the symbolic capital of Mount Tai—its long-standing historic and cultural significance—to emphasize the stability and longevity of the People's Republic of China.

Treating the state or local officials as having a single goal or viewpoint is quite problematic. As we have seen, attitudes change over time. Official policies about religious practice on Mount Tai have varied from benign neglect to outright hostility to large-scale restoration. Alterations to the site reflect a variety of perspectives. While the Lei Feng bust and the inscription about tree planting both reflect nostalgia for Communist ideals such as self-sacrifice, the first had no overt connection to Mount Tai while the latter is intimately related to the site. Officially the renovations preserve past historic sites for their cultural and aesthetic value as well as serving as investments for future tourism revenues, yet local officials may have personal spiritual motivations as well. Pomeranz convincingly demonstrates that the late Qing elites were divided in their attitudes toward the Goddess of Mount Tai, and it seems likely that a similar diversity of views exists among officials today (Pomeranz 2007).

CONCLUSION

Over the past sixty years the Chinese Communist Party (CCP) has attempted to appropriate the sacred space of Mount Tai in a variety of ways. Officials have sought to both secularize and revolutionize the space, and, in conjunction, to stamp out the remnants of what they saw as superstitious practices. Later they have also pursued an economic path, marketing the mountain as a tourist destination. Additionally, they have emphasized the historic and cultural significance of Mount Tai, and promoted it as a national symbol. Overall, promotion has certainly been successful. Official tallies from 1990 recorded three million visitors to Mount Tai (Zhang Zeyu 1991, 16). In episode five of the documentary that aired in 2000, the viewer is taken back and forth between the early morning flag raising ceremony in Tiananmen Square and watching the sunrise from the summit of Mount Tai (Shandong dianshitai). Connecting two potent symbols of Chinese nationalism, the documentary attempts to endow the flag raising with the enduring life-giving symbolism of Mount Tai. The modern praises of this ancient mountain focus on its potential for renewal, stability, and endurance—emphasizing the important role of history in making this mountain a national symbol. The development of secular characteristics for the mountain has been extremely successful, and has led to significant changes in the way people interact with Mount Tai. The result is that many people now travel to the site to enjoy nature, learn about culture and history, and to view a national symbol. In contrast, however, making the mountain into a site for revolutionary or "red" pilgrimage or tourism fell flat at Mount Tai. There were no important revolutionary events or personages directly associated with the mountain to make such an association resonate. Official acquiescence to this fact is demonstrated by the removal of the Lei Feng statue.

While secularization of the mountain has certainly been successful, this does not mean that sacred aspects of the mountain have been suppressed. Clearly this was the hope and intention in the prereform era. Subsequently, however, there has been a greater willingness on the part of officials to use religious worship as a means to encourage additional tourism, primarily for economic reasons. Religious worship on Mount Tai of course goes far beyond just providing another reason for tourism. Contemporary pilgrimage to Mount Tai reflects not only a continuation of past practices but also new rituals. While the state would like all visitors to approach the mountain as a historic and natural site, the religious values of many of the actions undertaken on the mountain remain at, or at least close to, the surface—viewing the sunrise being a prime example. Perhaps the change with the largest impact on visitors to the mountain in the last fifty years is the increase in literacy. In the past the vast majority of visitors to Mount Tai were traveling as pilgrims to pray to Bixia Yuanjun, while only a minority could read and appreciate the numerous inscriptions. Now many of the visitors, whether they self-identify primarily as tourists or as pilgrims, enjoy reading inscriptions as they ascend the mountain and a stop at the Tang imperial cliff inscription is mandatory for all groups. Every visitor to Mount Tai interacts with multiple aspects of the mountain's identities. Some might prioritize natural scenery over historic sites, while others would place religious worship before watching the sunrise. Whatever their goals are it is unclear what we gain by labeling them as either pilgrims or tourists. Even the tourism income from the mountain can be seen as spirit money.

NOTES

1. For more on the *feng* and *shan* sacrifices see Dott 2004, 41–52.

2. For more on Kangxi's and Qianlong's visits see Dott 2004, ch. 2. For more on Qianlong's self-aggrandizement see Crossley 1999, ch. 6, and Stuart 1998.

3. For more on this shift see Dott, 72–77. For more on the increasing popularity of goddesses see Yü 2001, 491.

4. While there would have been annual fluctuations in the number of pilgrims, and times when the pilgrimage was greatly diminished (such as the Ming-Qing transition, the Taiping northern expedition, and the Boxer Uprising), there is evidence that in some years the number of pilgrims exceeded four hundred thousand.

5. References to fieldwork come from trips to the mountain in 1994, 1995, 2000, 2006, and 2010, as well as trips to rural areas in Shandong in 1995.

6. See Strassberg 1994; Brook 1988; Pomeranz 1997; and Wu 1990, 1992.

7. There are a number of popular although apocryphal stories about Confucius's ascent, most of which emphasize the supernatural eyesight he had while on top of the mountain. Associations between eyesight and the Eastern Marchmount such as these help to explain why the Goddess of Eyesight is so closely linked to Mount Tai. For stories about Confucius at Mount Tai see *Li ji,* 716; Wang, *Lun heng,* j. 4, 56; and *Liezi*, 10.

8. Chapters 68 and 69 of the seventeenth-century novel *Xingshi yinyuan zhuan* ridicule what the author saw as the corrupting practices of pilgrim society leaders. For an English translation of the chapters see Dudbridge 1992.

9. The birthday of Bixia Yuanjun is currently celebrated on the fifteenth of the third lunar month, and that of Xiwangmu on the third of the third lunar month.

10. An excellent insight into seventeenth-century commercialism is an account by Zhang Dai (1597–1684?) of his experience of a package tour: "Dai zhi," 37; trans. in Wu 1992, 74.

11. "*Taishan jiding*." The inscription is in complex or traditional rather than simplified characters. In *The Temple of Memories* Jun Jing argues that the use of complex characters and classical Chinese in religious texts and rituals "safeguards the sacredness of ritual performance by rejecting everyday language" (110).

12. Jiang Fengrong 1995. Personal communication. At the time he was the director of the Religion Department of the Mount Tai Scenic and Historic Site Administration Committee.

13. This information is derived from a trip to visit this pilgrimage group in their hometown of Boshan, Shandong, in July 1995.

14. This six-hour documentary was produced by Shandong Television and filmed from 1995 to 1998. It examines the history, culture, religion, and natural environment of the mountain. In the summer of 2000 the series aired on national CCTV.

15. Personal conversation with Dr. Sally Bormann, who was the student's English professor at the time.

16. For more on the Kangxi and Qianlong emperors' interactions with Mount Tai see Dott 2004, ch. 2.

REFERENCES

Ban, Gu. 1962. *Han shu* (Book of the [Former] Han). Repr. Beijing: Zhonghua shuju.

Benguo dili (Our national geography). 1936. n.p.: n.p.

Brook, Timothy. 1988. *Geographical Sources of Ming-Qing History*. Michigan Monographs in Chinese Studies, no. 58. Ann Arbor: University of Michigan, Center for Chinese Studies.

Chang, Maria Hsia. 2001. *Return of the Dragon: China's Wounded Nationalism*. Boulder: Westview Press.

Chen, Yupu. 1992. *Taishan Bixia ci* (Mount Tai Bixia Temple). Tai'an: Tai'anshi daojiao xiehui.

Crossley, Pamela. 1999. *A Translucent Mirror: History and Identity in Qing Imperial Ideology*. Berkeley: University of California Press.

Dott, Brian R. 2004. *Identity Reflections: Pilgrimages to Mount Tai in Late Imperial China*. Harvard East Asia Monographs, 244. Cambridge, MA: Harvard Asia Center.

Dudbridge, Glen. 1991. "A Pilgrimage in Seventeenth-Century Fiction: T'ai-shan and the *Hsing-shih yin-yüan chuan*." *T'oung Pao* 77(4–5): 226–52.

———. 1992. "Women Pilgrims to T'ai Shan: Some Pages from a Seventeenth-Century Novel." In *Pilgrims and Sacred Sites in China*, ed. Susan Naquin and Chün-fang Yü. Berkeley: University of California Press, 39–64.

Eliade, Mircea. 1959. *The Sacred and the Profane: The Nature of Religion*. Trans. Willard Trask. New York: Harcourt, Brace.

Jing, Jun. 1996. *The Temple of Memories: History, Power, and Morality in a Chinese Village*. Stanford: Stanford University Press.

Kangxi. 1969. "Taishan shanmai zi Changbaishan lai" (Mount Tai's dragon veins originate in the Changbai Mountains). In *Kangxidi yuzhi wenji* (Collection of the writings of the Kangxi emperor). 4 vols. Repr. Taipei: Taiwan xuesheng shuju.

Lao, Taipo, pseud. 1934. *Taishan youji* (Mount Tai travelogue). Beiping: Dumai she.

Li ji (Book of rites). 1991. In *Shisan jing* (The Thirteen Classics), ed. Wu Shuping. Beijing: Beijing yanshan chubanshe.

Liezi, yizhu (*Liezi*, annotated). 1987. Ed. Yan Jie and Yan Beiming. Hong Kong: Zhonghua shuju.

Mencius. 1970. Trans. D. C. Lau. New York: Penguin.

Pomeranz, Kenneth. 1997. "Power, Gender, and Pluralism in the Cult of the Goddess of Taishan." In *Culture and State in Chinese History: Conventions, Accommoda-*

tions, and Critiques, ed. Theodore Huters, R. Bin Wong, and Pauline Yu. Irvine
Studies in the Humanities. Stanford: Stanford University Press, 182–204.

———. 2007. "Orthopraxy, Orthodoxy and the Goddess(es) of Taishan." *Modern
China* 33(1): 22–46.

Qiu Huanwen. 1961. Grave marker at the base of Mount Tai.

Shandong dianshitai. 1998. *Zhonghua Taishan* (China's Mount Tai). Jinan: Qilu Au-
dio and Video Publishing Company. 12-episode documentary on VCD.

Shandongsheng difangshizhi bianzuan weiyuanhui. 1993. *Taishan zhi* 泰山志
(Mount Tai gazetteer). Shandongsheng zhi, no. 72. Beijing: Zhonghua shuju.

Shang shu 尚書 (Book of history). 1991. In *Shisan jing* (The Thirteen Classics), ed.
Wu Shuping 吳樹平. Beijing: Beijing yanshan chubanshe.

Siu, Helen F. 1989. "Recycling Rituals: Politics and Popular Culture in Contemporary
Rural China." In *Unofficial China: Popular Culture and Thought in the People's
Republic*, ed. Perry Link, Richard Madsen, and Paul Pickowicz. Boulder: Westview
Press, 121–37.

Spence, Jonathan D. 1990. *The Search for Modern China*. New York: Norton.

Strassberg, Richard E., trans. and annot. 1994. *Inscribed Landscapes: Travel Writing
from Imperial China*. Berkeley: University of California Press.

Stuart, Jan. 1998. "Imperial Pastimes: Dilettantism as Statecraft in the 18th Century."
In *Life in the Imperial Court of Qing Dynasty China*, ed. Chuimei Ho and Cheri
A. Jones. Proceedings of the Denver Museum of Natural History 3(15). Denver:
Denver Museum of Natural History, 55–65.

Taian Investment Promotion Committee. 2007. "Mt Tai & Tai'an." www.tszs.gov.cn/
html/gyy/kfq/lykfq/english.htm (accessed 30 July 2007).

Tai'anshi lühua weiyuanhui. 1998. "Taishan zaolin beiji (Inscription commemorating
the creation of the Mount Tai forest)." Stone inscription at the base of Mount Tai.

Taishan fengjing mingshengqu guanli weiyuanhui. 1993. *Zhongguo Taishan* (Mount
Taishan in China). Beijing: Wenwu.

———. 2001. *Bainian Taishan: 1900–2000* (One hundred years of Mount Tai:
1900–2000). Ji'nan: Shandong huabao chubanshe.

UNESCO. 2007. "The World Heritage List." whc.unesco.org/en/list (accessed 29
July 2007).

Wang, Chong. 1974. *Lun heng* (Balanced discourses). Repr. Shanghai: Shanghai
renmin chubanshe.

Wu, Pei-yi. 1990. *The Confucian's Progress: Autobiographical Writings in Traditional China*. Princeton: Princeton University Press.

———. 1992. "An Ambivalent Pilgrim to T'ai Shan in the Seventeenth Century." In
Pilgrims and Sacred Sites in China, ed. Susan Naquin and Chün-fang Yü. Berkeley: University of California Press, 65–88.

Xizhousheng, pseud. 1993. *Xingshi yinyuan zhuan* (Marriage destinies that will bring
society to its senses). 17th c. Repr. Ji'nan: Qilu shushe.

Yan, Jingsheng. 1993. *Taishan fengjing mingsheng daoyou* (Guide to Mount Tai's
scenic and famous sites). Ji'nan: Shandong wenyi chubanshe.

Yang, En, and Xue Yao, eds. 1997. *Taishan* (Mount Tai). Beijing: Renmin meishu
chubanshe.

Yü, Chün-fang. 2001. *Kuan-yin: The Chinese Transformation of Avalokiteśvara.* Institute for Advanced Studies of World Religions. New York: Columbia University Press.

Zhang, Dai. 1954. "Dai zhi" (Annals of Dai [Mount Tai]). In *Langxuan wenji* (Collected works of Zhang Dai). Repr. Taipei: Danjiang shuju, 36–44.

Zhang, Zeyu. 1991. "An Open City at the Foot of Mt Tai." *Beijing Review* 34(35): 15–20.

2

Alchemy of the Ancestors

Rituals of Genealogy in the Service of the Nation in Rural China

Tim Oakes

In 1984, a group of performers from Caiguan village in southwest China's Guizhou Province were invited to the Autumn Arts Festival of Paris. Festival organizers that year had made Chinese opera a centerpiece of the festival program, and brought three opera troupes from around China to perform. They included a *kunqu* troupe from Nanjing, a *yueju* troupe from Shanghai, and this ragtag band of Guizhou villagers. Along with the opera troupes came a group of teahouse storytellers from Chengdu, puppeteers and musicians from Beijing, and choral groups from Xi'an, Chengdu, Beijing, and Suzhou. With kunqu and yueju, the festival featured two of the principal styles of traditional Chinese theater. Kunqu is performed throughout China, and was the dominant theatrical style between the sixteenth and eighteenth centuries, while yueju, also known as Shaoxing opera, is a well-known regional opera style originating in Zhejiang Province (see Siu 1997; Swatek 2002; Zheng 2005). Compared with these refined styles of opera, the Guizhou villagers performed a more rustic and primitive kind of theater, known as *dixi*—typically translated as "ground opera." Festival organizers called dixi a "living fossil" of Chinese opera, as if it were more a mysterious ancient ritual than a form of high entertainment.[1]

Dixi is a relatively recent term for a form of masked ritual theater commonly performed by "tunpu people," descendants of soldiers sent from central China in the early Ming to conquer the remnants of the Yuan dynasty and secure the southwestern frontier over six hundred years ago. The *di* in dixi is descriptive (a drama performed "on the ground" and not on a stage) as well as evocative, suggesting a performance that is unmistakably *of the earth* and *of the folk*. *Xi*, or "play, drama," then locates this earthy folk drama within a broader landscape of Chinese opera. Dixi explicitly subsumes local folk ritual under the umbrella of a national theater tradition. The term itself thus conveys something of the living fossil idea celebrated in Paris.

Before dixi was discovered by China's rising tide of ethnographic and folklore research—part of the broader "culture fever" and "roots searching" that galvanized Chinese intellectuals and cultural producers in the 1980s—tunpu villagers simply called it *tiaoshen*, or "leaping spirits." Tiaoshen was a masked exorcism ritual performed over a several-day period during New Year's celebrations.[2] In some tunpu villages, tiaoshen was performed during midsummer as well. Invoking heroic ancestors, legendary warriors, and protector deities, tiaoshen exorcised the community of evil spirits and entreated the gods' blessings for good harvest and fortune in the coming year. Tiaoshen was the primary form of religious practice among tunpu men, and local scholars and officials often refer to it as a form of ancestor worship (Zheng 2001; Wang and Shen 1994). But officially, tiaoshen amounted to what the Chinese government would call "superstition" (*mixin*). This made it illegal. And indeed, the practice was banned in many villages throughout central Guizhou during the Cultural Revolution.

But in turning tiaoshen into dixi, and suggesting by this renaming that it was a kind of "living fossil" of national cultural heritage, scholars and local officials colluded to make tiaoshen legible to the state. Throughout China in the 1980s, scholars were discovering in the countryside the remains of folk cultural traditions thought to have been stamped out by ideological zeal of the Mao era. Their training in orthodox Marxist evolutionary theory led to a spate of living fossil labels for any cultural practice that seemed to have survived encrusted in the sediment of China's "timeless" rural society (see Yan 1989; Zhang 1996). Rituals such as tiaoshen were thought to have missed out on the evolutionary developments theorized by Friedrich Engels (after Lewis Henry Morgan and Edward Tylor) and taken as a fact of history by a whole generation of Marxist Chinese scholarship. In the 1980s, masked "leaping" dramas all over rural China were seen in this light, as frozen specimens with a direct link to a distant past (Zhou 1996). Ironically, however, the living fossil label did not simply take a cultural practice "out of time" but allowed it to be understood from the materialist perspective of evolutionary social theory. Living fossil practices like tiaoshen were thus explained in a way that was acceptable to the state. Instead of a superstition, tiaoshen became part of the nation's ancient heritage, a primitive pre-opera form that occupied the key evolutionary transition from exorcism rituals to refined opera forms like kunqu and yueju (Shen et al. 1990; see also Tan 2006).

Dixi, then, is not officially regarded as a form of popular religion (which is viewed with suspicion), but as a form of national theater (to be promoted as cultural heritage). Dixi turns tiaoshen into a frozen cultural ob[ject] dynamic expression of faith or belief. Observing this trend, D[...] 864) notes the common practice of ascribing the living fossil label to China's vast repertoire of ritual theater. "Living fossil," he writes, seeks to link the origins of masked ritual theater "back to the *nuo* ritual of classical times, as mentioned in the Confucian Analects and as described so colorfully in Han dynasty sources. The intervening two thousand years are seen as an unbroken line of traditions." Thus, by linking the local folk ritual of tiaoshen to classical tradition on a national scale, the term *dixi* frames that ritual with a modernist logic, seeking to calcify it as a state fossil, as national heritage. Referring to a similar process of state-sponsored heritage production in Daoist temples of Southeast China, Kenneth Dean and Thomas Lamarre (2003, 257) argue that a modern logic tends to frame Chinese ritual activities "as remnants or survivals of traditional, archaic or premodern modes, thus ignoring the contemporaneity of ritual activities in Southeast China (as well as the history of ritual practices)."

The transformation of tiaoshen as popular religion to dixi as cultural heritage is more than a labeling exercise. For as an artifact of cultural heritage, dixi is now consumed on demand. Dixi is now performed not once or twice a year to cleanse villages of malevolent powers, but many times a day—in quick fifteen-minute versions—to generate income from tourists and "promote Guizhou culture to the world." Scholarship on dixi has become something of a mini-industry in the region too, with some villages being promoted as "research laboratories" of ancient Chinese culture. The situation appears to be one in which ancient ritual has been captured by the modernist logic of both the state and the market, rendering its original efficacious properties incapacitated. In fact there are villagers who themselves make this claim, complaining that dixi has become meaningless even as its importance in village daily life has increased beyond measure. "No one understands dixi anymore," one old performer told me with a sigh, "the tourists don't understand it, the villagers don't understand it. Even some of the performers don't understand it. It's just entertainment now."

In this chapter, however, I want to offer a more complicated interpretation of this modern framing of ritual, one that highlights the fundamental role of ritual as a contemporary *site of negotiation* between villagers and the broader powers of the state and the tourism industry. As Dean and Lamarre (2003, 267) point out, ritual practices in contemporary China find themselves at a dangerous intersection between the state and global capital. While this always puts ritual at risk of capture by outside powers, it also provides an avenue by which that power is negotiated and, indeed, made efficacious in its own risky ways. Just as tiaoshen performers masked themselves for protection from ritual danger when they conjured the gods and invoked the blessings of their

Figure 2.1.   Dixi performed on a stage for tourists. "It's just entertainment now." T. Oakes photo, July 2009.

powerful ancestors, dixi performers today risk the calamitous powers of tourists and state officials as they entreat the favors of policies and cash. In short, ritual efficacy in rural Guizhou is reconstituted through tourism.

RITUAL AND THE BOUNDARIES OF AUTHORITY

Ritual is typically viewed as a symbolic and representational activity, as opposed to the instrumental activity of everyday life (Asad 1993, 55). The term tends to evoke a kind of nostalgia for the world of enchantment, where symbolic acts carried deep meanings, and behavior was matched by faith and belief in a world beyond the here and now. But ritual is also a term that tends to carry with it the baggage of modern epistemology. Viewing ritual as symbolic action requires that those symbols be decoded (by "experts" and trained intellectuals). Ritual is thus approached as a "referent for meaning whose true essence resides only beyond the ritual itself" (Seligman et al. 2008, 4). Ritual becomes a mere instrument of conveyance for some deeper meaning, "something else" hidden behind a superficial world of symbolic practice. The symbols deployed in ritual acts, to draw on Roy Rappaport's recent definition (1999, 24), are "not entirely encoded by the performers."

Yet, as Talal Asad has pointed out, what matters for ritual practitioners is not the interpretation of some stable foundation of meanings, but the skills needed to do what is prescribed. "In other words, apt performance involves not symbols to be interpreted but abilities to be acquired according to rules that are sanctioned by those in authority: [ritual] presupposes no obscure meanings, but rather the formation of physical and linguistic skills" (Asad 1993, 62). Ritual is more about *doing* than about conveying meaning, and it can occur without much regard for meaning at all (Seligman et al. 2008, 4). And while the implications of this view of ritual are many, one significant outcome of thinking about ritual as action more than interpretation is to notice the ways ritual practice negotiates one's relationship to authority. Consider, for example, Catherine Bell's view of ritual efficacy:

> Ritual is the medium chosen to invoke those ordered relationships that are thought to obtain between human beings in the here-and-now and non-immediate sources of power, authority, and value. Definitions of these relationships in terms of ritual's vocabulary of gesture and word, in contrast to theological speculation or doctrinal formulation, suggest that the fundamental efficacy of ritual activity lies in its ability to have people embody assumptions about their place in the larger order of things. (Bell 1997, xi)

Tiaoshen invoked this "larger order of things" by enacting both the cosmos of ancestor deities and the social power relations that governed village life. Two of the most important ritual practices associated with tiaoshen—*kaixiang qingshen* ("opening the box; inviting the gods") and *kai caimen* ("opening the gate of wealth")—both enact clearly this larger order of celestial authority and the villagers' position within that order. *Kaixiang qingshen*—carried out prior to the actual masked performance—involves opening a reliquary box and inviting the masks stored there to come out. The masks are then marched through the village to temples, wells, ponds, roads, bridges, and gates. At all the prominent households of the village, *kai caimen* occurs as well, in which the spirits are entreated to bestow wealth upon the village. The deferential handling of the masks, and the reinforcement both of celestial power and material wealth enacted in these rituals, suggest precisely the embodiment of power relations highlighted in Bell's perspective above. As the authors of *Ritual and Its Consequences* similarly argue, "Ritual creates and re-creates a world of social convention and authority beyond the inner will of any individual" (Seligman et al. 2008, 11). They add that "ritual acknowledges authority relations and their consequences for human existence in the world by positing existing relationships between bounded entities, rather than by serving as an instrumental information code that conveys descriptive messages. Ritual both relies on and supports shared social convention" (15).

Like tiaoshen, dixi also invokes a "larger order of things" and enacts the villagers' place in that order. But unlike tiaoshen, dixi is now performed in a world where epistemological assumptions about deeper meanings underlying symbolic actions have come to shape and even enable its very existence as ritual. Dixi is something, in other words, requiring the interpretation of experts. As one villager told me, "These days we call tiaoshen dixi. . . . [They are] the same thing. People with culture, intellectuals, they call it dixi. The ordinary folks call it tiaoshen." The transformation of tiaoshen into dixi offers one instance of the state extending its authorizing power over the realm of Chinese culture, something it has done historically and continues to do today (see, for example, Nyíri 2006). In making tiaoshen legible as dixi, the state has enrolled ritual practice into the task of nation building, which is something heavily laden with symbolic action. Dixi has become a representational act ready-made for interpretation by experts. Framed in a modern epistemology, it is less important for what it *does* than for what it *means*. As such, dixi defines culture as the state's business and turns cultural practice into a "technology of government" (see Rose 1999, 51–55; Bennett 1998; Barnett 2001; Yúdice 2003). Dixi enacts the social conventions of state cultural authority, and the role of villagers as on-demand performers of a "culture" not entirely encoded by themselves. For dixi is encoded by a broader set of authorities as a living fossil, as national heritage, and as tourist attraction. Performing dixi is no longer an obligation to the ancestors but to the nation, and to the tourists who consume the nation. Ritual practice is thus not viewed here as a category distinct from other realms of everyday life—that is, a vestige of the past—but as an expression brought about by the obligations of everyday life in which dynamic and powerful authorities are always present.

But as the authors of *Ritual and Its Consequences* also argue, ritual both reinforces the boundaries of authority, *and* makes the transgression of those boundaries possible. This is because they view ritual not simply as expressive of boundaries, but also as *constitutive* of them. If we consider dixi a ritual not in terms of what it represents but in terms of what it *does*, we find something more complicated going on. Once ritual is viewed more as an enactment of the world than as its symbolic representation, it becomes possible to appreciate ritual acts as constantly negotiating the boundaries of authority. I have found some of this "negotiation" in the practice of dixi. With tourism as a major part of the development program to "Open Up the West" (*xibu dakaifa*) in China (Goodman 2004), ritual and lineage today serve as sites where villagers link themselves to dominant discourses of nation building on the frontier. A recycled state discourse of civilizing the frontier is brought to life through the touristic framing of tunpu ritual. But in dixi we find tunpu villagers act both as objects of the state's frontier cultural development strategies and active

Figure 2.2.   Dixi performed in a local deity temple for tourists. T. Oakes photo, May 2004.

negotiators of the boundaries of their own power, autonomy, and authority within a rapidly evolving cultural economy.

GOVERNING WITH CULTURE

There should be nothing surprising about the claim that the Chinese state is intimately involved in managing cultural production and ritual practice. Yet while there is a long history of cultural governance in China, that governance is now articulated with a global discourse in which culture is increasingly viewed as an expedient resource for specific modernization and development objectives. Around the world there has been a "cultural turn" in development policy and practice, with culture being valued as a resource both for the establishment of economic value chains and for community empowerment, "good governance," and "sustainability." Culture has been enshrined by such diverse institutions as UNESCO and the World Bank as a good in and of itself, both a consumable product and a vital tool in the ordering of society (see Shepherd 2006). Throughout the 1990s in China there was a growing trend toward cultural nationalism, expansion of culture and creative industries, and cultural strategies of rural development (see Wang 2001; Guo 2004; Oakes 2006).

Governing in China has long been seen as a project of managing the cultural beliefs, practices, and rituals of the masses. Wang Di (2003) has demonstrated this in his analysis of the municipal government's efforts to manage Chengdu street culture in the late nineteenth and early twentieth centuries. Elites and officials who viewed commoners as "indecent, stupid, vain, and dishonest, with 'nothing to do but play cards and then get drunk,'" looked to promote "civilization" as a technology of social order and governance (107). For the state, the rituals of popular culture and religion were both the core problem *and* the solution, and were thus subject to reinvention by elites: festivals were renamed, "vulgar" rituals were banned, new rituals were invented, old operas were censured, new operas were written, and healthy leisure was promoted in public spaces, such as bowling in teahouses.

As also noted by Dott in this volume, the Chinese state has for centuries sought to control acts of extraordinary devotion and has always held folk culture and popular religion in suspicious regard. Yet the state's reach into the world of everyday ritual practice throughout its vast territories was until the twentieth century rather limited, and tended to focus only on highly symbolic sites like Mount Tai, where maintaining a state-sanctioned cultural order was paramount. Nevertheless, local elites and officials throughout the empire gravitated toward the orbit of the state's cultural authority in many ways. While Wang's work on Chengdu street culture makes clear that by the late nineteenth century a discourse of civilization had developed to legitimize the state's cultural authority, that authority was articulated in other equally powerful ways during other historical periods. Local elites, for instance, were often instrumental in aligning local identity cults centered on territorial deities with the interests of imperial administration (see Thornton 1996).

David Faure's (1996) research on sixteenth-century Guangdong argues that territorial integration and hence increasing social control was achieved via a cultural shift in which local interests were expressed in terms of loyalty to the emperor. This expression involved the promotion by local elites of Zhu Xi's standardized rituals for ancestor worship, funerals, marriage, and filial piety. These were rituals centered on articulating one's identity according to common ancestry, with the emperor as the ultimate family patriarch. Local loyalties were thus redefined as lineage loyalty. Specifically, the building of ancestral halls was promoted by local elites as a means of upward mobility and as a "framework whereby communal interests could be expressed in a language acceptable to the state" (Faure 2007, 7). Ancestral halls replaced Buddhist monasteries as the most significant ritual spaces, and by the nineteenth century, according to Faure, no villager could be without an ancestral hall or written genealogy. All of this served to make Guangdong governable by making it Chinese in cultural terms, with genealogy becoming a marker of ethnic distinction and status. Once reframed in terms legible to the state, ritual practice served as the pivot of governance by enacting the state's cultural authority. Rituals of ancestor worship served as "the linchpin connecting state authority and local communities" (10).

Yet, while these rituals of lineage and genealogy constituted the boundaries of authority within which villagers were defined as subjects, the extent to which state-authorized rituals were actually followed is less clear. Recent work by Donald Sutton, Michael Szonyi, and others has argued that there is little evidence for symbolic and ritual conformity in the state's efforts to establish cultural governance (see Sutton 2007a, 2007b; Szonyi 2007). Instead, they argue that a "pseudo-orthopraxy" was probably more likely, in which local elites *claimed* ritual standardization but rarely achieved it in practice (Szonyi 2007, 50). As argued earlier, then, ritual is best viewed as an active negotiation of the boundaries of authority, rather than their simple reflection. Szonyi argues that the implication of "pseudo-orthopraxy" is less cultural coherence across the space of "Chinese civilization" than perhaps previously assumed: "The very notion of an integrated culture in China was 'a social and ideological fabrication'" (63).

The rarity with which rituals actually conformed to orthodox state models seems to suggest that the frontiers of the state would be particularly important spaces in which to establish standardized ritual practice and cultural authority. In this regard, the state's most valuable instrument in establishing cultural authority was the settlement of Han Chinese from China proper into frontier regions. And for such settlers, genealogy was—after the sixteenth century anyway—a crucial marker of their status as representatives of state cultural authority. As will be argued below, rituals of genealogy continue as important practices in which cultural authority is enacted and negotiated among tunpu villagers today. Ritual remains a focus of cultural governance as a discourse of nation building is recycled in the form of Beijing's campaign to "Open Up the West" and civilize the frontier.

OPEN UP THE WEST, CIVILIZE THE FRONTIER

Nation or empire building on the frontiers can occur in a variety of ways. Local cultural practices can, for instance, be appropriated, assimilated, and "standardized" according to state-sanctioned models of orthopraxy. Or heterodox local cultural practices may simply be subject to conquest or extermination. China's imperial expansion has long been thought to have followed an approach more akin to the former of these two extremes. But there has been recent debate regarding the extent to which frontier colonization, particularly in southwest China, could really be called a "civilizing mission" (Harrell 1995). Certainly a discourse of civilization via Confucian norms of ritual practice accompanied efforts to integrate frontier territories. But there is also evidence that frontier settlers from China proper were perhaps more interested in deploying cultural authority to maintain their distinction and distance from indigenes, rather than assimilate them via the kind of cultural shifts to Confucian orthopraxy described by Faure in Guangdong (see Millward 1996; Perdue 2005; Giersch 2006; Crossley et al. 2006).

Indeed, historical accounts of Ming and Qing frontier colonization challenge the idea that imperial expansion was a relatively benign process of assimilating the natives.[3] John Herman's recent study of the Ming colonization of Guizhou, for instance, portrays a brutal and bloody frontier where assimilating the natives was never a serious policy objective or practice. As Wang Zhou lamented in his *New Illustrated Gazetteer*: "Blood has been spilt on virtually every inch of Qian [since the province was founded in 1413]. Violence has become a way of life here" (Herman 2007, 118). Herman argues, "Frontiers can be and generally are extraordinarily violent places where common ground between colonizer and colonized is both precious and ephemeral. Ming China's military annexation of the southwest was, if anything, an uninterrupted campaign of state-sponsored violence. . . . Prior to the sixteenth century the Ming presence in the southwest was decidedly military, and even with the significant influx of Han immigrants in the sixteenth century the level of violence did not decrease; it increased. In short, Ming colonization of the southwest was not a 'civilizing mission'" (13). The frontier only achieves its power as a space of Chinese cultural governance *after* a myth of civilization has been applied to veil a more violent reality, and it is precisely these mythic qualities that lend cultural power to China's current campaign to Open Up the West.

For example, as the Open Up the West campaign got under way in 2000, according to Mette Hansen (2005, 160), officials and scholars—such as Tian Fang and Zhang Dongliang—began calling for a new round of organized Han migration into frontier areas. Hansen argues that the discourse of civilization remains fundamental as a resource for identity and cultural authority among Han settlers in frontier areas. Han settlers identify "as civilizers or, more precisely, as people whose right to resettle in any minority area within the borders of their state and engage in whatever legal economic activity that supports their own income is justified by an assumption that it brings indisputable advantages to the ethnic minorities" (7–8). Those advantages are expressed not merely in terms of economic development, but in terms of providing exemplary models for correcting "backward" cultural practices (see Bakken 2000). The belief that Chinese culture is exemplary, with the power to induce irresistible and inevitable assimilation by indigenes and ethnic others, contributes to a myth of civilization as a continuing component of nation building and cultural authority along China's borderlands today.

That power is clearly on display in the sites of tunpu tourism, where rituals of genealogy and ancestor worship enact the myth of civilizing the frontier. And yet, it is an awkward display of cultural authority that one finds in tunpu villages. For while a dominant discourse of frontier civilization provides a model for the cultural development of tunpu—a model in which modernization repeats the benign myth of inevitable indigenous assimilation to (superior) Chinese ways—the touristic framing of tunpu ritual practice enables the expression of cultural authority in ways that also suggest a counternarrative of frontier conquest, violence, and ethnic (Han) identity as *distinct* from minority peoples. This is a counternarrative in which the inevitability of assimilation plays little part. In ritual's constitution of the boundaries of authority, in other words, we find a cultural politics of ethnic distinction and Han cultural nationalism. For villagers themselves, dixi has become the ritual enactment of a history of violent conquest and of the centrality of genealogy to tunpu identity. Yet for scholars, officials, and other experts for whom dixi has come to symbolize something else, it is a symbolic ritual of civilization, a representation of national heritage preserved in pure form on the frontier. Tourists, then, in effect become the crucial witnesses to this ritual constituting of the nation.

FOSSILIZING TUNPU: PERFORMING THE FRONTIER MYTH

Many tunpu people claim to be the direct descendents of Ming soldiers sent in the late fourteenth century to conquer the remnants of the Yuan Mongols in Yunnan and then furloughed in garrisons where they guarded the post road, farmed land seized from indigenous people, and persisted for generations on the edges of the Chinese empire (see for example Weng 2001; Sun 2005). Scholarly interest in tunpu dates to 1980, when a local intellectual named Tang Moxiao wrote an essay about the rural women of central Guizhou and how their clothing was in fact like that worn by women in Nanjing during the early period of the Ming dynasty (Tang 1996). Tang said that contrary to popular perception, these people were actually Han. Citing early gazetteers, he called them "tunpu" people (the term is not a self-identifier, but instead means a fortress for stationing troops, such as a garrison). Tang argued that tunpu culture was of great value to scholars as a window on the past. His essay helped initiate a wave of local scholarly interest in tunpu culture. Already there was developing interest in dixi as a living fossil of ancient opera, and when scholars started spending more time in the villages where dixi was performed, they started to notice a whole new world of folk culture that no one had yet paid much attention to. Soon the living fossil label was being applied not simply to dixi but to the whole of "tunpu culture."

In this way, tunpu was reinvented as a fossil of the early Ming culture of downstream China, hidden away on the frontiers of civilization (Oakes and Wu 2007). A narrative of fossilization ensued: having conquered the frontier and ensconced themselves in fortress-garrisons, tunpu people sealed themselves off from the wheels of history, maintaining the rich cultural practices of Han China in the early Ming. Tunpu people were said to have preserved Han folk culture in a pure form, unsullied by the travails of revolution, modernization, or Westernization. While dixi was the most spectacular example of this, women's clothing, language, cuisine, architecture, and ancestor worship could all be interpreted in this way as well. Tunpu became a kind of academic industry in Guizhou, a resource for the recovery of Han tradition that had somehow escaped the destruction of the Cultural Revolution. And by the late 1990s, the local state had come to grasp the potential economic benefits of promoting tunpu for heritage-hungry urban tourists.

As commercial tourism development took hold in several villages, the tunpu cultural landscape began to undergo a transformation to reflect tunpu's status as a living fossil. Two qualities of this transformation stand out. On the one hand, more and more villages were fossilized by being "set in stone." Former white glazed tile and concrete building façades were covered with rough slate flagstone. Concrete-paved village lanes were resurfaced with the same flagstone. Villages that were formerly a mix of wood-frame, concrete-tile, and stone houses became increasingly monochromatic as dilapidated wooden structures were replaced with stone and unsightly "Westernized" concrete homes were disguised. Some local leaders referred to the process as "traditionalization" (*chuantonghua*) or "tunpuzation" (*tunpuhua*), and the effect was a landscape that concretized the metaphor of fossilization. But it also had the effect of concretizing the narrative of frontier conquest by transforming village landscapes into fortresses of stone. On the other hand, an overlay of "civilization" was also built into village landscapes, in which tunpu villages were represented as civilized outposts of downstream China, beacons of light in the dark wilderness. One village, for example, replaced wooden-plank bridges crossing the canal that ran through its center with little arched bridges (*gongqiao*) meant to evoke the graceful architecture of the Yangtze Delta "water towns" (see Svensson, chapter 8). Another village promoted its rich collection of elaborate courtyard architecture (*siheyuan* and *sanheyuan*) as an outpost of the "Confucian merchant" (*rushang*) townscapes found in Zhejiang, Anhui, and Jiangsu.

That a clear tension exists between tunpu as a landscape of violent conquest and tunpu as a landscape of civilization-in-the-wilderness is evident from the politics of tunpu identity that has been articulated in local evaluations of these landscapes for their tourism potential. Villages dominated by courtyard homes, for example, usually date only to the late Qing and were built by later-arriving Han migrants (referred to as kejia) who were for the most part merchants and not soldier-farmers. Leaders of villages that date to the original Ming conquest claim these later-arriving kejia villages (literally "guest family") aren't really tunpu because tunpu people were soldiers, not rich merchants. Leaders of kejia villages, on the other hand, claim to be more authentically tunpu because of their "civilized" architecture and their strong Confucian traditions of ancestor worship and education. Indeed, the kejia villages were, before the Communist revolution, typically wealthier. State preservation efforts have not themselves made a distinction and consider all of these landscapes to be equally tunpu, leaving it to villagers to make claims of authenticity as they compete with each other for tourists.

The debate over tunpu authenticity is itself ironic given the fact that at the center of the dominant narrative of fossilization is a claim that over the past six hundred years, tunpu culture has undergone no changes and has, like some erstwhile Peach Blossom Spring, escaped the wheels of history.[4] The ultimate tunpu symbol of this narrative of timelessness is of course dixi, which the original Ming soldiers are said to have brought to the frontiers from downstream China. The narrative of *liubainian bushuai* (no decline over six hundred years) is one in which the reality of long-term transformation and cultural borrowing on the frontier is marginalized while a national heritage of origins is prioritized. But in the performance of dixi lurks the same ambiguity found in the emerging landscapes of tunpu tourism. While dixi may be interpreted for tourists as a cornerstone of national heritage in its rawest form, its enactment continues to distinguish, for the villagers themselves, the conquerors from the conquered. In this ambiguity lies perhaps the ultimate irony, for the "conquerors" are not the only ones performing dixi in central Guizhou.

EXPEDIENT ANCESTORS: THE POLITICS OF GENEALOGY IN A TOURISM ECONOMY

Put a person in a group of his contemporaries and peers and he loses his uniqueness. See him, however, as the latest member of a lineage of forebears, and he automatically assumes a certain status. The narration of a genealogy inevitably

highlights the last member. Not only do the achievements of the ancestors ac-
crue to the most recent descendant, but the ancestors themselves appear to be
more forerunners pointing to what is yet to come. . . . Length of genealogy
confers prestige on an individual; likewise, length of history confers prestige
on a nation. Historical narrative produces the curious illusion of inevitability.
(Tuan 1980, 6)

The power of the narrative of fossilization has made ancestry highly political among tunpu people. Genealogy is regarded as the paramount measure of
authentic "tunpuness." And tunpuness forms the basis for claims of entitle-
ment to the proceeds of tourism development. Yet genealogy is complicated
by the ambiguity of tunpu as a heritage of either violent conquest or enlight-
ened civilization. This ambiguity lies at the heart of the frontier in Chinese
history, and it is an ambiguity that is repeated in the current campaign to Open
Up the West. Was the frontier, in short, an alien space of otherness or was it
merely the forward edge of Chinese civilization, passively lying in wait for
the inevitable transformation of civilization? Of course, these are far from
mutually exclusive representations of frontier. Indeed, they mutually constitute each other in a historical dialectic that has played out over the millennia
of Chinese imperial expansion.

During much of the Ming, Han settlers in Guizhou were remarkable to elites
for their stubborn refusal to be labeled as locals. When the peripatetic Xu Xi-
ake traveled through the region in the late fifteenth century, he noted this pe-
culiarity, remarking at one stopover, for instance, that "much of the economic
activity in Upper Fengning was in the hands of people from Jiangxi, who,
like the Yang family, still identified themselves as Han from Jiangxi, not Han
from Guizhou, even though their families had resided in southeast Guizhou for
several generations" (Herman 2006, 155). Guizhou provincial governor Tian
Wen similarly noted in his provincial history of 1690 that

the Han people in Guizhou came primarily from military farms, guards, and bat-
talions established earlier. Though we might now think of these Han as native to
Guizhou, they will tell you that their native villages are in China proper; not in
Guizhou. They are most adamant about communicating their non-native (*yuke*)
status to you. (160)

Guizhou, and China's southwestern region more broadly, has been defined
as a "land of immigrants" for at least half a millennium. Even those who
might be thought of as indigenous—the Miao, Buyi, Dong, and others—
claim immigrant, rather than native, origins. When the Ming founder Zhu
Yuanzhang queried his generals as to the nature of the region they had just
conquered, he was told that it was a region populated largely by immigrants.

"The idea that immigration characterized the southwest has prevailed in the popular mentality ever since" (Lee 1982, 280).

Yet subsequent waves of immigrants also had the effect of creating ethnic distinctions, in which indigenous status was attributed to earlier migrants by later arrivals (286). By mid-Qing times it had largely been forgotten by later arrivals that many of the rural Han in Guizhou were descendants of conquering soldiers. Indeed, it was often forgotten that they were even Han. Most Qing elites simply called them locals (*turen*). And they had strange customs. The women didn't bind their feet. They wore old-style gowns and headgear. They spoke a strange dialect. They ate strange food. And, like most of the locals in the region (including indigenes), they performed a distinctive form of masked ritual drama. Had they civilized the frontier, or had they succumbed to it? Had they learned their exorcism rituals from the indigenous people, or was it the other way around? At the time, no one could say. By the mid-Qing, these locals were seen as natives who were only now just starting to become *more Chinese*. An eighteenth-century picture book of frontier peoples (one of the so-called Miao Albums of late imperial armchair ethnology) depicted Guizhou *turen* as just another curious and exotic group to be found on the edges of civilization (see figure 2.3). Accompanied by a picture of a tiaoshen performance, the poetic text reads as follows:

> On New Year's Day sprites are welcomed, then exorcized
> Village after village beats drums, sings soulfully
> Gradually Turen are colored by Chinese styles—
> Recently it's been clothing and caps, what's next then?
> (Deal and Hostetler 2006, 66–67)

In gently lamenting the "coloring" of local customs by "Chinese styles," the text suggests a frontier of lost purity and authenticity. In doing so, the text also marks the kind of shift in discourse—from conquest to civilization—that characterizes frontier history. Along with conquest and civilization, then, comes inevitable corruption of purity, the inevitable despoiling of paradise (Oakes 2007).

The ambiguity of nation building that drives the politics of ancestry among tunpu people, then, involves not simply the tension between conqueror and civilizer, but also an ambiguity underlying civilization itself. What makes fossilization such a powerful metaphor, in other words, is its harkening to an original state of cultural purity. The inevitability and superiority of Chinese civilization, then, is shadowed by an equally inevitable loss of innocence, and straying from the true path. Many local scholars view tunpu culture as an excavated treasure chest of cultural purity. One book, in a deliberate reference to James Fenimore Cooper's classic *Last of the Mohicans*, was titled *Last of the Tunpu* (Zuihou de Tunpu) and characterized tunpu people as having

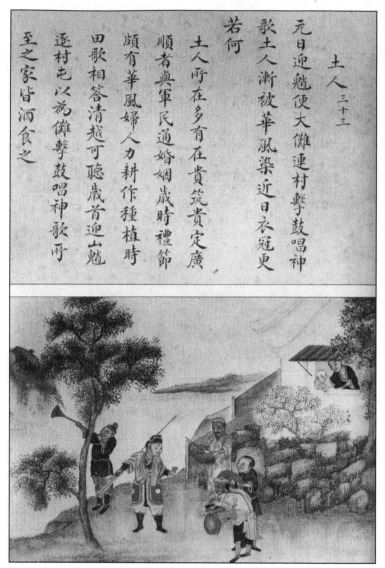

至之家皆酒食之

逐村屯以為儺擊鼓唱神歌所

田歌相答清越可聽歲首迎山魈

頗有華風婦人力耕作種植時

順者與軍民通婚姻歲時禮節

土人所在多有在貴筑貴定廣

若何

歌土人漸被華風染近日衣冠更

元日迎魈便大儺連村擊鼓唱神

土人 三十三

Figure 2.3. *Turen* (local people) from a late eighteenth-century Guizhou "Miao Album." Photograph ca. 1960s; text plates #33 and #18. Reproduced by permission of the Miao Manuscript Photographs, Freer Gallery of Art and Arthur M. Sackler Gallery Archives. Smithsonian Institution. Washington, DC. Photographer unidentified.

lived in frontier purity for six hundred years, only now to face the inevitable corruption of *today's* "Chinese styles": modernization, tourism, development (Zheng 2001; Overmyer 2002; Holm 2003).

Given the invention of tunpu as a culture of authentic purity, it makes sense that genealogy would become a highly valued resource for establishing one's credentials as a bona fide representative of tunpu. Family registers (*jiapu*) were important credentials for any family seeking upward mobility and entry into the imperial bureaucracy. But their content—tracing the descent pattern of the lineage and family branches—was tied to migration; a genealogy typically details the migration of the first family member to a different region (Kuah 2000). For tunpu, a genealogy can convey cultural purity vis-à-vis the present by linking that first migration to the dawn of the Ming. And so important is an original genealogy dating to the Ming conquest that villagers regularly invent or rewrite family histories to conform to this authentic norm. This has happened, for instance, in one of the kejia villages, where the village head has claimed ancestry dating to the original conquest, even though the village itself dates only to the late Qing or early Republican period. Meanwhile many villagers—disgruntled by his personal enrichment as a result of perceived corruption—articulate their grievances with the language of genealogy: "He's not really tunpu; his ancestors came from Shanxi—not Nanjing—only two hundred years ago. He shouldn't be in charge of our village tourism development; he doesn't even have a written genealogy."

Genealogy is far from stable history in China. Rather, genealogy is a "blueprint for action" (Freedman 1979, 31). Historically throughout China, genealogical records have been lost and re-created many times, and there have been several periods of genealogical reconstruction among tunpu people.[5] Tunpu tourism represents only the latest period in which it has become politically strategic to "perform" one's ancestry and thus deliberately link one's family narrative to that of the nation. Genealogies must of necessity, then, be written in a way that articulates the narrative of the nation. This is why genealogies are hidden and/or destroyed during periods of rebellion or upheaval. During the mid-Qing Xiantong rebellions in Guizhou, most of the tunpu genealogies were indeed destroyed. This was followed by waves of genealogical reconstruction during the early Republican and early Communist periods. They were again destroyed during the Cultural Revolution, and again rewritten with the onset of post-Mao reforms and the rise of tunpu tourism.

All of this has made the work of sorting out the various claims on the past challenging business for local scholars. As one explained to me,

> It's very hard to find the old genealogies. Many of the new genealogies have been modified [because of bad class backgrounds]. If they're written before Mao, they're always accurate. But you can't trust the ones written recently. Now genealogies are being written because of the promotion of tunpu; so there's interest in identifying oneself as tunpu. The two genealogies [we found in one

of the tourist villages] were written because of tourism. They can't be trusted. The people want to make claims to having come during the early Ming, so they can be authentic tunpu, but for many it's just not true. [A genealogy] is like a certificate of proof.

The imaginative geography of tunpu genealogy is centered on Nanjing because Nanjing was the original Ming capital. Identity with Nanjing not only confers civilized status upon descendants, but also connects the family history of those descendants directly to the history of the nation.[6] The desire to make this link often trumps the presence of any actual records. As another local scholar pointed out, writing genealogies only vaguely depends on records:

If they don't have the records, they just make it up. And if they have the records, they often try to embellish their family history, making it grander than it really was. . . . These days, there are so many historical records out there that if you're writing a new genealogy, you can easily borrow bits and pieces of your story from others and claim it as your own. It's easy to claim that your ancestors have an important name, or were important officials.

As Prasenjit Duara (1995) argues, national heritage must paradoxically include both ancient roots and progress toward modernity. Similarly, Frank Pieke has observed the role genealogies have played in turning history into the inevitability of progress and civilization. It is this latter quality that makes writing a genealogy a performative and political act.

A genealogy traces a descent line back to an ancestor who first moved from elsewhere in China to the area of residence (*shiqianzu*) and often even further back to mythical or legendary figures of China's great tradition, such as famous scholars, officials, or even emperors of the past. . . . This combination of local detail and a connection with the history of China makes genealogies very powerful statements that use Han Chinese patrilineal kinship ideology to turn the contested facts of imperial conquest, migration, and settlement of Han Chinese into the inevitable victory of civilization. (Pieke 2003, 105)

Today, tunpu tourism enables the fetishization of original ancestry. There is status and power to be gained by claiming ancestry dating back to the earliest settlements of furloughed Ming soldiers. People who can claim this original descent can claim a much higher prestige value. And so tunpu genealogical work today may be viewed as part of the state's construction of modernity and civility on the frontier, a kind of cultural governance, for these genealogies fuse local variations with an overarching state orthodoxy and nation-building project. Sometimes entire villages, which might in fact date only to the late Qing, claim to be original Ming settlements. In one of the most visited tunpu tourist villages, I have heard precisely this claim made repeatedly by village leaders, as well as local officials. Yet while a family with genealogical records dating to the first Ming settlement claims to have founded the village, local scholars have dated the village itself only to the mid-Qing era (Anshun shi wenwu guanlisuo 1994; Zheng 2001).

It should not be surprising, then, that it has become almost imperative for any village claiming authentic tunpu status to support its own dixi troupe. For dixi not only symbolizes original ancestry (in fossilized form), but itself calls upon the ancestors—both real and legendary—to bestow upon the villagers the blessing of "tunpuness" and all the benefits and status that derives from this thoroughly modern marker of identity. In the past, tiaoshen was not performed in all villages. But now, some village leaders are "reviving" dixi in places where it hadn't previously existed. While this is obviously meant to add credentials and attraction value to villages hoping to benefit from tunpu heritage tourism, it also illustrates how dixi has become a symbolic representation of genealogy. The presence of dixi conveys the ancestors' blessings on tunpu development and on village claims to represent the nation. This is because dixi is no longer the annual exorcism and warrior ritual of tiaoshen, but a ritual of tunpu as a symbol of national heritage and Han cultural purity.

As a hereditary ritual practice (fathers traditionally passed their performance skills on to their oldest sons) said to have continued unchanged for six hundred years, dixi is perhaps the ultimate performance of genealogy. Yet dixi's history itself is remarkably vague. There are no Ming-era records describing, or even referring to tiaoshen, nor are there any surviving tiaoshen artifacts dating to the Ming (Zheng 2001, 59). According to some village elders, soldiers originally performed tiaoshen for protection before going to battle: "In the beginning, they didn't use masks. It was all about fighting. It was performed at home, not outside. Eventually they started using masks and performing it outside." Eventually, some claim, tiaoshen became more of a community event, performed during Spring Festival with the objective of securing good fortune for the village. Elaborate ritual practices developed around the use of the masks. Since the masks conjured powerful spirits and ancestors, their handling needed to be kept to a minimum and required ritual sacrifices (such as chickens or pigs). Many villages also had strict rules regarding places where the masks could and could not be taken (such as restrictions on the number of times masks could cross a river during each twelve-year zodiac cycle).

Tunpu development, then, required that villagers reconsider the nature of ritual practices surrounding dixi. As a mechanism of cultural governance, it required that villagers take a more modern attitude to cultural practice while learning also to appreciate the representational value of that practice as a symbol of fossilized heritage. The following interview exchange illustrates this new kind of subjectivity encouraged by tunpu cultural governance:

Do you perform the kaixiang ceremony whenever tourists come?
Whether we do is based on the needs of the tourists. It used to be that once the box was closed, the masks couldn't be moved until the next year, but now that rule has been broken. It had to be broken so that we could do tunpu culture.

A troupe leader from a different village had a similar response:

Do you carry out the necessary rituals [kaixiang ceremony] every time you perform?
No, we only do that twice each year. So, when tourists come, or reporters, or scholars like yourselves, and you want to see us dance—we don't do the sacrifices every time. We might dance 365 days a year, but we won't do the sacrifices. This is right; it's good, it's opening to the world, it's promoting [tunpu] to the world.
And it's not a problem with the spirits that you perform so much without doing the sacrifices?
During Spring Festival, when I'm greeting the ancestors, I take some gifts, some wine, and I say to them, "Sorry, ancestors, but times have changed." This way they won't harm us.

And while there remains some ambivalence among elders regarding this sort of appeasement of the ancestors, most dixi troupe leaders feel that ritual continues to play a significant role in its reconstituted, tourist-oriented form:

So now you don't typically perform the sacrifices?
Not usually. Last year we were [performing] in Shanghai for Spring Festival. I called home and told them to burn some incense and paper, and invite a different troupe to perform [dixi in the village]. I wanted them to open the box for my family. You can't just have another troupe come and perform—they have to do the proper rituals.
Times have changed, haven't they? People come from all over to see you perform now.
Tourism is really good for the village—it gives the young people money to spend. I used to have to butcher pigs for a living. Now I just perform dixi. People say I should be getting more money, but my needs are taken care of. I'm training two younger people how to perform the box opening ritual, how to be troupe leader, how to protect the village. It's not in any books. They have to learn it from me.

As a ritual of genealogy, dixi bridges Duara's "aporia" of national history in which the atavism of authentic cultural heritage is paradoxically paired with the telos of modern progress and historical inevitability (Duara 1995). The very vagueness of dixi's history makes it malleable in the service of the nation. It is simultaneously ancient, unchanging, modern, and expedient.

CONCLUSION—RECYCLING DIXI IN SERVICE OF THE NATION

While dixi is said to lie at the heart of a distinctive tunpu cultural identity, tunpu villagers are not the exclusive performers of dixi. Indeed, in 2005 dixi was represented at China's "International Nuo Culture Week" in Nanchang by a troupe of Buyi villagers. Not only were they not tunpu; they weren't even Han! While the village that sent this troupe made no claims of tunpuness, they did print up a tourist brochure calling dixi a combination of six-hundred-year-old tunpu art (*tunpu yishu*) and Buyi culture. The village head told me that his dixi troupe had been selected to represent Guizhou because its performance was "updated" compared to tunpu dixi. Performers wore newly styled "modern" clothes with a variety of bright colors. And unlike tunpu dixi, this village performed *up on a stage*. The village head said this was because they thought it looked better on a stage. Implying that performing opera "on the ground" was symptomatic of poverty, he pointed out that since their village was located in the suburbs of a large city, they were relatively well off. Unlike most tunpu villagers, they could afford to build a stage.

The dixi of this Buyi village involved more theatrical dancing, with more action, and more performers. But they only performed one story—*Yang Jia Jiang* ("Generals of the Yang Clan")—rather than the many stories that tunpu troupes typically perform. This may have been the reason, the village head speculated, that their dixi was selected over tunpu troupes to represent Guizhou. *Yang Jia Jiang*—a series of Song- and Ming-era stories and plays—chronicles the exploits of four generations of the Yang military family during the final years of the Northern Song dynasty. The stories are exemplary of unflinching loyalty and of the virtues of patriotism (Edwards 1994, 89). "It's a very patriotic story," the village head said. "The leaders like that." But probably timing had as much to do with it as anything. In 2004, CCTV produced the television series *Yang Men Hu Jiang* ("Warriors of the Yang Clan"), followed in 2006 by *Shao Nian Yang Jia Jiang* ("Young Warriors of the Yang Clan"). Both were extremely popular throughout China. It was also around this time that Nintendo came out with its own video-game version of *Yang Jia Jiang*.

This is not to suggest that tunpu dixi troupes did not also make adjustments to match the times. Various troupe leaders told me how they had modernized their performances for tourists, adding more martial-style acrobatics, updating their clothes, and selecting patriotic stories to perform. One even mentioned that since it is now performed for an audience as entertainment, dixi would look better up on a stage. But the significance of a Buyi troupe representing dixi to China goes beyond what it tells us about the entrepreneurial subjectivity being encouraged by tunpu cultural development. It also marks an important moment in the shift from a frontier narrative of violent conquest to one of assimilation to civilization. As one local scholar explained:

> Long ago, the Buyi would never perform dixi, because dixi celebrated the oppression of the minorities and the superiority of the Han. So of course the Buyi would not want any part of it. But over the generations they forgot about all that. The tunpu people became more like minorities and the minorities forgot that the tunpu people had come to conquer them and take their land. So the Buyi started to perform dixi. But dixi itself—of course it came from the tunpu people. It's part of tunpu military culture. The spirit of dixi is the battle against the minorities. Dixi is a reminder of [the Ming colonization]. The actual stories are about fighting against minorities. . . . And everyone thinks of the enemies in the drama as representing the Miao. So the Miao have never adopted dixi, like some Buyi have. Of course, today many Miao will go and see dixi performed and won't really think about it. They don't get angry about it. And it's not written down anywhere that the enemies are supposed to be the Miao.

In fact, however, I know of at least one Miao dixi troupe as well. It seems that the ritual brokering of cultural governance is even too much for *them* to resist. And so perhaps dixi remains the key instrument of the same "cultural shift" that Faure believes occurred on the sixteenth-century Guangdong frontier as well, that is, a cultural shift toward governable subjects whose cultural rituals constituted the boundaries of authority in a multitude of ways. In central Guizhou, the rituals of dixi mark the boundaries of state power by enacting, for tourists, genealogical claims that link villagers to the nation. They do this not simply by enacting their place within the broader powers of state cultural authority, but by constituting the boundaries of those powers themselves. Those boundaries mark who is tunpu and who is not, who is authentic and who is not, who is Han and who is not. As should be clear though, this boundary construction is a political process of constant negotiation. In that sense, then, it remains fruitful to understand dixi as ritual, and not simply an inauthentic performance for tourists.

Yet it is tourism that energizes dixi as an ongoing ritual for tunpu villagers. Tourism has the power to recycle dixi in service to the nation, and it is tourism that reconstitutes dixi's ritual efficacy. Clearly, then, dixi is a very different ritual than tiaoshen was. It remains a ritual practice, brought about by the obligations of everyday life in which powerful authorities are always present. But if we view dixi as enacting the world rather than representing the world symbolically, we can appreciate its capacity to constantly renegotiate the boundaries of authority. Thus in performing dixi, tunpu villagers act as both objects of the state's project of nation building on the frontier and active negotiators of the boundaries of their own power, autonomy, and authority within a rapidly evolving cultural economy. And in this power to reconstitute boundaries, the ancestors remain potent resources, for they continue to be called upon to help their descendants garner benefits, eke out advantages, and otherwise succeed in the capricious world of the here and now.

NOTES

Research for this chapter was conducted in collaboration with Wu Xiaoping of Guizhou Nationalities University, and was supported by a grant from the National Science Foundation (BCS 0243045). This chapter was originally delivered at the 2005 Association of Asian Studies Annual Meetings in Chicago at a panel organized by Don Sutton and Xiaofei Kang entitled "Contested Claims: Religion, History and Tourism in Contemporary China." Many thanks to panel participants Kenneth Dean, Xiaofei Kang, Donald Sutton, and Rubie Watson for their discussion and comments. Earlier versions were also presented at the University of Oregon (in 2007), Vassar College, and the University of Toronto (both 2008), and I have benefited from many of the critical comments and questions received at those events. Thanks also to Colorado's Theory Thursdays reading group—Chris Anderson-Tarver, Joe Bryan, Afton Clarke-Sather, Abby Hickcox, Ted Holland, Travis Klingberg, Chris McMorran, Claire Simon, Emily Yeh, and Amy Zader—for their comments and suggestions.

1. The story of Caiguan's trip to Europe was recounted to me by village leaders during interviews, March 1994.

2. *Tiaoshen* was also referred to as *tiao xin chun*, or "new spring leaping."

3. The classic example of this view in Western scholarship is found in Wiens (1967).

4. Written by Tao Qian (Tao Yuanming) in the early fifth century, "The Story of Peach Blossom Spring" (*Taohuayuanji*) tells of a fisherman's accidental discovery of a utopian world hidden behind a mountain cave, inhabited by people who escaped the warfare of an earlier time, wear "old-style" clothing, and live in a timeless tranquil of harmony.

5. Wang Qiugui and Tuo Xiuming (1995), for instance, write of the Zhou clan of Cengong County, Guizhou, who trace their ancestry to Zhou Zhongrong, one of the so-called eighteen original generals of the Ming campaigns. Many non-Han people of Cengong invented genealogies that also claimed Zhou ancestry in order to avoid extermination by Ming armies.

6. According to one local scholar: "These days everyone says they're from Nanjing, but in fact according to the old genealogies, very few actually came from Nanjing at all. They were gathered in Nanjing before being sent to Guizhou; but they weren't from Nanjing. . . . But it's hard to tell exactly where the Nanjing idea comes from. Whether the villagers have heard it from others [who are promoting tunpu tourism] or whether it's simply been part of the story all along is hard to tell."

REFERENCES

Anshun shi wenwu guanlisuo. 1994. "Yunshantun Jianjie." In *Anshun Wenshi Ziliao 15: Anshun Tunpu Wenhua*, ed. D. Zhou. Anshun: Anshun Shi Wenwu Guanlisuo, 61–62.

Asad, Talal. 1993. *Genealogies of Religion: Discipline & Reasons of Power in Christianity and Islam*. Baltimore: Johns Hopkins University Press.

Bakken, Borge. 2000. *The Exemplary Society: Human Improvement, Social Control, and the Dangers of Modernity in China*. Oxford: Oxford University Press.

Barnett, Clive. 2001. "Culture, Geography, and the Arts of Government." *Environment and Planning D: Society and Space* 19: 7–24.

Bell, Catherine. 1997. *Ritual: Perspectives and Dimensions*. New York and Oxford: Oxford University Press.

Bennett, Tony. 1998. *Culture: A Reformer's Science*. London: Sage.

Crossley, Pamela K., Helen F. Siu, and Donald S. Sutton, eds. 2006. *Empire at the Margins: Culture, Ethnicity, and Frontier in Early Modern China*. Berkeley: University of California Press.

Deal, David, and Laura Hostetler. 2006. *The Art of Ethnography*. Seattle: University of Washington Press.

Dean, Kenneth, and Thomas Lamarre. 2003. "Ritual Matters." In *Impacts of Modernities*, ed. T. Lamarre and N. Kang. Hong Kong: University of Hong Kong Press, 257–84.

Duara, Prasenjit. 1995. *Rescuing History from the Nation: Questioning Narratives of Modern China*. Chicago: University of Chicago Press.

Edwards, Louise. 1994. *Men and Women in Qing China: Gender in the Red Chamber Dream*. Leiden: E.J. Brill.

Faure, David. 1996. "Becoming Cantonese, the Ming Dynasty Transition." In *Unity and Diversity: Local Cultures and Identities in China*, ed. T. T. Liu and D. Faure. Hong Kong: Hong Kong University Press, 37–50.

———. 2007. *Emperor and Ancestor: State and Lineage in South China*. Stanford: Stanford University Press.

Feng, Chong-yi. 1999. "Jiangxi in Reform: The Fear of Exclusion and the Search for a New Identity". In *The Political Economy of China's Provinces: Comparative and Competitive Advantage*, ed. Hans Hendrischke and Chong-yi Feng. Routledge, 249–76.

Freedman, Maurice. 1979. "The Chinese in Southeast Asia: A Longer View." In *The Study of Chinese Society: Essays by Maurice Freedman*. Stanford: Stanford University Press, 3–21.

Giersch, C. Patterson. 2006. *Asian Borderlands: The Transformation of Qing China's Yunnan Frontier*. Cambridge, MA: Harvard University Press.

Goodman, David, ed. 2004. *China's Campaign to Open Up the West: National, Provincial, and Local Perspectives*. Cambridge: Cambridge University Press.

Guo, Yingjie. 2004. *Cultural Nationalism in Contemporary China: The Search for National Identity under Reform*. London and New York: Routledge.

Hansen, Mette. 2005. *Frontier People: Han Settlers in Minority Areas of China*. Vancouver: University of British Columbia Press.

Harrell, Stevan, ed. 1995. *Cultural Encounters on China's Ethnic Frontiers*. Seattle: University of Washington Press.

Herman, John. 2006. "The Cant of Conquest: Tusi Officials and China's Political Incorporation of the Southwest Frontier." In *Empire at the Margins*, ed. Crossley, Siu, and Sutton. Berkeley: University of California Press, 135–68.

———. 2007. *Amid the Clouds and Mist: China's Colonization of Guizhou, 1200–1700*. Cambridge, MA: Harvard University Asia Center.

Holm, David. 2003. "The Death of Tiaoxi (The 'Leaping Play'): Ritual Theater in the Northwest of China." *Modern Asian Studies* 37(4): 863–84.

Kuah Khun Eng. 2000. *Rebuilding the Ancestral Village: Singaporeans in China*. Aldershot: Ashgate.

Lee, James. 1982."The Legacy of Immigration in Southwest China, 1250–1850." *Annales de démographie historique*: 279–304.

Millward, James. 1996. "New Perspectives on the Qing Frontier." In *Remapping China: Fissures in Historical Terrain*, ed. G. Hershatter, E. Honig, J. Lipman, and R. Stross. Stanford: Stanford University Press, 113–29.

Nyíri, Pál. 2006. *Scenic Spots: Chinese Tourism, the State and Cultural Authority*. Seattle: University of Washington Press.

———. 2010. *Mobility and Cultural Authority in Contemporary China*. Seattle: University of Washington Press.

Oakes, Tim. 2006. "Cultural Strategies of Development: Implications for Village Governance in China." *Pacific Review* 19(1): 13–37.

———. 2007. "Welcome to Paradise! A Sino-American Joint Venture Project." In *China's Transformations: The Stories Beyond the Headlines*, ed. L. Jensen and T. Weston. Lanham, MD: Rowman and Littlefield, 240–64.

Oakes, Tim, and Wu Xiaoping, eds. 2007. *Tunpu Chongsu: Guizhou Wenhua Lüyou yu Shehui Bianqian*. Guiyang: Guizhou minzu chubanshe.

Overmyer, Daniel, ed. 2002. *Ethnography in China Today: A Critical Assessment of Methods and Results*. Taipei: Yuan-Liu.

Perdue, Peter. 2005. *China Marches West: The Qing Conquest of Central Eurasia*. Cambridge, MA: Harvard University Press.

Pieke, Frank. 2003. "The Genealogical Mentality in Modern China." *Journal of Asian Studies* 62(1): 101–29.

Rappaport, Roy. 1999. *Ritual and Religion in the Making of Humanity*. Cambridge: Cambridge University Press.

Rose, Nicholas. 1999. *The Powers of Freedom: Reframing Political Thought*. Cambridge: Cambridge University Press.

Seligman, Adam, Robert Weller, Michael Puett, and Bennett Simon. 2008. *Ritual and Its Consequences: An Essay on the Limits of Sincerity*. Oxford: Oxford University Press.

Shen, Fuxing, et al., eds. 1990. *Anshun Dixi Lunwenji*. Anshun: Wenhua yishu chubanshe.

Shepherd, Robert. 2006. "UNESCO and the Politics of Cultural Heritage in Tibet." *Journal of Contemporary Asia* 36(2): 243–57.

Siu, Wang-Ngai. 1997. *Chinese Opera: Images and Stories*. Seattle: University of Washington Press.

Sun, Zhaoxia. 2005. *Tunpu Xiangmin Shehui*. Beijing: Zhongguo shehui kexue wenlian chubanshe.

Sutton, Donald. 2007a. "Ritual, Cultural Standardization, and Orthopraxy in China: Reconsidering James L. Watson's Ideas." *Modern China* 33(1): 3–21.

———. 2007b. "Death Rites and Chinese Culture: Standardization and Variation in Ming and Qing Times." *Modern China* 33(1): 125–53.

Swatek, Catharine. 2002. *Peony Pavilion Onstage: Four Centuries in the Career of a Chinese Drama*. Ann Arbor: University of Michigan Center for Chinese Studies.

Szonyi, Michael. 2007. "Making Claims About Standardization and Orthopraxy in Late Imperial China: Rituals and Cults in the Fuzhou Region in Light of Watson's Theories." *Modern China* 33(1): 47–71.

Tan, Chee-Beng, ed. 2006. *Southern Fujian: Reproduction of Traditions in Post-Mao China*. Hong Kong: Chinese University Press.

Tang, Moxiao. 1996. "Chuan Ming dai gu zhuang de funu." In *Qianshan zhailu lu*, ed. Zheng Zhengqiang. Guiyang: Guizhou renmin chubanshe.

Thornton, Susanna. 1996. "Provinces, City Gods and Salt Merchants: Provincial Identity in Ming and Qing Dynasty Hangzhou." In *Unity and Diversity: Local Cultures and Identities in China*, ed. T. T. Liu and D. Faure. Hong Kong: Hong Kong University Press, 15–35.

Tuan, Yi-fu. 1980. "Rootedness Versus Sense of Place." *Landscape* 24(1): 3–8.

Wang, Di. 2003. *Street Culture in Chengdu: Public Space, Urban Commoners, and Local Politics, 1870–1930*. Stanford: Stanford University Press.

Wang, Jing. 2001. "Culture as Leisure and Culture as Capital." *positions: east asia cultures critique* 9(1): 69–104.

Wang, Qiugui, and Shen Fuxing. 1994. *Guizhou Anshun Dixi Diaocha Baogaoji* (*Min-su quyi congshu* 15). Taipei: Shih Ho-cheng Folk Culture Foundation.

Wang, Qiugui, and Tuo Xiuming. 1995. *Guizhou Sheng Cengong Xian Zhuxi Xiang, Cenwang Cun, Laowuji Xi Nuoshen Diaocha Baogao* (*Minsu quyi congshu* 37). Taipei: Shih Ho-cheng Folk Culture Foundation.

Weng, Jialie. 2001. *Yelang Gudishang de Gu Hanzu Qunluo—Tunpu Wenhua*. Guiyang: Guizhou jiaoyu chubanshe.

Wiens, Harold. 1967. *Han Chinese Expansion in South China*. Hamden, CT: Shoe String Press.

Yan, Ruxian. 1989. "A Living Fossil of the Family—A Study of the Family Structure of the Naxi Nationality in the Lugu Lake Region." *Social Sciences in China* 3(4): 60–83.

Yúdice, George. 2003. *The Expediency of Culture: Uses of Culture in the Global Era.* Durham, NC, and London: Duke University Press.

Zhang, Ziwei. 1996. *Hunan Sheng Yongshun Xian Heping Shuangfeng Cun Tujiazu Maogusi Yishi* (*Minsu quyi congshu* 47). Taipei: Shih Ho-cheng Folk Culture Foundation.

Zheng, Lei. 2005. *Kunqu.* Hangzhou: Zhejiang renmin chubanshe.

Zheng, Zhengqiang. 2001. *Zuihou de Tunpu.* Guiyang: Guizhou renmin chubanshe.

Zhou, Shangyi, and Kong Xiang. 2000. *Wenhua yu Difang Fazhan.* Beijing: Kexue Chubanshe.

Zhou, Zhenhe. 1996. "Dixi qiyuan yice." In *Sui Wu Ya zhi Lu.* Shanghai: Sanlian Shudian, 335–40.

3

Pilgrim or Tourist?

The Transformation of China's Revolutionary Holy Land

Yu Luo Rioux

"*Jinggangshan shi budao shan, shang le shan guanyun yao fanyifan*' (Jinggangshan is the mountain of no collapse. The good fortune of a bureaucrat's career will double by scaling Jinggangshan). This saying is now popular in Beijing." It is difficult to confirm the popularity of this saying imparted to me one spring day during a visit to Jinggangshan in 2003. The young businesswoman who shared this saying left me wondering how a mere visit to a place like Jinggangshan could retain such importance. "It's like a prayer with incense offerings," she continued. "Whoever becomes a head has to come to see. It concerns whether or not the ruling power is to be stabilized!" The message conveyed here is clear: visiting Jinggangshan, and receiving its precious blessings, is imperative for the politically ambitious. Such sentiments seem to have elevated a Jinggangshan journey to that of a pilgrimage or a religious sacred rite.

To a certain degree, what occurs on Jinggangshan parallels what happens on Mount Tai. As illustrated in Dott's chapter in this volume, there exists a gap between actual practices (of tourism and pilgrim) and the state's intention to create new meanings for Mount Tai as an icon of national identity and pride. In modern times, for example, Mount Tai's attraction to pilgrims worshiping the Goddess of Mount Tai and Confucius continues because of its original connection to "natural renewal, life, birth, and rejuvenation" (p. 28). The state welcomes the profit from such "religious tourism"—that is, spirit money—but is "reluctant to encourage what it [has] traditionally condemned as superstitious practices" (p. 31). According to Dott, promotion of Mount Tai as a symbol of Chinese nationalism has been successful among all attempts of the state to appropriate Mount Tai's sacred space in the past half-century, ranging from religious faith to revolutionary devotion.

These purposes contrast sharply with "pilgrims" in the Maoist period, who came to commemorate revolutionary martyrs, with the goal of capturing and perhaps emulating their spirit. The new practices resemble somewhat the sacred pilgrimages of Judaism, Islam, and Christianity, in which "individuals [are given] a direct experience of the transcendent and an opportunity to show devotion and seek blessings" (Naquin and Yü 1992, 3). Although more concerned with blessings than with devotion, a journey to Jinggangshan seems to have taken on a purpose typically reserved for a religious pilgrimage. Ascending Jinggangshan becomes a vehicle for prayers and offerings from those who earnestly seek blessings.

Accounts of the inexplicable force of visiting Jinggangshan prevail, with remarkable stories of its miraculous power. According to some Jinggangshan residents, there is a particular order of major spots to visit for people of different trades, so that the wonders and good luck will take effect. Those who take up the administrative profession are advised to dedicate a floral basket to the Jinggangshan Revolutionary Martyrs' Memorial Hall (JRMMH) on the North Hill, and then go directly to the Huangyangjie Pass in order to be promoted continuously to a higher rank.

> Then you go all the way to the main peak. You may win promotion and get rich. Don't enter the mint; otherwise you'd become a corrupt officer. You have to consider how to arrange the tour. Those who take up the educational profession should follow the route for a political professional. Those who take up a commercial profession should enter the mint after the flora basket dedication. Then go all the way up to the Huangyang Pass, and buy a token hundred-yuan bill around the main peak. Put the bill in your pocket, and you may go anywhere [in Jinggangshan]. (Excerpt of an interview in 2003)

I have heard slightly different versions of the same story in Jinggangshan several times from different people, men and women, young and old, rich and poor. Some local residents who lived or worked there would be willing to tell me such quasi-legendary mysteries if I managed to approach them with such a loose social connection as a friend of an acquaintance's relative. "You have to go to *Bajiaolou* (the Octagon Building), and sit on the bench silently for fifteen minutes in order to have a good career," they would tell me matter-of-factly over the dinner table. The genuine concern in their tone made it hard for one to doubt their sincerity. "Some students from the National Defense Academy sat there for fifteen minutes, and they were all promoted upon returning [to the school]," one stressed.

The moral of these legendary stories on Jinggangshan is centered on the themes of job promotion and material wealth accumulation for the individual. Given that Jinggangshan has been revered as a revolutionary icon symbolizing the proletarian and atheist ideologies associated with Mao Zedong and his communist followers, there exists a big gap between one's presumption of what Jinggangshan is supposed to be and what is actually happening there today. There appears to be a contradiction between such mysterious beliefs of individual blessing and the once holy revolutionary memorial sites in Jinggangshan commemorating the sacrifice of one's personal interest for the people and the nation. Witnessing such changes and their inherent contrasts is astounding for a native-born Chinese scholar like me even though I had seen, read about, and heard of, the commercial trend in former revolutionary sites (including Mao's hometown in Shaoshan, Hunan) before I went to Jinggangshan in 2003. What is the link between a revolutionary memorial site and a sacred site in China? What is the connection between the revolutionary holy land and the development of tourism? How does the continuing practice of seeking personal blessings relate to the transformation from revolutionary sacred site to commercial tourism site?

The contradiction raises a series of broader issues and questions: How has tourism development affected the former revolutionary sacred sites in China? What are the cultural and political implications of the gap between dominant state discourses and goals of patriotism and moral righteousness in red tourism and the actual practices of tourists/pilgrims, practices that are enabled by market transformation? By addressing these issues, this chapter examines the relationship between revolutionary memorial sites and tourism development in China's reform era since 1978. I argue that unleashing market forces creates developments that the Chinese state cannot completely control. These market-driven developments in former revolutionary memorial sites include activities and prayers for personal blessings or benefits. Resulting from the commodification of revolutionary sites, popular religious practices (that had been regarded as superstitious) contradict the state-promoted goals of patriotic and moral education.

The revolutionary sacred sites in Jinggangshan are reproduced and commodified to a large extent as tourism attractions in the provincial economic development scheme of Jiangxi. The commercial trend is largely a result of fiscal decentralization during China's reform era. Commodification has eroded the state narrative of these revolutionary institutions as moral "educational bases" disseminating revolutionary ideologies. Although red tourism is promoted by the state to shore up this narrative, it is, in fact, more geared toward commercial tourism development strategies. Consequently, there exist certain contradictions among different interest groups involved in the memorial institutions. On the personal level, local residents seem to be more concerned with their own livelihoods than with official ideologies or revolutionary spirits, and this contrasts with the national agenda of strengthening the power of the state and the CCP through revolutionary heritage educational programs. I will start with the connections between revolutionary memorials and sacred space by introducing the historical background of the revolutionary sacred sites. Following that, I will illustrate how these sites in Jiangxi Province are transformed by the development of red tourism and green tourism, and in what ways "sacred space" of the revolution is contested and eroded by commercial and secular, as well as popular religious, practices.

FROM PILGRIMS TO TOURISTS

Rooted in the history of the CCP and the PRC, revolutionary memorials, monuments, and museums dedicated to revolutionary martyrs and key leaders were established all over the country as sacred sites of commemoration.

> After the founding of the People's Republic, the Center defined a series of places as of crucial importance for the Revolution. The selection of these places reflected the status of those leaders, such as Mao Tse-tung, who had emerged victorious in the various inner-party quarrels, as well as their ideological priorities. (Wagner 1992, 383)

In the early stages, there were three levels of importance for revolutionary memorials and museums on the national scale. "Peking, marked with a big red star, is a category all its own. Second-level places are marked with a red flag indicating 'Memorial Places of Revolutionary History'; the third level contains places without nationally relevant revolutionary charge" (383). These revolutionary memorials conveyed revolutionary ideologies: to sacrifice for the revolutionary cause and the liberation of the people. The memorials, museums, and monuments served to reinforce the revolutionary ideology of serving the people, the socialist state/cause for which the revolutionary martyrs had sacrificed even their valuable lives, and the leadership of the CCP. Visitors to these revolutionary sacred sites, therefore, could be thought of as revolutionary or patriotic "pilgrims."

A pilgrimage in the strict religious sense is a purifying tour seeking individual epiphany. Visitors to former revolutionary sites in China bear resemblance to spiritual pilgrims. Ever since their establishment, revolutionary sacred sites in China have been used for spiritual purification and moral elevation by party branches, schools, and work units to evoke patriotism and nationalism. Patriotic pilgrimages to these sites are meant to reinforce, among party members and youths, the underlying revolutionary ideologies of serving the people, the CCP, and the state.

Among all the *Geming Shengdi* (Revolutionary Holy Land), Jinggangshan has been one of the most highly regarded (figure 3.1, left), enjoying national fame due to its connection with Mao's victory and his "correct line." There are over one hundred revolutionary sites and relics in Jinggangshan, among which twenty-one are listed as national key artifact protection units, six listed as provincial key artifact protection units, and thirty-five as municipal artifact protection units (DPJMPC 2004, 2; Li 2003, 4; Luo 2000, 1; Xia 2004, 3). Included are the Revolutionary Former Residence and Former Sites Group in Ciping, the Red Army Hospital in Xiaojing, the Red Army Cave, the Huang-yangjie Pass, the Red Army Mint in Shangjing, and Bajiaolou and Xiangshan Temple in Maoping. The Former Residence and Former Sites Group in Ciping consists of seven national key artifact protection units: Mao Zedong Former Residence, the Former Site of the Headquarters of the Fourth Red Army, the Former Site of the Xiang-gan Border Defense Committee, and the Former Site of the Army Officer Training Unit (DPJMPC 2004, 13; Luo 2000, 18–22; Xia 2004, 3–5). The Huangyangjie Pass is one of the five large sentry posts in Jinggangshan where a scarce battalion of the Red Army force defeated the charges by four regiments of the Nationalists' army force in 1928, success-fully defending the Jinggangshan Revolutionary Soviet Base Area at the time (DPJMPC 2004, 15–16; Luo 2000, 9–10; Mao 2002 [2004], 48–50; Wang 1985, 5; Xia 2004, 44–47). Bajiaolou is one of Mao's residences and offices in Jinggangshan where he wrote the two famous works *Why Can Red Politi-cal Power Exist in China?* and *The Struggles of Jinggangshan.* Xiangshan Temple is the place where Mao married He Zizhen (DPJMPC 2004, 18; Luo 2000, 35; Xia 2004, 92). All these former sites have been visited as primary spots of revolutionary heritage and patriotic education in Jinggangshan, and are highlighted for the official promotion of red tourism.

The importance of Jinggangshan's contributions to the establishment of the PRC is evident in that Jinggangshan is honored as the "opening chapter" of the Chinese revolution, and as the cornerstone of Mao Zedong Thought (Mao 2002 [2004], 168). Jinggangshan was named "the first mountain of the world" by Zhu De in 1962 not for its height of 1,586 meters above sea level, but for its status and function in China's revolutionary history (Luo 2000, 102; Mao 2002 [2004], 3–4). There are many "firsts" in Jinggangshan in Chinese revolutionary history: China's first revolutionary base, the first Red Army, the first army hospital, and the first mint of the CCP (Li 2003, 7; Xia 2004, 7–8). The main peak of Jinggangshan, *Wuzhifeng* (Five Fingers Peak), is used as the background pattern of the one-hundred-yuan bill issued in 1990 for the fourth set of RMB bills, and becomes the symbol of Jinggangshan not only because the first revolutionary base area was established in Jing-gangshan, but also because the first "red" mint was set up there (DPJMPC

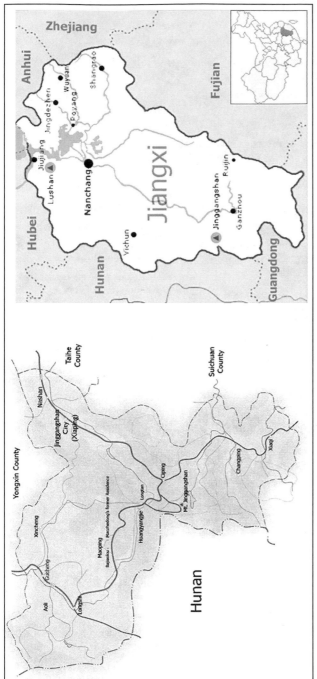

Figure 3.1. Map of Jinggangshan (left) and Jiangxi (right). Ye and Li 2002.

2004, 17; Li 2003, 115; Mao 2002 [2004], 208; Xia 2004, 164–66). The main peak has been renowned as the "most valuable mountain" and "the mountain of the God of Wealth" ever since 1990 (Li 2003, 115; Luo 2000, 17; Xia 2004, 65). Emphasizing the main peak of Jinggangshan as "the mountain of the God of Wealth" may be an effective commercial tourism development strategy to attract tourists who are seeking blessings of personal wealth and monetary fortune. Such appeal, however, seems to contradict the "revolutionary spirit" being promoted for patriotic education and for red tourism in the early twenty-first century.

Revolutionary museums and monuments in China have been incorporated into school education as an important tool of *geming chuantong jiaoyu* (revolutionary heritage education) since the founding of the People's Republic. Relevant activities of local Young Pioneers admission ceremonies, new party member inaugurations, and college student social practice programs have been held around these commemorative institutions all over the country. Jinggangshan is no exception. Just since 1978, Jinggangshan has seen domestic and international visitors exceeding 30 million from 150 countries (DPJMPC 2004, 2), including visitors for revolutionary education and tourists. Many top leaders of China, from Mao Zedong, Zhu De, Deng Xiaoping, Jiang Zemin, to Hu Jintao, Li Peng, and Zhu Rongji, have trodden Jinggangshan soil (Li 2003, 95–98; Luo 2000, 43–56; Mao 2002 [2004], 97–110; Sun and Zhan 2003, 118–28). The principal and perhaps most compelling reason to visit Jinggangshan "is meant to be root-searching, that is, searching for the root of the [Chinese] revolution" (Xia 2004, 2).

Jinggangshan is hallowed ground for the Chinese revolution to be sure, a divine place attracting the sort of reverence bestowed upon a sacred religious site. Journeying to the revolutionary sites in Jinggangshan, therefore, carries the connotation of pilgrimage. The feelings of a patriotic pilgrim are well illustrated in the poem composed by a famous contemporary Chinese writer, Wei Wei, who made a special trip to Jinggangshan in 1982 (Xia 2004, 6):

> Not coming to pay homage to gods or to pay reverence to saints,
> I am here on a pilgrimage mission to Jinggangshan.
> People say that you are five thousand and eight hundred chi,[1]
> I say that you are the first mountain in the world.

The beginning of Wei's poem clarifies that his trip to Jinggangshan was not for seeking personal blessings, but as a revolutionary pilgrimage. Such a visit is precisely what makes the state-promoted "pilgrimage" to Jinggangshan "patriotic." The sense of a revolutionary pilgrimage expressed in Wei's poem was strong among earlier visitors of the Mao era to Jinggangshan, with their ever-present devotion for Mao and their passionate longing to carry on the revolutionary heritage. During the Cultural Revolution, Red Guards from all over the country came to Jinggangshan like pilgrims (Chan 1985, Wagner 1992). At one point, the situation in Jinggangshan was quite serious with so many travelers:

> Tour activities to come to Jiangxi for visiting revolutionary heritage sites in the name of "the great union" mushroomed rapidly. Merely between August 1966 and June 1967, Jinggangshan had 900,000 Red Guards arrivals. By December 9th, 1966, 90,000 people had been detained in the entire area of Mt. Jinggang-shan, which had far exceeded the capacity of the city. The state had to airdrop food and medicine for the cold and hungry crowds. (Wen et al. 2000, 282)

Thus the cult of a revolutionary pilgrimage was carried to an extreme by the Red Guards of the mid-1960s who regarded Jinggangshan as a mecca of the revolution.

Red tourism promoted by the state at the start of the twenty-first century represents a form of revolutionary pilgrimage, but its nature is very different. The earlier visitors, as well as the elderly of today, may have identified with the revolutionary ideologies more spontaneously than do the youths who travel to Jinggangshan for "patriotic education." This new state-endorsed pilgrim-age links patriotic education with consumption and continues to be secular in discourse, as distinct from the practice of seeking personal blessings by paying homage to gods. The state, however, has proved incapable of maintaining hege-mony over pilgrimage once market mechanisms have been introduced.

Revolutionary/patriotic pilgrimages of recent years have been influenced by the overall economic development environment in China after the 1980s, although educational programs have continued in revolutionary sacred places since 1949. Ironically, during the early reform period, Jiangxi's revolutionary heritage was perceived as a root for Jiangxi's "backwardness." Based on this perception, provincial elites promoted "*Gan* culture" in the early 1990s in an at-tempt to evoke the neo-Confucian commercial roots of Jiangxi's traditional cul-ture (Feng 1999).[2] This Gan "cultural fever," which sought to replace Jiangxi's once glorious revolutionary heritage with its commercial heritage, however, was not successful. Nor did it change Jiangxi's economic status of ranking last among all six provinces in the central region of China in terms of gross do-mestic product (GDP) up until 2000 (Hu 2003, 5; Zhou and Yin 2002, 18–22). In 2001, a new provincial development strategic target of *cong zhongbu jueqi* (rising from the central region) was put forth by the Eleventh Session of the Jiangxi Provincial CCP Representative Assembly (Hu 2003, 8).

In order to "rise from the central region," Jiangxi endeavors to exploit its political, economic, historical, and cultural resources as geographical advantages (Hu 2003, 2004; Peng et al. 2004; Wang and Ma 2003). Capitalizing on Jiangxi's cultural resources, be they revolutionary or historical cultural heritage, is crucial for developing Jiangxi's tourism in the provincial scheme of generating economic growth (Ye 2004; Zhou and Yin 2002). The promotion of red, green, and classical tourism in Jiangxi's revolutionary sacred sites of Jinggangshan will be discussed in the coming section.

PILGRIM OR TOURIST?

Due to commercial tourism development, revolutionary pilgrims of the socialist era become more and more blurred with spiritual pilgrims in the post-Mao era. As mentioned in the previous section, revolutionary (or patriotic) pilgrimage indicates state-sanctioned activities of patriotic education in the dominant discourse whereas spiritual pilgrimage involves activities of prayers and offerings for personal blessings discouraged by the state. The rise of spiritual pilgrimage at Jinggangshan suggests that the state's efforts to control and secularize pilgrimage are not effective.

It is thus necessary to examine how spiritual pilgrims and patriotic pilgrims are intertwined in Jiangxi's tourism practices, particularly in the provincial efforts of simultaneously promoting red tourism and green tourism. Starting in 2001, Jiangxi's revolutionary heritage was labeled "Red Culture" and "Red Resources," and gradually assimilated into local tourism development and regional economic development schemes. In the Overall Planning for Jiangxi Tourism Development (2001–2020), red cultural tourism resources are seen to be a highly profitable resource for exploring new tourism routes (JTB and TPRC 2002, 259). In May 2002, the city of Jinggangshan started to promote a red tourism program of "*Shang Jinggangshan, yi chuantong, you hongjun guxiang, zou hongjun zhi lu*" (Ascending Jinggangshan, recalling tradition, touring the Red Army hometown, and walking the Red Army road; Tan and Wu 2002, 45). In the course of merely a few years, red tourism has developed into a sophisticated venture that is indispensable for Jiangxi's cultural tourism industry. The popularity of red tourism all over China is marked by a number of significant events, including the signing of Zhengzhou Declaration by seven provinces and municipalities to join forces in developing red tourism (Zhang 2004, 3), the initiation of the touring Jinggangshan Spirit Grand Exhibition (Chang et al. 2003, A1; Chen and Liu 2004, A1; Guo and Zeng 2003, A1, A3; Huang and Zhang 2003, 1; Wang et al. 2003, 4–9), and the launching of the first China (Nanchang) Red Tourism Fair (JPPGIS 2005).

The official definition for "red tourism" has yet to be finalized although many scholarly works discuss how to develop red tourism as a strategy for economic growth (Gao 2002, 4; Li 2002, 66; Lin 2003, 84; Tan and Wu 2002, 44; Wen 2004, 8; Zhang 2005, 9). As a working definition in this chapter, red tourism is a state-promoted tourism activity based on China's revolutionary cultural resources; it is essentially the state-endorsed commercial develop-ment in revolutionary memorial sites. One of the chief objectives for red tourism is to initiate economic development by capitalizing on red resources, that is, revolutionary heritage. But a second important goal of red tourism is to cultivate China's revolutionary spirit within the younger generation and party members.

Red tourism, however, is not promoted in isolation from other kinds of tourism in Jiangxi. During an interview in 2003 on red tourism of Jiangxi in revolutionary sacred sites, staff members of the Jiangxi Tourism Bureau (JTB) clarified that there are three types of tourism development in Jiangxi: green, or scenic tourism; red, or revolutionary heritage tourism; and classi-cal, or traditional heritage tourism. "The three types are inseparable," they emphasized, "and they are connected to each other." "This has to do with how tourism is positioned for the development of Jiangxi," one staff member explained. "That is, '*sange jidi, yige hou huayuan*' (three bases and a back garden), put forth by the Eleventh Session of the Jiangxi Provincial CCP Representative Assembly held in Jinggangshan in 2001." Staff members of the JTB were proud that tourism is closely related to Jiangxi's rise from the central region, and to constructing Jiangxi into the "*xiuxian hou huayuan* (leisure back garden)." My JTB respondents were excited that "the Provincial Committee and the Provincial Government regard highly the tourism industry in Jiangxi, positioning and nurturing tourism as a mainstay industry."

Obviously, red tourism is only one part of the overall provincial strategy of tourism development. "Red Cradle," "Green Homeland," and "Quaint Cul-ture" are "the three cards" in Jiangxi's scheme to construct the province into a leisure back garden for the eastern and southern coastal provinces and munic-ipalities including Guangdong, Jiangsu, Zhejiang, and Shanghai (LCCPGJTB and Zong 2003, A4). With this comparative advantage of close proximity to the developed coastal areas of the Pearl River Delta and the Yangtze River Delta, the provincial elites of Jiangxi plan to develop its tourism industry so that the province may be synthesized in the regional development system by way of, and by joining forces with, the relatively developed coast regions in China. Jiangxi people are called forth

> to help advance Jiangxi's rising from the central region, to help improve Jiangxi's
> international reputation and influence, and to help enhance Jiangxi's grand open
> strategy of "coordinating the Pearl River Delta and the Yangtze River Delta,
> and fitting into the world" by comprehensively introducing Jiangxi's beautiful

landscape and its three tourism features of "red, green, and classic colors" to the world based on the themes of "Rising Jiangxi," "Ecological Jiangxi," and "Safe Jiangxi." (Cheng and Fu 2004, 3)

Accordingly, the tourism theme of "Ecological Jiangxi and Leisure Garden" was underlined during the Jiangxi (Hong Kong) Investment Talks and Tourism Marketing Fair in 2002 (EC 2003, A4). As part of the "green action" to revitalize Jiangxi's tourism industry, the *Quanshun* tourism express line highlighted the slogan "Red Cradle and Green Homeland" in 2003 (EC and Zong 2003, A4).[3] A terminal for the tourism express bus line was set up in Nanjing Road, the busiest street in Shanghai.

As a key location for red tourism as well as "the three-color tourism" development in Jiangxi, the Jinggangshan administration is aggressive in advancing its tourism business and marketing. The development strategy for Jinggangshan City is explicitly expressed in the landscaping art in front of the municipal administration building. On one side of the lawn, bushes are planted to form the Chinese characters *kejiao lishi* (establishing the city with science), while on the other side bushes form the Chinese characters of *luyou xingshi* (revitalizing the city with tourism). Equal effort in publicizing both green and red resources finds expression in the official introduction to Jinggangshan's tourism resources. On glass-fronted billboards along the main street of the city, the Jinggangshan Municipal Party Committee's Department of Publicity represents Jinggangshan thus: "In Jinggangshan, there are two treasures; the history is red, and the mountain woods are good."

Jinggangshan is not only China's revolutionary historical cradle, it is also a key scenic spot, one of "China's Forty Best Tourism Resorts," "China's Excellent Tourism City," and a national "grade-AAAA" tourism district. Heroic achievements are intertwined with magnificent landscapes, forming Jinggangshan's unique scenic features. The glamour of Jinggangshan as a tourism resort and simultaneously a revolutionary pilgrimage destination lies in its most prominent feature—"*honglu huiying*" (the red intertwines with the green; the red complements the green). This "glamour" is evoked by the state policy sanctioning the "revolutionary pilgrimage" of patriotic education as part of red tourism. But, in order to enhance their profitability, revolutionary memorial sites in Jinggangshan and elsewhere in Jiangxi are promoted together with natural scenery and historical cultural relics.

Sightseeing and patriotic pilgrimage are thus equally important selling points for Jiangxi's (red) tourism marketing strategies, targeting consumers with differently focused interests. State-promoted and organized tours involved in the red tourism business qualify as pilgrimage in that their destinations are officially designated as "educational bases" for the participants. For some participants, the tour is a *"geming xili"* (revolutionary baptism) for the renewal of a faith in the revolutionary ideology and for the improvement of the individual. The synthesis of entertainment and natural scenery with revolutionary pilgrimage is promoted as more effective for both agendas.

Accordingly, some revolutionary heritage educational programs make use of the mountain's scenic beauty. Wuzhifeng, for instance, is integrated in the promotion of *Jinggangshan Jingshen* (Jinggangshan Spirit). The central poster for the Jinggangshan Spirit Grand Exhibition (figure 3.2, top) is represented by five large-scale billboards forming the shape of the Chinese character "hill/mountain," with "Jinggangshan Spirit" on the central billboard and a panorama of Wuzhifeng in the background spread over all five billboards (Wang et al. 2003, 5). The national reputation of Jinggangshan Spirit and that of Wuzhifeng on the back of the one-hundred-yuan bill (figure 3.2, bottom) mutually promote each other. Together they publicize Jinggangshan as a revolutionary pilgrimage site as well as a scenic tourism resort. In this regard, the one-hundred-yuan bill becomes "red" capital.

While the revolutionary memorials and relics are emblems of Jinggangshan's red tourism spots, Wuzhifeng and *Xiunu Pubu* (Fairy Waterfall) with *Longtan* (Dragon Pond) are representatives of its green tourism spots. According to one of the managerial staff members of the JRMMH who has been to Jinggangshan, "The development of Longtan and Wuzhifeng does not have much to do with the revolution. It's influenced by the reputation of Jinggangshan." The scenic spot of Wuzhifeng features a billboard introduction to the one-hundred-yuan bill both in Chinese and in English, a photo service stand, and gift stalls selling token one-hundred-yuan bills. Longtan is similar regarding the setup of photo services and gift stalls. What is unique about Longtan is the use of a bamboo raft, a local transportation specialty more commonly used during the Red Army era, with a chair on which tourists may take pictures. All these devices are meant to make a profit by offering tourists the experience of "being there." The line of gift stores near Longtan are selling souvenirs one can buy anywhere around Jinggangshan: Mao's badges, bamboo screens inscribed with Mao's poems about Jinggangshan, bamboo wares from pen holders to massagers, cloth bags, and Jinggangshan snacks. When I asked the owners how they decide what to stock, they said that they would stock anything that sells, mostly handicrafts. Their business does not have much to do with the revolutionary heritage or moral education, but it helps create a tourism experience of entertainment and consumption for both the sightseers and patriotic pilgrims while generating economic growth in previously poor and remote areas.

Figure 3.2.   Central poster for the *Jinggangshan Spirit* Grand Exhibition (top); Wuzhifeng on the back of the one-hundred-yuan bill. *Jiangxi Pictorial* 2003, 5. A. Luo Rioux photo, April 2003.

The elements of red tourism and green tourism are mixed in the "Jinggangshan Revolutionary Heritage Educational Tour Guide" of 22 April 2004, an informal pamphlet geared toward the needs and interests of an organized group from Wuhan. According to the pamphlet, the purpose of a Jinggangshan tour is to "launch heritage education, enhance the friendship of comrades, activate institutional life, mold a cadre's temperament, and further develop the learning and educational activity of 'creating the image for organizational cadres.'"

For this organized group, both red and green tourism sites were included in the itinerary. The logic for combining the red tour with the green tour can be drawn from the words of the managerial staff member of the JRMMH who has been to Jinggangshan:

> Jiangxi's notable characteristic is that there are a few revolutionary base areas in the province. The value of Jinggangshan would be a lot less if it had not been developed together with tourism. It would be boring to develop merely revolutionary former sites. Tourism, leisure, and education should be coordinated. There is more developing space for tourism and leisure. The infrastructure is a lot better. The houses for the former sites cannot be changed, but the content may be adjusted and improved with further research efforts.

Considerations of Jinggangshan as a revolutionary sacred site and simultaneously a scenic spot are oriented to the subject of the consumer market—the tourists. Incorporating sightseeing into a revolutionary heritage educational tour is becoming more and more common, and one can argue that seeing the beautiful rivers and mountains of the motherland may evoke patriotism and nationalism among the Chinese. Likewise, the mysterious force of Jinggangshan legends associated with Mao and the Red Army attracts spiritual pilgrimage for personal prayers and blessings as well as the above-mentioned officially sanctioned patriotic pilgrimage.

The point here, however, is that revolutionary heritage educational programs are transformed by the market forces within which they are promoted. Pure sightseeing tours might not be endorsed by the official organizers due to their potential connection to public funds abuse and potential corruption, whereas a pure revolutionary heritage educational tour might not generate enough interest or passion among participants. These official organizers range from the party committee of a city/township or work-unit to the Communist Youth League committee of a college or a university.

By analyzing how the revolutionary sacred space of Jiangxi has been transformed, the next section will illustrate how an ideological tension exists between officially sanctioned discourse and actual practice in developing red tourism with green (and classical) tourism.

TRANSFORMATION OF REVOLUTIONARY HOLY LAND

Economic growth and commercial development are perhaps the most noticeable transformation for the revolutionary sacred sites of Jiangxi. Jinggangshan is heralded for having

> realized the new leap from "the revolutionary sacred place" to "the tourism resort," further glorifying its revolutionary achievements and beautiful landscape. Jinggangshan has become a famous historical cultural city as well as a tourism resort bringing together humanistic landscape and natural landscape. It is one of the tourism hot spots along the grand (Bei)jing-jiu(long) railroad line. Every year, millions of people come here for sightseeing and revolutionary tradition learning. (Li 2003, 5)

Jinggangshan has changed into a commercial tourism site through the combined efforts of the government and private investors. The initial passive commitment of administrative agencies in the tide of reform and economic development was pushed onto an active business engagement in Jiangxi on the part of the former revolutionary memorial institutions.

This transformation of Jinggangshan translates into visible landscape changes. The town of Ciping, as shown in a photograph taken in 1959, was only a circle of buildings scattered around a vast open space of farmland along the foot of the surrounding hills (He 1959, 5–7). By the time I visited Jinggangshan in 2003, Ciping had already become a sprawling city. Construction of new houses, new office buildings, new market places, and new hotels, normally restricted in other tourism resorts such as Lushan—a more straightforward scenic resort in northern Jiangxi—was seen every day in Jinggangshan. In addition to the old and the new guest houses, reception centers, and training bases, over a hundred well-equipped hotels, mansions, and mountain villas have been built (Luo 2000, 255–59; Xia 2004, 235–39).

With a closer look at the parenthetical characters on hotel signboards, one can easily see that some hotels are simultaneously guest houses, receptions centers, or training bases of certain public institutes. Dujuan Hotel, for example, is the original Jinggangshan Municipal Guest House; Yinshanhong Hotel is also the Planning Committee Training Center; Jingxiu Mountain Villa is the original Power Industry Employee Training Base. The original guest houses, reception centers, and training bases are pushed onto the market to gain profit. While these businesses do serve the purpose of ideological training centers for some of the revolutionary pilgrims within their respective systems of work-units, they may not necessarily discourage potential abuse of public funds in disguise of moral education. A tourist guide I met in Jinggangshan told me that more and more organized group tours sponsored by work-units or governmental institutions tended to choose Jinggangshan over Lushan as a destination in order to avoid potential criticism. Most of these publicly funded tours actually incorporated sightseeing into revolutionary heritage education since "*yu jiao yu le*" (incorporating recreation into education) is quite acceptable. Leisure tourism, on the other hand, may inevitably take the form of a revolutionary educational tour. Infrastructure construction in the name of training center construction may also escape regulations. The dilemma of good intention and unexpected outcome in the commercial development of tourism, therefore, may well render some revolutionary heritage educational programs superficial and ineffective except for financial profit.

Given their passion for moral education and renewal of the revolutionary faith, there may be no doubt about the party and the state's sincerity to foster a patriotic younger generation. A much wider range of interests in journeying to the revolutionary sacred sites, however, surfaces in the transformation of the revolutionary holy land. During my field research, I met generally three types of visitors. On one end of the continuum are those who voluntarily pay respect to revolutionary sacred sites. These visitors usually bear strong enthusiasm for the history of the CCP and the hardship the revolutionaries had gone through for the interests of the Chinese people. They include descendants and family members of the commemorated. Visitors of the second type comprise organized students, employees, cadres, party members, and soldiers who may or may not readily identify with the state's hegemonic ideology. Among them are the faithful pilgrims of the revolutionary spirit and the sightseers seeking pleasure. On the other end of the continuum lie those spiritual pilgrims who seek personal blessings and individual interests.

A series of contradictions is manifested in the mixture of red tourism and green tourism development in Jinggangshan. Discrepancies exist between officially sanctioned discourse of patriotic/moral education and actual practices of superstition. Quite unexpectedly, nationalism and patriotism are contested by individual agendas. The revolutionary "culture" is turned into "red culture" and employed as a red resource for tourism development. The extraction of revolutionary symbols and the reinvention of a revolutionary culture work more as a tourism development strategy than as a revolutionary pilgrimage. Revolutionary monuments stand alongside service stalls for profit. Bajiaolou is partly used as a temple for personal blessings and good fortune, and this has nothing to do with patriotism or nationalism. A journey to Jinggangshan can take one quite far from the state's objective of a revolutionary baptism. Quite the contrary, seeking personal interests is directly counter to the revolutionary ideology of "serving the people" or "constructing the socialist nation."

Even Mao Zedong himself, an atheist, is mystified into a deity, and worshiped as a secular god. The continuing cult of Mao is popular in his birthplace of Shaoshan, and throughout China (Barmé 1996; Dutton 1998, 232–82; Han 2001, 225–31). In Jinggangshan, I ran into a middle-aged woman prostrating herself in front of Mao's statue raised on a pedestal set up in one of the gift stores (figure 3.3). I did not have any opportunity to talk to the woman and inquire why she was offering prayers. Her motivations were probably typical of many who revere Mao—for prosperity, a sick family member, college admissions, a job promotion, or other like reasons. Her act, as well as similar rites, may be a sign of the disappointment with the outcomes of the reforms, and a crisis of faith. The Mao cult can be interpreted as an indication of nostalgia for Mao's era, and for Mao's ideal of an egalitarian society in which the poor are empowered and the proletariat, or the people, are the masters of the nation to be served (*renmin dangjia zuozhu*). It may also be a sign of popular dissatisfaction with some corrupt officials in the reform era, and nostalgia for the upright cadres in Mao's era. The irony of Mao's podium exchanged for Mao's altar lies in the ideological contrast. Mao the atheist is now mythologized and reinvented with

Figure 3.3. Worshiping Mao's statue. A. Luo Rioux photo, April 2003.

the supernatural power of a deity, but he was adamantly opposed to such superstitious activities.

If visits by the Red Guards and revolutionary heirs during the Cultural Revolution, and organized tour groups during the reform era, were patriotic pilgrimages, then visits similar to the one by the woman worshiper in Jing-gangshan are spiritual pilgrimage. In this privately owned gift store, the accumulation of incense ashes in the burner and that of offerings in the box show how similar activities are not occasional, but quite common. In one direction, there has to be a need on the pilgrim's part to worship a deity for prayers; in another direction, there has to be a need on the part of a business owner for profit from Mao's altar. It may also be the business owner's initiative to set up the altar to mystify Mao in order to better sell the souvenirs since people are more willing to spend money for personal blessings and for their reverence for Mao. The popularity of the Mao cult reveals that Jinggangshan and its connection to Mao become mystified in a commercial cultural sense for some visitors' as well as business owners' emotional investment and ties.

The emotional investment itself in the revolutionary sacred space is therefore not weakened as a result of the commercial trend in Jinggangshan. But the focus has been redirected. During the earlier days, ordinary people were more willing to identify with the CCP's agendas to serve the people, and to sacrifice personal interests for the cause of the nation and the collective as a result of the good models the revolutionary martyrs and the selfless leaders set up. Nowadays, due to disillusionment with the bad examples of some corrupt CCP members and government officials who are concerned more about personal interests than about the interests of the people, ordinary people tend to identify with the state and the CCP's agendas less willingly. This is where revolutionary heritage educational bases are called on to strengthen the power of the state and the CCP by evoking nationalism and the ideal of serving the people and of sacrificing for the benefit of the collective. Ironically, the promotion of this agenda mingled with commercial development strays from the state's original intentions.

The official agendas of evoking nationalism and sacrifice for the people, in the same vein, are constrained by the internal paradox of red tourism development, which is complicated with the promotion of green tourism. Although economic growth may empower the state economically, the free market ideology of seeking ultimate capital and personal benefits contradicts the ideology of sacrificing personal interests for the benefit of the people. In a free market economy, a personal interest is satisfied in the example of the gift store owner. The owner pursues maximum profit, setting up the Mao altar with the hope to attract the multitudes. Books are offered, statues and trinkets, any item that might possibly tempt a visitor to part with some money.

CONCLUSION

After the establishment of the PRC, memorials, museums, and monuments were set up to commemorate revolutionary martyrs who had sacrificed their lives for the nation. These memorial sites once enjoyed the status of sacred space, having their own devoted followers in the form of revolutionary pilgrims. Starting from the reform era, these sites have experienced a dramatic transformation associated with tourism development. As a result of fiscal decentralization and growing provincial pressure, revolutionary memorials and museums have been pushed onto the market. The commodification of sacred revolutionary spaces has expanded prominently in the operation and promotion of red tourism that emerged in 2002. One of the most renowned revolutionary sacred sites, Jing-gangshan in Jiangxi Province, is particularly marketed for its revolutionary "red history" and its beautiful "green scenery."

Development-oriented commercialism has eroded and transformed these "sacred spaces" of revolutionary memorials in China during the reform era. Histories and symbols of the revolution are advocated as major tourist attractions by way of reinvention and selectivity. In the commercial development of red tourism in parallel with green tourism, the divine is "naturalized," and the sacred becomes secularized. The fetishism of Mao's statue, for instance, is developed mainly for the well-being of the individual on the part of the "pilgrims" and for monetary gains on the part of business owners. Yet in another direction, the secular and the human evolve into the divine. Mao the human is deified for business and profit, which represents an ironic reversal of Mao's proletariat worldview of atheism. The demarcation between the secular and the divine is thus reconstituted in the revolutionary sacred sites undergoing tourism development.

Consequently, the state-endorsed tourism development produces very unpredictable outcomes that the state cannot fully control or maintain hegemony over. The moral educational programs strongly promoted for red tourism, for example, are intended to strengthen revolutionary ideologies of serving the people. In reality, however, many organized trips feature leisure tourism and recreation at the public expense in the name of moral education. As a result of the transformation, a growing conflict arises between individualism and collectivism, and between commercialism and patriotism. This is because the commodification of revolutionary sites as tourist destinations opens up opportunities for the reenactment or reconstitution of popular religious practices, such as praying for personal blessings. While the state promotes red tourism partly to maintain the moral upper hand, the market transformation encourages those practices that challenge the state's dominance. The above-mentioned controversial ways of using the revolutionary memorial sites have diminished the sacred status of revolutionary holy land among which Jing-gangshan is representative.

NOTES

I wish to heartily thank the National Science Foundation (NSF) doctoral dissertation research improvement (DDRI) award (#BCS-0202018) for funding my fieldwork in Jiangxi, China, in 2003, to thank the Developing Area Research and Teaching (DART) program at the University of Colorado at Boulder for a grant during the summer of 2004, and to thank relevant institutions and numerous individuals in China for facilitating my research. An earlier version of this chapter was presented at a panel organized by Tim Oakes and Donald Sutton for the 2006 annual meeting of the Association of Asian Studies in San Francisco, CA. I appreciate their feedback.

1. *Chi* is a popular Chinese unit of length. One *chi* is one-third of a meter, which equals to 1.094 feet.
2. *Gan* is the historical term and the abbreviation for Jiangxi. The *Gan* culture is thus Jiangxi's historical cultural tradition.
3. *Quanshun*, meaning "completely smooth" in Chinese, is the chosen brand for the tourism express line.

REFERENCES

Barmé, Geremie R. 1996. *Shades of Mao: The Posthumous Cult of the Great Leader*. New York and London: M.E. Sharpe.
Chan, Anita. 1985. *Children of Mao: Personality Development and Political Activism in the Red Guard Generation*. Seattle: University of Washington Press.
Chang, Gen, Jing Zhang, and Jiyan Huang. 2003. "Jinggang Spirit Shines Over Beijing: The Media of the CCP Central Committee and the Capital City 'Focus On' Jinggangshan Spirit Grand Exhibition." *Jiangxi Daily*, 13 November, A1. [长根，张晶，黄继妍。《井冈精神耀京华·中央及首都媒体"聚焦"井冈山精神大型展览》。《江西日报》11月13日，A1版].
Chen, Fang, and Fuming Liu. 2004. "Heat Waves of Revolutionary Heritage Education Surging Along the Lakeside of Xizi Lake, Jinggangshan Spirit Grand Exhibition Enters Zhejiang Province for an Exhibition Tour." *Jiangxi Daily*, 23 March, A1 [陈方，刘福明。《西子湖畔涌动革命传统教育热潮·井冈山精神大型展览进浙巡展》。《江西日报》3月23日，A1版].
Cheng, Yuanyuan, and Chuanwei Fu. 2004. "Based on Themes of 'Rising Jiangxi,' 'Ecological Jiangxi,' 'Safe Jiangxi,' Pushing Jiangxi Character onto the Entire World." *Information Daily*, 17 July, 3 [程媛媛，傅传蔚。《以"崛起江西"、"生态江西"、"平安江西"为主题·把江西特色推向全世界》。《信息日报》7月17日，第3版].

Department of Publicity, Jinggangshan Municipal Party Committee (DPJMPC), ed. 2004. *Jinggangshan Today—A General Introduction to Jinggangshan City* [井冈山市委宣传部编印。《今日井冈山—井冈山市情概况》].

Dutton, Michael. 1998. *Streetlife China.* Cambridge: Cambridge University Press.

Editorial Collective (EC). 2003. "Concept, Thoughts, and Creativity." *Jiangxi Daily*, 21 July, A4 [编委。《观念·思路·创新》。《江西日报》7月21日，A4版].

Editorial Collective (EC), and Huan Zong. 2003. "Green Action—Plan for Revitalizing the Tourism Industry in Jiangxi." *Jiangxi Daily*, 21 July, A4 [编委/文，宗欢/摄。《绿色行动—江西旅游业振兴计划》。《江西日报》7月21日，A4版].

Gao, Shunli. 2002. "Thoughts on Developing Red Tourism." *China Tourism News*, 21 August, 4 [高舜礼。《发展红色旅游的思考》。《中国旅游报》8月21日，第4版].

Guo, Dehong, ed. 2001. *The East Is Red When the Sun Rises—Historical Records of the CCP's 80-Year Journey.* Nanchang: Jiangxi People's Publishing House [郭德宏，主编。《日出东方红—中国共产党80年历程纪实》。江西人民出版社，6月].

Guo, Ping, and Weimin Zeng. 2003. "Let Jinggangshan Spirit Shine Over China; *Jinggangshan Spirit Grand Exhibition* Preludes the National Exhibition Tour in Tianjin." *Jiangxi Daily*, 17 December, A1 and A3 [郭平，曾为民。《让井冈山精神光耀神州·〈井冈山精神〉大型展览在天津拉开全国巡展序幕》。《江西日报》12月17日，A1及A3版].

Han, Min. 2001. "The Meaning of Mao in Mao Tourism of Shaoshan." In *Tourism, Anthropology, and China*, ed. C. B. Tan, S. C. H. Cheung, and H. Yang. Bangkok: White Lotus Press, 215–35.

He, Daxing. 1959. "Ciping—Center of the Revolutionary Cradle Jinggangshan." *Jiangxi Pictorial* no. 2 (August): 5–7 [贺大行/摄。《茨坪—革命摇篮井冈山的中心》。《江西画报》8月，第2期，5–7页].

Headquarters of Red Guards at Jiangxi Middle Schools and Colleges (HRGJMSC), General Headquarters of Revolutionary Faculty, and Staff and Students at Jiangxi Colleges (GHRFSSJC). 1967. "Enhance the Thorough Revolutionary Spirit of Jinggangshan, Becoming Avant-Garde Pioneers of 'Fighting the Selfish, and Critiquing the Revisionists.'" *Jiangxi Daily*, 7 October, 4 [江西省大中学校红卫兵司令部，江西省大专院校革命师生总指挥部。《发扬井冈山彻底革命精神，做"斗私，批修"的急先锋》。《江西日报》10月7日，第4版].

Hu, Ping, ed. 2003. *The Land Loved and Hated— Interpretation of Jiangxi and the Central Region.* Nanchang: Jiangxi People's Publishing House [胡平，编著。《爱并恨着的土地—江西及中部的解读》。江西人民出版社，7月].

———. 2004. *Observing Jiangxi with a Third Eye.* Nanchang: Jiangxi People's Publishing House [胡平，编著。《第三只眼睛看江西》。江西人民出版社，4月].

Huang, Jiyan, and Changgen Zhang. 2003. "Jinggangshan Spirit Grand Exhibition Started Ceremoniously in Beijing." *Jiangxi Daily*, 16 November, 1 [黄继妍/文，张长根/摄。《井冈山精神大型展览在京隆重开展》。《江西日报》11月16日，第1版].

Jiangxi Provincial People's Government Information Service (JPPGIS). 2005. *2005 China (Jiangxi) Red Tourism Fair*. www.jxcn.cn/hsly/ (accessed 28 October 2005) [江西省人民政府新闻办公室，主办。《2005·中国（江西）红色旅游博览会》。中国江西网].

Jiangxi Tourism Bureau (JTB), and Tourism Planning Research Center at the Institute of Geographic Sciences and Resources in China Science Academy (TPRC), ed. 2002. *Overall Planning for Jiangxi Tourism Development (2001–2020)*. Beijing: China Travel and Tourism Press [江西省旅游局，中国科学院地理科学与资源研究所旅游规划研究中心。《江西省旅游业发展总体规划（2001–2020）》。北京：中国旅游出版社8月].

Leading CCP Group of Jiangxi Tourism Bureau, the (LCCPGJTB), and Huan Zong. 2003. "Waves of Constructing the Back Garden Are Surging." *Jiangxi Daily*, 21 July, A4 [江西省旅游局党组/文，宗欢/摄。《贯彻落实省委十一届四次全会精神，全省旅游行业积极行动—后花园建设，大潮正起》。《江西日报》7月21日，A4版].

Li, Congming, ed. 2003. *Sacred Jinggangshan*. Nanchang: Jiangxi Fine Arts Press [李从明，编著。《神圣的井冈山》。江西美术出版社].

Li, Rui. 1999 [2001]. *Minutes of Lushan Conferences*, 3rd ed. Zhengzhou: Henan People's Publishing House [李锐。《庐山会议实录（增订第三版）》。河南人民出版社].

Li, Zongyao. 2002. "On Functional Diversity of 'Red Tourism': Also on Comprehensive Development of the Tourism Industry in Yedian Town in Mengyin County." *Journal of Shandong Agricultural Management Cadres' Institute* 18(4): 66–67 [李宗尧。《论"红色旅游"功能的多样性—兼谈蒙阴县野店镇旅游业的综合开发》。《山东省农业管理干部学院学报》第18卷第4期，66–67页].

Lin, Mingtai. 2003. "A SWOT Analysis of and Developmental Measures for Red Tourism in Putian." *Journal of Putian University* 10(4): 84–88 [林明太。《莆田发展红色旅游的SWOT分析与对策》。《莆田学院学报》12月，第10卷第4期，84–88页].

Luo, Jinqing. 2000. *Resorts and Tours of Jinggangshan*. Hohhot: Inner Mongolia University Press [罗锦清，编著。《井冈名胜与旅游》。内蒙古大学出版社].

Mao, Binghua. 2002 [2004]. *The First Mountain of the World*. Nanchang: Jiangxi People's Publishing House [毛秉华，主讲。《天下第一山》。江西人民出版社].

Mao, Zedong. 1991 [1951]. *Selected Works of Mao Zedong,* vols. 1–4. Beijing: People's Press [中共中央文献编辑委员会。《毛泽东选集，一至四卷》。人民出版社].

Naquin, Susan, and Chün-fang Yü. 1992. "Introduction: Pilgrimage in China." In *Pilgrims and Sacred Sites in China*, ed. S. Naquin and C.-f. Yü. Berkeley: University of California Press, 1–38.

Peng, Chunlan, Yuqi Wang, and Hua Li, eds. 2004. *Are We Ready: Shocking Waves of Tell How Forum*. Nanchang: Jiangxi People's Publishing House [彭春兰，汪玉奇，李华，主编。《我们准备好了吗—泰豪论坛冲击波》。江西人民出版社].

Sun, Jiaye, and Kaixun Zhan, eds. 2003. *Jinggangshan Shone in Red and Green*. Nanchang: Jiangxi People's Publishing House [孙家烨，詹开逊，主编。《红绿辉映井冈山》。江西人民出版社].

Tan, Dongfa, and Xiaobin Wu. 2002. "'Red Resource' and Poverty Relief Development." *Old Liberated Areas Construction* 7: 44–45 [谭冬发，吴小斌。《"红色资源"与扶贫开发》。《老区建设》，第7期，44–45页].

Wagner, Rudolf G. 1992. "Reading the Chairman Mao Memorial Hall in Peking: The Tribulations of the Implied Pilgrim." In *Pilgrims and Sacred Sites in China*, ed. S. Naquin and C.-f. Yü. Berkeley: University of California Press, 378–423.

Wang, Wusheng. 1985. "One of the Five Large Sentry Posts in Jinggangshan—The Huangyangjie Pass." *Jiangxi Pictorial* 1: 5 [王午生/摄。《井冈山五大哨口之一—黄洋界》。《江西画报》11月，创刊号，第5页].

Wang, Yuqi, Wenlan Liu, Yuan Tai, Hong Xi, and Gen Chang. 2003. "Torch Burning in the Bosom—A Report on the Large-Scale Exhibition of Jinggangshan Spirit." *Jiangxi Pictorial* 6: 4–9 [汪玉奇，刘文兰/文，泰垣，曦洪，长根/图。《火炬在心中燃烧—来自井冈山精神大型展览的报告》。《江西画报》第6期，4–9页].

Wang, Yuqi, and Xuesong Ma. 2003. *Jiangxi: Walking Towards Rising*. Nanchang, Jiangxi: Baihuazhou Artistic Press [汪玉奇，马雪松。《江西：走向崛起》。南昌：百花洲文艺出版社].

Wen, Rui, Xinchun Liao, Yinzai Guo, Haihua You, Haiquan Xu, and Yingming Zhang. 2000. *Dramatic Changes in One Hundred Years and the Dream of Revitalization—On Twentieth Century Economy in Jiangxi*. Nanchang: Jiangxi People's Publishing House [温锐，廖信春，郭银仔，游海华，许海泉，张英明。《百年巨变与振兴之梦—20世纪江西经济研究》。江西人民出版社].

Wen, Xiu. 2004. "Red Tourism: Observation of Progress." *China Tourism News*, 29 March, 8 [温秀。《红色旅游:前进中的审视》。《中国旅游报》3月29日，第8版].

Xia, Mengshu. 2004. *Jinggangshan Tours*. Haikou: Hainan Press [夏梦淑。《井冈山旅游》。海南出版社].

Xiong, Wei, Shunmin Xu, and Guohong Zhang. 1998. *Lushan*. Beijing: China Architecture Press [熊炜，徐顺民，张国宏。《庐山》。中国建筑工业出版社].

Xu, Shunmin, Wei Xiong, Xiaogang Xu, Guoquan Wang, Guo-hong Zhang, and Wei He. 2001. *Lushan Studies—On Lushan Culture*. Nanchang: Jiangxi People's Publishing House [徐顺民，熊炜，徐效钢，汪国权，张国宏，贺伟。《庐山学—庐山文化研究》。江西人民出版社].

Ye, Mingzhi, and Zhanggen Li. 2002. *Jinggangshan: Handbook for Free Individual Tourists*. Beijing: China Travel and Tourism Press [叶明智，黎章根。《井冈山—自助旅游手册》。北京：中国旅游出版社].

Ye, Qing. 2004. "Research on the Development Strategies for Jiangxi's Cultural Industry." In *Blue Book of Economy: Analysis and Prediction of Jiangxi's Economic Situation in 2004*, ed. Fu, Bai-yan. Nanchang: Jiangxi People's Publishing House, 221–35 [叶青。《江西文化产业发展战略研究》。傅伯言，主编，《经济蓝皮书—2004年：江西经济形势分析与预测》江西人民出版社].

Yin, Chaohai. 2001. *Lushan Walking into the World*. Beijing: China Social Press [尹超海。《庐山走进世界》。中国社会出版社].

Zhang, Binbin. 2005. *Research on the Development and the Distribution of Red Tourism in China*. Master's thesis, East China Normal University [张彬彬。《中国红色旅游发展与布局研究》。华东师范大学硕士论文].

Zhang, Xuntao. 2004. "Develop 'Red Tourism' with Joint Efforts, Seven Provinces or Municipalities Signing *Zhengzhou Declaration*." *China Tourism News*, 12 January, 3 [张洵涛。《共同发展"红色旅游", 七省市签署〈郑州宣言〉》。《中国旅游报》1月12日, 第3版].

Zhou, Shaosen, and Jidong Yin. 2002. *The Strategies for Jiangxi to Rise from the Central Region*. Nanchang: Jiangxi People's Publishing House [周绍森, 尹继东。《江西在中部地区崛起方略》。江西人民出版社, 6月].

Zou, Wenkai. 1967. "Political Power Comes from Inside Gun Barrels." *Jiangxi Daily*, 7 October, 4 [邹文楷。《"枪杆子里面出政权"》。《江西日报》10月7日, 第4版].

The most obvious loci of ethnoreligious tourism in the region are the Tibetan monasteries, the Tibetans being the largest ethnic group in the Aba region, which has the administrative title Autonomous Tibetan and Qiang Nationalities Prefecture of Aba (Aba Zangzu Qiangzu zizhizhou). Bön monasteries in the Upper Min valley north of Songpan have been revived since the 1980s, and find themselves conveniently situated along the only tourist highways from Songpan to the World Heritage sites of Huanglong and Jiuzhaigou. In the 1990s, taking advantage of their locations, five of the Bön monasteries in the Songpan area followed a new business pattern in China's burgeoning "religious tourism" and contracted their monasteries out to Han Chinese businessmen from outside Songpan. The businessmen paid for the monasteries' renovation, expansion, maintenance, and the monks' salaries, and shared a fixed amount of the monasteries' tourist revenue. In return, the monasteries became the designated stops for tourist buses and tourist guides. Sales agents, most of them Mandarin-speaking Han ignorant of Tibetan language or culture, were hired to showcase Tibetan religion (Baimacuo 2004; interview with Gesang, 1 August 2004).[1] Critics of this trend told us in 2004 that Bön and various sects of Tibetan Buddhism had been lumped together as "Tibetan Buddhism." Cheap replicas of religious paraphernalia, such as Thangka and statues of Bön gods, were sold at the souvenir shops set up at the monasteries' entrances. Female tour guides wandered in the various quarters of the monasteries that used to be "monks only." In one monastery, a designated elder monk would don a lama's robe whenever a bus of tourists arrived, and the tour guides would introduce him as a highly cultivated Tibetan lama who "could go for 365 days without eating and drinking, and could fly from one mountain peak to another in an instant" (interview with Gesang, 1 August 2004). Local Tibetans who practiced their daily worship in the monastery were kept apart or away so that tourists could focus on buying incense and souvenirs.

This overtly commercial display of religion quickly produced tensions. While administrative committees disposed of extra income from tourism, some of the lamas and monks resented the violation of their religious space. Some left for other monasteries or returned home, in one case reducing the number of monks from thirty-two to eleven between 1999 and 2001. There were also complaints from tourists about aggressive sales agents and tour guides. And the contract business disrupted the traditional pattern of each monastery's links with its neighboring community. As the five open monasteries drew more and more tourists, local Tibetans' sense of their sacredness was diminished. One Tibetan villager commented, "The large monasteries are open to the public. They are no longer mysterious and the gods are no longer efficacious. We only go to smaller monasteries now [meaning worship halls in the backrooms of the large monastery and some village-based monasteries not open to tourists]" (interviews 19 June 2005). Another young monk and his Tibetan villager friend ridiculed the commercialization of their religion: "Kha-btags are offered one by one, lungta are flying everywhere, 'Tashi Delek' is worthless" (interviews 26 June 2005). Kha-btags are long white silk scarves Tibetans offer to respectable guests, prestigious people, or gods. Lungta are square paper prints of horses and dragon that Tibetans throw at high places for blessings. "Tashi Delek" is a common Tibetan greeting phrase. All three have been heavily used in the tourist industry as representations of Tibetan religion and culture. Two local monasteries that opted out of the tourist business gained popularity and credibility (Baimacuo 2004).

State agencies had tolerated the commodification of Bön monasteries. Indeed the Office of Religious Affairs served as a key intermediary with outside business entrepreneurs, and was said to share business profits with the monasteries through private arrangements with individual committee heads. But when the conflicts among the different parties intensified, and tourists, monks, and local Tibetan communities complained formally and informally to the county government, the office assumed a more public role. In 2002, it issued new regulations forbidding any involvement of outside businesses in religious establishments. However, it also encouraged tourist entrepreneurship by the monasteries themselves, stipulating that all senior ranking religious professionals, such as lama, kanbu, or living Buddhas would have to wear an ID when they provide services to tourists. Fees and gate money could be levied at a rate fixed by the Prefectural Office of Religious Affairs and the Bureau of Pricing. Tour guides were to be monks from within the monasteries (Baimacuo 2004, 104–5). How much the new policy has strengthened Tibetan religion in the villages remains a question. The regulations, after all, consider religion as a tourist commodity and ignore the still prevalent feelings of many Tibetan monks and villagers that the sacred power of gods and monasteries depends on exclusiveness and secrecy, and that the intrusion of outsiders can compromise the sacred link between monasteries and their supporting local communities.

Tibetans suffered a setback at the World Heritage site in Huanglong, where they had hoped to gain or recover a foothold. In the winter of 2003–2004 the Huanglong administration did rebuild the old Middle Temple (the largest surviving religious structure apart from the Rear Temple) in Tibetan style, but did not allow for any Tibetan presence. This was a characteristic effort to display religious symbols while denying them an institutional home, ritual expression, or any function outside display for the benefit of tourists (Kang and Sutton 2008; Kang 2009). But as we suggest, this was perhaps all that tourists wanted and expected.

Yet Tibetans themselves are finding other means to benefit from tourism and still maintain their local institutions. Like the numerous Tibetan-run hotels, restaurants, souvenir shops, and teahouses along the highway north of Songpan, notably at Chuanzhusi, the monasteries are also taking advantage of tourism to prosper. Many monasteries are now running souvenir shops and organizing tours on their own. Some monks provide spiritual services to tourists, who according to the monks, are vulnerable to the ghosts of traffic accident victims in the rough and unfamiliar terrain. Others are on the lookout for rich and devout tourists from the coastal areas whose donations could help in renovation. But in the meantime, almost all Bön monasteries have demarcated public and private zones. All visitors can walk the lines of great prayer wheels in their covered corridors. All can enter the main hall, if there are no rituals or meditations in progress, and pass counterclockwise (in Bön fashion) past the great images. Tourists are decked with a yellow scarf of welcome, given the option, but not pressed, to donate, and exit through the souvenir shop with monks standing behind counters offering hand prayer wheels, bells, embroidered and printed cloth, thanka, and other goods. For local villagers, by contrast, the monasteries have reserved a smaller hall on the side or in the rear. So the monastic committees now decide what to display, trying to balance the different needs of tourists and local communities.

The opportunity to exhibit regional religious performances to tourists has not been taken. The great festivals, though in principle annual, are now rare, requiring much expense and special official permission. Despite the festivals' great visual and aural appeal, they are not organized with tourists in mind, perhaps because their infrequency makes them inconvenient for tourist agencies. There are performances that could be abstracted from a religious setting, for example the famous Hwa shang (Heshang) dance associated with Rinspungs (Linbo Monastery). On one occasion it was performed at the tourist destination Huanglong, but for unknown reasons the experiment was never repeated (see Schrempf 2006). Though the principal mountain circumambulation at Bird Cemetery Mountain preceding the annual festival at the Dga' mal monastery (Gamisi) has become popular among some local Han, the six- to ten-hour circuit would be too arduous for tourists as well as inconveniently timed. Tibetan costumes are shown in stage performances in the tourist towns, the great horns are sounded, and throat singing is done in the local style, but all in a highly truncated form (see below). In short, while Tibetan monasteries can be visited, religion is not practiced and performed in the presence of tourists.

THE REVIVAL OF HUI MOSQUES

Tourists see rather less of the local mosques than the monasteries. This is not so much a matter of demand (tourists might like to see them) as of of-

Figure 4.1. Tibetan festival at Gamisi, without tourists.

ficial tourist policy. From official perspectives, tourism in Songpan and the whole Aba Prefecture revolves around displaying Tibetan and Qiang ethnic cultures. Hui are not considered to have much to offer. More important, however, is the strong preference of the mosques themselves not to be subject to the tourist gaze.

For the Hui are a distinct community unified by mosque and religion, at least by the idea of religion. Now mosques are revived in every Muslim village north of Songpan City, and splendid large mosques have been rebuilt inside and just outside the city. There are also two Sufi *gongbei* mosques. As elsewhere in China, better communications among the regions and attendance at several well-known schools in Shaanxi and Yunnan have helped to increase the role of Islam in Hui identity (Gladney 2003, 174–76). The government prefers the mosques to have a purely local identity, and is said to watch contacts among different regional Hui communities. The state applies the same restrictions as on Tibetan monasteries.

Religiously imposed diet is the clearest everyday marker of identity. Though young Hui people rarely observe the five daily prayers or wear the skullcap for men or chador for women, they avoid eating pork. Most expect to marry Hui fellow Muslims or Han who will cook *qingzhen* and eventually convert, and while they don't yet go to the mosque, they expect to do so when they become forty or fifty years old. In the Hui case, ethnic membership depends not on language (their dialect is indistinguishable from the Songpan variety of Chengdu or Sichuan Chinese) but ultimately on religion and its related dietary practices. In a society where hospitality by feasting plays such a central role, Han and Muslim cannot easily socialize because Han with their ritually unclean kitchens and pork consumption are not able to reciprocate.

Hui themselves emphasize the purity, the "qingzhen" nature of their mosques, and indeed the entire history of Islam underlines the preeminent need for purity. Despite strong notions of hospitality, they do not expect to see non-Muslims in the precincts of mosques. Han residential areas are separate, in the northern part of the city and just outside the walls, and in villages farther north. Given this habitual separation from local Han, it would be surprising if Han from outside Songpan would be actively recruited as tourists. The caretaker of the rebuilt mosque in the quarter outside the North Gate does not admit Westerners except in the courtyard, even if, following Islamic practice, they make to take off their shoes. By contrast the mosque in Songpan City, along with most village mosques, welcomes non-Muslim outsiders quite warmly and of course appreciates guest donations, but makes no particular effort to market the mosque.

This does not mean that the Hui reject the idea of tourism. It is important to stress that up to 1949 leading Hui were at the top of Songpan society, enjoying cultural prestige (in Chinese terms), and economic wealth in the old city. For centuries they had controlled much of the tea and horse trade. With the coming of the People's Republic their businesses were ruined, their properties confiscated, and their sons and daughters reduced to peasant status with little chance of education or advancement. The reform era from 1978 did not improve their situation as rapidly as that of the Tibetans. Songpan Hui of well-connected, middling, and poor backgrounds readily shared with us their feeling that they had been left behind in the recent wave of prosperity.

Tourism in fact has led to economic improvement for Hui. Many Songpan Hui are actively involved in taxi companies, motels, souvenir shops, Internet bars, and the many qingzhen restaurants, including the best restaurant in town. But what Hui would like to do is to promote their culture and identity to outsiders, though not in the mosques. We know active members of the Hui community who position Hui as an ethnic group good at singing, dancing, and playing folk music instruments, like their Tibetan and Qiang neighbors. They resent the fact that all visual and textual presentations of Songpan invariably feature Tibetan and Qiang dances and ethnic costumes without images of Hui. Instead of showing off their religion, they seek to display Hui ethnicity in a secular form, through ethnic performances; skill at singing and dancing is always ascribed to China's ethnic minority groups. In competition for public and official attention with others of the fifty-five minority nationalities, the Hui too would like to perform their membership in their own nationality. No doubt this would need invention, since there is not even the memory or name of historical customs along the lines of the local Guizhou dances revived or reinvented for tourism, as described in Tim Oakes's chapter. Recently, for example at the Huanglong official festival in 2004, the local custom has been for Hui men to perform sober dances brandishing (plastic) flower baskets. Hui were glad to be invited, but some felt the dance did not sufficiently show off the richness of Songpan Hui culture. What the content of that culture would be was not clear. (One of our informants, who made his own instruments, was enthusiastic about the local music of the Xinjiang Muslims, but that probably wouldn't qualify.) But they feel the pressure of competition from other more colorful nationalities. They would like the Hui to have more representation in official tourist literature, so that they would no longer be marginalized in the tourist economy. So the Songpan Hui today are a community that has found religion or rediscovered it but is still in search of a distinctive minority culture to put on display.

SONGPAN CITY RELIGION AS A POTENTIAL TOURIST ATTRACTION

Songpan's religious buildings were largely destroyed in Tibetan rebellions around 1860 and in 1911 (*Songpan xianzhi* 1924, j 3: 45b–56a) and totally eliminated during Maoist times. Religious revival and urban reconstruction occurred simultaneously after 1978, but the old Chinese temples and shrines that once defined the city neighborhoods have not been rebuilt. After the county government made tourism its first priority in local development, the city thrived as a "transit hub" (Nyíri 2006, 46) on the tourist bus route from the Sichuan provincial capital of Chengdu to the two newly developed scenic parks: Jiuzhaigou, 70 kilometers north of Songpan, and Huanglong, 55 kilometers northeast of Songpan.

What then of the pull of religion? If Dazhai could invent its own Buddhist temple, as the introduction notes, why could not Songpan? Unfortunately tourist policy focuses on the ethnic appeal of this center in the Aba Autonomous Prefecture, and there is no attested historical Tibetan (or Qiang) religious presence in the city. A religious monument was rebuilt in splendid style before 2002, but against the express wishes of local officials. The five-hundred-year-old City God (*chenghuang*) Temple, partly converted into a cemetery for revolutionary martyrs and mostly demolished in the Mao years, now stands again overlooking Songpan from halfway up the great western hill. The most celebrated event at the Songpan City God Temple, however, was and still is the Songpan City God Temple Festival (*Chenghuang hui*) on the twenty-first of the third lunar month, which is the god's birthday. In the good old days, as the locals recall today, the Songpan City God Temple with its three courtyards and commanding view of the city from the west slope was the most magnificent of all. The front halls housed the statues of netherworld yamen runners and paintings of the ten hells traversed by the newly dead; the huge statue of the City God occupied the second set of main halls, and the third quartered images of his wife and family, as in other City God temples offering a humanizing touch to his awful majesty. On the temple festival day, elaborate rituals and a procession would be performed. The City God would don the golden dragon robe and be carried out on the imperial carriage (*banfu luanjia*) by eighteen adult bearers and escorted by eight twelve-year-old boys riding on horses. Its first stop was the county government offices, where local officials would pay homage, make offerings to the god, and then march in the front of the procession. The carriage would make its descent into the outer city in the south, where Han Chinese communities lived, and then enter the city through the South Gate. It then proceeded through the main thoroughfare of the city, moving from the Chinese quarters in the south, to the ethnically mixed central parts, then to the north where Hui Muslims predominated. It would finally arrive at the Northern Altar (*beitan*) outside of the North Gate, and here officials and local people made offerings to Heaven and brought the god back to the front hall of the temple. He presided there throughout the temple fair celebration, and was retired to the main hall when the festival was over. During his procession, every household would have its family members holding incense at the front door to greet the god. Hui Muslims were not expected to offer incense but otherwise greeted the god just like everyone else. The Cultural Revolution destroyed much of the old temple along with its traditions.

Along with local place gods (*tudi shen*), the City God is not an approved deity in the People's Republic, perhaps because it encourages particularistic local identification as against loyalty to the state; the official line is that its festivals do not represent "healthy" customs. In Songpan, the location of the temple high up on the mountain slope and far away from the highway and main commercial streets was out of the tourists' reach and therefore government planners saw no point in renovating it. In the 1990s two men of middle age, experts in painting and construction respectively, led a number of Songpan women in raising money to rebuild the temple complex. When officials refused to give permission, they went ahead with the project anyway. Buddhism is considered more respectable than Daoism or folk religion in official circles, so they began by building a series of shrines for Buddhist gods in the

complex and finishing them with statues and altars lit daily for worship. Officials, who came up from many city departments to ask them to stop, may
have seen through this subterfuge, and they were right: in the project's last
stage what was unmistakably a City God hall was erected, with a front and
rear sections, complete with sidewalls occupied by the fearsome traditional
bodyguards of that god and the usual wall paintings depicting the sufferings
of hell. The official attempts to discourage the project had failed because of
the evasiveness and intransigence of the two main authors, the support of
many Songpan people, and, some say, the intervention of senior Han officials'
wives. Elaborate feasts are served to local worshipers at the traditional time
of the City God's birthday, on the twenty-first of the third lunar month, but
its processions have not been renewed.

Besides the extra-official reconstruction of the City God temple none of
the old temples that once served every part of old Songpan City has been
rebuilt. The rebuilding has focused on surfaces, on what can be seen, with
no attempt to restore what once lay behind the façade. One Han temple, the
Guanyin Pavilion, which overlooks the western part of the city, has been allowed to stand, though it seems in fairly poor repair. It has a caretaker who
keeps the incense lit in the various halls, and the few tourists who venture
there as individuals are drawn by the picturesque way it protrudes from the
high ledge of the western hills rather than its religious or architectural appeal.
A temple to the Wuxian gods near the small West Gate survives in a decrepit
state, patronized by some of the villagers living on the western hill. Just outside the former South Gate, there is also an active little Guanyin temple in
part of what was once the Temple of Dongyue, associated with death and the
underworld, but it is cramped and lacking an impressive façade. Like the tiny
temples in most villages it is supported by the neighborhood elders but is not
on any tourist itinerary.

The refurbishing of Songpan city streets and city walls in 2004 was only the
first step on the county government's new design for Songpan as the "Great
Tang City of Song." The new Songpan would be divided into two parts: the old
and the new district, with space within the city walls to be devoted to tourism.
A museum of Songpan history and its ethnic groups will be built on top of the
walls above the North Gate, and a street of "ethnic snacks and crafts" will appear on the southern part of the city. As part of reenacting Songpan's historic
flavor, the City God Temple will after all be included, and other key buildings
in old imperial cities—the long-gone Temple of Literature, the Temple of Wu,
the City God Temple along with the late Qing county government office—will
all be restored to their "original" likeness. In the meantime, the current county
government offices, the office of the Songpan People's Congress and People's
Political Consultative Conference, built on the old site of the Temple of Lit-

erature, will be moved to the vacant lots of the "New District" north of the city, along with new residential houses built for relocating those who lost their houses in the restoration of the city walls and city gates (*Sichuansheng Songpan xian lüyou fazhan zongti guihua* 2002, 82–84).

But the proposed restorations of these religious buildings can by no means be taken as signs of government enthusiasm for religious revival. Holding to the view that religion is a feudal relic, party people have agreed to finance temple rebuilding to help local economies, as in the east where overseas tourists were keen to visit gods worshiped in Taiwan, Hong Kong, Macau, and beyond (see Dean's chapter in this volume). Outside regions of heavy minority presence in Sichuan, the Han Buddhist temples at Mount Emei, and the great Buddha at Leshan have been developed as tourist attractions, but in this ethnic periphery officials have given moral support to Tibetan monastic projects and the construction of Qiang hamlets (*zhai*) rather than Han temples.[2] This selective official toleration offends some Han Chinese worshipers who grumble privately of a double standard.

The local people know well that official sponsorship of local temples would also mean official monopoly of temple resources. Once the City God Temple was rebuilt, the county government decided to make the best of the situation and turn it into a tourist attraction after all. Officials now include it as a key site on the old "Silk and Horse Trade Route" that once passed through the West Gate, and offered money in 2007 to enhance it. Tempted by this offer but wary that they might lose, as at Huanglong, the autonomy they have so far enjoyed, the Han Chinese "activists" at the City God Temple are looking for leverage to negotiate with the government. They are eager to seek legitimacy and tourist resources in order to promote the City God Temple, but in the meantime, they also worry about possible pollution tourists would bring to the temple. They have their own ideas of what should be on display at the annual temple festival they host and the temple structures they build. They would be proud to display this site to the tourist as long as they, not the county government, ultimately control the merit donation boxes in front of the god.

The temple offers an important ritual space for local Han as well as Tibetan communities to burn incense, paper money, and barley bread to honor their dead at the "Home-Looking Terrace" for all dead souls and under the ancient pine trees in front of the temple. Its images—the stern-looking god, his awe-inspiring runners, and the gruesome details of hells in the temple—are still part of local cultural memory. In imperial times the magistrate and the City God divided the tasks of ruling the living and the souls of the dead. Although the City God's bureaucratic power has lost its significance in socialist times (officials never pay their respects), some Han still understand him to be the ruler of the underworld for all Han, Qiang, and Tibetans in Songpan. This is why the temple has long been a vital marker of Songpan's regional identity. Statues of Buddha and other Buddhist deities figure in the main halls of the new City God Temple, because they would help attract not only Han but also Qiang and Tibetans who after all, many locals say, "are all Buddhists." More importantly, such a display of Buddhism provides some protection from official supervision and censorship. Altogether the god, the hells, the Buddhas, and the mix of Han, Tibetans, and Qiang and occasionally some curious Hui visitors would make a scene that the locals believe is uniquely Songpan. But Songpan culture, with its distinct dialect, its open-air changba gatherings in the summer, its sense of distinction from outsiders, is not to be emphasized. The state's version of the fifty-five minority nationalities marks them and their religions off from the Han, who are considered on principle to be more advanced and less superstitious. So this version of Songpan culture is not suitable for display to tourists.

Showing off ethnic culture is always subordinated to the governing national policy of ethnic unity and harmony, one that contrasts, for example, with Spain's model, where regional identity (notably in the case of Catalonia) stands juxtaposed assertively to the central state. The PRC policy is to guarantee ethnic harmony by avoiding minority linguistic education and dissemi-

Figure 4.2.   The rebuilders of the Songpan City God Temple at the Home-Looking Terrace.

nation, by banning corporate representation outside the party, by excluding minority languages from radio broadcasts, by subordinating *minzu* identity within loyalty to the state, and, significantly for this chapter, by minimizing all but visible cultural differences. Will the minzu eventually wither away and be homogenized into a Han Chinese state? The officials who dressed local shopkeepers in Tang (not minority) clothes to celebrate the rebuilding of the wall in 2005 may envisage such a future. A huge canvas picture hung by the middle bridge in Songpan portrayed the tourist city of the future, with inhabitants—looking almost Japanese in their flowing gowns—portrayed as elegant Tang ladies and gentlemen mingling among Caucasian tourists. A second version in a similar vein replaced it in 2007. Missing from these portrayals were the everyday sights of Hui men with their hats or Tibetan men and women in their long russet wraparound coats. In the imagined future of the touristified "Ancient Tang City of Song," ethnic identity would be merged into a common Han (or Tang) culture.

SYMBOLIZING HARMONY AMONG THE MINZU

Reconstruction at Songpan has, then, focused on surfaces: on walls and fa-çades, not what is within them. The state is not in the business of accurate and complete restoration of former religious sites. It has no plans to revive religious activities like the processions that once wound through the narrow streets. The motif is harmony among the minzu, and displaying their colorful, almost interchangeable identities, not on restoring former objects of identity that might divide or detract from patriotic loyalty to the state.

The message of patriotism and national unity is explicit. Religious institutions have to make clear that their loyalty to the country supersedes their religious faith. The declaration, whether wholeheartedly or for mere self-protection, is put on public display. Two huge signboards, for example, hang above the temple gate of the City God Temple. The bottom one reads "Chenghuang miao" (City God Temple), and the top one, with even bigger size characters, reads, "Love Our Country and Love Our Religion." The Chengguan Mosque in the city posts similar messages at its entrance. Almost all temples and mosques we have seen in Songpan (and elsewhere in China) have similar patriotic slogans and the "Compact for Practicing Religion" in display windows or walls near their entrances.

A large statue stands outside Songpan's main (north) gate, dominating the approach from the north, and every tourist wants to snap a picture of it. Its significance is that it is the only artistic representation of local and ethnic identity. It must be read as a local statement of national faith, expressing contemporary

Chinese nationalism in a form peculiar to this frontier. Tibetans might present a challenge to the evolutionary historical model of minorities always trailing Han political and economic advances. The Tibetan empire, after all, fought and co-existed with the Tang empire from the seventh to the ninth centuries. The larger-than-life statue represents Songzen ganbu (Sron btsan sgampo ([r. 618–641]; aka Khri sron brtsan), along with his bride, a happy-looking Tang princess. An engraved text nearby, drawn directly from the *New Tang History*, notes that this Tibetan ruler in 638 had mobilized a large army and threatened invasion of Tang territories unless he were given a princess in marriage. Taizong eventually assented, giving him Princess Wencheng. (No Tibetan version or English or Japanese translation is given.) Although such intermarriage was an Inner Asian form of diplomacy, Sron btsan sgampo's other wife being a princess from Nepal, it is here recruited as an example of Han Chinese-style ethnic blending. The erection of the double statue symbolized the local party-state's desire to draw a line under one hundred years of devastating clashes (1860–1959) between Songpan City's inhabitants and various bands of local "Fan" or Tibetans.

The symbolism of the double statue is complex and fascinating. Peace follows war by voluntary agreement, in which the dominant side is Tibetan. The

Figure 4.3.   The statue at Songpan's North Gate of Songzenganbu and the Chinese Princess Wencheng.

implication is that the local territory fell into Tang hands by peaceful means after initial confrontation, sealing a long-standing pact between peoples.[3] The representation of Tibetans by a male warrior, instead of the minority woman common in other minority representation in the PRC, resembles the performances put on for tourists, in which the characteristic Tibetans are aggressive young male dancers. Princess Wencheng represents the Chinese civilizing influence that has won the Tibetans over, but though physically dominated by her cloaked and wild-haired husband she stands upright—not the dutiful wife of Confucianized late imperial China but a smiling partner.[4] Made out of a single block (of pink sandstone), they are indivisible—just as (by implication) the Tibetans and Han are today in Songpan and Aba Prefecture. Since the prince was the founder of the Tibetan kingdom, his marriage would give his descendants a genetic relationship to later Chinese. Thus both kinds of Chinese influence that have traditionally been understood to absorb the minorities— ancestral and cultural—are brought into play (Ebrey 1996). While the shared character "Song" of Songpan and his own name (Songzen ganbu) was an accident of transliteration, and while there is no historical evidence that attaches his confrontation with Taizong to this city, the prince's smile and gesture identify him unambiguously with Songpan: he is portrayed facing north, with right hand raised. Behind him on the city wall stand facsimiled guns and siege weapons, and two armed statues of cavalrymen flank the tunnel-like gate entrance. It is a reminder perhaps that the Tibetans (unlike in Republican times) are now permitted to live within the city walls. For the Han Chinese he is "one of us," a minority within the all-embracing Chinese national history. Thus he is represented not attacking Songzhou (Songpan), but protecting it, presumably from unreconstructed minorities advancing from the north. (Not of course the Qiang minority: the old sign still affixed to the North Gate in Republican times, "Repel the Qiang," has been tactfully removed.)

The North Gate with its statue still marks a symbolic boundary, but its symbolism is reinterpreted so that the boundary is no longer external. Securely encompassed within multiethnic China, Sron btsan sgampo, with his Tang wife, is defined from a thoroughly Chinese cultural standpoint. He is not the independent founder of the Tubo empire but the Tang's submissive and partly sinified former enemy. Located firmly within China, the statue signifies not the Chinese-Tibetan confrontation of the *Tang History* text, copied on a signboard, but wishful Han-Tibetan cooperation suitable for the current regime of ethnic harmony under the Han-dominated party-state. This story is widely referred to in the Chinese media as a justification for Chinese rule (see Millward 2008).

This patriotic view of things is hard to argue with, especially in the form of a statue. There are, of course, other possible interpretations of this famous story. A historian might identify the common enemy to be the Tuyuhun, whom the Tang and Tibetans joined to wipe out in the mid-seventh century. The Tibetans have more than one interpretation of this Sino-Tibetan saga, understandably giving more attention to their own dynastic founder. Colin Mackerras refers to a Tibetan spoken drama of 1981 that reduces the princess to a minor role and omits all Chinese characters, and an older version that portrays the Tang emperor Taizong as "rather deceitful" and the Tibetan king's ambassador as so clever that he overcomes Taizong's opposition to the marriage by besting rival ambassadors in all five competitions that the emperor sets (Mackerras 1992, 5, 30).

These alternative narratives with a Tibetan slant are absent in Songpan public art, but the patriotic version of the statue at the North Gate, with its emphasis on the inclusive harmony brought by Han-Chinese dominance on the frontier, does not go unchallenged. There is a current joke among the young men in the Muslim communities outside the gate, on the Chuanzhusi road, that the prince's gesture, hand upraised, along with the north-pointing guns on the wall, is actually directed against them! This counternarrative reflects surely the Muslim sense of being underdogs in a prefecture run by Tibetans and Qiang under the direction of Han party people, as its name indicates: the Aba Tibetan-Qiang Autonomous Prefecture. This feeling cannot be openly expressed but under the authoritarian state takes the form of private humor (see Bovington 2002).

Several other patriotic themes of official literature and statuary are noteworthy. In our studies of the World Heritage site at Huanglong, we have discussed the patriotic narrative of the Yellow Dragon, who assisted the Chinese culture hero Yu the Great in harnessing the rivers of the region and is identified as "the symbol of the Chinese nation." Since Yu the Great was the ancestor of the Qiang minority as well as the Han, their association spells out a history of ethnic harmony. Similarly the rebuilt Tibetan Middle Temple is dominated by the Chinese dragon's Rear Temple. Daoism too is recruited as a national symbol even though officials do not allow it to be practiced on the site (Kang 2009; Sutton and Kang 2009).

This patriotic meaning ascribed to the tourist landscape is enhanced by the environmentalist message at Huanglong and Jiuzhaigou. Since World Heritage status was achieved in 1992, stringent sanitary arrangements and a path system overseen by numerous attendants have been introduced to cope with the swarms of tourists. There are the picture boards identifying local fauna and flora arranged along the path for educational purposes, and other displays align the management behind the global conservation movement. Like the management, tourists from the eastern seaboard identify themselves with these modern trends. They seem proud of the protected environment in these World Heritage parks. Photographing a bird next to the path, a man at Jiuzhaigou said playfully within our earshot to a child (perhaps his daughter): "Birds aren't afraid of people in America. Now in China birds aren't afraid of people either! We are making progress!" Here is an expression of national sentiment embedded in global awareness as China modernizes. The wider landscape of new hotels, improved roads, and an airport near Chuanzhusi reinforces the general rationalizing and secularizing effect—an implicit modern narrative that disenchants, and thus challenges the older sacred narratives.

The most obvious political symbol in the region is the patriotic-revolutionary monument to the heroes of the Long March at Chuanzhusi. It is a metal statue of a soldier with rifle and left hand raised triumphantly above his head, with a tall brass plate below it that catches the sun every evening as one looks up from Chuanzhusi. Nearly at the foot of the hill is a faux-stone monument of struggling figures in several groups, representing the steadfastness and suffering of unnamed Red Army soldiers who died fighting in three campaigns through Songpan in 1934 and 1935. Further down is a new marble museum of the Long March, with two floors of maps, paintings, photographs, calligraphy, and framed descriptions of events on the march. The themes of the monuments and writings about them are the martyrdom of these men and women and their indispensable contribution to the sacred task of revolution; not just the victory of the Communist Party but China's national unity and patriotic resurgence were the results. Much space is given to the efforts of the minority groups encountered during the Long March, the material and moral help they are said to have volunteered, and the recruits they supplied. Visiting this site, an academic cannot fail to be struck by its religious atmosphere and reminded of the sacred component of nationalism that scholars have noted in China (DuBois 2005, 131; see Rioux's chapter 3 in this volume) and other nations (e.g., Ozouf 1988; Smith 2005; Goody 2002; see also Bellah 1967), in the course of revolutionary unification. The three parts of the monument, and the performances sometimes held below it, exist to keep alive the faith in nation as embodied in the party and its heroes.

HAN TOURISTS AND THE QUESTION OF AUTHENTICITY

How successful are these various patriotic messages arrayed for tourists from the urban east, each medium with its ethnic undertone? These days the Red Army monument is not nearly as popular as it used to be after it was built in 1989. It never seems particularly crowded, even after the morning flights from Chengdu arrive. Most tourists these days are anxious during their standard one-and-a-half or two days in the region to see the natural beauties of

Jiuzhaigou and Huanglong, which lie an hour or so in different directions. In general, however, our discussions with tourists and tour guides at the main sites and in the tourist hotels suggest that the patriotic Han-centered view of things is very persuasive to them even if the party and its monument have lost a little of thier sheen. The discovery of diversity, relative poverty, and cultural backwardness in the borderland cannot fail to remind them flatteringly of their Han identity and their dominant role in the nation.

Tourists, it has been argued, are content with superficial representations— with what has been called "staged authenticity" (MacCannell 1976; Oakes 1998). In the Chinese case, superficiality goes with the theme of patriotism.[5] As Pal Nyíri (2006) notes, the content of ethnic shows is fully consistent with hegemonic media representations of the nation and its parts. Our visits confirmed this. Take onstage nationality performances at the main hotel centers, Jiuzhaigou and Chuanzhusi. Their organizers know what tourists like: loud music, flashing disco lights, ethnic pop songs, fast synchronized dancing by groups of dancing male and female troupes in colorful ethnic costume. Religion makes a brief appearance, usually at the start, as men dressed as monks blow huge horns amid dry ice mist against a mountain backcloth, and a "lama" intones a few unexplained words in Tibetan. The few performances with traditional instruments or throat singing, however expert, are coolly applauded, despite fulsome introductions about the players' national fame. The pieces seem too long and too slow, and the elderly players not glamorous enough. Tourists enjoy most what they are used to on TV, and are not disposed or equipped to seek authenticity. Cute minority children dash out at intervals to present flowers to the glamorous performers—an illustration of the minorities-as-children trope in Han thinking (Harrell 1995). At the start of one performance at Jiuzhaigou in 2007, a long-haired Tibetan compère dressed in high boots and brightly colored clothes sang a sort of Chinese pop song in Tibetan after his own introduction in Mandarin. A tourist from Shandong turned to Don (we had been chatting before the performance) and said, "This is really traditional!" The tone was not at all ironic. The performer fitted an image of Tibetans from the media, one labeled traditional but lacking the threat of the unfamiliar (on representation of a "macho" image of Tibetans, see Hillman and Henfry 2006).

The objectification of the internal other is facilitated by the intimate identification of place and people: for Han Chinese tourists today, as for Qing officials and travelers, the non-Han of the west merge with the rugged features of the region (see Teng 2004, 103; Sutton 2006). The local people are essentialized as part of a scarcely changing landscape. In the past the association was sometimes fixed by drawing territorial boundaries between Han and the other, as with the Yao in Guangxi (Faure 2006), and the Plains Aborigines in Taiwan

(Teng 2004, 120–21). The power and persuasiveness of official stereotypes rooted in a sense of place were evident in our field research, for example, in a conversation we overheard on a park bus in Jiuzhaigou between a Tibetan primary school teacher (our interpreter) and a visiting Han Chinese from Shenzhen. No doubt noticing the Tibetan's slightly suntanned complexion, the Shenzhen tourist said to him:

"Are you Tibetan? It must be wonderful to live in this beautiful countryside."

The teacher, who was on his first visit and had earlier complained to us bitterly that ordinary Tibetans could not afford to enter the park, replied diplomatically: "Actually I don't live in Jiuzhaigou. We think it must be wonderful to live in skyscrapers like you."

The bus was now passing one of the hamlets specially constructed in the park in the traditional Tibetan style:

"Look at those houses: they are so well built."

"Yes, but Tibetans live in many poor places elsewhere."

The Shenzhen tourist, no doubt calling to mind the pastoral nomads pictured in magazines and on TV, then asked: "Do you move from one valley to another every year?"

"You are thinking of the people on the plateau. I live in Songpan City."

This tourist cannot be blamed for naïveté; he was simply expecting to confirm what he already knew from many magazine articles and television programs, and what he might already have seen after his arrival in the region, for local stage performances are invariably set against the backdrop of the romanticized high plateau with its yaks and horse riders. Judging from such encounters, the setting familiar from state propaganda is inseparable from the conception of the Tibetan other, and as in the past plays a clear role in the process of Han self-construction.

Finally, in these days of mass tourism by bus (the gradual rise of automobile tourism may introduce some more leisurely and discriminating visitors), the experience is not only rushed but it is largely visual. The shepherded tours and paths (one-way at Huanglong, fleets of buses through Jiuzhaigou) allow little discovery. The ritual of picture taking, usually combining family members in sights already glimpsed in advertisements or films shown on TV, guarantees the reduplication of what is already branded. The consumer ritual of bargaining for local ethnic products is a different act of appropriation with the same result, enabling each tourist to take home something local (Sutton 2010). The most powerful effect of these tours is to confirm the media's images of a backward periphery, backward but advancing local ethnic groups, and a beautiful if crowded landscape. There is little room for appreciating religion. The message is of the quasi-religion of Chinese nationalism, of the tourists' proud place in the nation as its most advanced and majority ethnic group.

This then is the faith that China's western periphery most strongly reinforces for visitors. Yet the visitors are ready to experiment with actual religious practice, learning from the locals. Ritual, it has recently been argued,
is about making and breaking boundaries, playing with hypothetical "as if"
roles (Seligman et al. 2008). In this place of differences of all kinds, many
Han Chinese tourists of all ages find themselves in the "as if" mode of ritual
as for example at Huanglong when they arrive after their long climb at the
Rear Temple. Thus one frequently sees tourists from Chinese cities imitating the local pilgrims in offering incense—asking the resident priest where
to light and place the incense sticks, having him divine for them, making
donations, and taking away a strip of red cloth for good luck on the journey
home. To tourists, the periphery seems to have changed less than the east.
It is a place to recover Chinese culture, whose visible remains are sparse in
post-Maoist cities. Folk religion, despite two generations of atheistic socialist
education, is momentarily at least part of Chineseness. Nostalgia, Chinese
patriotism, and Han chauvinism fuse in this unfamiliar setting, opening some
tourists to faith of a more traditional sort.

CONCLUSION

We have shown the basic strains in tourist policy: How can religion be tolerated yet kept within bounds? How can the symbols of religion be commodified without encouraging religious expression? How can locals or tourists
share the enthusiasm for party history as an object of reverence? During Maoist times, all religious establishments in the old Songpan lost their political
significance and were eventually destroyed. In the age of market economy,
local state agencies tolerate religion but keep it firmly under control. They use
the state power to exploit its market value but dwell on visible surfaces—on
religion reduced to folklore. The restoration of old Songpan City, including its religious symbols and infrastructures, is designed simultaneously to
maximize tourist profits for economic development and to subordinate all to
nationalism and patriotism, for both locals and tourists.

Despite the unusually tight administrative measures set up by state authorities, religious expression tends to slip out of state control, always straining at
the limitations, going a little further than officials expect. Different religious
and ethnic communities play active roles in negotiating with the state to
display, or not display, their religions and ethnicities in their own terms. For
some local Han, especially middle-aged and retired women, Guanyin, Huanglong, and the City God remain sources of solace in a time of uncertainty, and a
focus of free time sociability. For many Tibetans and for most Muslims, iden-

tities remain stubbornly ethnoreligious; participating in religious activity is partly who they are, and unremitting pressure for religious expression is hard for the officials to resist. Thy take different paths to practice their religions and to extract an income from tourism. As for Han tourists, they accept the version of the nation presented to them because it confirms their Han Chinese self-image as the vanguard of the nation and the official media's representation of their younger-brother-and-sister minorities of the backward west; yet they too slip out of expected channels when they light incense and behave like pilgrims of the past. What we see in the religions displayed both inside and outside Songpan City is emblematic of an ongoing struggle in which the increasingly market-oriented Chinese state confronts the various ethnic, religious, and regional communities that are seeking to empower themselves with the same market forces but not necessarily to admit tourists to the rituals of their faiths.

NOTES

This chapter draws on a manuscript in progress jointly written by the authors, bearing the provisional title, *Contesting the Yellow Dragon*.

1. We used pseudonyms for all the people we interviewed in the field in order to protect their identities.

2. The Songpan Chenguan mosque was rebuilt and finished in 1988. It had three financial sources: local Muslim donations, about 60,000 yuan; local government, 50,000 yuan; and state loans, 60,000 yuan. The Northern Mosque (*beisi*) had government sponsorship of 20,000 yuan. See Ma 1989, 28. Four Tibetan monasteries in the Songpan area were rebuilt in 1980. Total funds available were 609,000 yuan, including 424,000 from Chinese government contributions. The Gelug Maoergain monastery received 408,000 yuan, dGa'mal 9,000 yuan, Houshi in Mini xiang 3,000 yuan, and Kaya in Xiyun xiang 3,000 yuan. *Songpan Zang chuan Fojiao gaikuang*, 37–38, cited in Desjardins (1993, 36). Our conversations with some employees at the Songpan Office of Religious Affairs confirm that Tibetan monasteries also received some government funding in their revival.

3. Subsequent history somewhat undermines the intended meaning. Princess Wencheng and her entourage indeed played an important role in Lhasa for forty years, but almost two hundred years of confrontation and conflict ensued, throughout the apogee of the Tibetan empire, during which Lhasa allied for a time with Tang enemies like the Western Turks and the Nanzhao kingdom against the Tang, took over the southern Silk Road and much of the Tarim basin and Qinghai, and after the An Lushan rebellion deprived the Tang of southern Gansu and the rest of Qinghai, with their pasturelands vital for the supply of horses (Beckwith 1987; Twitchett 2000; Wang 1958).

4. See Millward (1994) for the famous case of the Uyghur "fragrant concubine."

5. This is another Chinese variation on a common theme in tourism. According to Tom Selwyn, "Tourist perceptions, motivations, and understandings about destinations are shaped by a preoccupation with harmonious social relations, ideas about community, [and] notions of the whole. These are the preoccupations which are mythologized in the tourist's view of Nepal, the English West Country or whatever—and are in this sense 'overcommunicated.'" (1996, 3). Cited in Burns 1999, 112.

REFERENCES

Baimacuo. 2004. "Songpan Benjiao siyuan lüyou diaocha fenxi," *Yunnan shehui kexue* 5: 102–6.

Beckwith, Christopher I. 1987. *The Tibetan Empire in Central Asia: A History of the Struggle for Great Power among the Tibetans, Turks, Arabs, and Chinese during the Early Middle Ages.* Princeton: Princeton University Press.

Bellah, Robert N. 1967. "Civil Religion in America." *Daedalus* 96: 1–21.

Bovingdon, Gardner. 2002. "The Not-So-Silent Majority: Uyghur Resistance to Han Rule in Xinjiang." *Modern China* 28(1): 39–69.

Burns, Peter M. 1999. *An Introduction to Tourism and Anthropology.* London and New York: Routledge.

Desjardins, J. F. Marc. 1993. "A Preliminary Field-Report on the Bön Community of the Songpan Area of North Sichuan." Master's thesis, McGill University.

DuBois, Thomas. 2005. *The Sacred Village: Social Change and Religious Life in Rural North China.* Honolulu: University of Hawai'i Press.

Ebrey, Patricia. 1996. "Surnames and Han Chinese Identity." In *Negotiating Ethnicities in China and Taiwan*, ed. Melissa J. Brown. Berkeley: University of California Press, 11–37.

Faure, David. 2006. "The Yao Wars in the Mid-Ming and Their Impact on Yao Ethnicity." In *Empire at the Margins: Culture, Ethnicity and Frontier in Early Modern China*, ed. P. Crossley, H. Siu, and D. Sutton. Berkeley: University of California Press, 171–89.

Gladney, Dru. 2003. *Ethnic Identity in China: The Making of a Muslim Minority Nationality.* Mason, OH: Cengage.

Goody, Jack. 2002. "Bitter Icons and Ethnic Cleansing." *History and Anthropology* 13(1): 1–12.

Harrell, Stevan, ed. 1995. *Cultural Encounters on China's Ethnic Frontiers.* Seattle: University of Washington Press.

Hillman, Ben, and Lee-Anne Henfry. 2006. "Macho Minority: Masculinity and Ethnicity on the Edge of Tibet." *Modern China* 32: 251.

Izutsu, Toshihiko. 1983. *Sufism and Daoism.* Berkeley: University of California Press.

Kang, Xiaofei. 2009. "Two Temples, Three Religions, and a Tourist Attraction: Contesting the Sacred Space on China's Ethnic Frontier." *Modern China* 35(3): 227–55.

Kang, Xiaofei, and Donald S. Sutton. 2008. "Purity and Pollution: From Pilgrimage Center to World Heritage Park." In *(Im)permanence: Cultures In/Out of Time*, ed. Stephen Brockmann and Judith Modell. University Park: Pennsylvania University Press, 2008.

Lipman, Jonathan. 1997. *Familiar Strangers: A History of Muslims in Northwest China.* Seattle: University of Washington Press.

Ma, Yucai. 1989. "Songpan Chengguansi luocheng qiyong." *Zhongguo Musilin* 2: 28.

MacCannell, Dean. 1976 [1999]. *The Tourist: A New Theory of the Leisure Class.* Berkeley: University of California Press.

Mackerras, Colin. 1992. "Integration and the Dramas of China's Minorities." *Asian Theatre Journal* 9(1): 1–37.

Millward, James A. 1994. "A Uyghur Muslim in Qianlong's Court: The Meaning of the Fragrant Concubine." *Journal of Asian Studies* 53(2): 427–58.

———. 2008. "China's Story: Putting the PR into the PRC." 18 April. www.opendemocracy.net/article/governments/how_china_should_rebrand_0.

Nyíri, Pal. 2006. *Scenic Spots: Chinese Tourism, the State, and Cultural Authority.* Seattle: University of Washington Press.

Oakes, Tim. 1998. *Tourism and Modernity in China.* London: Routledge.

Ozouf, Mona. 1988. *Festivals and the French Revolution.* Trans. Alan Sheridan. Cambridge, MA: Harvard University Press.

Peng, Wenbin. 1998. "Tibetan Pilgrimage in the Process of Social Change: The Case of Jiuzhaigou." In *Pilgrimage in Tibet*, ed. Alex McKay. Surrey: Curzon Press, 184–201.

Schrempf, Mona. 2006. "Hwa shang at the Border: Transformations of History and Reconstructions of Identity in Modern A mdo." *Journal of the International Association of Tibetan Studies* 2 (August): 1–32.

Seligman, Adam B., Robert P. Weller, Michael Puett, and Bennett Simon. 2008. *Ritual and Its Consequences: An Essay on the Limits of Sincerity.* London and New York: Oxford University Press.

Selwyn, Tom, ed. 1996. *The Tourist Image: Myths and Myth Making in Tourism.* London: Wiley.

Sichuansheng Songpan xian lüyou fazhan zongti guihua: 2001–2015 (The master plan for tourist development in Songpan county, Sichuan province, 2001–2015). 2002. Compiled and published by Songpan xian renmin zhengfu and Sichuan lüyou guihua sheji yanjiuyuan.

Smith, Anthony D. 2005. "Nationalism in Early Modern Europe." *History and Theory* 44(3): 404–15.

Songpan xianzhi (Songpan county gazetteer). 1924. Comp. Fu Chongju and Zhang Dian.

Songpan xianzhi (Songpan county gazetteer). 1999. Compiled by Songpan xianzhi bianzuan weiyuanhui. Beijing: Minzu chubanshe.

Sutton, Donald S. 2006. "Ethnicity and the Miao Frontier in the Eighteenth Century." In *Empire at the Margins: Culture, Ethnicity and Frontier in Early Modern China*, ed. P. Crossley, H. Siu, and D. Sutton. Berkeley: University of California Press, 190–228.

————. 2010. "Transfers of a Ritual at a Northern Sichuan Site: Tibetan and Han Chinese Pilgrims, and Han Chinese Tourists." In *The Dynamics of Ritual, Transfer,* ed. G. Dharampal-Frick and R. Langer. Frankfurt: Harrassowitz Verlag (in press).

Sutton, Donald S., and Xiaofei Kang. 2009. "Recasting Religion and Ethnicity: Tourism and Socialism in Northern Sichuan, 1992–2005." In *Casting Faiths: The Construction of Religion in East and Southeast Asia,* ed. Thomas DuBois. New York: Palgrave Macmillan, 190–214.

Teng, Jinhua Emma. 2004. *Taiwan's Imagined Geography: Chinese Colonial Travel Writing and Pictures, 1683–1895.* Cambridge, MA: Harvard East Asia Center.

Twitchett, Denis. 2000. "Tibet in Tang's Grand Strategy." In *Warfare in Chinese History,* ed. Hans van de Ven. Leiden: Brill, 106–79.

Wang, Zhong. 1958. *Xin Tang shu Tubo zhuan jianzheng.* Beijing: Kexue chubanshe.

5

Minzu, Market, and the Mandala

National Exhibitionism and Tibetan Buddhist Revival in Post-Mao China

Charlene Makley

Mini China welcomes you!

Is it possible to walk the length and breadth of China within a single day? One place you could do just that is at the Chinese Ethnic Culture Park, south of the Bird's Nest and within the Olympic Green. The huge park has been a labor of love and precisely re-creates life in all 56 of China's ethnic groups.

—*China Daily*, 15 July 2008

The Chinese government's frenzied preparations and unprecedented spending for the Beijing 2008 Olympics represented the culmination of national exhibitionism in a new global era. That process of state and corporate collaboration in packaging and branding a newly cosmopolitan city and nation-state rivals on the world stage the world's fairs and expos of old. Yet, as the excerpt above points out, the traditional allure of ethnic tourism still plays an important role in offering visitors a state-sanctioned vision of the substance and reach of the host polity. Indeed, the display of China's colorful ethnic others figured prominently in the massive opening ceremonies of the Olympics. Like the Midway displays of ethnic others outside the 1893 Chicago World's Fair, the Chinese Ethnic Culture (or Minzu) Park next door to the new Olympic grounds in Beijing sells tickets to view ethnic "villages" and "landscapes" representing the fifty-six "nationalities" (Ch. *minzu*) that constitute the multiethnic PRC (Ch. *duo minzu guojia*). The park would seem to instantiate nicely the themes of national harmony and market-based development that accompany the Olympic brand. But those claims were strongly countered in, among other things, the unprecedented scope of unrest and protests in Tibetan regions just months before the opening of the 2008 Games.

The extraordinary events of 2008 give me new impetus for thinking through the meanings and implications of Chinese ethnic theme parks, and in particular, the display and commodification of religion as a feature of ethnicity. My interest in this was first piqued during my fieldwork on Tibetan Buddhist revival in the PRC in the 1990s and early 2000s (see Makley 2007). At that time, I met several young Tibetans from where I was living in Amdo regions (now the PRC's western provinces of Qinghai and Gansu) who told me about their experiences working at the ethnic theme parks in China's rapidly developing eastern coastal cities. In the summer of 2002, I finally had the chance to visit the Beijing Ethnic Culture Park and experience for myself the context in which those young Tibetans' tourism work took place. On a pleasant Sunday in early June, I strolled around the extensive grounds. They seemed strangely empty because the few Han Chinese couples and families exploring the exhibits and taking pictures there seemed dwarfed in the wide pathways and carefully labeled "plazas" (Ch. *guangchang*) between the exhibits. I chatted with some of them and talked to young Amdo Tibetan and other minority workers as I viewed the exhibits myself. Over the course of the day, I felt strongly that this park, built at precisely the time of my 1990s fieldwork in Amdo, encapsulated a cultural politics of the nation-state that had been profoundly reshaping Amdo Tibetan homelands hundreds of kilometers west. And that contested process arguably came to a head in 2008 when for the first time large numbers of Tibetans in Sichuan, Qinghai, and Gansu provinces (that is, Tibetans living outside the Tibetan Autonomous Region) participated in anti-China unrest.

ETHNIC TOURISM PARKS AS TRANSACTIONAL ORDERS

In this chapter, I draw on my research in Tibetan regions of the PRC to interrogate the Chinese state's social, economic, and political premises in the national exhibitionism of the Beijing Ethnic Park. I do this by focusing on the implications of Tibetans' own participation (as workers and performers) in the park. After all, since the 1990s especially, Tibetans' eastward migration to work in the Buddhist-themed Tibet exhibits of the park, along with the westward travels of Han urban tourists to Tibetan regions, embodied the ongoing links between interethnic and political economic interactions in the nation's capital and those out west (see Oakes and Schein 2006; Schein 2000; Oakes 1998). By considering this central tourism site from the perspective of the Tibetan Buddhist frontier, I treat it not, as the state would have it, as a benign, even trivial sideshow in Beijing, but as an important site for reframing and incorporating Tibetans and Tibetan Buddhism within the post-Mao

PRC nation-state, a project that participates in the ongoing clash (and mutual constitution) of social orders that has characterized Inner Asian politics since the late Qing dynasty especially.

In this light, rather than see them as benign backdrops for selling experiences of the ethnic or alternatively as sinister sites for the destruction of ethnic authenticity, I take national ethnographic exhibits like the Beijing Ethnic Park to be important means by which state officials, park investors, and designers attempt to define and instantiate certain *transactional orders*, or institutions for producing and channeling the circulation of people and values, that are deemed essential to nation-state building. The Ethnic Park then must be seen as an ever-evolving attempt, in the face of the actual unruliness of real people, to structure and render pleasurable citizens' and visitors' participation in the core categories, hierarchies, and thus values of the ascendant PRC. Even in such hypergroomed spaces, value, as social relations of evaluation and exchange, is always in the making.

To be more specific, in the extraordinarily didactic design of spaces and architecture, flows of people and money, displays of persons and objects as evidence and ideal types, and interactions between spectators and exhibited persons, such exhibitions are transactional orders in which park officials attempt to recruit people to embody the objectifications that make national governance and economies possible (see Hinsley 1991; Macdonald 1998). In fact, perhaps even more than state-sponsored social science, ethnic parks and museums work to instantiate the all-pervasive, yet abstract secular space of the "social" (distinguishable from "religion," "economy," and the "state") because they mediate between elite and popular or "public" forms of realist knowledge, while backgrounding the very situated (and state-sponsored) nature of that knowledge (Asad 2003, 191–92). In China's ethnic parks, the common sense subjectivity of the citizen on offer for participants was that of *minzu* ("nationality") identity.[1] That designation, embossed on all citizens' state identity cards, was supposed to represent one's primary loyalty to the state's secular policies over the commitments and timeframes associated with "religion" (Ch. *zongjiao*).

However, by considering parks and their participants as dynamic transactional orders, I argue that the Tibet exhibits at the Beijing Ethnic Park did not guarantee such a neat containment of religion. Thus I focus on Tibetan performers and workers there as historically situated people with the capacity to divert meanings and values along alternative lines, even as they cope with the often crushing weight of shifting state and market pressures (see Oakes 1998). For as we will see, the dangers of tourism participation for Tibetans in the PRC hinged on complex value shifts, which no one completely controlled, that were emerging in intensified competitions for newly mobile and transnational capital. From this angle, we can see both ethnic tourism and Tibetan Buddhism in a new light—not as static and discrete sets of places and ideologies, but as the simultaneous and intermingled experiences and aspirations of real people. And we can thus better understand the broader stakes and hazards of Tibetan Buddhist revival in post-Mao China.

MINZU AND THE MANDALA

Contrary to recent popular notions of Tibetan Buddhism as an eminently peaceful, individualist or ultrarationalist set of philosophies, Tibetans had adopted specifically tantric forms of Buddhism from India that, especially with the rise of the Dalai Lamas' Geluk sect, amounted to highly hierarchical, even martial, institutions and forms of governance. Indeed by the waning years of the Qing dynasty, Tibetan Buddhist institutions in many regions represented full-scale alternative polities, formidable opponents to Chinese would-be modern state builders. As Toni Huber (1999) and others have pointed out, the successful spread of Tibetan Buddhism across Inner Asia (and even to the Qing court) hinged on the uniquely Tibetan subject of the incarnate lama (Tib. *sprul sku*). As the incarnation of both a Buddha and a predecessor lama, incarnate lamas were heirs to both political economic estates (Tib. *bla brang*) and the tantric Buddhist capacity to violently tame enemies of the Dharma and command legions of protector deities. Thus, through close alliances with their subordinates, lay male leaders, and through elaborate ritual pageants and everyday worship practices, the Geluk sect trulkus in the frontier zone, as elsewhere, sought to "mandalize" the region. That is, they worked to construct their jurisdictions as Buddhist polities and patronage centers on the model of a transcendant tantric Buddhist mandala palace—mandalas laid out as ideal transactional orders for human affairs under Buddhist auspices. In the principal tantric rituals (Skt. *sadhana*, Tib. *sgrub thabs*, lit. means of achievement), accessible only to initiated men, mandalas were essentially repertoires of ordering tools for emplacing and exhorting vast pantheons of deities as coparticipants nonetheless subordinated to the current event and goals of a practitioner (see Makley 2007; Berger 2003, 89; Hanks 1996, 180). Divine embodiment as Buddhist incarnations thus worked to both substantiate and legitimate incarnate lamas as key pivots between the relative and the absolute, between mobile nomadic patrons and the settled monastic community, between the local and the translocal.

But CCP leaders also worked to posit natural correspondences for people between micro- and macrocosmic spaces. From the 1950s on, they countered Geluk mandalization efforts in the frontier zone by creating competing transactional orders aimed at marginalizing Tibetan incarnate lamas and establishing rival authorities as *unmarked*, that is, as disembodied or all-pervasive disciplinary and arbitrating agencies, centered nonetheless in Beijing (see Makley 2007). For example, the authority of the local officials of the new Religious Affairs Bureau (RAB, now the State Administration for Religious Affairs) was supposed to supersede that of local lamas, yet RAB officials' authority was grounded in the secular offices of the Beijing State Council. For CCP leaders all along, but especially after the 1980s reforms, the category of minzu was pivotal in their attempts to establish competing intermediary frameworks for embodying Tibetans as citizens of the new PRC nation. State-sanctioned minzu identity as Tibetan "minorities" (Ch. *Zangzu*), one of fifty-six recognized groups, was supposed to be the ground of membership in a new "multiethnic" national community, and the basis of Tibetans' participation in new local state careers.

As an alternative secular identity, minzu was also a dangerous and shifting category of new national personhood for CCP leaders vis-à-vis Tibetan authority. It promised to liberate non-Han men from local hierarchies (like networks of kinship, prestige, and Buddhist patronage) in new institutions and careers for men's translocal and social mobility. And yet I argue that it was most importantly a category designed for the ideal "incarceration of the native" (see Appadurai 1996; Gupta and Ferguson 1992; Malkki 1997, 52)— not only as less civilized, tradition- and place-bound inhabitants of marginal regions targeted for resource extraction, but also as limited political actors confined to local minzu "autonomous" (Ch. *zizhi*) districts, where a majority of the government (not necessarily party) cadres were supposed to be Tibetan. At the same time, defining Tibetans as Zangzu lent state administrative weight to a translocal identity that had arguably never existed among Tibetans.

A STATELESS NATION: MARKETING MINZU

With the 1980s economic reforms and subsequent "consumer revolution" (Davis 1999) in the PRC, ethnic theme parks in Chinese cities began to proliferate (Hai Ren 1999, 2). At that time, hundreds of young Tibetan men and women, a large number of them from Amdo regions, were recruited to work and perform at the parks. The Folk Cultural Villages in Shenzhen, which included a Tibetan "village," was in 1991 the first of the ethnic theme parks to be built on a large scale. At that time, it rivaled the massive theme park in the same city opened two years earlier called Splendid China (Jinxiu Zhongguo), which featured among China's wonders a miniature replica of the Dalai Lamas' Potala Palace (see Anagnost 1997, 163; Oakes 1998; Hai Ren 1998, 1999, 2007).

The theme park that presented itself, however, as the culmination of this vaunted "museumization" of ethnicity in China was the huge park built on 45 hectares at the northern perimeter of Beijing. This park, begun in 1992 and completed by 1996, was structured as a combined Chinese Ethnic Museum (Zhonghua Minzu Bowuguan) and Chinese Ethnic Culture Park (Zhonghua Minzu Yuan). Park planners, a consortium of state work-units and entrepreneurs in Hong Kong and Taiwan who took advantage of China's bid for the 2000 Olympics to push for a national showcase park next door to the new Olympic grounds, explicitly announced the park (at a projected cost of 120 million yuan) as a more comprehensive and "accurate" exhibition than the Folk Cultural Villages in Shenzhen, and claimed that it would encompass all fifty-six minzu in the PRC (Hai Ren 1998, 81; Anagnost 1997, 214; Gladney 2004, 39).

Of course, the revolutionary and modern secularist rhetoric of CCP nation-state builders notwithstanding, the decision to locate such a park in Beijing strongly recalled the empire-building strategies of the Manchu Qing emperors at court. The Beijing Ethnic Park recalls Qing emperors' efforts to construct an overarching social order by bringing the peripheries to dynastic centers in ethnically marked imperial villas (see Foret 2000; Berger 2003). Such alternate capitals, as James Hevia describes them, were elaborately arranged to construct the Qing empire as a realm of multiple lords, and to orchestrate hierarchical encounters establishing Qing emperors as superior overlords and visiting ethnic others as subordinate, tribute-paying lords and subjects (1995, 32).

And yet, as many have pointed out, Tibetan Buddhist lamas, as incarnated Buddhas and exclusive purveyors of tantric prowess based in particular monasteries, situated themselves as superiors in "patron-preceptor" relations (Tib. *yon mchod*) with emperors, relations that in turn stood for relationships between entire regions (Petech 1950). Thus, within the intricate orchestrations of guest ritual at Qing courts, trulkus and emperors "vied to hierarchize each other" (Hevia 1995, 48) by asserting the transcendence of the transactional orders they embodied to a variety of ends, even as they recognized each other as powerful men—that is, as *commensurate* agents operating at the upper reaches of authority and mediating the highest forms of value. A kind of "calculated ambiguity" (Berger 2003, 184) was essential in the negotiations of Chinese and Tibetan authorities.

In important ways then the main state disciplinary effort of Qing imperial ethnic capitals was reproduced in the Ethnic Park under CCP auspices in the 1990s: juxtaposing spaces representing selected, discrete ethnic others at the regime's center were efforts in time-space compression—visualizing and materializing an impossibly massive realm while asserting the primacy of state authorities' agency to define and arbitrate ethnic diversity within it (Hevia 1995, 48). This logic of privileged knowledge and vision of the other is perhaps what most strongly linked Han CCP authorities' jurisdiction claims over Tibetan regions with those of past dynasties, allowing them to locate themselves and Tibetans in an unbroken "Chinese" legacy of definitive historiography and rule.

Indeed, just as Qing emperors initiated encyclopedic projects based in the capitals to map and know the empire (see Perdue 2005; Hostetler 2001; Millward 1999; Elliot 2000), the Ethnic Park's colorful brochure and ticket tout it as an "anthropological museum" and research institute, heir to some fifty years of CCP state-directed social science research on China's "minorities." And the park motto, prominent on both in large, bold letters, proudly proclaims that one can "sightsee in one day 10,000 km of rivers and mountains" and that "all of China's 56 minzu are in one park!" Finally, the park's main didactic function vis-à-vis the nation and the world is encapsulated in the principal slogan heading up all printed materials and reproduced throughout the grounds: "Let the world experience/know China, let us recognize/know ourselves" (Ch. *rang shijie liaojie Zhongguo, rang woman renshi ziji*).

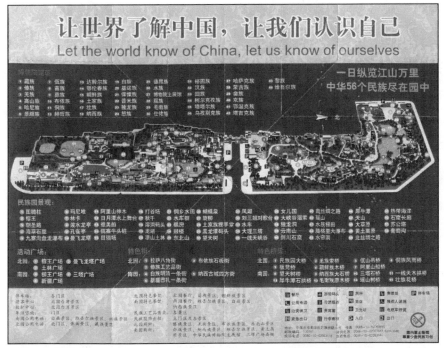

Figure 5.1.   Fold-out map in the Beijing Minzu Park ticket. The Tibetan (Zangzu) exhibit is labeled number 1 at the top left corner of the right ("north") half of the park. C. Makley photo, Summer 2002.

In many ways, then, the park's remarkably explicit project to define and shape ethnic identity and thus the nation is a gesture back to imperial efforts to define dynastic realms. Yet the spatial politics of the Beijing park, and its representations of Tibetanness, also constitute the very different ideology of citizenship and political authority of a nation-state, one which Chinese leaders sought to characterize as explicitly post-Mao and economically developed or "civilized" on a par with other "modern" nations (see Enloe 1989, 31). Indeed, such an elaborate effort at ethnographic exhibition in reform-era China must be seen as taking up the modernist project of competitive national exhibitionism that was first institutionalized and universalized in the mid-nineteenth century with the rise of World Fairs in Europe and North America (Hinsley 1991, 344). Crucially, the secularizing and relativizing detachment of the modern citizen that such sites offered to visitors was effected through the display of "primitive" others from the colonial peripheries juxtaposed with the wonders of industrial machinery exhibited there.[2]

As a site for the ideal consumption of ethnicity in a depoliticized public space, the Beijing Ethnic Park is a paradigmatic transactional order for experiencing a reform-era *stateless* nation as itself a collective market subject aspiring to modern knowledge and comfortable living (see Munson 1999, 1; Duara 1995; Fitzgerald 1996). Indeed, in addition to its association with the international image politics of the Olympics, the park was established just after Deng Xiaoping, faced with increasingly public discontent among the citizenry after Tibetan demonstrations in Lhasa and Chinese students' demonstrations in Tiananmen Square, attempted to divert attention from the state's military crackdown on those demonstrations and urged the populace to "jump into the sea" (Ch. *xia hai*) of the market economy. In the wake of such unruly popular aspirations in the midst of market reforms, it is easier to appreciate the extremely regulated nature of the exhibits at the Beijing Ethnic Park.

Unlike other types of ethnographic display (like some dioramas) in which human subjects are presented with minimal framing, leaving wider leeway for viewers' interpretations, the Beijing park's minzu "landscapes" are meticulously labeled in signage and ubiquitous park media—this transactional order is meant to generate particularly regulated consumption on behalf of a national economy. In fact, the collaboration of state officials and Han entrepreneurs in establishing such a park was enabled by the new national "visual language" (Dias 1998, 49) of ethnicity since reforms that depicted various minzu groups as clusters (or better, packages) of visible features of language, lifestyle, and beliefs fixed in particular locales (see Gladney 1994; Schein 2000; Bulag 2002). Thus, in contrast to the conflicts between nineteenth-century social scientists and capitalist investors over the nature of ethnographic visibility at the World Fairs (i.e., in contextualizing museum exhibits vs. exoticizing carnival displays; see Hinsley 1991), the Beijing Ethnic Park design reflects a deep national consensus over the visual terms of ethnic difference in the post-Mao PRC—ethnic groups, for example, should have colorful costumes and dances, a set of festivals, and distinct forms of local architecture.

The park then does for ethnicity what Dai Jinhua (1996, 32) argues was happening all over China in the 1990s: it displaces the revolutionary plaza for the (orderly) shopping plaza as the preferred venue for bringing the masses (Ch. *qunzhong*) "face to face with themselves" (Benjamin 1968, 234) in a new multiethnic nationspace that yet remained under CCP rule. That is, the design of the park works to recruit citizens to participate in the new common-sense frameworks of a market secularism that allows for a sense of relative autonomy from state discipline (see Anagnost 1995; Schein 2000; Dutton 1998; Yang 1999).

My encounter with the young Tibetan workers in the park's Zangzu Land-scape Area (Ch. Zangzu Guanjing Qu) clarified for me the dilemmas such a transactional order presented to minority citizens. I arrived at the Zangzu area just as the Tibetan workers were finishing their afternoon circle dance for an audience of Han tourists in front of the centerpiece of the Zangzu exhibit: the large and meticulously rendered replica of the great Jokhang (Sakyamuni Buddha) Temple in Lhasa. I sat on a bench with the other tourists, behind a young, pimply faced red-robed monk, and watched as the four pretty young women in matching Lhasa-style dresses and a single young man in thigh-length robe halfheartedly danced to recorded music, arms flapping lazily, making no eye contact with each other or the tourists, even when a few Han women got up to join the dance.

When the brief dance ended, the dancers unceremoniously scattered, and some congregated around the table manned by other young Tibetan laymen, to watch as tourists strolled over to the gift shop or tried on Tibetan clothes for pictures.

I got up and followed the young monk, who had crossed to the bench in front of the temple building and sat listlessly watching the courtyard. After his initial shock at being addressed in my rusty Tibetan, he and I chatted as some of the other Tibetans came to listen with great interest. Akhu Tenzin told me in his nomad-accented Amdo dialect that he was one of only two monks at the park, and he had only arrived three months earlier, having accompanied this group of about ten young dancers (all nineteen years old) from the county song and dance troupe in Qinghai's Chabcha (Ch. Guinan county seat). Just as I had heard from other young workers at the park, Akhu Tenzin said they made only 300 yuan per month in wages (less than a quarter of Beijing aver-age monthly incomes then), and lived in dorms provided by the park orga-nized by minzu category and sex. Akhu Tenzin's job was to take tourists on tours of the Jokhang building (built, he said, in 1994) and he dutifully got up to show me around.

The Zangzu area, with its Jokhang replica, pilgrim path, Khampa village house, Lhasa Barkhor street, a row of prayer wheels, a pile of rocks carved with mantras, garden, and the requisite gift shop and ethnic clothing photo-op booth, is the first and largest of the minzu exhibits; its main exhibits were among the most elaborate in the park. That day I noticed that whereas many other exhibits stood empty, their colorfully garbed workers idle, the Zangzu exhibit was bustling with visitors. Recalling the importance of Tibetans at the Qing court, the high status of the exhibit in the park also reflected the refigured prominence of Tibetanness in PRC nation-state building, especially after Tibetans in the diaspora organized to counter CCP narratives about the national incorporation of their homelands.

But the spatial organization of the exhibits as icons of minzu categories reflects an effort to domesticate Zangzu ethnicity in an absolute and all-pervading nationspace dominated by Han as the unmarked norm. Thus, for example, the park's main museum hall was located in the center of the "southern" section of the park and contained an assortment of objects representing Han history as "our" quaint, rural legacy ("The Common People: Our History, Our Roots"). But the park itself is a geographic hodgepodge. The "north" and "south" halves of the grounds refer not to the homelands of minzu groups, but to the cardinal orientation of the park itself in Beijing. Inside them are juxtaposed exhibits for wildly different and distant groups of people (mostly from China's north-south frontier zone in the western provinces), presented in bullet-listed signs as precisely enumerated minority populations living in particular provinces, each represented by selected cultural icons, a language, a "religion," and a "festival." Most are associated with a characteristic landscape so that representations of mountains, rivers, loess plateau, farm fields, village huts, and monuments intermingle in a fantastic pastiche of a space ultimately referencing nowhere but itself.

And yet, as against the more common pattern among Tibetans of narrower translocal migration routes that ranged mostly across the western provinces, Beijing Ethnic Park recruiters had succeeded in bringing Akhu Tenzin and his young peers from their largely nomad region hundreds of kilometers east to participate in their own embodiment as "Zangzu" in a radically objectified way. Indeed, the cosmopolitan aspirations of the young Tibetans I met in 2002 had followed the state-sponsored lines of appropriate rural-urban mobility—into a hypermanaged space constituting a transactional order of consumption (Hai Ren 1999, 24) that subordinated them as underpaid workers and objects of tourist voyeurism. That is, "the people" directly addressed by the park exhibits did not include them. As against their own aspirations, their job at the park was to literally embody the new visibility of colorfully backward ethnicity that constituted the *in*visibility or unmarkedness of both civilized Hanness and Chinese state authority (see Yang 1999, 50; Oakes 1998; Schein 2000). In this way, the young Tibetans' move to Beijing countered those of millions of domestic migrants from poorer western and central provinces in China. The unmanageable movements of those migrants in search of work in urban areas in the east had been unleashed by the market reforms of the 1980s, in which economic development policies privileged eastern cities (Marshall and Cooke 1997, 1340; also see Wang and Hu 1999). In the context of Han urbanites' anxieties and intensifying policing strategies directed at the unsightly backwardness of rural-ethnic others in cities (see Dutton 1998), the young Tibetans' participation in the park, despite the tactical defiance expressed in their bored and haphazard dance, was markedly accommodating.

REVALUING TIBETAN DIVINITY

The park also features live cultural performances. Every morning real lamas from the Tar Monastery of Qinghai province chant Tibetan Buddhist sutras to pray for peace at the Tibetan monastery, while a dongba priest burns incense and says his prayers at the Naxi village.

—*China Daily*, 15 July 2008

But such cheesy objectifications of ethnicity for Han audiences as staged folk dances, I argue, had far less potential to transform Tibetans' worlds than Tibetans' own participation in transactional orders that erased or compromised Tibetan men's privileged relationships to divine agencies. Those, in fact, were the relations and values that had underpinned the power of many Inner Asian polities. My awkward tour of the park's "Jokhang Temple" with the young monk Akhu Tenzin pointed this up for me.

I had been on many monastery tours in Amdo regions, but none prepared me for the radically reordered nature of that space in the Jokhang replica. Akhu Tenzin ushered me into the echoingly empty main hall first. As he led me into the first room to the left of the main door, a space that in the Lhasa Jokhang should have been a deity shrine (see Larsen and Sinding-Larsen 2001), the young monk was proudly telling me that even though there were only two monks here in the park, we are "real monks" (Tib. *ngo ma red*), unlike the fake ones who had led tours in previous years. I was listening and was thus unprepared for finding myself in the strange environment of that room. We had stepped directly from the main hall through a doorless opening into a well-lit exhibit of five wrathful protector deities. Two of them I recognized as worldly gods (one a *zhidak* or mountain deity, the other a red-faced *tsan*), and the other three were tantric protector Buddhas. All five of the large statues, their ferocious faces, popping eyes, and bared white fangs glinting in the stark electric light, were of similar size and were arrayed not on altars, as are the main images residing in monastic protector deity shrines or in the Lhasa Jokhang, but side by side against bare walls and on a raised platform with no other accompanying context.

An important part of my status as a female in Tibetan regions was that I had never been inside a protector deity shrine before. Those dark and guarded spaces in revitalized Tibetan Buddhist monasteries out west were strictly off limits to all but (initiated) males. However, I knew from descriptions and occasional glimpses from outside them that this was an extremely disorienting way to encounter such deities. After all, protector deities like these were supposed to be "under the feet" of incarnate lamas, tamed and subdued by lamas' tantric ritual prowess to serve Buddhist orders.

With Akhu Tenzin watching, I was completely nonplussed. I had no idea what he expected me to do. We looked at each other and I stammered that I had never seen such deities this way before. Akhu Tenzin explained dryly that whereas at home we (including himself as a neophyte monk) could not enter such a temple, here this is a site for tourist looking. The Tibetan neologism for tourist site he used (*lta skor lta sa*, lit. site for tourist looking) emphasizes the core activity of *voyeurism* that distinguishes tourism from Buddhist pilgrimage especially (Tib. *gnas skor 'gro pa*, lit. go to encircle abodes of Buddhist divines; see Huber 1994b; Urry 2002). Like the tourist I was in that space, I asked if I could take a picture, and with only a slight hesitation, the young monk said yes. As I quickly and shamefacedly snapped two, I noticed that even though there were no altars, people had nonetheless placed a few paltry offerings of artificial flowers and small change in front of each. Perhaps thinking that this would negate what I had just done, I awkwardly placed a few yuan in front of each, explaining to Akhu Tenzin that I was worried about a relative's health. I was touched when he, without comment, obligingly recited a prayer for me.

Exposing the Tibetan protector deities to the mass gaze of tourists in the nation's capital seemed to me to epitomize the secular displacement of Tibetan Buddhist authority in post-Mao China. Here the protectors were disclosed outside the expert auspices of Tibetan laymen and initiated monks and lamas. The five statues, unremarkable for their craftsmanship, were not displayed as individual examples of "primitive art." Instead, as a group, they stood as icons of an ideal type, a class of Tibetan deities that in turn indicated *not* divine agency, but the ethnographic expertise of the exhibit designer (see Kirshenblatt-Gimblett 1991, 396). Just as the Jokhang exhibit arrayed the worldly deities as categorically equivalent objects alongside their superiors, the Buddha protectors, all in turn accessible to me, a foreign female, this reordering threatened, in some ways *more* than direct state violence, to eradicate the vital mandalic hierarchy that before and after reforms had positioned Tibetan laymen and incarnate lamas in the frontier zone as exclusively empowered defenders of local interests centered on monasteries (see Makley 2007). Thus, while Chinese tourists are generally not put out by, or even expect, the "staged authenticity" (Oakes 1998) of ethnic tourism sites as part of the festive re-creation that they pay for, Tibetan workers like Akhu Tenzin could be very concerned to emphasize the "realness" (Tib. *ngo ma* or *kho thag*) of Buddhist commitments and transactions in those settings.

I argue that this was so *not* because such exhibits reduced Tibetan deities to "inauthentic" commodities separated from Tibetan ritual use, but because they constituted a crucial *value shift* in an increasingly diversified and capitalist transactional system in which everyone was arguably caught up (cf. Lopez 1998, 153; Maurer 2006). That is, the transactional order of the Beijing Minzu Park is ultimately geared toward exploiting ethnic visibility in order to accumulate investment capital and to attract the increasingly mobile global capital so vital to China's reforms (see Hai Ren 1999; Oakes 1998). As Oakes (1998) and Anagnost (1997) point out, under globalizing competitive pressures in the 1990s, the main role of theme parks organized at a variety of administrative scales in the PRC was to provide visual "enticement" for longer-term capital investments in the relevant region, always in complex alliances or rivalries with other regions (see Oakes 2000). Thus Tibetans' participation in the national minzu park, even their countermoves, worked to incorporate them into a new transactional order in which translocal capital under central state auspices displaced trulkus' place-based tantric prowess as the highest value. Indeed, according to Hai Ren, 85 percent of the total capital for the initial construction of the park came from two wealthy businessmen from Hong Kong and Taiwan, while the rest came from various Chinese government agencies in Beijing (1998, 53).

In other words, we should consider the "Jokhang" protector deity exhibit *not* as an objectification that ruined some original, authentic presence (see Benjamin 1968). Instead, it epitomized the capitalist imperatives of a new minzu "aesthetics of decontextualization" (Appadurai 1986, 28) in China in which the value of certain objects and persons, their exoticness, is enhanced by the way their surface features seem to indicate their distance from an *imagined and reified* original ethnic context.

I was struck by the variety of ways Akhu Tenzin positioned himself counter to this effort throughout our tour, for example, by proudly insisting on the realness of his monastic commitment and interceding via prayer in my offering-exchange with the protector deities, even as those very efforts seemed to enhance park officials' claims that they had captured authentic ethnicity in the exhibits. But his most important countermove came significantly as soon as we left the disorienting protector deity exhibit. Akhu Tenzin made sure to point out the dusty color photograph (strategically?) placed on the wall right outside it. As he reverently explained, the photo depicted lamas and monks from the nearby state-sponsored central Buddhist Studies Institute in Beijing in the midst of conducting a *rapnay* ritual, the final consecration, or better, vivification ceremony, inside the meticulously crafted Kalacakra (Wheel of Time) mandala temple that stood outside in the center of the Zangzu exhibit.

The Kalacakra temple was the first structure erected in the Zangzu exhibit, and it was funded by a wealthy Hong Kong businessman in 1993 and constructed by monk artisans under the direction of a trulku from Lhasa at the Beijing Institute. It is said to be the only Kalacakra temple in the PRC outside of Tibetan and Mongolian regions.[3] Notably, the mandala temple, its circular outside walls painted with gorgeously rendered protector Buddhas, was the only building I saw on the entire park grounds that had no signage and was closed to tourists that day.[4]

The rapnay ceremony so conspicuously displayed in the wall photo was the process through which the presiding lama, a young incarnate lama, according to the photo's caption, from a Geluk monastery in Sichuan, invited the central

Figure 5.2.   The Kalacakra temple in the Zangzu area at the Beijing Minzu Park. C. Makley photo, Summer 2002.

deity Kalacakra (along with his retinue) to inhabit his statue in the center of his newly constructed three-dimensional mandala palace.[5] Among Tibetan Buddhists, rapnay ritual must be done in order to transform a building, sculpture, or image from an inert object to the abode (or "support," Tib. *rten*) of a divine presence, thereby establishing it in the history and transactional order of a particular incarnate lama (see Bentor 1993, 1997; Huber 1994a; Lopez 1998).

Even though Tibetan Buddhist exegesis downplays such material abodes as expedient means for ordinary minds who cannot perceive the abstract omnipresence of Buddhas (see Bentor 1997, 234), in rapnay ritual, incarnate lamas (the preferred ritual agents for important abodes like the Kalacakra temple) assert the tantric prowess of lamas by mandalizing representations of Buddhas. That is, as in all tantric ritual, here the lama officiant, appropriating the subjectivity of the central deity, transforms the deity's omnipresence into an emanation localized in a specific representation, thus also subordinating him or her to the contemporary event and to those of future acts of worshipful transaction (Tib. *mjal ba*).

In this sense then, the most important omnipresent divine agent established in rapnay ritual is the incarnate lama, *not* the deity. Thus we could see the Kalacakra rapnay at the Beijing Ethnic Park as a key countermove on the part of Tibetan lamas in the PRC. As Akhu Tenzin's reverent reference to it years later indicated, it was in part a successful effort to replace the secular market transactional order of the park with a Buddhist mandalic one. That is, the Kalacakra rapnay ritual was an attempt to displace unmarked secular state authority at the park as the main arbiter of transactions there for that of embodied lamas instead. In effect, after the rapnay ritual, the divine presence of Kalacakra under the auspices of lamas mandalized the Zangzu area of the park, reasserting vital hierarchies of divine agencies for Tibetans (thus for example closing off the deity from unregulated viewing and putting the protector Buddhas back in their proper peripheral positions guarding the mandala palace of the central deity).

Indeed, as Dru Gladney reports, during his visits to the park in the fall of 1995, he met with Tibetan monk workers from what must have been one of the first Tibetan contingents at the park after the Zangzu area opened. According to the monks, they were recruited and paid monthly wages (300 yuan/month) like all the other minzu workers, but unlike other minzu groups represented, Zangzu were represented by a group of fifteen young monks from the great Geluk monasteries of Sera and Drepung in Central Tibet. Most importantly, the monks Gladney spoke with, along with his Yizu park guide, insisted that the Zangzu site, and especially the Kalacakra temple, were "real religious sites." In addition, the monks went further than the tour guide and insisted that the Zangzu area was *not* part of the park (2004, 46). From this

perspective on transactional orders as people's efforts to regulate the circulation of values, we would have to see such statements not as mere assertions
of "religious" authenticity countering secularizing commodification, but as
themselves (counter)circulations of value on behalf of particular Tibetans'
agendas. The conflict set up for Tibetan participants at the Ethnic Park was
not essentially one between religious versus secular realms, but between
competing institutions facilitating asymmetrical exchanges across value registers (see Maurer 2006, 22).

To appreciate this, we need to see the cultural politics of Buddhist transactions within a much longer history of South and Inner Asian political
economies. As Benevides (2005) points out, the rise of Buddhism from its
inception in India has been bound up with centralizing states and shifts to
monetized economies. From this angle, we could understand the historical
capacity of Buddhist orders to translocalize (to make Buddhism, as some call
it now, a "world religion") as in part due to the capacity of the transactional
systems of Buddhist ritual to commensurate different scales of time and space
in particularly compelling ways. That is, through the ubiquitous and constant exchanges and circulations of values in Buddhist rituals, Buddhist acts
and offerings, just like modern forms of money, operate as hinges between
worldly and transcendent spaces, and between short- and long-term transaction orders (Maurer 2006, 24).

This is one way to understand the ongoing and pervasive practice of the
pious copy among Tibetans (see Berger 2003, 161; Bentor 1993, 119). The
most important aspect of many Buddha representations for Tibetans was
not their authentic originality, but their exchangeability for the long-term
and lifetime-transcending reward of karmic merit (Tib. *dge pa*), but also for
other mundane and relatively immediate social or bodily values (see Ohnuma
2005).[6] Indeed, it was this capacity to offer both transcendent *and* immediate worldly values mediated and embodied by the incarnate lama, that made
Tibetan forms of tantric Buddhism so vital in the political economic transactions of late imperial *and* Republican-era China (see Tuttle 2005). And this, I
would argue, is at least one important reason why Tibetan forms of Buddhism
have been so highly amenable to the capitalist reorderings that are part and
parcel of its contemporary global appeal.[7]

Thus in the case of deity images, lamas' rapnay ritual does not just render
deities present in them, but it also transformed them into potentially Buddhist
transactional fields, opening the way to their mediation of the higher values
of Buddhist registers of exchange, linking short- and long-term goals (see
Bentor 1993, 112). Deities for Tibetans, materially manifest in the image,
could be both autonomous agents in exchange as well as relative objects of
exchange, depending on the relevant spatiotemporal framework (see Mills

2003). From this perspective then, we are in a better position to grasp the full import and hazards of Tibetans' participation in the Beijing Ethnic Park. Under the extraordinarily explicit market and state pedagogical auspices of that transactional order, we could consider the Tibetan lama officiants at the park's Kalacakra temple rapnay ritual as oppositional entrepreneurs. All the while accommodating post-Mao state policies requiring Tibetan Buddhist institutions to be innovative in seeking ways to be economically "self-sufficient" (see KZC 1978; Kai Wa 1995), the lama officiants exercised the entrepreneurial agency so vaunted in state-sponsored media by collaborating with the Hong Kong Chinese entrepreneur-patron to restructure the tourist setting as a Tibetan Buddhist transactional order, (re)inserting themselves as indispensable embodied agents in the process. But this process, as it played out throughout Tibetan regions, had dangerous implications for both monastic officials and state authorities.

GLOBALIZING THE MANDALA

In effect, in the Kalacakra rapnay and its wall photo display, Tibetan lamas vied with state officials and private entrepreneurs to attract and channel mobile global capital by appealing to the aspirations and acquisitive desires of both tourist-consumers and patron-investors (see Oakes 1998). In the context of increasingly mobile capital flows and broadening transnational Chinese business networks in the 1990s, we have to consider the particular threat of such Tibetan Buddhist mandalization efforts at the Beijing Ethnic Park.

As Oakes (1998) and Ong (1999) argue, the main conflict in emerging forms of Asian capitalism and modernity is between central PRC state officials and increasingly cosmopolitan Chinese businessmen over the control of both fluid capital and the moral shape and geographic center of a "Greater China" (see Young and Shih 2004). Hence the first major theme parks as sites for the enticement of foreign direct investment in the PRC were in Shenzhen, that special zone of precariously unregulated transnational capital, and they were owned by a Hong Kong–based firm (see Hai Ren 2007). The decision a few years later to allow a major ethnic theme park to be built back up north in the nation's capital could then be seen as in part an effort to repatriate investment flows to the nation-state's center in anticipation of the turnover of Hong Kong to CCP rule and the 2000 Olympic bid. And still, as Gladney notes, the PRC Minzu Affairs Commission participated only to approve the construction, while the park itself was established as a profit-seeking joint venture between government units and Hong Kong– and Taiwan-based entrepreneurs (2004, 41).

The entrepreneurial efforts of Tibetan Buddhist lamas to mediate private capital flows from overseas Chinese patrons thus threatened the precarious balance between state and transnational Chinese capitalist interests in such settings. And this process, I argue, was playing out not only abroad, but *across* Tibetan regions of the PRC by the mid-1990s (see Makley 2007; Tuttle 2005; Zablocki 2005; Moran 2004). For example, Arjia Tshang, the central trulku at the famous Geluk sect Kumbum Monastery in Qinghai, was one of the most prominent Tibetan Buddhist trulkus in the PRC in the late 1980s and early 1990s, holding several political appointments in national and Qinghai provincial bureaus.[8] Known especially for his skills in mandala design, as abbot of Kumbum in the late 1980s and early 1990s, he designed and built there what is considered to be the largest three-dimensional Kalacakra mandala in the world. He was also particularly active in embracing the museumization of Tibetanness as an (oppositional) "pedagogy of the people," helping to construct exhibits on Tibetan Buddhism in several Chinese cities.

In addition, in the 1980s and 1990s increasing numbers of wealthy Han and overseas Chinese urbanites became disciples and patrons of Tibetan lamas in the PRC, a phenomenon that had much to do with the remarkably vigorous reconstruction of Tibetan Buddhist monasteries in Amdo by the mid-1990s. We could then see the Beijing park's Kalacakra temple, as well as Arjia Tshang's museum efforts throughout the PRC, as different bids in Geluk Tibetan lamas' very successful efforts to expand their "patronage spheres" (Lopez 1998, 206) in the 1990s and thus to globalize the scope of their mandalization efforts (see Zablocki 2005; Moran 2004). In this light, the choice of Kalacakra as the mandala temple for the park becomes very significant. This is so because the utopic frameworks offered in the Kalacakra teachings for the triumph of Buddhist authority over multiethnic lay subjects would seem to be ideally suited for appropriation by Tibetan Buddhist incarnate lamas faced with their compromised positions under the CCP.

Indeed, as one of the few Indian Buddhist tantric lineages that in Tibet came to be associated with mass empowerment ceremonies (in which the lama officiant admits thousands of people to the mandala), the Kalacakra in recent years has been the preferred transactional order for global mandalization efforts among Geluk lamas especially, both inside and outside of the PRC. As Lopez (1998, 207) and others have noted, the fourteenth Dalai Lama encouraged its practice in the diaspora as a way to both teach the world about Tibetans and contribute to world peace (see Samuel 1993, 517; Bryant 1993; Kohn 1997; Andreson 1998; Huber 1994b; Zablocki 2005). Beginning in the early 1970s, he has given the Kalacakra mass empowerment over twenty times and endorsed museum exhibits of Kalacakra sand mandalas. Over the past few decades, his audiences have expanded to include hundreds of thousands of attendees from all over the world.[9]

The Kalacakra tantra was one of the last and most complex of tantric cycles to have been transmitted to Tibet from India at a time when Indian Buddhists were under imminent threat of Muslim invasion. The teachings thus offer the Buddhist utopia of Shambhala both as the ideal contemporary site for the practice of that tantra and as the future country in which the compassionate Buddhist king will have led his armies to destroy invading non-Buddhist barbarians and demons. After that victory, the country becomes an ideal society for a Buddhist lay-monastic alliance centered on the Kalacakra mandala, where lay subjects, including erstwhile Hindu brahmans, are all practitioners of tantric Buddhism, and most inhabitants will attain Buddhahood in one lifetime.

Donald Lopez ends his controversial book *Prisoners of Shangri-La: Tibetan Buddhism and the West* (1998) by noting that since all initiates to the Kalacakra mandala plant the seeds to be reborn in Shambhala in their next lifetime, lama officiants like the Dalai Lama could be said to be recruiting the troops of the future Shambhala king in order to defeat the contemporary enemies of Buddhism (i.e., he implies, the Chinese state) and realize that ideal Buddhist world (1998, 207). But in the PRC, the threat to the state of Tibetan lamas' Kalacakra mandalizing need not be referred only to the utopic future timeframes of the teachings. Indeed, the Kalacakra's unusual form of *mass* mandalization, and the escalating numbers of attendees in the PRC in recent years, provided occasions for lamas and their retinues to incorporate flows of offerings and vast arrays of participants into a Buddhist order literally centered on the lama's embodied divinity, even as state policy aimed at confining religion (Ch. *zongjiao*) to a circumscribed and inconsequential realm of activity. Perhaps the most successful of these efforts were those of the sixth Gongtang Tshang (1926–2000) at Labrang Monastery (in Gansu Province), who was arguably the most widely known and beloved of trulkus there by the mid-1990s.

As one of the four "Golden Throne" trulkus, the Gongtang lineage enjoyed extremely high prestige and by the early twentieth century, the Gongtang estate was among the wealthiest at Labrang.[10] After his release from prison in 1979, where he had spent twenty-one years, insisting all along on remaining a monk, Gongtang's integrity and tireless efforts in Tibetan cultural revitalization in the early reform years attracted interregional and international respect and patronage, so that his estate was the wealthiest and most powerful in the region by the time I met him in 1993. As the Tibetan trulku scholar Dor Zhi notes, Gongtang had had a particularly intimate relationship with the Kalacakra teachings since he was young. Apparently, when the ninth Panchen Lama (1883–1937) visited Labrang in 1936, at precisely the time the Kuomintang (KMT) official Ma Haotian was there (as the Panchen Lama's state-appointed escort) advocating the national need for Tibetans' "unity through assimilation," the Panchen Lama gave a mass Kalacakra empowerment and

Figure 5.3. The sixth Gongtang Tshang and his main Chinese American disciple in Chengde. Publicity photo, 1993.

initiated the ten-year-old Gongtang, expressly charging him with the task of disseminating that tantra's teachings (1995, 4).

Gray Tuttle's recent work (2005) has shed new light on the later life of the ninth Panchen Lama, himself exiled from central Tibet in the early 1920s after clashing with the Tibetan government in Lhasa over control of his estates. From Tuttle's account, at that time of great political upheaval, it seems that the Panchen Lama played crucial roles in collaborating with Chinese Buddhist leaders, and eventually with Chinese government leaders, as well as in helping to instigate an unprecedented boom in popular Chinese interest in Tibetan Buddhism by the early 1930s. Key to the Panchen Lama's politics in Chinese regions as he maneuvered to return to Tibet was his expanding use of mass Kalacakra empowerment rituals. In the face of nationalist gov-

ernment officials and secularist intellectuals' virulent efforts to eradicate the
"superstitions" and immoral extractions of "popular religion" (Duara 1995),
the Panchen Lama's Kalacakra events expanded his patronage sphere so
much that he had to open a business office dedicated to handling the influx
of funds. He did this even as KMT officials attempted to recruit him as their
representative in Sino-Tibetan affairs. Indeed, his Kalacakra teachings were
important occasions for advocating the inseparability of Buddhism and governance under nationalist pressures (Tuttle 2005, 171).[11]

It seems then that the Panchen Lama, and not the Dalai Lama, first initiated
new globalizing Kalacakra events as he negotiated the political economic
minefields of early modern China. Since he initiated Gongtang Tshang into
the mandala at Labrang, we would have to see Gongtang as in the direct lineage of these modernizing Tibetan Buddhist mandalization efforts. The ninth
Panchen Lama died a year later in 1937, before he realized his goal of returning to Tibet, but Gongtang continued those efforts beyond even the CCP
victory in 1949. When he came of age, Gongtang gave mass Kalacakra empowerments fully six times in the ten tumultuous years surrounding the CCP
victory and takeover of Labrang (Dor Zhi 1995, 4), even as CCP work teams
began to implement land reforms and collectivization efforts in the Sino-
Tibetan frontier zone. Gongtang's final Kalacakra was held in February 1958
for thousands of Tibetans at a branch monastery in Amchok, just two months
before PLA troops attacked Tibetan rebels there (see Tenzin Palbar 1994).[12]
We can imagine the threat such events might have posed to beleaguered PRC
state officials as Tibetan laymen's guerrilla resistance in the surrounding
mountains intensified into the late 1950s. He was then a natural target for the
party's lama-purging arrests during the 1958 military crackdown, accused
like others of being a reactionary criminal deliberately fomenting rebellion
(see Tenzin Palbar 1994, 79).

After his release in 1979, Gongtang's various state-appointed titles, including head of Labrang Monastery's new Democratic Management Committee,
and vice chair of the Gansu Province Political Consultative Committee, had
little to do with the expanding audiences at his Kalacakra empowerments.
When he gave his tenth mass empowerment in 1994, the summer before I
arrived for my fieldwork, lay and monastic attendees from all over the PRC
and abroad descended on the Sangkok grasslands upriver from Labrang in the
hundreds of thousands—as many exclaimed to me later, such numbers were
unprecedented (see Wang 1997, 246; Dor Zhi 1995). For that two week period, I was told, public security officials patrolled nervously as the grasslands
grew white with the mass of tents pitched there, so that, as one old village
man reminisced to me, it seemed to have snowed up there (Tib. *khangs bab
dang 'dra mo red*).

CONCLUSION: THE DANGER OF BEING DEFANGED

In 1994, the Kalacakra temple rapnay in the Beijing Ethnic Park took place just weeks before Gongtang Tshang's mass Kalacakra empowerment began back on Labrang's Sangkok grasslands. Together, the two events encapsulate well the cultural politics of revitalizing Tibetan Buddhist divinity in post-Mao China. The state violence of the Maoist years and the late 1980s had demonstrated to many Tibetans the precarious status of minority minzu identity in the CCP-ruled nation-state. And by the 1990s, the ongoing incorporation of Tibetans as Zangzu in the PRC hinged on renewed efforts to domesticate Tibetan masculinity via the allure of a new market secularist "aesthetics of decontextualization." While the Ethnic Park in the nation's capital could be said to be the ultimate transactional order for such state-sponsored projects, Gongtang's mass Kalacakra was a culmination of Geluk trulkus' oppositional mandalization efforts on an unprecedented scale in Amdo Tibetan homelands.

In the light of this article's analysis, we can better appreciate the multiple dangers inherent in Tibetan Buddhist lamas' various efforts to reassert their tantric prowess under the press of CCP-sponsored capitalism in tourism sites. As before, the main effect of the power of incarnate lamas was to (re)hierarchize the spatiotemporal frameworks of exchange and circulation and their appropriate agents in a mandalic transactional order under the lama's all-pervasive presence and authority. But the exigencies of capitalist exchange under a repressive state meant that trulkus' oppositional participation could also be the "trojan horse

Figure 5.4. Monks look on at Gongtang's Kalacakra empowerment ritual on Sangkok grass-lands west of Labrang, Gannan TAP, Gansu Province. Tourism brochure photo, Summer 1994.

of value shift" (Appadurai 1986, 57). It seems to me that lamas' participation in ethnic museumization efforts like the Beijing Ethnic Park epitomized the general hazards for Tibetan divine authorities of close accommodation with the state and global capital in post-Mao China. In the hypermanaged transactional order of the park, their very efforts to reassert tantric prowess could not but contribute to its defanging. That is, the officiating lama's rapnay ritual in the Kalacakra temple animated the mandala and its deities as Buddhist emanations and transactional fields, but that move also indicated his willingness to access capital *via* the state's terms of minzu and market secularism.

Arjia Tshang's translocal efforts on behalf of (Geluk) Tibetan Buddhism perhaps epitomized this dynamic. His untiring work paid off handsomely at his home monastery of Kumbum in the 1990s. Between 1991 and 1995, he brought in millions of yuan in donations from non-Tibetans in order to help fund the construction of his own Kalacakra temple there as well as a massive renovation of the monastery's buildings, in addition to his local school and disaster-relief projects. Millions came from overseas Chinese patrons, including 3 million from the Hong Kong and Singapore based foundation of the famous film magnate Sir Run Run Shaw. But the largest amount by far, 37 million yuan, came from the PRC State Council itself with president Jiang Zemin's express approval, in part to develop Kumbum Monastery, just south of the provincial capital, as one of the premier tourism sites in Qinghai (see TIN 1998; Kolas and Thowsen 2005, 66; Liu 1999; Bodeen 2001).

In some ways, Arjia Tshang's close involvement with the state in presenting Tibetan Buddhism to translocal audiences recalled the importance at the Qing court of Tibetan incarnate lamas from Amdo (see Wang 2000; Tuttle 2005). But as Arjia Tshang later discovered, the transactional orders for collaborations between Tibetan Buddhist lamas and state leaders had radically shifted since Qing times. When Jiang Zemin visited Kumbum in the mid-1990s, wishful rumors spread among Tibetans there that a photograph of Jiang showing respect in front of a Buddha image indicated his status as a true patron of Buddhism (Liu 1999). But the development of the Zangzu exhibit in the Beijing Ethnic Park, as well as that of Kumbum Monastery in Qinghai, was decidedly *not* premised on the strategic patron-preceptor alliance that had framed, for example, the Jangjya lama's and the Qianlong emperor's joint efforts in the eighteenth century to construct Tibetan temples in the Qing imperial capitals (see Berger 2003). Instead, the spatial politics at the Ethnic Park, and operative at Kumbum, held the peril for Tibetans of categorical incarceration in the PRC nation. That is, by animating Tibetan divinity within the confines of the Zangzu exhibit on the outskirts of Beijing, lamas and monks, along with the young lay dancers, participated in their own incarceration as purveyors of a circumscribed, exotic "religion" positioned as ultimately inconsequential both to the secular concerns of well-off urbanite consumers and to the political loyalties expected of Tibetans by the state—an absolute dichotomy between apolitical "religion" as individual consumption and (legitimate) politics was eminently suited to the exigencies of the post-Mao Chinese state.

Exposed and packaged as tourist objects (even though animated by offerings), the wrathful protectors in the Zangzu exhibit illustrate well the defanging of Tibetan Buddhist authority, a process that threatened the foundations of Tibetan monastic revitalization back in Amdo. Despite the heady possibilities of a world opened to global capital, the capacity of Tibetan leaders to arbitrate transactional orders for value creation and circulation had been greatly curtailed. Indeed, the everyday pulse of activity in and around the park's Jokhang and Kalacakra temples was not that of lamas, monks, or lay worshipers, but that of Han tourists and, importantly, young Tibetan laymen and -women whose secular aspirations had brought them hundreds of kilometers away from their Amdo homelands to participate. And even though Chinese state leaders seemed absent from the Ethnic Park grounds or from the local mandalic order that Arjia Tshang was helping to rebuild at Kumbum, Arjia Tshang was to feel the full weight of their presence when central leaders' tensions with the Dalai Lama came to a head in 1995 over the choice of the eleventh incarnation of the Panchen Lama.[13]

The expansion of Geluk mandalization efforts in Tibetan regions, such as those of Arjia Tshang and Gongtang Tshang in the early 1990s, helps explain state anxieties over the outcome of the Panchen Lama decision, a process that had dragged on for some five years. While I was in Labrang, state officials' rejection of the Panchen Lama recognized by the Dalai Lama in exile and his replacement with a state-arbitrated candidate illustrated to many the state's willingness to radically reorder older patron-preceptor transactions (see Lopez 1998, 207; Goldstein 1997). As one monk remarked to me matter-of-factly during our discussion about Tibetans' avid interest in the Panchen Lama affair that year, whereas the Qing emperors who donated money to Tibetan lamas had been true believers in Buddhism, so that Tibetans had worshiped them as emanations of the Bodhisattva Manjusri, now the government was just "exploiting religion" (Ch. *liyong zongjiao*).

In that context, Arjia Tshang discovered that the obligations conferred in his lucrative CCP-arbitrated transactions of the early 1990s entailed his public avowal of the incarceration of religion in a display of his political loyalties to the state. In the end, he found that he had entered into a very different relationship with state leaders than had his Qing counterparts—in this case, the "calculated ambiguity" of Sino-Tibetan transactions had betrayed him. In his later account of those years, Arjia Tshang expresses his great indignation at having been forced to attend the state's recognition ceremony for the Panchen Lama in Lhasa despite his official protest. During the "patriotic education" campaign in Tibetan monasteries launched in the aftermath of the Panchen Lama affair, Arjia Tshang and monks at Kumbum, as elsewhere, were required to publicly denounce the Dalai Lama. As he tells it, this was ultimately too direct an imposition, which meant "participating in government practices that went against my religion and my personal beliefs" (TIN 2000) and he secretly fled to the United States in 1998, leaving behind the monastic community he had worked so hard to revitalize.[14]

One of the first things Arjia Tshang did when he arrived in the United States was to complete a gorgeous three-dimensional model of the Kalacakra mandala, which he presented to the Dalai Lama. It now resides in another key site for a national pedagogy of the people: the American Smithsonian museum in Washington, D.C.

NOTES

1. Here I agree with Stevan Harrell (1995) that the Chinese term *minzu*, with its long history of appropriation from Japanese contexts, and its multiple connotations of "race," "ethnicity," "lineage," and "nationality," is virtually untranslatable in English. I thus choose to leave it untranslated.

2. As Frederick Putnam, the ethnologist in charge of the human displays at the 1893 World's Columbian Exposition in Chicago put it, "After such a stroll amid the scenes [of native peoples living in their natural habitats] one will visit the other departments of the Exposition . . . with an appreciation which could only be aroused by such contrasts" (cited in Hinsley 1991, 348).

3. Hai Ren, personal communication, January 2007.

4. The Kalacakra temple is also the only conspicuous structure in the park's ticket map that is unlabeled.

5. Note that the photo was captioned in Chinese, not Tibetan. And the name of the presiding trulku *had been ripped off.* Perhaps the monk's comment that the lama was now in the United States had something to do with that.

6. Thus as Clare Harris (1999, 85) rightly points out, Tibetans long ago developed forms of mechanical reproduction (the woodblock, the stamp, the stencil) in order to efficiently produce multiple copies of texts, clay deity or stupa icons (Tib. *tsa tsa*), or scroll paintings of deities and mandalas (Tib. *thang ka*) as meritorious acts and offerings, as well as objects for sale or for patrifilial exchange.

7. Abraham Zablocki (2005), in his fieldwork in Taiwan in the late 1990s and early 2000s, as did Peter Moran in Nepal (2004), found a surge of interest among Taiwan Chinese in Tibetan forms of Buddhism. He found that most Chinese devotees and popular consumers of Tibetan ritual items were most interested in the tantric ritual efficacy promising worldly wealth and well-being that they associated with Tibetan lamas. Further, in what seems to be an unprecedented development, Zablocki found that it had become common practice for businesses to hire Tibetan Buddhist monks and lamas to perform offering rituals for prosperity on their premises.

8. Arjia Tshang is of Mongolian descent and is recognized as the incarnation of the father of Tsongkhapa (hence his Tibetan title of "A rgya," meaning Father).

9. There is even a website dedicated to the Kalacakra mandala called the International Kalacakra Network.

10. Danzhu and Wang (1993, 235) state that in the first half of the twentieth century, the Gongtang estate included 500 patron households, about 200 mu of land, 3 regions of forests, 600 head horses, 3,000 cattle, 500 sheep, and over 1,000,000 yuan of capital accumulated from trade and loan business (see Zha Zha 1993; Liu 1993; Dor Zhi 1995; Wang 1997).

11. The Panchen Lama gave mass Kalacakras to huge crowds in Inner Mongolia in the late 1920s, he gave another in Beijing in 1931 as "state preceptor" (Ch. *guoshi*) within the Forbidden City itself, and another for seventy thousand Chinese attendees in the erstwhile Chinese Buddhist core region of Jiangnan (Tuttle 2005, 185).

12. Importantly, the timing of Gongtang's Kalacakra empowerments, all supposedly given upon the invitation of lay and monastic subjects, coincide with the years building up to the CCP takeover (and the sudden death of the fifth Jamyang Shepa) and then the subsequent crackdown on Tibetan resistance to collectivization and property expropriation. According to Wang Yunfeng, Gongtang gave Kalacakra empowerments in Labrang territories south and west of the monastery in 1946, 1948, 1949 (just a month before PLA troops arrived in the valley), 1956, 1957, and 1958 (1997, 242). He was arrested two months after his final one.

13. The tenth Panchen Lama, so beloved in Amdo especially for his courageous advocacy of Tibetan issues during the later Maoist years and during the early reform years, died at only age fifty-one in 1989. As I discovered when I arrived in 1995, one of the most popular Tibetan songs at the time was a lament and prayer for the Panchen Lama, grieving over the loss of the tenth and praying for his speedy reincarnation.

14. In the light of the expanding power of Gongtang Tshang at Labrang during the 1990s, it seems possible that CCP leaders were actually cultivating Arjia Tshang and Kumbum as a regional and national counterweight to Labrang, the erstwhile and revitalizing monastic power center of Amdo. Indeed, by late 1995, Gongtang had resolutely refused the state's demand that he himself choose a Panchen Lama. As a consequence, in the late 1990s he was increasingly surveilled, his political positions removed and his movements limited. He passed away in 2001. His incarnation, the seventh Gongtang trulku, was finally discovered and confirmed by a joint lama-state official commission in 2004.

REFERENCES

Anagnost, Ann. 1995. "A Surfeit of Bodies: Population and the Rationality of the State in Post-Mao China." In *Conceiving the New World Order: The Global Politics of Reproduction,* ed. Faye Ginsburg and Rayna Rapp. Berkeley: University of California Press.
———. 1997. *National Pastimes: Narrative, Representation and Power in Modern China.* Durham, NC: Duke University Press.
Andreson, Jensine. 1998. *Kalacakra: Textual and Ritual Perspectives.* Ph.D. diss., Harvard University.

Appadurai, Arjun. 1986. "Introduction." *The Social Life of Things: Commodities in Cultural Perspective,* ed. Arjun Appadurai. Cambridge: Cambridge University Press.

———. 1996. *Modernity at Large: Cultural Dimensions of Globalization.* Minneapolis: University of Minnesota Press.

Asad, Talal. 2003. *Formations of the Secular: Christianity, Islam, Modernity.* Stanford: Stanford University Press.

Benevides, G. 2005. "Economy." In *Critical Terms for the Study of Buddhism,* ed. Donald S. Lopez, Jr. Chicago: University of Chicago Press.

Benjamin, Walter. 1968. "The Work of Art in the Age of Mechanical Reproduction." *Illuminations: Essays and Reflections,* ed. Hannah Arendt, trans. Harry Zohn. New York: Harcourt, Brace and World.

Bentor, Yael. 1993. "Tibetan Tourist Thangkas in the Kathmandu Valley," *Annals of Tourism Research* 20: 107–37.

———. 1997. "The Horseback Consecration Ritual." In *Religions of Tibet in Practice,* ed. Donald S. Lopez, Jr. Princeton: Princeton University Press.

Berger, Patricia. 2003. *Empire of Emptiness: Buddhist Art & Political Authority in Qing China.* Honolulu: University of Hawai'i Press.

Bodeen, Christopher. 2001. "Monks, China Police Coexist Uneasily." Associated Press, collected from *World Tibet News,* December 3.

Bryant, Barry. 1993. *The Wheel of Time Sand Mandala: Visual Scripture of Tibetan Buddhism.* New York: Samaya Foundation.

Bulag, Uradyn. 2002. *The Mongols at China's Edge: History and the Politics of National Unity.* Lanham, MD: Rowman and Littlefield.

Dai, Jinhua. 1996. "Redemption and Consumption: Depicting Culture in the 1990s." *positions: east asia cultures critique* 4(1): 127–43.

Danzhu Angben (don 'grub dbang phan) and Wang Zhouta ('brug thar). 1993. Lishishang de Labuleng Si (Labrang Monastery in history). In *Zangzu Wenhua Sanlun* (Collected writings on Tibetan culture). Beijing: Zhongguo youyi chuban gongsi.

Davis, Deborah, ed. 1999. *The Consumer Revolution in Urban China* (Studies on China, 22). Berkeley: University of California Press.

Dias, Nelia. 1998. "The Visibility of Difference: Nineteenth-Century French Anthropological Collections," In *The Politics of Display: Museums, Science, Culture,* ed. Sharon Macdonald. New York: Routledge.

Dor Zhi (Duo Shi) (dor zhi gdong drug snye mas blo). 1995. Di shi ci shilun Jingang Guanding fahui jianjie (A brief introduction to the fourth Kalacakra initiation ceremony). In *Xianmi* 1.

Duara, Prasenjit. 1995. *Rescuing History From the Nation: Questioning Narratives of Modern China.* Chicago: University of Chicago Press.

Dutton, Michael. 1998. *Streetlife China.* Cambridge: Cambridge University Press.

Elliot, Mark. 2000. "The Limits of Tartary: Manchuria in Imperial and National Geographies." *Journal of Asian Studies* 59(3): 6046.

Enloe, Cynthia. 1989. "Nationalism and Masculinity." In *Bananas, Beaches and Bases: Making Feminist Sense of International Politics,* ed. C. Enloe. Berkeley: University of California Press.

Fitzgerald, John. 1996. "The Nationless State: The Search for a Nation in Modern Chinese Nationalism." In *Chinese Nationalism*, ed. Jonathan Unger. Armonk, NY: M.E. Sharpe.

Foret, Phillipe. 2000. *Mapping Chengde: The Qing Landscape Enterprise*. Honolulu: University of Hawai'i Press.

Gladney, Dru. 1994. "Representing Nationality in China: Refiguring Minority/Majority Identities." *Journal of Asian Studies* 53(1): 923.

———. 2004. *Dislocating China: Muslims, Minorities, and Other Subaltern Subjects*. Chicago: University of Chicago Press.

Goldstein, Melvyn. 1997. *The Snow Lion and the Dragon: China, Tibet and the Dalai Lama*. Berkeley: University of California Press.

Gupta, Akhil, and James Ferguson. 1992. "Beyond 'Culture': Space, Identity and the Politics of Difference." *Cultural Anthropology* 7(1): 3.

Hai Ren. 1998. "Economies of Culture: Theme Parks, Museums and Capital Accumulation in China, Hong Kong and Taiwan." Ph.D. diss., University of Washington, Seattle.

———. 1999. *Imagineering Government*. Paper written for the symposium on "Vernacular Cultures," Center for Chinese Studies, University of California at Berkeley.

———. 2007. "The Landscape of Power: Imagineering Consumer Behavior at China's Theme Parks." In *The Themed Space: Locating Culture, Nation, and Self*, ed. Scott A. Lukas. Lanham, MD: Lexington Books.

Hanks, William. 1996. "Exorcism and the Description of Participant Roles." In *Natural Histories of Discourse*, ed. Michael Silverstein and Greg Urban. Chicago: University of Chicago Press.

Harrell, Stevan. 1995. "Introduction: Civilizing Projects and the Reaction to Them." In *Cultural Encounters on China's Ethnic Frontiers*, ed. Stevan Harrell. Seattle: University of Washington Press.

Harris, Clare. 1999. *In the Image of Tibet: Tibetan Painting After 1959*. London: Reaktion.

Hevia, James. 1995. *Cherishing Men from Afar: Qing Guest Ritual and the Macartney Embassy of 1793*. Durham: Duke University Press.

Hinsley, Curtis. 1991. "The World as Marketplace: Commodification of the Exotic at the World's Columbian Exposition, Chicago, 1893." In *Exhibiting Cultures: The Poetics and Politics of Museum Display,* ed. Ivan Karp and Steven D. Levine. Washington, DC: Smithsonian Books.

Hostetler, Laura. 2001. *Qing Colonial Enterprise: Ethnography and Cartography in Early Modern China*. Chicago: University of Chicago Press.

Huber, Toni. 1994a. "Why Can't Women Climb Pure Crystal Mountain? Remarks on Gender and Space at Tsa-ri." In *Tibetan Studies: Proceedings of the 6th Seminar of the International Association for Tibetan Studies, Fagernes (1992)*, ed. P. Kvaerne. Vol. 1, Oslo.

———. 1994b. "Putting the Gnas back into Gnas-skor: Rethinking Tibetan Buddhist Pilgrimage Practice." *Tibet Journal* 19(2): 20.

———. 1999. *The Cult of Pure Crystal Mountain: Popular Pilgrimage and Visionary Landscape in Southeast Tibet*. New York: Oxford University Press.

Kai Wa. 1995. "Lun Dangqian Zangzu Siyuan Jingji jiqi Daoxiang Wenti (On the economy of contemporary Tibetan Buddhist monasteries and the problem of guiding it)." *Qinghai Minzu Xueyuan Xuebao* 4: 53.

Kirshenblatt-Gimblett, Barbara. 1991. "Objects of Ethnography." In *Exhibiting Cultures: The Poetics and Politics of Museum Display*, ed. Ivan Karp and Steven D. Levine.

Kohn, Richard. 1997. "A Rite of Empowerment." In *Religions of Tibet in Practice*, ed. Donald S. Lopez, Jr. Princeton: Princeton University Press.

Kolas, Ashild, and Monika P. Thowsen. 2005. *On the Margins of Tibet: Cultural Survival on the Tibetan Frontier*. Seattle: University of Washington Press.

KZC. 1978. *Kansu'u zhing chen gyi nang bstan dgon pa do dam byed rgyu'i tshod lta'i lag len byed thabs* (Preliminary methods for the management of Buddhist monasteries in Gansu Province).

Larsen, Knud, and Amund Sinding-Larsen. 2001. *Lhasa Atlas: Traditional Tibetan Architecture and Townscape*. Boston: Shambhala.

Liu, Melinda. 1999. "China's Balkan Crisis." *Newsweek International*, April 19.

Liu, Yu. 1993. "Jinxi Dashi Gongtang Cang" (The great Golden Throne teacher Gongtang Tshang). *Tuoling* 4: 8–50.

Lopez, Donald. 1998. *Prisoners of Shangri-La: Tibetan Buddhism and the West*. Chicago: University of Chicago Press.

———. 2006. *The Madman's Middle Way*. Chicago: University of Chicago Press.

Macdonald, Sharon. 1998. *The Politics of Display: Museums, Science, Culture*. New York: Routledge.

Makley, Charlene. 2007. *The Violence of Liberation: Gender and Tibetan Buddhist Revival in Post-Mao China*. Berkeley: University of California Press.

Malkki, Lisa. 1997. "National Geographic: The Rooting of Peoples and the Territorialization of National Identity Among Scholars and Refugees." In *Culture, Power, Place: Explorations in Critical Anthropology*, ed. Akhil Gupta and James Ferguson. Durham, NC: Duke University Press.

Marshall, Steven D., and Susette T. Cooke. 1997. "Tibet Outside the TAR." Washington, DC: International Campaign for Tibet. (CD-ROM).

Maurer, Bill. 2006. "The Anthropology of Money." *Annual Review of Anthropology* 35: 16.

Mills, Martin. 2003. *Identity, Ritual and State in Tibetan Buddhism*. London: RoutledgeCurzon.

Millward, James. 1999. "Coming Onto the Map: 'Western Regions' Geography and Cartographic Nomenclature in the Making of Chinese Empire in Xinjiang." *Late Imperial China* 20(2): 68.

Moran, Peter. 2004. *Buddhism Observed: Travelers, Exiles and Tibetan Dharma in Kathmandu*. London: Routledge.

Munson, Todd. 1999. "Selling China: www.cnta.com and Cultural Nationalism." *Journal for Multimedia History* 2. www.albany.edu/jmmh/.

Oakes, Tim. 1998. *Tourism and Modernity in China*. London: Routledge.

———. 2000. "China's Provincial Identities: Reviving Regionalism and Reinventing 'Chineseness.'" *Journal of Asian Studies* 59(3): 6692.

Oakes, Tim, and Louisa Schein, eds. 2006. *Translocal China: Linkages, Identities and the Reimagining of Space*. London and New York: Routledge.

Ohnuma, Reiko. 2005. "Gift." In *Critical Terms for the Study of Buddhism*, ed. Donald S. Lopez, Jr. Chicago: University of Chicago Press.

Ong, Aihwa. 1999. *Flexible Citizenship: The Cultural Logics of Transnationality*. Durham, NC: Duke University Press.

Perdue, Peter. 2005. *China Marches West: The Qing Conquest of Central Eurasia*. Cambridge, MA: Harvard University Press.

Petech, Luciano. 1950. *China and Tibet in the Early 18th Century: History of the Establishment of Chinese Protectorate in Tibet*. Leiden: E.J. Brill.

Samuel, Geoffrey. 1993. *Civilized Shamans: Buddhism in Tibetan Societies*. Washington, DC: Smithsonian Press.

Schein, Louisa. 2000. *Minority Rules: The Miao and the Feminine in China's Cultural Politics*. Durham, NC: Duke University Press.

Tenzin Palbar (Alags Tsa yus tshang). 1994. *nga'i pha yul gyi ya nga ba'i lo rgyus* (The tragic history of my fatherland). Dharamsala: Narthang Publications.

TIN (Tibet Information Network). 1998. "Key Religious Leader Leaves Tibet for America." November. www.tibetinfonet.net/.

———. 2000. "A Violation of Belief: The First Public Statement by Agya Rinpoche in Exile." March. www.tibetinfo.net/publications/docs/rspeech1.htm.

Tuttle, Gray. 2005. *Tibetan Buddhists in the Making of Modern China*. New York: Columbia University Press.

Urry, John. 2002. *The Tourist Gaze*. London: Sage Publications.

Wang, Shaogang, and Hu Angang. 1999. *The Political Economy of Uneven Development: The Case of China*. Armonk, NY: M.E. Sharpe.

Wang, Xiangyun. 2000. "The Qing Court's Tibet Connection: Lcang skya rol pa'i rdo rje and the Qianlong Emperor." *Harvard Journal of Asiatic Studies* 60(1): 1264.

Wang, Yunfeng. 1997. *Huofu de Shijie* (The world of a Living Buddha). Beijing: Minzu Chubanshe.

Welch, Holmes. 1972. *Buddhism Under Mao*. Cambridge, MA: Harvard University Press.

Yang, Mayfair. 1999. "From Gender Erasure to Gender Difference: State Feminism, Consumer Sexuality, and Women's Public Sphere in China." In *Spaces of Their Own: Women's Public Sphere in Transnational China*, ed. Mayfair Yang. Minneapolis: University of Minnesota Press.

Young, Nick, and June Shih. 2004. "Philanthropic Links between the Chinese Diaspora and the PRC." In *Diaspora Philanthropy and Equitable Development in China and India*, ed. Geithner et al. Cambridge, MA: Harvard University Press.

Zablocki, Abraham. 2005. *The Global Mandala: The Transnational Transformation of Tibetan Buddhism*. Ph.D. diss., Cornell University.

Zha Zha (bkra bkra). 1993. "Labuleng Si Si (4) Da Saichi Shixi Shulue" (Brief history of the four Golden Throne lamas of Labrang Monastery). *Anduo Yanjiu*, Chuankan hao (Inaugural issue of Amdo Research) 1: 66.

6

Economic Development and the Buddhist-Industrial Complex of Xishuangbanna

Susan K. McCarthy

In late October 2008, an entourage of senior Thai officials visited a Buddhist temple in the village of Manchunman, located in the Xishuangbanna Dai Autonomous Prefecture in China's southwestern province of Yunnan. Manchunman is a village of about five hundred people, all of whom are Dai; the Dai are one of China's fifty-five minority nationalities and are related to Tai peoples in Thailand, Laos, and the Shan State of Myanmar. The visit by the Thai officials was no ordinary sightseeing tour. Instead it was a merit-making event during which an envoy of Thailand's King Bhumibol donated royal vestments, ceremonial objects, and funds for temple upkeep. This was the third such royal donation ceremony held in Xishuangbanna, which many Thais view as an ancestral homeland. In 1998 and 2004 envoys of King Bhumibol donated similar gifts during ceremonies at Xishuangbanna's Central Buddhist Temple, the most important Buddhist temple in the prefecture and the highest-ranking Theravada temple in China.

Accompanying the Thai entourage this day were several Chinese officials. Among these were Dao Shuren, deputy secretary of the national Buddhist Association and the head of its Yunnan branch; Ai Xiangzai, head of the Minority and Religious Affairs Bureau in Xishuangbanna Prefecture; and Yang Sha, deputy chief of the prefectural government. Also in attendance were eighty-one monks and over a thousand laypeople from Manchunman and nearby communities. The monks chanted sutras, while visiting dignitaries and laypeople made offerings of cash, incense, lotus buds, food, and other objects in addition to the royal gifts. The event was both a religious and a political ceremony, one that reaffirmed Sino-Thai relations. As the deputy chief of the prefecture explained, the ceremony would "strengthen communication between the two countries, and promote mutual exchange and cooperation in the areas of religious culture, trade, and the development of tourism."[1]

Although royal donation ceremonies such as this one are rare, they are emblematic of the way in which religion, politics, and economics intertwine in contemporary Xishuangbanna. The ceremony also illuminates key features of the religious expansion taking place throughout China. First, it highlights the vibrancy and variety of religious institutions, communities, and practices, despite the Chinese state's official atheism and periodic crackdowns on activities it deems threatening. Second, it shows that the state does not merely tolerate religion, it often promotes it. The resurgence of Han and minority religious life is in part a consequence of post-Mao state retrenchment. Yet it is also the product of active state promotion and intervention. Third, the Manchunman ceremony illustrates the "locality" of much religious and cultural production in what is often viewed as a highly centralized regime. Nearly all of the Chinese government personnel who participated in the donation ceremony were from Xishuangbanna, and most were Dai, including Dao Shuren, the national representative of the Buddhist Association who is a member of the pre-1949 Dai aristocracy.[2] National policies form the backdrop against which such events take place; however, local officials exercise considerable discretion in how they police and promote religion (Dean 1997, 172).

Yet there are aspects of the donation ceremony that set it apart from the religious and cultural revival sweeping China. Many scholars note the robustness of cultural practice in contemporary China and its importance to political and economic projects. Many also note the Han-centrism of the state's cultural policies, especially as they pertain to China's geographic and demographic periphery. The state deploys Han Chinese culture and the Han themselves to modernize and civilize China's border regions and peoples. As Dott in this volume demonstrates, traditional Chinese institutions, beliefs, and practices associated with the Han are celebrated as touchstones of morality and identity, insofar as they encourage identification with the nation and adherence to state-sanctioned ideals of modernity.

The Dai, however, are an ethnic minority whose language, religion, and traditional political institutions place them squarely outside the mainstream of Chinese culture and society. They are a peripheral people, inhabitants of an ethnic and geographic borderland (Giersch 2006). Their cultural revival connects them not so much with a historical Han Chinese collectivity but to an imagined community of the Tai, an ethnolinguistic group that spans several neighboring states. In general, the Chinese government decries foreign "meddling" in matters of religion (especially minority religion) and tries to limit the influence of outside organizations on domestic groups. In the case of the royal donation ceremony, the state facilitated a religious event that encouraged Dai identification with a foreign monarch and a transnational Tai collectivity.

Why would the state do so? One reason is summed up in the deputy prefectural chief's statement: religion and other cultural practices are economically useful. This is particularly so in less developed minority and border regions. As Oakes says in this volume, culture is "the state's business." In Xishuangbanna, Dai culture, including Theravada Buddhism, is the bedrock upon which trade and especially tourism are founded. Temples and other institutions are sources of revenue, and help spur growth in the hospitality sector. Religious traditions shared with transnational Tai communities function as social capital that can be deployed to forge trade agreements and regional development schemes.

Other interpretations of state-led minority cultural production see it as in fact tied to the state's agenda of nation building and consolidation. The "internal orientalism" thesis, for example, holds that the construction of minorities as traditional (if not primitive), feminized exotics helps to produce, in dialectical fashion, a modern, advanced, masculine Han Chinese subject (Schein 1997). As Makley notes in this volume, state-led minority cultural promotion may also be an effort to domesticate and depoliticize nonmainstream practices and identities by turning them into commodities for nonminority tourist consumption. If these interpretations are correct, the nonassimilative policies of the current regime are much less of a departure from Maoist policies than they appear, insofar as they seek to more fully subordinate minorities to a Han-centric national identity and ideal.

This chapter explores the role of Buddhism in Xishuangbanna's development experience, and the impact of that development on Buddhist institutions and practices. In particular, it examines the nexus of state, capital, and Buddhism—what I only half-jokingly call the "Buddhist-industrial complex"—with the aim of understanding official promotion of Buddhism and the ways in which Dai Buddhists respond. All of the above-mentioned explanations of party-state support for minority culture have merit, and can be applied to the Dai case—especially the argument that sees Buddhism as a resource for economic development. Yet none of these fully explain the dynamics of the relations among state, capital, and religion, nor do they fully explain Buddhist revival. There is no question that Buddhism is promoted because it serves the economic and political interests of the state and its entrepreneurial allies. However, it does not follow that either the state or business controls the Buddhist revival, its meanings or its direction. Buddhism enhances political and economic resources, but the reverse is also true. Like the Tibetan Buddhists analyzed by Makley in chapter 5, Dai cultural activists—who include monks, laypeople, and some local officials—are finding ways to mobilize state and economic resources to revitalize and strengthen Theravada Buddhism. Tourism, trade, and state sanction of Theravada Buddhism have created opportunities for the enhancement of Dai religious identity and practice.

BUDDHISM IN DAI SOCIETY AND HISTORY

The Xishuangbanna Dai Autonomous Prefecture is located along China's borders with Laos and Myanmar (see figure 6.1). It consists of two counties, Menghai and Mengla, and the county-level municipality of Jinghong. The prefecture is home to about one-quarter of the 1.3 million Dai in Yunnan Province. Within Xishuangbanna the Dai compose 34 percent of the population of roughly 1 million inhabitants. The next largest group is the Han. The Han population of Xishuangbanna, tiny before Liberation, swelled in the decades after 1949 as waves of migrants from Hunan and other interior provinces settled to work on newly established state farms. The 1990s saw the start of another wave of predominantly Han in-migration, driven by the search for opportunities created by reform. Xishuangbanna is also home to significant numbers of Jinuo, Hani, Yi, Lahu, Bulang, and several thousand Hui Muslims (McCarthy 2009, 72–73). Though multiethnic in composition, Xishuangbanna is identified officially and in popular consciousness as a Dai prefecture.

For centuries the area formerly called Sipsongpanna was a more-or-less independent polity, one of several interlinked yet competitive Tai principalities in mainland Southeast Asia (Hsieh 1995). Sipsongpanna's independence waxed and waned over the centuries, and by the middle of the Qing dynasty it had been significantly incorporated into the imperial Chinese order. Yet Sipsongpanna remained geographically and culturally isolated from mainstream Chinese society well into the twentieth century, even after the founding of the PRC in 1949. This isolation created challenges for the CCP in its efforts at state and party building in the region. As is true of many Chinese minorities, a section of Sipsongpanna's traditional elite was absorbed into the new party-state apparatus. Sipsongpanna's last ruler became the head (*zhouzhang*) of the Xishuangbanna Dai Autonomous Prefecture when it was established in 1954, a post he held for approximately forty years.[3]

Theravada Buddhism had long been integral to the social and political fabric of Sipsongpanna. Buddhist ritual and institutions also facilitated relationships between Sipsongpanna and other Tai polities, as well as with the Chinese imperial state (Giersch 2006, 59–60 and 194–97). After the establishment of the PRC, the CCP allowed traditional Dai religious and other cultural practices to persist for several years relatively unimpeded. In the late 1950s, however, Xishuangbanna and its minorities fell victim to the leftist radicalism that was transforming the rest of the country. From that point on the Dai were

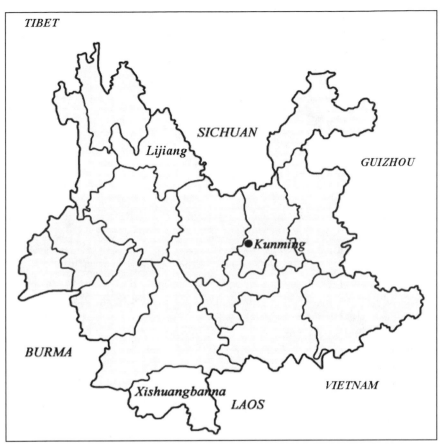

Figure 6.1.   Map of Yunnan with Xishuangbanna Prefecture and Lijiang indicated.

subject to "the cut of one knife," uniform policies that disregarded minorities' "special characteristics" and relegated religion and other traditions to the dustbin of history. Monks were forced to defrock and return to lay society, although some fled to Burma and Laos. Temples were destroyed or converted to secular and political use as meeting halls and granaries. From the Great Leap Forward through the end of the Cultural Revolution, Buddhism in Xishuangbanna practically ceased to exist.

THERAVADA BUDDHISM UNDER REFORM

In the post-Mao period, Deng Xiaoping's economic reforms were accompanied by a marked shift in CCP minority and religious policy. Even before new policies were formally announced, in the years following Mao's death many Dai began renovating temples and openly practicing Buddhism. Also reestablished was the novitiate, the practice whereby young boys and men serve as novice monks for a period of a few months to several years. Because of a dearth of trained religious personnel, many villages hired senior monks from Tai communities in neighboring states to staff rural temples and train novices, a practice that has continued to the present. By 1981, about one-fifth of all temples in the prefecture had been reopened. At present over 570 temples dot the mostly rural landscape of Xishuangbanna, one for every one or two villages. These temples are staffed by over 700 senior monks and approximately 3,800 novices (Xi 2006, par. 3). Cross-border and regional religious networks are active, contributing to religious regeneration. Today, many Dai journey to temples and festivals in neighboring countries. Many also follow influential Buddhist leaders from these countries and travel long distances to events over which these leaders preside (Cohen 2000). Dai monks study at Buddhist institutions in Thailand, Laos, Sri Lanka, and Myanmar, a practice that has become de rigueur for religious career advancement within Chinese Theravada Buddhism. The Buddhist revival in Xishuangbanna has clearly benefited from transnational linkages, just as it has helped to cement them.

Another sign of the revitalization of Buddhism is the public attention garnered by certain religious leaders. Guba Longzhuang Meng, the abbot of the Central Buddhist Temple in Jinghong as well as the new Mengle Great Temple, is a case in point. Like other prominent religious leaders in China, Longzhuang is an official figure. He serves as a deputy head of the national Buddhist Association and its Yunnan branch, and he heads the association's Xishuangbanna branch and the prefectural Buddhist Studies Institute. Longzhuang is also a member of the provincial China People's Political Consultative Committee (CPPCC), and deputy secretary of the CPPCC in Xishuangbanna. Longzhuang is also chief *guba* (*guba meng*). The title of *guba* (in Thai, *khruba*) signifies high rank in the *sangha*, the community of monks, and as chief guba Longzhuang is the most senior Theravada monk in China. Abbot Longzhuang attained that position in 2004 at a ceremony attended by party-state officials, Buddhist leaders from around China, and members of Xishuangbanna's former royal family (Xie and Wan 2004). At the ceremony, the head of the Yunnan Province Religious Affairs Bureau presented Longzhuang with a government certificate approving his promotion. Though there are other monks with guba status, Longzhuang is the first monk to be promoted to guba meng since 1933, and thus the first monk to achieve that status since the founding of the PRC. The previous guba meng died in 1974.

BUDDHISM AND DEVELOPMENT IN XISHUANGBANNA

The public attention paid to Theravada Buddhism signifies its importance in contemporary Xishuangbanna. Increasingly, Buddhism is described as indispensable to Xishuangbanna's economic transformation. Yet for decades scholars and officials questioned its compatibility with economic modernization. Philosophically Theravada Buddhism emphasizes world renunciation to a greater degree than does the Mahayana tradition, the dominant form in China, and Dai Buddhism has been portrayed as contrary to the acquisitiveness at the heart of a market economy. Such views were more prevalent in the early years of the reform era, but they persist today. Even Dai officials have expressed concern over the allegedly retarding influence of Buddhist detachment and Dai habits of life. As one senior Dai official and member of the former royal family explained to me in a personal interview, Buddhism "hinders competition and leads to a resigned attitude towards life. It teaches that all life is suffering, and because of this Dai people tend to be satisfied with what they have, rather than striving for more." As a result of their religious worldview, "Dai people's 'struggle spirit' is lacking (*fendou jingsheng bu gou*)." The official pointed to the Jinuo minority of Xishuangbanna as a counterexample of a non-Buddhist ethnic group among whom (in his view) the entrepreneurial spirit was well developed. This high-ranking individual, who in his youth served briefly as a novice monk, stated that he "respected" Buddhism but was not himself a believer.[4]

Monks themselves are sometimes blamed for impeding the "struggle spirit" so necessary for economic development. A 2006 report by the Xishuangbanna Buddhist Association on the state of the "religious culture industry" (*zongjiao wenhua chanye*) laments the weakness of "market consciousness" among senior monks, along with their lackadaisical attitude toward the commercial aspects of temple management (Xi 2006, par. 8). Monks are held in high esteem by ordinary people, and many are indeed indifferent to economic development. They see their role as promoting moral and spiritual development, not economic growth. As one temple abbot explained, "Whether or not this area develops is of no concern to me. I don't oppose development, but I don't promote it either. My purpose is to help people live in accordance with Buddhist principles."[5]

Certain Dai traditions have complicated state goals. One example is the novitiate. As mentioned, this is the practice whereby young boys and men spend a limited period of time as monks, studying Buddhist scripture, philosophy, history, the Dai written language, and other subjects in temple schools. Today, young novices from the ages of about eight to the midteens are a common sight at temples throughout the prefecture (see figure 6.2). Although this underscores the vitality of Buddhism in Xishuangbanna, the reestablishment of temple schools sparked an exodus of boys from the state-run school system (McCarthy 2009, 78–80; Hansen 1999, 119–22). Dai novices continue their studies in the temples, but the religious education they receive normally does not include instruction in the Chinese language, Chinese history, or other subjects compatible with the state's modernizing agenda.

Officials have tried to combat this trend without violating the sensibilities of the Dai or directly suppressing religious practice. In some instances senior monks have been induced to offer special courses in temples for novices; in other cases they are made personally responsible for seeing that their young charges show up for class at state schools, delivering them in person if necessary. Classes at some state schools in the prefecture are segregated by sex, to help novices abide by monastic strictures. Officials also accommodate the religious calendar by providing tutors during periods when full-time attendance at the temple is required, such as the period after the Door-Closing Festival. A key ally of the state in these efforts is Guba Longzhuang. In the 1980s long before he attained high position, Longzhuang garnered attention for his efforts to improve education among Dai novices in the village where he first served as abbot ("Guba Longzhuang" 2007, par. 7).

While some traditional practices and habits of mind have complicated the drive to create a modern workforce and economy, Xishuangbanna has undergone a profound transformation. Its location, long a liability, is now advantageous. The prefecture has benefited from increasing trade and closer ties between China and nearby Southeast Asian countries. China is a member of the Greater Mekong Subregion (GMS) economic cooperation program, which promotes regional development and trade among member states, which include Laos, Myanmar, Cambodia, Vietnam, and Thailand. One of the main foci of the GMS in recent years has been the construction of an expressway, completed in 2008, stretching from Kunming to Bangkok via Xishuangbanna. The 2001 opening of the Lancang River to commercial navigation between China and neighboring countries has helped turn the prefectural capital of Jinghong into a small but increasingly busy international port. According to Xishuangbanna officials, this focus on Southeast Asia and especially the Dai-Thai connection is paying off: in 2008, the number of Thai visitors to the prefecture increased fourfold over the previous year to more than 48,000, or 44 percent of all overseas tourists.[6]

It is tourism more than any other sector that has transformed Xishuangbanna's economic, political, and even religious landscape. Xishuangbanna has long been characterized as a land of lush mountains, verdant jungle, picturesque paddy fields, and quaint villages inhabited by a colorful, sensuous, docile, leisure-loving people (Gladney 1994; McKhann 1995). These

Figure 6.2. Novice monks study Buddhist scrolls written in the Dai language, Damenglong. S. McCarthy photo.

stereotypes of Xishuangbanna and the Dai were energetically promoted in the 1980s with the birth of the tourist industry and China's opening to the West. The expansion of domestic tourism in the 1990s accelerated the packaging and promotion of the prefecture, its people, and their culture. Local government reports describe tourism as the "dragon's head" of the local economy, the dynamic force leading the way. Between 1997 and 2007 when Xishuangbanna's economy grew at an average annual rate of 9.3 percent, the service sector, which includes tourism, grew 13.8 percent per year (Xishuangbanna Prefecture E-government 2008, par. 4). Millions of Chinese and foreign tourists have visited Xishuangbanna over the last two decades, and tourism is a billion-yuan industry.

However, tourism, like development in general, is a double-edged sword. Xishuangbanna was one of the first places in Yunnan to capitalize on its scenery and perceived exoticism. Its success has encouraged officials in other parts of the province to develop ethnocultural tourism, and many domestic and foreign tourists are bypassing Xishuangbanna in favor of areas like Lijiang and Shangri-la in Yunnan's northwest. In part this is because Xishuangbanna has gained a reputation for being overly developed. Rapid growth and poor planning have turned the formerly sleepy town of Jinghong into a dirty, noisy, overbuilt city, complete with sprawl and traffic jams. Newly prosperous villagers in the surrounding countryside have replaced traditional wooden stilt homes with multistoried, tiled concrete homes common in other parts of Asia. Much of the exoticism on display is, quite simply, kitsch—state and business promotion of Dai culture has produced some profoundly inauthentic products, including daily celebrations of the ostensibly annual "water-splashing festival" unmoored from seasonal context, staged displays of Dai women bathing in the Lancang River, and transvestite performances of the allegedly traditional "Peacock Dance," to name a few. The large-scale song and dance performances held nightly in Jinghong embody a Vegas-meets-Bangkok aesthetic (if it can be called that) rather than traditional Dai sensibilities. Consequently, the reaction of many tourists to what is packaged as traditional minority culture is underwhelming. Economic growth is killing the prefecture's golden goose, its exoticism and beauty.

Officials and entrepreneurs have sought various solutions to the problems created by economic modernization. One strategy is to create planned "Dai culture villages" that showcase, and hopefully preserve, traditional crafts, architecture, and ways of life. Many of these are little more than tacky souvenir stands thrown up alongside the actual villages whose residents staff and operate them. However, the more ambitious of these villages fuse commerce and recreation with actual, preexisting Dai settlements. In theory, they aim to provide glimpses of, and even the experience of, "authentic" Dai culture,

This engaged participation, which inevitably involves appropriation of cultural objects as one's "own," generates an experience of authenticity that watching an ethnic dance performance most likely cannot. Despite differences between Theravada and other Buddhist traditions, religious practices and beliefs are avenues through which non-Dai Buddhist visitors to Manchunman may experience a variety of the authentic firsthand.[8]

Producing a steady supply of authenticity (or "authenticity") is, however, no easy task. Some visitors find the slick packaging of both Dai-ness and Buddhism in Manchunman off-putting. One group of Taiwanese Buddhist tourists I spoke to in 2002 expressed skepticism that the village and temple were authentic. They found the Dai Garden as a whole overly commercial, and stated a desire to visit a real Dai village and temple. I explained that they were in a real Dai village, and that Manchunman was a real temple, a very important one in fact. "No, they're not," retorted one member of the Taiwanese group; "they're fake!" Ironically, our conversation took place on the day of the Door-Closing Festival, an important holiday that was being celebrated in the temple as we spoke.

Generating the appearance of authenticity may even require that the actual (authentic?) wants, needs, and habits of village residents be disregarded. Conversely, villagers' efforts to satisfy their "real" wants can work against the plans of those managing these scenic spots. In Manting as in much of Xishuangbanna, the scourge of modern construction methods is eroding its traditional character. As of May 2008, nontraditional, "Western"-style buildings (*yanglou*) accounted for 15 percent of all houses and one-quarter of all commercial and residential space in Manting, and more were in the works. On several occasions work teams from the property management bureaus of Menghan Township and Jinghong Municipality have tried to prevent villagers from putting up multistory cement buildings (Wang 2008). For reasons that are unclear, despite work team efforts and the objections of other villagers, some residents continue to flout architectural restrictions, refusing, as Oakes puts it, "to become willing performers in the performance of 'folk culture' in terms that are deemed acceptable" to Chinese state and capital (1998, 12).

The quest for Dai-ness may also entail fundamental changes in the demographic character of Dai settlements. Mannongfeng, a not-yet completed Dai cultural village on the outskirts of Jinghong, exemplifies this phenomenon. Mannongfeng is adjacent to the Theravada Buddhist Cultural Center, a major tourist attraction that opened in late 2007. However, the village's proximity to Jinghong has resulted in the original settlement being nearly swallowed up by urban expansion. Monks and local officials do not want the ideals and aesthetic of the center compromised by its environs. Officials also would like to see Mannongfeng capitalize on its proximity to the center, but to do so it must appeal to tourists. Consequently the village is the subject of a cultural redevelopment plan not unlike the one implemented in Manting. A key element of this project is a plan to showcase and market traditional arts and handicrafts. However, the current inhabitants farm rice and rubber, and lack either the time or skills to engage in traditional performance and craft production on a commercial scale. Project developers have advertised throughout the region for artists, performers, and craftspeople willing to relocate to Mannongfeng. Officials from the Jinghong Business Initiative Bureau admit that getting current residents on board the project will require stepping up education and thought work (*sixiang gongzuo*).[9]

It must be emphasized that Dai cultural revival is not driven only or primarily by the need to appeal to non-Dai Chinese and foreign tourist consumers. Cultural and religious revival is in great part a grassroots, bottom-up endeavor, aimed at and for Dai people. The use of Dai culture for economic purposes is made possible because of this popular foundation. Many cultural events and institutions supported by the party-state are organized by and for ordinary Dai people as well as the Dai elite. These express and affirm, and sometimes contest, relationships among and expectations of the state, minority elite, and ordinary Dai people. Some of the more ambitious endeavors intertwine commerce with Dai traditions and religion in surprising ways.

The centrality of Manchunman in the creation of the Xishuangbanna Dai Garden highlights the complicated way in which tradition and tourism intersect. Manchunman is a Chinese transliteration of the Dai name of the settlement: "man" is a transliteration of the Dai word for village, while "chunman" is a transliteration of the Dai word for garden. In pre-1949 Sipsongpanna, villages were responsible for performing specific tasks in service to the local nobility or the king, the *chao phaendin*. Manchunman was designated as the garden playground of the *chao phaendin*, a place for his enjoyment and relaxation. Its reorganization as an AAAA scenic spot pays homage to and builds on its traditional function (Duan and Yang 2001).

The temple itself possesses historical and religious importance. In Dai Buddhism temples are organized hierarchically, and historically temple rank corresponded with the status of villages and their residents within the Dai class structure. In the pre-Liberation era, the Manchunman temple was the highest-ranking temple in Menghan district and one of the most important in Sipsongpanna. Officially the traditional class structure has disappeared; yet Manchunman's temple retains its significance. That significance is affirmed by tourist-oriented development, as well as by events like the Thai king's donation ceremony. Given its historical importance, it is no surprise that the Manchunman temple was selected to host the royal donation ceremony. The only other temple to have hosted such events is the Central Buddhist Temple in Jinghong.

Manchunman's significance was also very much on display during the temple's ceremonial rededication in 1997, well before the Dai Garden project was completed. In the 1980s and 1990s temples across Xishuangbanna were being renovated, and although reopenings were typically marked by ceremonies, few were as large or public as the one staged in Manchunman. Funds for the temple's reconstruction came from the prefectural Buddhist Association, local private donors, tourism revenues, and Thai Buddhists. As listed on a plaque in the temple compound, the Kunming-based Thai consul donated 225,800 yuan to the reconstruction, while the president of the Thai Senate gave the auspicious amount of 198,888 yuan. The actual rededication ceremony, which I attended, took place during a three-day festival that included banquets, performances by dance troupes and pop music groups, and a rocket festival. During the ceremony the temple overflowed with people, including the Thai consul, local government officials, members of the former Sipsongpanna royal family, dozens of monks, and hundreds of local residents. Monks chanted from scripture while the visiting dignitaries made cash offerings and requested blessings for their families and the community. The ceremony was followed by a banquet and then a raucous rocket festival on the banks of the Lancang River a few hundred yards from the temple. Groups of men from villages throughout the township launched homemade rockets, competing to see whose flew the farthest. Winners were awarded cash prizes in the form of wads of hundred-yuan notes by the dignitaries, who were seated on a reviewing stand apart from the thousand or so spectators watching from the banks. The prize giving was as much a spectacle as the competition. The victors in each heat danced and sang their way to the reviewing stand where they hoisted the chairs of the dignitaries (still seated) up in the air, setting them down only when the winners were satisfied with the size of their prize.

Festivals like King Bhumibol's donation ceremony and the rededication of the Manchunman temple create publicity for Xishuangbanna and contribute to its mystique and desirability as a tourist destination. They also serve as venues for officials, especially Dai officials, to demonstrate their commitment to Dai autonomy and influence, at least locally. They affirm Dai political, economic, and social position in a prefecture they once dominated, but where demographics have been altered tremendously by waves of Han migrants from the interior. By making offerings, requesting sutras for their families, awarding prizes in the rocket competition, or accompanying the envoys of the Thai king, party-state officials affirm Dai distinctiveness and their right to engage in cultural and social endeavors (mostly) unique to them as a people. At the same time, Dai members of the local and provincial party-state apparatus assert their role as mediators between the central state and the Dai people.

Theravada Buddhism has contributed greatly to Xishuangbanna's economic revitalization. That said, the ways in which economic revitalization has contributed to Theravada Buddhism cannot be overlooked. The symbiosis of Buddhism and commercial development has enriched Buddhism and augmented its public role and stature. One shining, gaudy, yet impressive example of this is the aforementioned Theravada Buddhist Cultural Center (*nanchuan fojiao wenhua yuan*), perched on a hillside on the outskirts of Jinghong. The center, which opened in the fall of 2007, includes Mengle Great Temple, as well as several smaller temples, shrines, and stupas. It also houses the brand-new campus of the Xishuangbanna Buddhist Studies Institute, comprising multiple classroom buildings (including expanded computing facilities) and dormitories. The prefectural Buddhist Association and related bodies have also relocated to the center. There are acres of paths where visitors can wander and engage in contemplation, and gift shops where they can purchase incense, amulets, and other souvenirs. Visitors must pay an entry fee of 100 yuan, unless they are both Xishuangbanna residents and Theravada Buddhists (e.g., members of the Dai and Bulang minorities), in which case they may enter for free. Ninety percent of ticket revenues are retained by the property development firm based in the northeastern city of Shenyang that put up most of the 350 million yuan in capital used to construct the center.[10] The remaining 10 percent goes to the Buddhist Studies Institute to be spent as its directors, led by Guba Longzhuang, see fit.

The center's opening has entailed a geographic shift in the locus of Buddhist activity in the prefecture. The Xishuangbanna Buddhist Studies Institute and other organizations previously were housed at the Central Buddhist Temple several miles away, as were many of the monks who now live at the center. Guba Longzhuang has himself relocated to the Theravada Buddhist Cultural Center; the day he moved into his new residence was marked by a morning-to-night celebration attended by party and state officials, monks from around Yunnan Province, the media, members of the former royal family, and hundreds of well-wishers (see figure 6.3). The move in practice makes the Mengle Great Temple the new "central" Buddhist temple in Xishuangbanna, although the original retains its name and official status.

Theravada Buddhist organizations thus have a new, more modern home in Xishuangbanna. This modernization of infrastructure parallels other modernizing activities being spearheaded by the guba, the Buddhist Studies Institute, and other bodies. These include the preservation, publication, and digitizing of Dai religious texts, an effort touted in tourist promotional materials and government reports on the state of the religious culture industry (Xi 2006). Another example is the institute's Internet-based promotion of a new program, begun in early 2008, that allows lay Buddhists to briefly par-

Figure 6.3. Ceremony at the Mengle Great Temple, with the city of Jinghong in the background. S. McCarthy photo.

take of the monastic life and study the philosophy and meditation techniques of Theravada Buddhism.[11] This decidedly untraditional program is geared toward a mainly Han Chinese audience regardless of Buddhist affiliation, and is funded by fees as well as donations from lay Buddhists and Buddhist organizations around China. The length of the program varies according to the interests of individual participants; there are three-day, seven-day, one-month, three-month, and longer programs. During their stay, participants live and study at the temple in Manting, part of the same Dai Garden Village complex that includes Manchunman. Interestingly program materials state that women are welcome to participate, despite the fact that, unlike Mahayana and Tibetan Buddhism and Theravada in other countries, there is no tradition of women serving as nuns in Xishuangbanna.

There is no question that the Theravada Buddhism Cultural Center is part of a multipronged strategy aimed at revitalizing and expanding the tourist industry in Xishuangbanna. Overdevelopment and competition from other scenic and exotic localities in Yunnan have forced officials and business to pursue strategies aimed at grabbing the attention of travelers seeking an experience of rustic minority culture. Big, attention-grabbing projects like the

Theravada Buddhist Cultural Center represent the analogue of an "arms race" among competing localities and their business allies. The revenue potential of such projects helps local officials cement linkages with private sector investors, such as the Shenyang-based firm behind the center's construction.

Pecuniary motives aside, Buddhism also benefits. Aside from providing new digs for monks and Buddhist organizations, the linking of tourist sites with Buddhism augments popular interest in Theravada Buddhism. Its public profile is also enhanced. After decades of suppression and marginalization, Buddhist institutions, identity, and leaders are again prominent in the public realm. Major Dai Buddhist festivals are state events as much as cultural and religious ones, and Buddhist leaders like Guba Longzhuang are publicly recognized for their contributions to local cultural revitalization and the construction of the harmonious society. Official sanction of traditional Dai culture and especially Buddhist institutions and identity has created opportunities for activists to pursue cultural and religious goals that, although connected to the projects of state and capital, are distinct from them. Religion serves the state, but the state also serves religion.

HOME OF BUDDHIST LIGHT

State-led cultural promotion has helped make Buddhism a resource that can be mobilized for a variety of ends. One example of this is the case of Home of Buddhist Light (*Fo Guang Zhi Jia*), an organization of Dai monks and laity that promotes HIV/AIDS awareness throughout Xishuangbanna. The organization also provides social support for people living with the disease. Home of Buddhist Light began as an informal effort of monks and laity who saw a need for expanded HIV/AIDS education, especially in the Dai language, and who felt that linking AIDS education to a Buddhist message would facilitate its reception by ordinary people. For a number of years Home of Buddhist Light (HBL) was based out of the Central Buddhist Temple, though it recently moved operations to the Mengle Great Temple. Several years after its founding HBL was absorbed into the prefectural Minority and Religious Affairs Bureau, turning what was a religious nongovernmental organization (NGO) into a government program. Although they work out of offices at the temple, paid lay staff members are bureau employees.

HBL's origins are intertwined with the revival of Dai culture and religion after 1978. The suppression of Buddhism in the Mao era produced a dearth of trained religious personnel, and as Dai temples began reopening in the 1980s, many communities hired monks from Laos, Myanmar, and Thailand to staff them. Newly ordained Dai monks also traveled to these countries for Theravada study and training that was lacking in China. Many of those who went abroad in the 1980s and 1990s encountered the ravages of AIDS, particularly in Thailand and Myanmar. In Thailand, some also encountered a grassroots Buddhist response to the disease. In the 1990s Thai monks in Chiang Mai began a program that melded Buddhist teachings with HIV prevention education and care for the afflicted. On returning to Xishuangbanna the Dai monks and several laypeople began brainstorming how they too might organize a Buddhist response to the epidemic.

The Thai organization, known as Sangha Metta, influenced the genesis of HBL in other ways. Several years after it was founded, UNICEF began funding its programs and promoting the Sangha Metta model throughout Buddhist regions of Southeast Asia. In Yunnan, UNICEF was already carrying out AIDS projects including the Greater Mekong Subregion HIV/AIDS Prevention and Care Project. After a series of consultations, UNICEF convinced the Chinese government to invite leaders of the Thai organization to Xishuangbanna to conduct training sessions for Dai monks. Subsequent training sessions have been held in the years since, and Xishuangbanna monks periodically travel to Thai, Lao, and Burmese Theravada Buddhist communities for additional education, and to exchange ideas with other monks. In 2003, monks and laymen at the Central Buddhist Temple formally established HBL. They continue to be part of and receive funding through the UNICEF initiative. Since the late 1990s, over 560 monks in Xishuangbanna have been trained in HIV/AIDS prevention education.[12]

Xishuangbanna has so far been spared the worst of the AIDS epidemic, and the infection rate is still low. Recent reports state that there are over 550 people in the prefecture known to be infected with HIV—relatively a very small number.[13] HBL staff members admit, however, that the actual number of infected individuals is underreported. Yunnan, moreover, is one of the provinces hardest hit by the epidemic. The largest cluster of cases has erupted in Dehong, another Dai Autonomous Prefecture that borders Myanmar (Van Zant 2004). Though Xishuangbanna is several hundred miles from Dehong, officials and others are concerned that a similar disaster might unfold at home. HBL is one of several organized responses to HIV/AIDS in Xishuangbanna.

HBL has implemented a variety of programs. Monks from rural areas receive training at the Central Buddhist Temple, after which they return to their villages where they incorporate HIV/AIDS education into their normal religious duties. At religious fairs and during key Buddhist holidays, monks give sermons on prevention and hand out literature printed in both Chinese and the Dai script. One of the most important conduits for disseminating information is the temple school; senior monks incorporate AIDS awareness lessons into the regular religious curriculum. Because of the large number of

Dai boys who serve as novices, this approach has the potential to reach thousands of impressionable young men who are not expected to remain celibate upon their return to civilian life.

Buddhist principles are central to HBL's message. HBL stresses the applicability of the Five Precepts to life habits that can raise or reduce risk. For instance, the Fifth Precept demands abstention from intoxicants, crucial in a region where injection drug use is the chief means of disease transmission. The Four Noble Truths of Buddhism, which address suffering, its origins, causes, and cessation, also figure prominently in HBL teachings. Participants in HBL workshops are not simply provided with information about HIV and how to combat it. Instead, they are encouraged to reflect on the meaning and ethics of the disease, and the behaviors that prevent or transmit it. HBL also seeks to improve the quality of life of people with the disease. Monks counsel affected individuals as well as their families and neighbors. Through the monks' example, family members and neighbors of AIDS sufferers also see that physical proximity, sharing a meal, and even physical contact with the affected are not dangerous. The monks' attention and care also gives "face" to HIV/AIDS sufferers, who are typically shunned and even attacked if their condition becomes public (Liu 2005). All of these actions demonstrate "loving-kindness" (*metta*), one of the Four Sublime States of Buddhism and a guiding principle of Home of Buddhist Light.

Buddhism as an institution is also important to HBL's existence. As mentioned, the group's offices were located at the Central Buddhist Temple, though they recently were moved to the Theravada Buddhist Cultural Center. Dai language materials are produced using the printing press at the Buddhist Studies Institute. The organization's founders and leaders hold important positions in local government and official bodies; its formal leader and spokesman is Guba Longzhuang Meng. The guba periodically speaks at AIDS workshops held either for monks or rural people. According to HBL staff, at events where the guba speaks, attendance skyrockets and the audience listens in rapt attention.

Despite its nonstate origins, HBL's official linkages are clear. State actions have influenced the group's development in other ways. China's cultivation of trade and diplomatic relationships with the countries of the Greater Mekong Subsystem, particularly Thailand, facilitated the transfer of knowledge from a religious Thai NGO to the monks of Xishuangbanna. Without this favorable political and economic environment, the religious exchanges that generated HBL might never have occurred. Dai activists, both clerical and lay, have skillfully deployed the financial, institutional, and symbolic resources of the state to promote the goal of spreading AIDS awareness among the local population. Their ability to carry out their mission is helped by the

Figure 6.4.   A Home of Buddhist Light staff member leads an AIDS prevention workshop for Dai villagers, while Marx and Engels look on. S. McCarthy photo.

fact that the aims of HBL dovetail with the interests of the Chinese state. Official support and incorporation of this religious organization makes sense insofar as HBL helps the state manage and influence the health and behavior of its citizens; as with minority religious revival in other contexts (Litzinger 2000), HBL enhances the governing capacity of the Chinese state. If it succeeds, HBL may help minimize the catastrophe of AIDS while promoting an ethic of selfless, compassionate public service.

CONCLUSION

In recent decades China has experienced a vibrant and wide-ranging revival of religion and cultural practice. This rediscovery and expansion of a variety of cultural identities and institutions have resulted from a confluence of forces. State retrenchment from social and cultural life has made it possible for Chinese people to reestablish traditions suppressed during the Maoist era. The loss of community, values, and identity as China has exchanged collectivism for ruthless individualism has led many to seek replacements in tradition. The move to a market economy and the need for new sources of revenue has encouraged the development of tourism, an industry whose success frequently depends on the cultivation of religious sites and other manifestations of meaning, mystery, and the exotic. As market imperatives and state retrenchment have accelerated the disintegration of the Maoist social safety net, traditional and especially religious organizations have tried to offer material and spiritual substitutes.

The cultural turn has a political dimension as well, and reflects the continuing role of the state in economic matters. Capitalism with Chinese characteristics has entailed not laissez-faire but the active involvement of party-state officials in economic matters, especially at the local level. Thus the promotion of culture for economic reasons is frequently a state-led strategy, albeit one involving private entrepreneurs and market incentives rather than bureaucratic planning. Politics informs the cultural turn in other ways. The promotion of traditional values and customs is part of a broader strategy of national identity construction (or reconstruction), a strategy based on propagating state-sanctioned norms of civilization and progress. It is also a legitimation strategy, made necessary by the Chinese Communist Party's abdication of socialist ideals and by widespread corruption, both of which have greatly undermined popular trust. State-led or state-sanctioned cultural and religious endeavors are an attempt by the party-state to ground its authority in ostensibly Chinese traditions and values.

Of course, the revival of folk culture and tradition is not wholly controlled or directed by the state, nor is it unproblematic. State support for cultural and religious activities is often a response to developments that have already occurred at the local level. Certain forms of religious practice continue to be deemed threats to state authority and national unity, as exemplified by crackdowns on Islam, Tibetan Buddhism, underground Christianity, and Falun Gong. Practitioners of these are often blamed for fomenting unrest; however, the state also justifies repression by highlighting such movements' deviance from what it claims is authentic Chinese tradition. The cultural dimensions of projects like the "Open Up the West" campaign illustrate state efforts to counter deviant identities and practices with others believed more amenable to party-state control. Not surprisingly, these efforts at cultural governance have a pronounced Han-centric tone.

In light of these developments, the Dai case at first glance appears paradoxical, if not counter to the general trend. In Xishuangbanna, the party-state and its business allies enthusiastically promote Dai Buddhist identity and institutions. The seeming paradox is that state support for Buddhist revival encourages Dai identification with a non-Chinese, transnational imagined community of the Tai, which includes the Thai state and monarch. However, the paradox disappears once Buddhism's contributions to the state-sanctioned goal of economic modernization are recognized. Dai religious tradition is promoted because it serves Chinese modernity. Moreover, as the example of HBL demonstrates, Dai Buddhism can facilitate regime governance by providing conduits for the dissemination of official norms and the management of citizen behavior.

In contemporary Xishuangbanna, Theravada Buddhism increasingly serves government and business agendas concerning development and foreign relations. Though Dai Buddhism has long been blamed for contributing to the underdevelopment of this somewhat remote corner of China, more recently the so-called religious culture industry of Xishuangbanna has come to be seen as fertile ground for the development of new commodities and markets. Buddhist practices and institutions, along with other aspects of Dai culture, are promoted in order to preserve the exoticism of the prefecture, viewed as essential to the health of the tourism industry. The broader religious expansion taking place throughout China contributes to this trend. Chinese people are embracing religion in record numbers, and the promotion of Buddhism to center stage in Xishuangbanna helps draw visitors to the prefecture, regardless of their faith.

The deployment of Dai Buddhism in this fashion raises questions regarding the extent to which Buddhist revival in Xishuangbanna is driven by tourism and by the interests of state and capital. The pecuniary and political goals of the Buddhist-industrial complex notwithstanding, religious and cultural interests are also served by state and business attention to religion. Dai Buddhist laypeople and religious leaders have benefited tremendously from temple expansion; new infrastructure; government and business interest in closer ties with Thai, Lao, and Burmese Tai communities; and broad acceptance of the legitimacy of Buddhism in the public life of Xishuangbanna. Local activists, both lay and clerical alike, are pursuing projects they hope will improve the cultural as well as physical health and vitality of the Dai people. Certainly many products of the cultural revival have been generated not for the Dai but for tourists desiring to glimpse and experience Dai exoticism, or their idea of it. However, the activities of the state and its business allies have also created space for the Dai to regenerate Buddhism, restore its public prominence, and, through institutional innovations like Home of Buddhist Light, modernize aspects of this ancient religious tradition.

NOTES

1. "Taiguo guowang yuzhi jiasha bushituan dao Xishuangbanna Manchunman fosi jushi bushi huodong" (Thai king's royal monastic vestments donation group

holds ceremony at Manchunman Buddhist temple), par. 2, *Xishuangbanna Mengla Da Fosi Wenhuayuan* (Xishuangbanna Mengla Great Temple Cultural Center), 4 December 2008, www.zgncfj.com/Article/news/fojiexinwen/200812/1212.html (accessed 15 December 2008).

2. China Central United Front Work Department, "Dao Shuren," www.zytzb.org.cn/zytzbwz/hkmatai/renwu/200804/t20080430_376038.htm (accessed 15 December 2008).

3. In officially designated minority areas like Xishuangbanna, top government posts must be held by members of the titular minority or minorities. However, the most powerful person is the Communist Party secretary, a position with no ethnic restrictions. In Xishuangbanna and elsewhere, the party secretary has typically been a Han.

4. Author interview with Dai official, Jinghong, March 1997.

5. Author interview with temple abbot, Damenglong, April 1997.

6. There were approximately 110,000 foreign tourists in 2008. By way of contrast, over 6.2 million domestic Chinese tourists visited the prefecture, a figure that includes those from Taiwan, Hong Kong, and Macau. Xishuangbanna Ministry of Commerce, "Xishuangbanna: Dazao dongnanya Dai minzu xungen fangyuan zhi suo" (Xishuangbanna: Constructing a place for the Southeast Asian Tai people's search for roots), 6 May 2009, xsbn.mofcom.gov.cn/aarticle/dxsw/200905/20090506224410.html (accessed 12 July 2009).

7. *Communitas* is Victor Turner's term, cited in Sangren (1987, 189).

8. The complexities of authenticity with regard to tourism in general and Chinese ethnic tourism in particular have been well plumbed (Oakes 1997, 1998; Notar 2006). What I stress here is the way in which participation in religious ritual can entail a relationship to culture and an experience of meaning that are quite different from what is involved in observing the ceremonies and religious artifacts of the exotic other. By way of analogy, consider an American Catholic tourist in Rome, who along with all the other tourists makes the requisite visits to the Sistine Chapel, St. Peter's, and other historical Catholic sites. Come Sunday, that American Catholic may then attend Mass in an Italian Catholic church, maybe even in St. Peter's, not simply as a tourist but as a Catholic. She may even attend despite not really wanting to do so, but because that is what Catholics are required to do. Of course, that American Catholic might feel there is something particularly authentic and meaningful about attending Mass in Rome, compared to, say, attending church in her hometown parish, though doctrinally there is no difference. In this case, the experience of authenticity emerges from the interplay between self and other, one's "own" religious culture and that of Italy and history, and from the ability to inhabit rather than simply observe the culture of the other.

9. "Mannongfeng pianqu xingguang canlan" (Splendid Mannongfeng), *Xishuangbanna Business Initiative Bureau*, www.xsbndjq.cn/ReadNews.Asp?NewsID=50&BigClassID=7 (accessed 27 October 2008).

10. "Xishuangbanna touzi 3.5 yi yuan dazao nanchuan fojiao wenhua zhongxin" (Xishuangbanna invests 350 million yuan to construct the Theravada Buddhism Cultural Center), *Yunnan Xinhua Net*, 4 November 2007, www.yn.xinhua.org/newscenter/2007–11/04/content_11576417.htm (accessed 30 November 2007).

11. "Duanqi chujia bidu—hewei duanqi chujia?" (Short-term monastic life and study—What does the short-term monastic experience entail?), *Zhongguo Nanchuan Fojiao wang* (China Theravada Buddhism net), 5 October 2008, www.zgncfj.com/Article/College/xuebu/200810/1166.html (accessed 11 January 2009).

12. "Monks Teach, Practice Tolerance for HIV-AIDS Victims," *People's Daily Online*, 26 October 2005, english.people.com.cn/200510/26/eng20051026_216985.html (accessed 3 February 2007).

13. "2007 Foguang Zhi Jia gongzuo jihua" (2007 work plan for Home of Buddhist Light], *China Sangha Metta*, 4 April 2007, www.chinasanghametta.org/article/news_view.asp?newsid=573 (accessed 15 May 2007).

REFERENCES

Cohen, Paul T. 2000. "A Buddha Kingdom in the Golden Triangle: Buddhist Revivalism and the Charismatic Monk Khruba Bunchum." *Australian Journal of Anthropology* 11(2): 141–54.

Davis, Sara L. M. 2005. *Song and Silence: Ethnic Revival on China's Southwest Borders*. New York: Columbia University Press.

Dean, Kenneth. 1997. "Ritual and Space: Civil Society or Popular Religion?" In *Civil Society in China*, ed. Timothy Brook and B. Michael Frolic. Armonk, NY: M.E. Sharpe, 172–94.

Duan, Ying. 2001. "Xiandai bianyuan de Manchunman: Xiandai lüyou yu minzu yishi de ge'an yanjiu" (Manchunman on the modern periphery: A case study of contemporary tourism and minority consciousness). Yunnan University Department of Anthropology website, www.channelwest.com/FILES/friends/yndxrlx/xsyd/01_01.htm (accessed 11 July 2009).

Duan, Ying, and Yang Hui. 2001. "Quanli bianyuan de Manchunman: Lüyou zuo wei xiandaixing yu minzu yishi de ge'an yanjiu." In *Lüyou, renleixue yu Zhongguo shehui* (Tourism, anthropology and China), ed. Yang Hui. Kunming: Yunnan University Press, 94–115.

Giersch, C. Patterson. 2006. *Asian Borderlands: The Transformation of Qing China's Yunnan Frontier.* Cambridge, MA: Harvard University Press.

Gladney, Dru. 1994. "Representing Nationality in China: Refiguring Majority/Minority Identities." *Journal of Asian Studies* 53(1): 92–123.

"Guba Longzhuang Wannaxili da zhanglao" (Abbot Guba Longzhang Wannaxili). 2007. *Zhongguo Foxue* (China Buddhist studies), 16 October. www.china2551.org/Article/fjrw/s/200710/1401.html (accessed 5 October 2008).

Hansen, Mette Halskov. 1999. *Lessons in Being Chinese*. Seattle: University of Washington Press.

Hsieh, Shih-chung. 1995. "On the Dynamics of Tai/Dai-Lüe Ethnicity: An Ethnohistorical Analysis." In *Cultural Encounters on China's Ethnic Frontiers*, ed. Stevan Harrell. Seattle: University of Washington Press, 301–28.

Litzinger, Ralph. 2000. *Other Chinas: The Yao and the Politics of National Belonging*. Durham, NC: Duke University Press.

Liu, Qihong. 2005. "'Fo Guang zhi Jia'—rang aisibing huanzhe zouchu yiny-ing" ('Home of Buddhist Light'—Bringing AIDS sufferers out of the shadows). *Fojiao Xinxiwang* (Buddhist Information Net), 5 April. news.fjnet.com/jjdt/jjdtnr/t20050805_12710.htm (accessed 15 December 2006).

McCarthy, Susan K. 2009. *Communist Multiculturalism: Ethnic Revival in Southwest China.* Seattle: University of Washington Press.

McKhann, Charles F. 1995. "The Naxi and the Nationalities Question." In *Cultural Encounters on China's Ethnic Frontiers*, ed. Stevan Harrell. Seattle: University of Washington Press, 39–62.

Notar, Beth E. 2006. "Authenticity Anxiety and Counterfeit Confidence." *Modern China* 32(1): 64–98.

Nyíri, Pal. 2006. *Scenic Spots: Chinese Tourism, the State, and Cultural Authority.* Seattle: University of Washington Press.

Oakes, Tim. 1997. "Ethnic Tourism in Rural Guizhou: Sense of Place and the Commerce of Authenticity." In *Tourism, Ethnicity and the State in Asian and Pacific Societies*, ed. Michel Picard and Robert E. Wood. Honolulu: University of Hawai'i Press, 35–70.

———. 1998. *Tourism and Modernity in China.* London: Routledge.

Sangren, P. Steven. 1987. *History and Magical Power in a Chinese Community.* Palo Alto: Stanford University Press.

Schein, Louisa. 1997. "Gender and Internal Orientalism." *Modern China* 23(1): 69–98.

Swain, Margaret B. 1990 "Commoditizing Ethnicity in Southwest China." *Cultural Survival Quarterly* 14(1): 26–29.

Van Zant, Eric. 2004. "Fatal Attraction." *Asian Development Bank Review* 36 (May–June): 3. www.adb.org (accessed 27 November 2008).

Wang, Tao. 2008. "Daizuyuan de daijia zhulou zai bei 'canshi'" (Dai Garden traditional architecture being 'nibbled away'). *Xishuangbanna Cultural Tourism Information Net*, 26 August. www.xsbncti.gov.cn/newshow.asp?id=321 (accessed 29 November 2008).

Xi, Yunhua. 2006. "Xishuangbanna zongjiao wenhua chanye fazhan: diaocha baogao" (Research report on the development of the Xishuangbanna religious culture industry). *Shandong Culture Industry Net*, 22 April. www.sdci.sdu.edu.cn/detail.php?id=8469 (accessed 24 February 2008).

Xie, Xianbin, and Wan Yinjiang. 2004. "Du Long Zhuang jincheng wei Xishuangbanna guba meng" (Du Long Zhuang promoted to chief guba in Xishuangbanna). *Jinghong City Government Information Net*, 3 February. www.jhs.gov.cn/newshow.aspx?id=249 (accessed 15 January 2009).

Xishuangbanna Prefecture E-government. 2008. "Jingji yunxing qingkuang tongji fenxi di shiqi qi: yanzhe gaige kaifang sanshi nian de zuji" (Circumstances of economic transformation, statistical analysis no. 17: Following the course of thirty years of reform), 10 November. xxgk.yn.gov.cn/canton_model24/newsview.aspx?id=327460 (accessed 5 December 2008).

7

Naxi Religion in the Age of Tourism

Persistence and (Re)creation

Charles F. McKhann

Hailed as a solution to lagging economic growth, ethnic tourism has over the last two decades become a major industry in southwest China.[1] In the political climate of the Maoist period (1949–1976), when class tensions were highlighted, ethnic differences and the marked expression of ethnic identity were downplayed or even suppressed. Not so in recent years. In the reform era (1980–present), ethnic culture has become increasingly valued as a commodity, and peoples once geographically and culturally marginalized are learning to present their culture to outsiders (mainly other Chinese) in a variety of ways. While the state and the consuming public largely shape the new forms of minority cultural expression, the producers of culture also help to condition consumer taste, and are themselves transformed as they participate in the creation of new forms and come to internalize those forms as authentic. This chapter considers one such arena of cultural production: *dongba* religion among the Naxi of northwest Yunnan Province.

Like many other Chinese nationalities, the Naxi (pop. 300,000) hold a variety of religious beliefs. Different strains of Buddhism have entered the region through Tibet, lowland China, and the former Nanzhao kingdom (ca. 720–902, near present-day Dali). The region supports several Tibetan Buddhist monasteries (belonging to both Karmapa and Gelugpa sects), and today a good number of the resident monks and even two *trulkus* (incarnate *lamas)* are Naxi.[2] Daoist and Confucian beliefs concerning nature, the body, health, ancestors, filiality, and funerary rites are also widespread, owing to a history of Han immigration dating to the Ming dynasty (1368–1644). And in the early twentieth century, Dutch, German, and English Protestant missionaries also had some success in the region. These originally alien beliefs and practices have been adopted to varying degrees by many Naxi, with social class, geographical location, and personal inclination often serving as contributing factors.

Aside from these outside traditions, the Naxi have two main kinds of indigenous religious specialists: *sainiis* and *dongbas*.[3] Sainiis (shamans) are persons considered to have the ability—stemming from birth or some catastrophic life event, such as near-death illness—to travel to alternate worlds and to divine processes in them. As with spirit mediums and soul-callers in the Han tradition, they have been denounced by the Communist government as purveyors of wasteful and potentially harmful "superstitious activities" (*mixin huodong*), and accordingly have been pushed deep underground over the last fifty years. Dongbas have been more tolerated by the government, in part, as I mean to show, because they better fit the government's idea of orthodox religious specialists. Their art is learned through years of study, inscribed in texts, and displayed in relatively standardized ritual performances, involving recognized expressive arts, including chanting, dancing, and music. It is these Naxi "priests" who will chiefly concern us here, although in the past the two kinds of specialists often worked together.[4]

In their practices and organization, dongbas are closer to the lesser known ritual specialists in some neighboring Tibeto-Burman groups—for example, Premi (Pumi) "*anji*," Nuosu (Yi) "*bimo*," and Jingpo (Kachin) "*dumsa*"—than they are to the more familiar Tibetan lamas or to Chinese (Han) Buddhist monks and Daoist priests.[5] Like these others, the dongba tradition is diffused. There is no organized dongba "church" and no hierarchy of positions; nor do dongbas build or operate from any sorts of temples or monasteries. They are village-based, part-time specialists—all male—who also farm, herd, run pack trains, and do most of the other kinds of work associated with Naxi men in the mountain villages. They typically learn their art by apprenticing with their father or a paternal uncle, so that there are whole lineages of dongbas, as well as dongbas who are attached to non-dongba lineages as customary providers.

Before the founding of the Communist state in 1949, dongbas were quite common throughout the Naxi countryside. Every village typically had one or two, and in areas where villages were closely spaced, there could be a dozen or more within a couple hours' walk. During the Maoist period this system largely collapsed. Dongbas were pressured to reduce in scope or eliminate altogether many of their rituals, and the training of new dongbas was discouraged. The late 1980s represented a low point in terms of numbers of dongbas and ritual performances. Although political restrictions began to ease off in the late 1970s and early 1980s, there was a lag period: old dongbas were dying off faster than young ones were being trained. Likewise, because of the still-uncertain political climate, formerly banned practices were slow to revive.

In the 1990s, the situation began to shift. Traditional dongba practices returned in some (mainly remote) areas, and a few young men there began to study the arts. At the same time, a new kind of interest in dongba religion was being generated in the towns and in Naxi academic circles. The starting point for the latter movement had more to do with ideas of preserving and developing Naxi cultural heritage than with issues of belief or practice, and in this respect it dovetailed nicely with the growth of (secular) tourism. Before turning to these transformations, however, let me review some of the features of dongba religion as it was practiced traditionally, and is now being "naturally" revived in some of the remote rural areas (mainly to the north and west of Lijiang Town (a.k.a. Dayanzhen), see figure 6.1, p. 161).

Dongbas traditionally performed divinations and a variety of rituals, either in home settings for individuals or families (weddings, funerals, naming ceremonies, house raisings, curing rites, rites to bring wealth and prosperity, etc.), or in public spaces for lineages or entire village populations (collective sacrifices to heaven, to village tutelary deities, to ward off plagues, etc.). They were paid for their services with gifts of food, clothing, and usually some cash. Often they worked together in small groups, with the more senior among them taking the leading roles, and/or in conjunction with sainii.

The use of an arcane pictographic script for recording their ritual chants is a distinctive feature of the dongba tradition. The pictographic manuscripts—written on long, narrow sheets of handmade paper, not unlike Tibetan books, but a little smaller and sewn along the left-hand edge—are not "texts" per se, for they are grammatically incomplete and therefore "unreadable" in the ordinary sense of the word. Rather, they represent a sophisticated mnemonic prompt for helping the dongba to recall long chants that are in the first place learned by ear and memorized.[6] This makes for a fairly long period of apprenticeship—about ten years. Along with variation in the type and form of the rituals themselves, there is considerable local variation in the dongba texts, reflecting both the isolating topography of the region (high mountains and deep valleys) and the tradition of apprenticing with a master and copying his texts. Nonetheless, there is sufficient coherence across the region that most scholars are comfortable speaking of a single "dongba religion" that is distinct from some similar, neighboring traditions (see above).[7]

Dongba rituals may last anywhere from a few hours (for naming a newborn infant, for example) to several days (in the case of funerals and some lineage- or village-wide rituals). Almost always there is some kind of altar established where offerings are made to ancestors or gods, or to placate demons, and in the longer rites there may be several of these, in different places, at different times, and associated with different subceremonies. The altars are sometimes elaborate and may require hours of preparation (see figure 7.1 later in this chapter). Offerings frequently include live sacrifices of chickens, goats, pigs, and cattle, and are accompanied by chanting from the ritual texts, dancing, and music. Persons on whose behalf the rituals are performed generally also play active roles in the proceedings. Some rituals are private, involving only immediate family members, for example, but in many cases dozens or even hundreds of guests attend and are fed, sometimes several times. Expenses for larger private rituals can be enormous—several years of household income. Rituals performed for the village as a whole are generally cheaper—each participating household contributing to the feast, or sometimes preparing and eating their own food separately.

THE CLASSIFICATION OF DONGBA RELIGION

Chinese ethnologists, following guidelines set by the Chinese Communist Party that have their source in both Marxist and Confucian ideologies, have tended to classify the religions of China's nationalities according to a linear evolutionary scale. Those traditions that are characterized by (1) a fairly high degree of central organization—that is, have ranks of professional, full-time practitioners and dedicated temples, monasteries, churches, and the like—and (2) have codified their beliefs in scriptures are classified as "religions" (*zongjiao*). These include Buddhism (Fojiao), Tibetan Buddhism (Zangchuan Fojiao), Daoism (Daojiao), Confucianism (Rujiao), Islam (Yisilanjiao), Catholicism (Tianzhujiao), and others. At the other end of the spectrum are the practices and beliefs of part-time specialists and their clients, who have no temples or sacred texts. These "lesser" practices get coded in several ways. If they occur among Han populations, they may be labeled as "heterodox" (*yiduan*) or "superstitious" (*mixin*). Such practices were disparaged by Confucian elites in former times, and are disparaged by Communist elites today. Falun Gong—the health cult that has been so strongly attacked by the Chinese government in recent years—has written texts (which some might even call "sacred"), but otherwise is a pretty good example of this.

In the case of China's minority nationality religions, if they lack full-time, ranked specialists, temples, texts and the like, they are generally labeled as "primitive religions" (*yuanshi zongjiao*). The fact that they possess ritual texts—even if they are written in a "primitive" script—and that there is so much clear borrowing from the Tibetan Bön and Buddhist traditions puts Naxi dongba religion somewhere in the middle. This kind of classifying is quite evident in the "nationalities brief histories" (*minzu jian shi*) and "nationality county survey" (*minzu xian gaikuang*) series.[8] More advanced nationalities will have whole sections devoted to their "religious beliefs" (*zongjiao xinyang*), while the religions of backward minorities are buried in sections labeled "customs" (*xisu, fengsu xiguan*, or some variant thereof), where the word "religion" (*zongjiao*) may never appear.[9]

The hierarchy of religions is sometimes overt and sometimes implied. In a small book concerning a Yi nationality autonomous county we learn that "before Liberation the Yi nationality practiced polytheism" (*Yizu zai jiefang qian shengxing duoshen congbai* [*ESYZZZXGK* 1986, 20]), where the phrase "*duoshen congbai*" (lit. many gods worship) implies a stage in the evolution of religious thought, most famously outlined by Sir Edward Tylor (1970). More overt hierarchizing can be found in the recent "county gazetteer" (*xian zhi*) series. The 1999 Weixi County (Yunnan) gazetteer, for example, lists the following sections in its chapter on "Religions": The Primitive Religion of the Lisu Nationality, The Primitive Religions of Other Nationalities, Tibetan Buddhism, Daoism, Catholicism, and Protestantism (*WXLSZZZXZ* 1999, 188–98). In the gazetteer from neighboring Deqin County the section on "Religious Beliefs" includes only Tibetan Buddhism, Islam, and Catholicism. A host of "folk" religious beliefs belonging to the several nationalities that reside in the county are listed in the following chapter on "Customs and Habits" (*fengsu xiguan; DQXZ* 1997, 321–38).

The Naxi and Naxi religion are intermediary cases when viewed in terms of this hierarchy. The Naxi have one of the highest levels of education of all the minority nationalities; they produced a large number of scholar-officials during the imperial era, and continue to produce many advanced modern degree holders today. In the Ming (1368–1644) and early Qing (1644–1911) dynasties their native chiefs (*tusi*) were highly literate and well cultivated in the Chinese and Tibetan arts, and gentlemen from Republican-era (1911–1949) Lijiang prided themselves in their appreciation of the finer things Chinese—such as the Taoist-inspired *dongjing* music that Helen Rees (2000) has written about.

In the late Qing dynasty and early decades of the twentieth century, Naxi elites under the influence of assimilationist policy from the Chinese center turned away from their native dongba religion. Dongbas were ridiculed and their pictographic writing demeaned as "the ugly faces of oxen and horses" *(niu tou ma mian;* Yang 2003, 22). It is ironic then that sixty years later, in the 1980s and 1990s, it was the grandsons and granddaughters of these same Naxi intelligentsia who came to promote dongba religion as an essential (and glorious) sign of Naxi culture and identity.

Three important changes associated with the reform era (1978–present) have led to a revitalization of dongba religion—a liberalization of government policy toward religion, a positive shift in the value of minority nationality identity and culture, and the rapid development of tourism in the Lijiang area. Due to this particular combination of factors, the revitalization of dongba religion and what I like to think of as "dongba consciousness"[10] has proceeded along two, interrelated lines: the revival of traditional practices in remote villages, and the valorization of dongbas as carriers of Naxi culture in urban, national, and international discourses. If the former, to borrow Clifford Geertz's well-worn phrase, is "a story [the Naxi] tell themselves about themselves," the latter is one they are now telling everyone else.

The main expressions of this new consciousness include various kinds of staged performances, and most obviously a much-expanded use of the dongba script. Traditionally, the script was employed only by dongbas and only for recording their chants. In the last three decades it has come to signify Naxi culture more broadly, and appears in works of fine art, adorning handicrafts for sale in the tourist trade, and on signs in and around the town of Lijiang, the cultural center of Naxi modernity. The two stories are not unrelated, however. The rise of dongba stock in the town (and globally) has influenced rural markets. Some dongbas have migrated to urban areas to seek their fortunes in tourist-related industries and, conversely, the tacit approval granted to some religious practices by the post-Maoist state has fed the revival of traditional religions in some rural areas. At this point, the two stories are thoroughly intertwined, as can be seen, for example, in the rise of a new kind of dongba—one trained in the urban context (research institute, museum, or academy), far removed from the rhythms and contours of village social life that underlie the traditional religious practices.

THE RISE OF TOURISM IN LIJIANG

At the beginning of the reform era, Lijiang was a sleepy rural county seat with a population of about fifty thousand. There were two hotels—the government-run Number One and Number Two Guest Houses—and during the 1983 Spring Festival when I first visited Lijiang with my friend Wang Donghai both were virtually empty. Such an occurrence would be unimaginable today. During China's three major holidays—Spring Festival, May Day, and National Day—the town's many hotels fill to capacity, often requiring overflow tourists to seek lodging in neighboring towns and private residences.

Tourism on any notable scale began in the mid-1980s as a small, foreign, backpacker phenomenon. Lijiang and Dali were opened to foreign tourism in 1985, and word spread quickly that Lijiang was populated by friendly and colorful ethnics, that it had a charming Old Town that preserved traditional architectural styles that were fast disappearing in other places, and that it was situated amid picturesque mountains and gorges, ideal for trekking and a possible "backdoor" to Tibet, which had not yet been "opened" to tourism. Since that time, tourism in Lijiang has developed at a spectacular rate into a multimillion dollar industry, which processes upward of two million tourists a year. Foreign backpackers have been utterly eclipsed by Chinese from Kunming, Shanghai, Beijing, and other big cities, flush with new wealth and eager to explore the Wild West. The great majority come on organized package tours lasting three to four days, with mornings spent traveling to nearby scenic spots on comfortable air-conditioned buses, and afternoons and evenings wandering and shopping in the Old Town, sampling local delicacies at the many new restaurants, and attending shows and concerts at popular nightspots.[11] With a ban on logging since the late 1990s, tourism is being promoted as Yunnan's new "green industry," and departments of tourism development and economics have sprung up in provincial universities and local colleges. The provincial government has had a large hand in promoting tourism, and television audiences throughout the country are familiar with Lijiang's charms due to nationally broadcast television specials.

The impact of tourism on Lijiang has been enormous. It provides service sector jobs for thousands (likely *tens* of thousands) of locals, especially young people, who have flocked to the town from across the region, leaving some villages short on agricultural labor, so that grain production in particular has declined. At the same time, the increased demand for meat and produce at area restaurants has been a boon to farmers in nearby villages, and Lijiang's bustling markets offer foods that in quantity, quality, and variety far outstrip those of neighboring county seats. Lijiang's star has also risen politically. It is regarded as one of the province's key areas, and for much of the late 1980s and early 1990s the provincial governor, an appointed position, was a Naxi— He Zhiqiang—from Lijiang.

The social and cultural impacts of tourism include a much more cosmopolitan population. Internet access is ubiquitous, and the cultural horizons of the area's young people far exceed those of their grandparents' generation. At the same time, the maintenance of a robust local culture is key to Lijiang's continued success as a destination tourist town. People are keenly aware of this fact, with the result that many traditional cultural forms—music, dance, dress, architecture, handicrafts, and cuisine—are being revived and transformed to meet current needs.

While the rise of tourism has spurred the process on greatly, the kind of cultural revival the Naxi are experiencing is not unique. With a population that is 92 percent Han, China's leaders are very sensitive about international attention to policies directed toward the country's fifty-five officially recognized minority nationalities.[12] In order to deflect accusations of "Great

Han Chauvinism" (*Da Han Zhuyi*) since the end of the Cultural Revolution (when Han chauvinism certainly *was* imbedded in the period's radical social policies), the government has made a point of promoting ethnic equality and advertising the contributions of minority nationalities to China's national culture. As Louisa Schein (2000) and others have shown, the volume in state-run media of images of minority people—prosperous and content—far exceeds what their actual numbers would suggest. Lijiang's tourism boom has its roots in government advertising. Ordinary citizens learned a great deal about the country's minority cultures from watching their televisions in the 1980s and 1990s. As one of the Naxi's most distinctive institutions, and one that has received a lot of scholarly attention dating back nearly a century, dongba religion features prominently in Lijiang's current cultural imaginings.

VILLAGE REVIVAL

The "natural practice" of dongba religion—that is, as performed unself-consciously, as a matter of habit in the small village context—has declined radically since 1949. Most scholars who study dongba religion identify only a few remote areas of the Naxi homeland where it persists. These include primarily Sanba Township in Xianggelila (Shangri-la, formerly Zhongdian) County, Eya Township in Muli County, and Ludian and Tacheng town-ships in Lijiang County. In these areas, although the rate of recruitment may ultimately be too low to sustain the tradition, there are now a number of young dongbas (but probably no more than sixty to seventy in all) who have started training and practicing. Elsewhere in the Naxi homeland, older dongbas are not being replaced by younger trainees, and the practices are dying or dead.

Eagleback Village[13] is one of the few places where traditional dongba re-ligion continues to flourish. This is mainly due to its remote location—two days' walk over steep terrain from the nearest jeep road, but not without some modern amenities.[14] A hydroelectric generator—carried in by a score of men and reassembled on-site—provides electricity to all of the 120 or so households in the village, powering low-watt electric lights, a public address system, home stereos (some with quite impressive outdoor loudspeakers!), and in the last few years a couple of dozen rooftop television dishes. The most recent additions include a satellite telephone at the township government building and personal cell phones.

In and about Eagleback, there were (in 2006) about half a dozen senior dongbas (age fifty-five or older) and a dozen younger trainees. I visited the village twice in 1996, 2006, and 2009, for a total of nine weeks, and on virtually every day there was some kind of dongba-led ritual, and sometimes two or three. I personally attended rituals associated with the construction or occupation of new houses, weddings, funerals, the naming of newborn infants, and the protection of household members. I also learned about the regular performance of personal healing rituals, and community rituals for the abatement of infectious diseases affecting livestock (a chicken epidemic), for the serpent-like mountain deities (Shu Ggv), and for the village tutelary deities. The only major ritual that has not been revived in some form is the Sacrifice to Heaven (Mee Biuq; see figure 7.2 later in the chapter).[15]

The revival of dongba practice in Eagleback and similar locales is almost wholly a grassroots movement.[16] Township (*xiang*) level officials—a mix of Han, Tibetan (Premi), and Naxi ethnicities—do not at this time participate much in the everyday social activities of the villagers, although they played a stronger role during the Maoist period when they were held more responsible for implementing government policies.[17] Village-level officials, on the other hand, are all native Naxi and deeply involved in everyday affairs, but tend to keep their distance from dongba activities. The stigma attached to religious rituals persists, and officials at all levels remain leery of too close an association. At the same time, many life cycle events—naming ceremonies, house raisings, weddings, and funerals—require the presence of a dongba, and in these contexts village officials are no different than anyone else. They will invite dongbas to perform in their homes, and attend events in their neighbors' homes where dongbas are working.[18]

By all visible indicators, traditional dongba practices have rebounded quite well in Eagleback. The dongbas are busy with work and command obvious respect in the community. The lure of salaried work away from the village is a new wrinkle. Two government-funded work-units in Lijiang—the Dongba Culture Research Academy and the Dongba Culture Museum (along with several private enterprises, including the Dongba Palace and the Dongba School)—have a need for experienced dongbas to live and work on the premises. The salaries they offer are attractive—very high by Eagleback standards, in fact—and there are other opportunities to make money in town through private engagement with the tourism economy (copying and selling pictographic manuscripts or paintings, for example), so that the draw is quite strong. One senior dongba from near Eagleback now teaches at the Dongba School, and all of the other organizations mentioned have at least one or two resident dongbas from similar remote villages where the natural religion is still quite strong. The kinds of work they do and the effect that urban life has on their outlook are subjects I explore below.

CREATING DONGBA CONSCIOUSNESS:
THE DONGBA CULTURE RESEARCH ACADEMY

The first dongbas to come to Lijiang to work in the reform era came at the behest of the Dongba Culture Research Academy.[19] The Dongba Academy was established in 1979 by a group of Naxi historians and ethnologists—including Fang Guoyu, He Zhiwu, and Guo Dalie—under the leadership of He Wanbao, a Communist Party official, who was educated at the prestigious Southwest United University (Xinan Lianhe Daxue) during the War of Resistance Against Japan (WWII), and one of the first Naxi to join the Communist Party. Like many other officials, He Wanbao's status fluctuated wildly during the Maoist period. After riding high in the 1950s, he was "struggled" against and "sent down" during the Cultural Revolution (1966–1976), and then rehabilitated in the late 1970s as a senior Naxi representative at the Yunnan Province Nation-alities Commission (Yunnan Minzu Weiyuanhui), and as director of the new Dongba Academy. Overseen by the Lijiang County government and the Yunnan Academy of Social Sciences (YASS), the Dongba Academy was established to conduct research and publish on subjects relating to "dongba culture."

The concept of "dongba culture" (dongba *wenhua*) was coined and pro-moted by He Wanbao and his colleagues in the late 1970s as a means to two ends: to deflect potential criticism away from scholars and work-units (*dan-wei*) whose main object of study was dongba *religion* (dongba *zongjiao*), and to legitimate a series of subdisciplines, including dongba literature (*wenxue*), dongba art (*yishu*), and dongba dance (*wudao*). Since then the concept has ex-panded to encompass a broad range of things Naxi, but especially things that incorporate dongba pictographs, whether or not they contain any religious content. For example, one can buy T-shirts produced for the tourist market in Lijiang with the brand label "Dongba Culture" stitched inside the collar.

The Dongba Culture Research Academy is the premier institution associ-ated with the study of Naxi religion. Besides the studied use of the term "cul-ture" in its name, the Dongba Academy has fended off political criticism by distinguishing the dongba textual tradition from actual practice, and focusing on the former as a genre of sacred classics (*jingshu*), inscribed with traditional Naxi wisdom. The strong association in the dominant Chinese (Han) cul-ture between writing (*wenzi*) and culture (*wenhua*; lit. to transform through writing) facilitates this distinction. For its first two decades, the academy's dozen-and-a-half members, including at least three or four senior dongbas at any given time, worked primarily on researching and translating into Chinese the corpus of dongba classics—indeed, it was they who largely established it as a "corpus"—a project that concluded in 2001 with the publication of a magnificent hundred-volume set.

The academy's emphasis on texts and translation obscures the messiness of everyday reality; namely, that people in Eagleback and other places believe the stuff that is in the texts, and act on those beliefs in a variety of ways, some of which at various times have been officially glossed as "superstitious activities" (*mixin huodong*) or even considered "illegal" (*fanfa*). The academy's interest in dongba *performance* has been expressed in village-level field research and publication by some of its members, but mainly through the staging on the academy grounds of some of the major rituals, including the Sacrifice to Heaven, the Propitiation of the Wind Spirits, the Funerary Rites for a Dongba, and the Sacrifice to Mountain Deities. The production of these rituals has been costly and elaborate, and although the main participants are the academy dongbas, researchers, and their families, close attention is paid to reproducing ritual objects and procedures as authentically as possible. In accordance with village tradition, each performance is overseen by a lead dongba, with others assisting. Because the dongbas come from different places around the Naxi homeland, their versions of individual rituals differ and academy researchers recognize that there is no one "right way" to perform them. Still, they confer among themselves to determine which of the dongbas seems to know a ritual best, and on that basis invite him to take the lead.[20]

The Dongba Academy's mission is strongly "salvage" oriented. Their main purpose in studying the dongba manuscripts is to produce a good series of translations with interpretations while there are still enough knowledgeable dongbas alive to do it. Likewise, the goal of the staged performances is to create a visual record. Performances are photographed and videotaped, and the materials archived. Interested natives or tourists who stumble onto the performances are generally allowed to watch from the sidelines, but kept back so that they do not interfere. The camera operators generally try to avoid capturing spectators in their images, which are widely reproduced in books and other visual media. As some of these rituals are revived in their natural settings, the perceived need to preserve them through artificial enactments may diminish, but this remains unclear.

With the rise of tourism in Lijiang, and of capitalism and the private sector in China more generally, the Dongba Academy (like other academic institutions) has felt increasing pressure to turn a profit. Opinions within the academy differ as to the appropriateness of a scholarly work-unit participating directly in the tourist economy, but it is a trend in fact: the academy bookstore has expanded to include arts and crafts, they rent out part of their compound for a private Dongba School (about which more below), and some academy dongbas and researchers now have sideline businesses in calligraphy and painting that earn them considerably more than their academy salaries.

In recent years, the Dongba Academy has increasingly marketed its expertise for profit. This trend began in the mid-1990s with the staging of dongba rituals at several of the "nationality village" (*minzu cun*) theme parks that cropped up around the country at that time, and has expanded since then, including the following curious incident.[21] On 4 February 1996, a major earthquake hit the Lijiang region, killing more than three hundred people and toppling buildings over a wide area. The epicenter was quickly determined to be almost directly below the region's most prominent land-form, 19,000 foot Jade Dragon Mountain, home to the god Saddo, tutelary deity of the Lijiang basin. Within days, rumors spread to the effect that Saddo had caused the earthquake as punishment to the Naxi for promoting tourism on the mountain. Particularly implicated were employees of the Jade Dragon Mountain Tourism Development Corporation, a joint venture of city and county governments, which had built a chairlift up to one of the lower meadows, and was just in the process of installing the towers for a massive gondola system to access the broad glacier high on the mountain's eastern shoulder.[22]

To deflect the rumors, in June the Tourism Development Corporation contracted the Dongba Academy to perform the Sacrifice to the Mountain Spirits (Shu Ggv) on their behalf. The structure of that performance illustrates the ongoing evolution of dongba rituals under the influence of tourism and globalization. Performed "naturally" in only a few places today, the Mountain Spirit Sacrifice was an annual rite that involved all the members of a village, at a nearby water source—typically a river or spring—where serpent-tailed mountain spirits (*shu*) are thought to dwell.

The location, timing, and participants in the 1996 Jade Dragon performance of Shu Ggv distinguished it both from these traditional performances, and from those that have in recent years been staged for broader audiences (to be discussed in detail below). These differences can be roughly summed up in table form, shown in table 7.1. At the Development Corporation's request, the 1996 ritual was held on the flank of Jade Dragon Mountain, in the piney woods, just near the base of the first gondola tower to be erected (see figure 7.1). In this respect, it also served as a kind of "groundbreaking" ceremony

Table 7.1. Dongba Performance Types

Performance Type	Traditional	1996 Jade Dragon	Fully Staged
Participants	entire village	corporate group	disconnected audience
Location	natural water source	pine forest	variable, often on a stage proper
Timing	annual (in spring)	crisis	random (as scheduled)

Figure 7.1. He Kaiqiang performing Sacrifice to the Mountain Spirits at Jade Dragon Mountain, Yunnan, 1996. Chas. McKhann photo.

for the new gondola, which some regarded as an act of pure hubris. This interpretation was stimulated by the astonishing occurrence of a significant aftershock right in the middle of the performance. Some brushed it off as a coincidence, but when it became known back in town it further fueled the rumors of Saddo's ire over the rise of tourism on the mountain.

BROADCAST DONGBA: REACHING THE GLOBAL AUDIENCE

Four years before the earthquake, my wife, Tricia, and I were married by one of the academy dongbas. The wedding too was notable from the standpoint of participants, location, staging, and audience. I had known He Jigui for six years. We worked together closely on my doctoral dissertation and he was my main mentor in Naxi religious studies. A few years earlier he had casually mentioned that when I was ready to marry, he wanted to perform a traditional Naxi wedding ceremony. I was enthusiastic about the idea, both because such ceremonies are virtually never seen in the Lijiang basin these days—even Naxi scholars who specialize in dongba religion don't hire dongbas for their or their children's weddings anymore[23]—and because He Jigui and I were close friends; it would be a very personal thing between us.

At least, that was how it started . . .

In June 1992, Tricia and I were officially wed in Washington State, which we followed with a "honeymoon" to Lijiang, accompanied by my sister. About halfway through our three-week visit, He Jigui reminded me again of our plan. I was game, but as a member of the Dongba Academy he needed to consult the higher ups, and the next day, the director of the academy took me aside. Would we really like to do this thing? If so, he could make the arrangements. A traditional Naxi log house with the requisite hearth and seating platform had been moved to the academy property, so location would not be a problem. He could also enlist academy researchers, friends, and family members, who could stand in for the various "roles" one would typically find at a traditional wedding—a senior bride's side man to lead the wedding party, a counterpart from the groom's household, surrogate parents before whom to kowtow at appropriate moments, a bride's retinue to bear the dowry (chests, blankets, clothes, and cooking utensils—all borrowed from friends), and of course, a dongba—He Jigui. Even my sister got a role—groom's sister: she was a natural.

I assumed it would be a small affair—perhaps He Jigui knew differently— but Director Zhou saw immediately that the wedding would make good propaganda for the Dongba Academy—a way to highlight their work salvaging traditional Naxi religion.[24] So my sister, Tricia, and I found a goat to sacrifice, and Director Zhou got all the other people and stuff together . . . and then he invited newspaper reporters and a television crew.

On the big day, Tricia and I were dressed (with considerable attention) in traditional Naxi clothes, and led through the paces: bridal procession, call and response at the groom's house, the ceremony for the house god (Seel Kv), dabs of yak butter on our foreheads, kowtows before "the elders," and a feast of overcooked goat. That night and for two following nights, we got to experience it all over again—on television. Director Zhou had meant to promote the Dongba Institute before other Naxi cultural institutions in town, but by the time the county television station edited the piece, it was about foreigners coming to Lijiang and falling in love—with each other incidentally, but mainly with Naxi culture.

And that wasn't the end of it. When I arrived back at Whitman College in September, my colleague in the Chinese language program called out to me across the quad: "Hey, Chas! I saw your wedding on TV. I made a copy of it for you off of global satellite." It turned out that the original Lijiang piece had been redacted twice since we had seen it—once for Yunnan Province television, and again for Chinese national television—CCTV 1. At each step, predictably, the length of the piece had been shortened, and the message modified to fit the audience and the broadcaster's intent. What began as a personal thing between He Jigui and me was now a national thing concerning foreign guests, minority nationalities, and the government's implied support of both.

TRAINING AT THE DONGBA ACADEMY

As part of its efforts to preserve dongba religion, one of the academy's projects has been to train young dongbas. Because the researchers rely daily on the dongbas' expertise to interpret rituals and texts, at least a couple of dongbas-in-residence are needed at all times. When the original group began to die off in the 1990s, academy leaders decided to bring in a few young trainees for intensive study. Most of those selected were kin of the older dongbas— patrilateral grandsons or grandnephews—who, it was hoped, would be more devoted to learning and could help care for their senior kinsmen.

The results from this project have been mixed. The trainees have learned a great deal, but the social context has not been altogether conducive. On the one hand, the academy compound and its scholarly productions are a poor substitute for a natural social environment in which to train and perform—that is, by invitation from fellow villagers. The trainees learn the technical aspects of the rituals, but not the nuances of the genuine human interactions they entail.

The temptations of life in a tourist town have also been a problem for single, young dongbas with money in their pockets. The ready availability of late night party spots with gambling, prostitutes, and alcohol has seriously undermined the academy's goal. More than one young trainee has been let go because he was unable to maintain a working balance. Some of the senior dongbas have also developed alcohol problems, due in part to feelings of dislocation in the fast-paced cosmopolitan town that Lijiang has become.

JET-SET DONGBAS

Minority nationalities (*shaoshu minzu*) were hot in the Chinese cultural scene of the 1990s. *Minzu* chic was expressed in clothing styles, popular art, television song and dance spectaculars, a bloom of ethnic restaurants, and by nationality theme parks (*minzu cun*) in big cities like Kunming, Beijing, Shenzhen, and even Miami. Staff members at the Dongba Academy were instrumental in arranging dongba performances at a number of the theme parks and at various minority festivals, and most of the first-generation dongbas to work at the academy got to make trips to these places. In 1998, He Jigui was invited to the University of Zürich to perform in connection with an exhibit of dongba texts and artifacts at the Völkerkundemuseum.[25]

He Jigui and the other first-generation dongbas at the Dongba Academy are all dead now. Several younger ones have come and gone, and there are now two younger and one middle-aged dongbas-in-residence. One of these, He Xiudong, came to my hometown of Walla Walla, Washinton, in 2003, as part of a semester-long program in Naxi studies.[26] He Xiudong began his training at a young age with lineage elders in rural western Lijiang County, and joined the Dongba Academy in 2002 when he was just twenty-two. We invited him to Whitman College to perform an abbreviated version of the Sacrifice to Mountain Spirits (see above), which is one of the Dongba Academy's favorite choices for "outsider" performances because of its strong environmental/ecological themes, which academy members regard as relatively universal and accessible to non-Naxi audiences.[27]

After two weeks of student-assisted preparation, the ritual was held in a small glen on the college campus—a spot made suitable by the natural flow of spring water and surrounding mature trees. The abbreviated rite lasted three hours: the gods were invited, a chicken was sacrificed and the demons propitiated with its blood, the mountain spirits were given various offerings, and a hundred students were purified with water and juniper smoke, and received the gods' blessing. Our visiting Naxi scholars and some local assistants donned traditional Naxi garments that I had collected over the years, and He Xiudong pronounced the event a big success. Even the college president was good humored about the unadvertised chicken sacrifice.

The next U.S. trip was in October 2004, when another young academy dongba, Yang Yuhua, came to New York and together we did an hour-long lecture-display at the American Museum of Natural History. I call our performance a "lecture-display" because although Yang set up altars, and danced and chanted briefly, despite my introduction there was little context in which to place the artifacts or his actions. We were confined to an auditorium setting where there was no audience participation, and a large part of Yang's "performance" was actually a demonstration of pictographic writing using an overhead projector. He explained to the audience that it would be inappropriate to call the gods to such a place, and he later complained that the experience felt quite strange: lecture, teach-in, demonstration, exhibition? Whatever it was, it was nothing like a proper sacrifice to the *shu* spirits.

The sense of disjuncture was perhaps even greater for He Xiudong when he went to Washington, D.C., to participate in the "Mekong River: Connecting Cultures" portion of the 2007 Smithsonian Folklife Festival. The festival runs for a week and a half, around the Fourth of July. Participants set up performance and demonstration spaces under large tents on the Washington Mall, which are clustered around several small stages and one large one. Opening day began in the big tent, with speeches by congressmen, Smithsonian leaders, and representatives from the embassies of the participating countries—China, Vietnam, Cambodia, Laos, and Thailand. Each country's troupe put on a short performance, culminating in an Olympic-style opening parade.

He Xiudong shared a tent with three other cultural performers from Yunnan Province—a candy maker, a paper cutter, and another dongba, He Guoyao, who was demonstrating pictographic writing. He Xiudong had performances twice a day, for half an hour each. The rest of the time, for ten days, he was expected to stand by his display of ritual paraphernalia—a kind of makeshift altar—and talk with interested visitors about dongba religion with the help of an interpreter. Despite the organizers' best intentions, it was not a pleasant experience. He speaks no English and very little Chinese, and it was predictably hot and humid, making his heavy garments of wool and silk brocade exceedingly uncomfortable. His main complaint, however, was that he had nothing to do. Except for the half-hour performances—which he deemed too brief to convey much meaning—he had little to *show* people, other than himself and his ritual gear.

One of He Xiudong's daily performances was a dance with He Guoyao; the other a much-abbreviated version of the Sacrifice to Mountain Spirits (Shu Ggv). I served as his "presenter" for the first two days—a job which involved introducing He Xiudong and his "acts," interpreting with his audiences, drawing in passersby, and answering questions. He was not happy with the ritual set up in the tent, but at least there was a big tree nearby which he used as one of the poles for his ritual stage (see figure 7.2). Like Yang Yuhua in New York, he complained that the context was wrong and the performances too truncated. The gods were unlikely to come to such a place, under those conditions, and it was disrespectful and dangerous to summon them.[28]

DONGBA ARTS AND CRAFTS

At the same time that the Dongba Academy began promoting the study of dongba literary culture (early 1980s), a small group of young Naxi painters began to experiment with incorporating dongba pictographs into their drawings and paintings. They called their group the Contemporary Dongba Art School (Xiandai Dongba Meishu Xuehui), and several of their number have gone on to very successful careers, exhibiting their works across China and internationally.

Many of these painters were trained in Yunnan's leading art academies in the late 1970s and 1980s and their work reflects the ideals of the so-called Yunnan school, which was popular at the time. Among the many intellectuals who were "sent down to the countryside" (*xiaxiang*) during the Cultural

Figure 7.2.   He Xiudong performing Sacrifice to the Mountain Spirits at The Mall, Washington, D.C., 2007. Chas. McKhann photo.

Revolution (1966–1976), some wound up in minority nationality villages in the southwest, and a number of the artists among them responded by making minority peoples and customs the subjects of their art. When the schools reopened in the late 1970s, they returned to teaching and the Yunnan school was born. The school is characterized by its romantic primitive and erotic portrayal of southwestern minorities—not unlike some depictions of American Indian subjects—and its heavy borrowing of European modernist techniques, especially cubism (Cohen 1988). Many of the paintings have a dreamlike quality in which people and nature are melded together through the use of mythic symbols, and when Naxi artists took up the style they naturally turned to their own dongba pictographs for inspiration. Some Dongba School painters use the pictographs to portray key scenes in actual myths from the dongba corpus. Others apply them to more mundane subjects. Zhang Yunling, for example, is famous for his whimsical pictographic depictions of everyday village life. Regardless of their particular emphasis—some religious, some secular—all the members of the Contemporary Dongba Art School must be counted as Naxi intelligentsia, and their paintings as conscious attempts to develop their Naxi cultural identity through experimental visual forms.

The use of dongba pictographs in more traditional Han-style painting and calligraphy is another recent development—for example, watercolor and ink paintings with pictographic calligraphy, poetic couplets on vertical strips (*dui lian*), calligraphic scrolls, and so forth. Sometimes the content is derived from traditional dongba poetics, sometimes it derives from Han (Chinese) language phrases, and sometimes a Chinese character translation appears alongside pictographic Naxi phrases, to render them readable by a broader audience. One of the senior dongbas at the Dongba Academy in the 1980s and 1990s, He Kaiqiang, was a pioneer at fusing dongba content with traditional Han calligraphic forms. He was quite prolific and made a good side income from this work. Since then, many others, including some non-Naxi calligraphers, have developed these styles.

An important repercussion of the growing market for dongba art is the expanded interest among Naxi (and some others) in learning to read and write the pictographs. Formerly used only by dongbas in reproducing their ritual texts, the pictographs are visible everywhere now, especially in the Old Town section of Lijiang and other tourist locations. Besides arts and crafts for sale, they appear on large wall murals, business signboards, T-shirts and other clothing, even business cards.

Many of Lijiang's tourist shops are operated by outsiders (mainly Han) who have moved to the town only recently, and they offer products that are commonly found at other tourist locations in Yunnan—jades, tea, batik clothing, silver jewelry, antiques, and so on. Products that incorporate dongba pictographs, however, are immediately identified as Lijiang-specific, and therefore popular as mementos or as gifts to family and friends back home. These include stone "chops" with one's name rendered in pictographs, wooden plates carved or painted with pictographs, and pocket dictionaries or wall charts showing common pictographs and their Chinese and/or English equivalents.

Competition for the tourist trade and the expanded use of dongba pictographs in all kinds of nontraditional contexts has led to debates over what constitutes dongba art and handicrafts. Traditionalists—dongbas, scholars, academic artists—insist that in addition to incorporating pictographic elements, the subject matter should also derive from the religious texts—for example, depict a god or hero, relate to a particular legend or myth, or incorporate a direct quote. Others, often less knowledgeable about the religion, are predictably less concerned with historical veracity and more open to experimenting with secular meanings. Overall, there is an extremely wide range in this regard. Traditional religious artifacts—*thangka*-style cloth paintings, wooden slats with images of deities and demons drawn on them, and pictographic manuscripts—make up a very small percentage of what is sold as "dongba art" in Lijiang today. T-shirts, key chains, and other inexpensive tourist artifacts are much more readily available.

MAKING A MONASTERY? THE DONGBA CULTURE MUSEUM

Tibetan Buddhist monasteries are a familiar sight in northwest Yunnan. There are several small ones in the Lijiang area, and a large one (Songzanlin) in neighboring Shangri-la Country. In the Tibetan tradition, monasteries are important sites for religious teaching and devotion, for pilgrimage, for rituals and festivals, and for the display of religious art (see Makley, chapter 5). Dongba religion has no such grand places, only small shrines and temporary altars. With its display and teaching functions, and its ornate compound architecture, however, the Dongba Culture Museum (est. 1984) arguably stands as a kind of secular monastery for the dongba tradition.

Dongba rituals often employ representations of supernatural beings—gods, ancestors, malevolent demons—painted or drawn on cloth or wood, carved from sticks, or molded from a dough of roasted barley and water or butter. Some of these are similar to (and almost certainly derive from) Tibetan Buddhist religious arts—for example, thangkas and five-lobed painted "crowns" (Naxi *kol*; Tib. *rigs lnga*), but they are never displayed in public places (or in private homes), except during the performance of a ritual. Some dongbas say this is because Naxi gods are too powerful to be left out on their own—I was once chastised by a dongba for collecting fragments of a demon board (*kua biuq*) that had been discarded along a village path after having been ritually "killed"—which raises questions about the appropriateness of displaying supernaturally charged dongba ritual objects in a museum setting. And yet, museums have become the quintessential loci for cultural collections, and the Dongba Cultural Museum is no exception.

I (somewhat hesitantly) call it a "monastery" because of the strong teaching function it has also taken on—not in terms of the general public, but specifically aimed at Naxi children from Lijiang whose understanding of traditional Naxi culture is perceived as threatened by tourism and globalization. In 1995, the Dongba Museum established the Lijiang Naxi Dongba Culture School, at which resident dongbas taught "dongba culture" in a classroom setting to tuition-paying students. This model has since been taken up by an offshoot of the Dongba Academy, and has been extended to some of the area's primary schools. It must be emphasized, however, that the instruction provided at these schools is quite unlike the training that apprentice dongbas receive in natural village settings. There, the emphasis is entirely on dongba as a *practiced* religion: that is, on the performance of rituals for client households or larger collectives, and acquiring the skills to do so—for example, creating altars, fashioning ritual artifacts, chanting from ritual texts, and appropriate action sequences. In the new schools, the emphasis is on cultural content, not performance: students learn the pictographs and their meanings, myths, legends, art, and dance forms, but not how it all (traditionally) goes together. In 2004, *China Daily* reported that the Dongba Museum had also started to provide funds to local households to invite dongbas to perform traditional wedding, funeral, and other ceremonies (*China Daily* 2004).[29]

SAGES ON STAGES: A NEW KIND OF PERFORMANCE

Dongba has always been a performance art. Through words and acts, dongbas create new alignments in the cosmos and in society, with the aim of improving the lives of their clients. Gods and ancestors are propitiated, demons are driven off, children are named, sick people are cured, houses are made habitable, and the spirits of the dead are comforted, controlled, and directed. Oftentimes, everyone present at a ritual might be counted as a performer—an entire household receives a blessing, for example, or all the families of a village make offerings to the gods together. In other instances, there is an audience *per se*, as in a naming ceremony, or funeral, or wedding, where kin and neighbors are invited in large numbers to feast, but even here—where they may not engage directly in ritual activities—the audience is implicated in the performance. Because of the close-knit quality of village social relations, everyone there ultimately has a stake in the outcome. Indeed, everyone present is likely to be kin (see figure 7.3).

With the rise of global tourism in Lijiang, new genres of dongba performance are emerging, and their participants—actors and audiences—are being reconfigured in myriad ways. In addition to the staged rituals orchestrated by the Dongba Academy, the Dongba Museum, and other scholarly organizations (described above), dongba performances that fall more under the heading of "pure entertainment" have been emerging at some Lijiang tourist venues. One of the best known of these is the Dongba Palace (Dongba Gong), which was opened about ten years ago by a leading Naxi cultural figure and former county official. The Dongba Palace puts on nightly folk art performances, which include Naxi and other minority singers, dancers, and musicians. The house seats about 250 people (generally all tourists), and it is usually full. Tickets are 20 yuan (about $3), on top of which there are CDs and DVDs for sale at the entrance. [30]

Included in the Dongba Palace show are performances by two Naxi ritual specialists—a sainii shaman and a dongba. The staging and setup are profes-

Figure 7.3. Dongbas preparing funerary cloth, Eagleback Village, Sichuan, 2006. Chas. McKhann photo.

sional. Performers work on a raised stage, with entrance and exit wings, colored flood and spotlights, and a professional sound system. Most are dressed in gussied up versions of traditional local clothing styles, while an emcee in a Confucian-style men's robe—Naxi have ironically retained some traditional Chinese garments long after they went out of fashion in Han areas—announces the acts and tells jokes. He is an intellectual and long-time culture worker, well known in the community.

I count these nightclub performances as their own type because their detachment from dongba religious content is almost complete, although in some respects they grade into the kinds of performances put on by academic dongbas at nationality theme parks, the Smithsonian, and so on. Traditional sainii performances involve entering into alternative states of consciousness (trancing) and traveling between alternate time-space dimensions (dancing) in order to contact various supernatural beings. Sometimes they work in conjunction with dongbas, who will typically divine the causes of illness or misfortune and call forth the gods prior to the sainii's transcendental tripping.

In Dongba Palace performances, the roles of sainii and dongba are highly stylized—the former as barbarian wild man, the latter his gentleman counterpart.[31] With long, unkempt hair and dressed in animal skins, the sainii gyrates, moans, and shouts incomprehensibly, while rattling a hand drum, and shaking his spear. The action starts slowly, as he enters into a faux trance, and builds to a crescendo. After an enormous rattling drum roll, he collapses, spent.

Later in the show, his older, more dignified counterpart does his thing. Dressed in flowing silk robes, laced with gold brocade and a five-pointed crown painted with images of the great founder, Dongba Shilo, and other gods, a sixty-five-year-old dongba, with wizened mien and long, gray beard enters the stage, posture erect, cadence slow and dignified. After a courteous bow left and right to the audience, he is joined on either side by two young Naxi women—maidens by their dress—each bearing a yak horn trumpet, which they offer to the elderly dongba, held high with both hands, a sign of respect. He receives one, then the other, puts them both to his lips, and blows. The sound is incredible, magical—an eerie dissonant chord that seems to last forever.

From the standpoint of dongba religion, however, it is a complete sham. No dongba ever took a horn from a girl like that: this psychosexual drama is a wholly modern entertainment. And ironically, what a dongba does most— speak—this one never does. He comes on stage, blows his horns, and leaves. The wild man and the mute. During the daytime, dressed in his ritual garb, the old dongba sits in the entryway to the "palace"—*tristes montagnes*, a silent advertisement for the evening's entertainments.[32]

CONCLUSION

There is no simple way to sum up the status and direction of dongba religion in the first decade of the twenty-first century. Organic village revival proceeds apace with previously unthinkable transformations brought on by tourism. The line between the two runs through government policy. Yan (2003) characterizes the Chinese government as increasingly distant from private life in recent years, and this has certainly made possible the return of traditional dongba practices that we see in some villages. At the same time, government-sponsored tourism development and changing attitudes toward minority nationality culture—coupled with intense pride in that culture by minority elites—have led to a reimagining of dongba religion in urban, national, and international contexts. The link between (contemporary) dongba culture and (traditional) dongba religion is tenuous, but persistent and evolving. To outward appearances, the dongba culture movement is successful and here to stay. Whether the religion can survive in forms that would be recognizable to earlier generations remains to be seen. Much will depend on the ability of today's young village dongbas to meet the changing needs of their rural clients, and to inspire young urban Naxi to find meaning in beliefs and practices from a world very different to the one they now inhabit.

THE LAST DANCE

A year after the Dongba Academy finished its translation of the complete dongba corpus, my friend and mentor, He Jigui, made the ultimate performance. On a moonless night, he left his spartan room in the academy compound, walked out the back gate toward the latrine, and drowned himself in the big cistern on the hill. He didn't leave a note, so nobody knows all of the reasons for his act, but one of them certainly was a profound sadness over the direction of dongba religion. Despite the opportunities for travel, wealth, and fame, he loathed the commoditization of his art, and frequently said so publicly. The last time I saw him, in 2001, he seemed withdrawn—working hard at the texts, but alone in his room much of the time. A year later, the work of translation—two decades—was done, and in Lijiang there was little for an old dongba to do that didn't involve dancing for ignorant audiences. Five years earlier, he and I and another friend from the Dongba Academy made a month-long trip into southern Sichuan Province, tracing the route that the souls of the Naxi dead are said to follow. All along the way, He Jigui told us he was trying to memorize the landforms so that he wouldn't get lost when he came again. None of us suspected his leaving would be so soon, or under such heartbreaking circumstances.

NOTES

1. This paper is dedicated to the memory of He Jigui—mentor, pater, and beloved friend.

2. In Chinese, trulkus, such as the Dalai Lama, are termed "*huofo*" (living Buddhas).

3. My spelling for "*sainii*" follows the convention of Naxi pinyin, which I will use as a standard. By that convention, the second term should be "*dobbaq*" (the *q* serving as a tone marker), but I will defer to the Chinese pinyin spelling "*dongba*" because it is so widely recognized.

4. A similar division is present among the ritual specialists of some neighboring groups as well. The Naxi distinction between dongba and sainii, is paralleled by the Premi *anji* vs. *somi* (Wellens 2006) and the Nuosu (Yi) *bimo* vs. *sunyi* (Bamo 2000; Liu 2001). Ortner 1989 and Samuel 1993 point to a similar tension among Sherpa and Tibetan lamas, between those whose powers are acquired through institutional channels (study and knowledge), and those whose powers are innate (magical and charismatic).

5. For more on these other religious specialists, see Wellens 2006, Wang 1997, and Bamo 2001.

6. The manuscript pages are divided into a series of rectangular blocks in three rows, read left to right and top to bottom. Each box contains several pictographs, which together stand for one phrase in the chant. The written phrases are nongram-

as embodied in architecture, aesthetics, crafts, food, religion, and even the rhythms of daily life.

One example is the Xishuangbanna Dai Garden (*Xishuangbanna Daizu yuan*), created out of the administrative village of Manting about one hour's drive from the capital of Jinghong. Manting comprises five natural villages including Manchunman, the site of King Bhumibol's donation ceremony described at the start of this essay. In China tourist sites are classified according to rank (Nyíri 2006), and the Dai Garden is designated an AAAA international scenic spot, the second highest ranking. The Dai Garden was not established out of thin air; rather, it is coterminous with the preexisting villages, their residents, and, ostensibly, their everyday lives. Villagers continue to live in their houses, although these have been upgraded in a fashion meant to retain their traditional charm. Thanks to ticket and souvenir sales some villagers have abandoned farming, though most continue to carry out agricultural and sideline activities. Entry into Manting requires the purchase of a ticket, the price of which is typically included in the cost of packaged bus tours, which is how most tourists visit. Dozens of tour buses arrive daily to discharge their passengers for an hour or so of shopping, eating, strolling, and—if so interested—praying. For the heart of Manting is Manchunman village, and the heart of Manchunman is its Buddhist temple. Buddhism is central to the concept of Dai-ness promoted in the Dai Garden.

Many of the groups that visit are Buddhist groups from Taiwan, Hong Kong, Thailand, and other parts of China. Other visitors possess varying degrees of belief in and devotion to Buddhism. Regardless of their faith, most visitors tour the temple, and many light incense or purchase religious objects and publications. Their behavior highlights an interesting and advantageous dimension of religious as opposed to other types of ethnocultural tourism, and of the use of religion as an element in tourist attractions. Tourists are outsiders and spectators, and while they wish to encounter what they perceive as authentic local culture they cannot be of it (nor do they desire to be, for the most part). They observe and consume cultural products generated in great part for their benefit. Yet religion can allow the tourist-outsider to encounter culture in a way that, in terms of the tourist's subjective experience, collapses or at least reduces the outsider-local distinction. In arguing this I am not suggesting that religious tourism dissolves disparate social categories in an experience of "*communitas*"; as Sangren argues, such tourism (i.e., pilgrimage) and the experience of cultural transcendence it facilitates are themselves "culturally located," made meaningful through localized and differentiated cultural forms (1987, 189–206).[7] What I am highlighting is the mode of participation involved in religious as opposed to ethnic tourism, which is one of active engagement and cultural coproduction, rather than passive consumption of the spectacle of the ethnic "other."

matical in the sense that not all of the words spoken in the chant are present as pictographs on the page. The dongba must fill in the missing words from memory.

7. Dongbas can generally "read" each other's manuscripts, although the texts and the chants that go with them may be a little different.

8. Much of the work for these series was conducted in connection with the early work of nationality identification (*minzu shibie*) in the 1950s and early 1960s, but most were not published until the 1980s.

9. The downgrading or erasure of some minority religions is extreme in the case of the Wa. The only hint of Wa religion in the official "A Brief History of the Wa Nationality" comes in the final chapter: "Marriage, Funerals and Material Life" (*WZJS* 1986).

10. Following "Krishna consciousness" from the 1970s in the United States, with which it has some profound similarities.

11. I have described some of the spectacular infrastructural developments associated with Lijiang's tourism boom elsewhere (McKhann 2001a, 2001b), but to give some sense of the scale it is perhaps enough to note that Lijiang now supports dozens of large hotels, including the province's first five-star hotel, and countless smaller guesthouses. An airport, opened in 1994, receives fifteen to twenty full-sized jet-loads of tourists each day, mostly from Kunming, but also on direct flights from Beijing, Shanghai, Guangzhou, and Shenzhen.

12. Fear of potential minority separatist movements ranks high on the Chinese government's list of long-term concerns, and activities even remotely connected with the possibility are strongly suppressed. Hypersensitive to global attention in the year of the Beijing Olympics, immediately following small-scale riots in Lhasa and other Tibetan areas in the spring of 2008 (see this volume, chapter 5), the government canceled without explanation a major international anthropology conference in Kunming, and shut down travel and scholarly research in many Tibetan areas. Ironically, many of the Chinese organizers of the conference were the very same minority intellectuals on whose support in matters of minority policy the government usually depends.

13. A pseudonym.

14. As Steve Harrell 2001, Erik Mueggler 2001, Du Shanshan 2002, and others have so powerfully demonstrated, even in the most remote mountains of southwest China there are virtually no places where minority or local Han culture has not been profoundly changed by Communist policy over the past sixty years. Exponentially more so than any previous government, the current regime has penetrated local society to its deepest roots.

15. This formerly important ritual celebrating the patrilineal kin group is, so far as I know, no longer being performed in any village locations. It was staged at the Dongba Culture Research Institute in Lijiang in 1986 (McKhann 1992).

16. A similar grassroots revival of native religion is ongoing among the Nuosu (Yi) and some other neighboring ethnic groups. Because of their much larger numbers, the long-term success of the *bimo* revival among the Nuosu seems fairly certain, however, whereas this is not the case with Naxi dongbas (see Bamo 2001).

17. Yan Yunxiang writes at length about the withdrawal of the state from everyday affairs in his *Private Life Under Socialism* (2003).

18. The job of village leader (*cunzhang*) is particularly sensitive. They are at once responsible for implementing policies handed down from above, and for protecting the interests of villagers against a state that has proven its capacity for excess. In minority areas, their intimate understanding of local customs is key to their success in performing this buffering role. In short, they need to defend local practices without being seen to do so, especially when those practices directly contradict higher-level policy. The implementation of marriage law is a good example of this. In Eagleback and many neighboring communities, marriages are often out of accord with national laws, but local officials generally turn a blind eye.

19. The Dongba Culture Research Academy was created as a "research institute" (*yanjiusuo*) in 1979, but upgraded to "research academy" status (*yanjiuyuan*) in 2005, although there has been little obvious change in its organization or operation. For convenience, I will refer to it as the Dongba Academy, although the history of the name change should be born in mind.

20. The question of local variation extends to the textual translations as well. Volumes of translations published by the Dongba Academy include the name of the dongba who read the texts, along with the name(s) of the translator(s). Dongbas-in-residence at the Dongba Academy are invited by the academy leaders. At its establishment in 1979, about seventy senior dongbas from across the region were invited to a gathering in Lijiang. Their knowledge was assessed—by each other and by academy researchers—and a few were invited to take up residence at the academy. Numerous others have worked on particular academy projects over the years.

21. I know they made a trip to Shenzhen for this purpose around 1994, and I think there were others, probably including the one on Lake Dianchi, near Kunming. See this volume, chapter 5, for more discussion on nationality theme parks.

22. Original plans to develop a ski area on the mountain were abandoned due to insufficient and irregular snow cover, but the gondola system was completed in 1999. A round-trip ticket—with time at the top to play in the snow, a key attraction for lowland southerners—costs more than 100 RMB, or about ten times the daily wage for a laborer in a village like Eagleback.

23. Actually, I think this is less true today than when we got married in 1992. It was absolutely true then—no one in the Lijiang area was doing dongba weddings—but there have been more in recent years, reflecting the general revival of dongba religion that is the subject of this chapter.

24. Chinese often use the word "propaganda" (*xuanchuan*) to describe what in English would be termed "promotion" or "public relations." The Chinese term *xuanchuan* lacks the negative connotations of its English equivalent.

25. *Thing, Myth, Pictograph* was curated by museum director Michael Oppitz, and featured weekly lectures by invited experts on dongba religion, and in one-week performances by He Jigui.

26. Whitman College and the Freeman Foundation sponsored semester-long courses in Naxi painting and cultural history, taught by visiting Naxi scholars Zhang Yunling and Yang Fuquan, and an exhibition of traditional and contemporary dongba art that showed in Walla Walla and Seattle and Portland, Oregon (McKhann et al. 2003).

27. According to Naxi myth, the mountain spirits (*shu*) are the half-siblings of human beings, and are responsible for caring for the wild animals and birds, meadows, forests, and so forth. Because we humans habitually poach on their domain, it is necessary to placate them with regular offerings.

28. He Xiudong's jet-setting continues. Quite by accident and much to their mutual surprise, he and my wife ran into each other in the summer of 2008 near the Brandenburg Gate, Berlin. Dressed in his ornate dongba robe, he cuts a wide swath.

29. Unfortunately, I have no recent information concerning this program.

30. There is some irony to the fact that these Naxi cultural performances are mainly attended by non-Naxi. In the 1970s and 1980s there was a large cultural center in the New Town square where locals gathered nightly for popular, inexpensive arts performances. In the 1996 earthquake, the old cultural center was destroyed, and its replacement—a controversial hypermodernist structure—is most often used for national and international conventions that the general Lijiang public is unlikely to attend. In some respects, Naxi are getting "priced out" of their own culture. (See also Yan 2003 for a discussion on the decline of community sociality in China.)

31. This opposition rather neatly replicates the state's views on superstition (*mixin*) versus religion (*zongjiao*).

32. Dongbas and (faux) sainii who work in such shows are clearly hired as much for their physical appearance as for their skills and talents. In the 1990s, a few elderly dongbas— including my friend He Jigui—became almost iconic figures. The cameras loved them, and their images were everywhere.

REFERENCES

Bamo, Ayi. 2001. "On the Nature and Transmission of *Bimo* Knowledge in Liangshan." In *Perspectives on the Yi of Southwest China*, ed. Stevan Harrell. Berkeley: University of California Press, 118–31.

Bamo, Qubumo. 2000. "Ghost Boards and Spirit Pictures." In *Mountain Patterns: The Survival of Nuosu Culture in China*, ed. Stevan Harrell, Bamo Qubumo, and Ma Erzi. Seattle: University of Washington Press, 58–64.

Chao, Emily. 1996: "Hegemony, Agency, and Re-Presenting the Past: The Invention of *Dongba* Culture Among the Naxi of Southwest China." In *Negotiating Identities in China and Taiwan*, ed. M. Brown. Institute of East Asian Studies, Monograph #46, Berkeley: University of California Press, 208–39.

China Daily. 2004. 6 August. www.china.org.cn/english/culture/103193.htm (accessed 4 June 2009).

Cohen, Joan L. 1988. *Yunnan School: A Renaissance in Chinese Painting*. Minneapolis: Fingerhut Group.

Du, Shanshan. 2002. *"Chopsticks Only Work in Pairs": Gender Unity and Gender Equality Among the Lahu of Southwest China*. New York: Columbia University Press.

DQXZ. 1997. *Deqin xian zhi*. Kunming: Yunnan minzu chubanshe.

ESYZZZXGK. 1986. *Eshan Yizu zizhi xian gaikuang*. Kunming: Yunnan minzu chubanshe.

Harrell, Stevan. 2001. *Ways of Being Ethnic in Southwest China*. Seattle: University of Washington Press.

Liu, Xiaoxing. 2001. "The Yi Health Care System in Liangshan and Chuxiong." In *Perspectives on the Yi of Southwest China*, ed. Stevan Harrell. Berkeley: University of California Press, 266–82.

McKhann, C. F. 1992. *Fleshing Out the Bones: Kinship and Cosmology in Naqxi Religion*. Ph.D. diss., University of Chicago.

———. 2001a: "The Good, the Bad and the Ugly: Observations and Reflections on Tourism Development in Lijiang, China." In *Tourism, Anthropology, and China*, ed. Tan Chee Beng, Sidney Cheung, and Yang Hui. Bangkok: White Lotus Press, 147–66.

———. 2001b. "Tourisme de masse et identité sur les marches sino-tibétaines: Réflexions d'un observateur." *Anthropologie et sociétés* 25(2): 35–54.

McKhann, C. F., Yang Fuquan, and Zhang Yunling, eds. 2003. *Icon and Transformation: (Re)Imaginings in Dongba Art*. Walla Walla, WA: Sheehan Gallery Press.

Mueggler, Erik. 2001. *The Age of Wild Ghosts: Memory, Violence, and Place in Southwest China*. Berkeley: University of California Press.

Ortner, Sherry B. 1989. *High Religion: A Cultural and Political History of Sherpa Buddhism*. Princeton: Princeton University Press.

Rees, Helen. 2000. *Echoes of History: Naxi Music in Modern China*. Oxford: Oxford University Press.

Samuel, Geoffrey. 1993. *Civilized Shamans: Buddhism in Tibetan Societies*. Washington, DC: Smithsonian Institution Press.

Schein, Louisa. 2000. *Minority Rules: The Miao and the Feminine in China's Cultural Politics*. Durham, NC: Duke University Press.

Tylor, E. B. 1970 [1873]. *Religion in Primitive Culture*. Gloucester, MA: Peter Smith.

Wang, Zhusheng. 1997. *The Jingpo Kachin of the Yunnan Plateau*. Program for Southeast Asian Studies Monograph Series. Tempe: Arizona State University Press.

Wellens, Koen. 2006. *Consecrating the Premi House: Ritual, Community and the State in the Borderlands of East Tibet*. Ph.D. diss., University of Oslo.

WXLSZZZXZ. 1999. *Weixi Lisuzu zizhi xian zhi*. Kunming: Yunnan minzu chubanshe.

WZJS. 1986. *Wazu jian shi*. Kunming: Yunnan jiaoyu chubanshe.

Yan, Yunxiang. 2003. *Private Life Under Socialism: Love, Intimacy, and Family Change in a Chinese Village 1949–1999*. Stanford: Stanford University Press.

Yang, Fuquan. 2003. "The Modern *Dongba* Painting School in Historical Perspective." In *Icon and Transformation: (Re)Imaginings in Dongba Art*, ed. C. F. McKhann, Yang Fuquan, and Zhang Yunling. Walla Walla, WA: Sheehan Gallery Press, 19–24.

8

Tourist Itineraries, Spatial Management, and Hidden Temples

The Revival of Religious Sites in a Water Town

Marina Svensson

EXPERIENCING WUZHEN DURING MAY HOLIDAY 2007

In the outskirts of Wuzhen the soft chanting of monks can be heard from the Ciyun Temple. A group of elderly women from Hangzhou who have come to stay for forty-nine days in the temple also take part in the service. After the service the women take off their black robes and go to the dining hall where they share a simple lunch consisting of rice and vegetables with the monks. The women follow the services throughout the day until they take an early night's rest in the newly built dormitory belonging to the temple. For board and food they pay a mere five yuan per day, but many of the women also give donations to the temple during their stay. It is thanks to their donations, and the sale of incense and candles, that the temple has been able to build the new dormitory and is building a new hall. The abbot has already bought several statues that now stand wrapped in plastic in the courtyard while the hall is being finished.

Not far away from the Ciyun Temple, the Xiuzhen Daoist Temple is bustling with people. Tourist group after tourist group pushes into the temple. One can distinguish the different tourist groups from each other as people from the same group often wear the same colorful caps. Local guides usher the tourists through the different halls while giving a scripted overview of the temple and certain Daoist practices. Many tourists perform religious acts such as offering incense, praying to the deities, and having their fortunes read by the Daoists in the temple. Although some of the tourists seem to know how to proceed others look more awkward and lost. Tourists are encouraged by the guides to buy wooden amulets with the *bagua* (eight trigram) that is said to

211

bring luck and protect the family. Business is rather brisk although the amulets cost 200 yuan and upward. A young man hesitates to buy an amulet that costs 600 yuan but obviously feels somewhat pressured to buy the smaller one for 200 yuan and not disappoint his girlfriend, who might otherwise think he is not sincere about their relationship. The couple has already spent a lot of money on their trip to Wuzhen. The entrance ticket to Wuzhen East Street alone costs 100 yuan per person, or 150 yuan if they also want to see the newly opened West Street.

The old women wouldn't dream of visiting the Xiuzhen Temple, although they know about it and of Wuzhen's success as a tourist attraction. It is not only a question of loyalty to the abbot and different faiths. The women and the Ciyun monks also question the Daoist temple's management and the authenticity of its religious practices. The majority of the tourists visiting Wuzhen, on the other hand, do not know about the Ciyun Temple as it is not on the tourist itinerary, and as they stay safely within the prescribed guided path. These two temples, so close geographically but yet so far apart, offer very different religious experiences and target different groups of people. They also present different religious narratives and have different spatial practices,

Figure 8.1. Tourists throng the Xiuzhen Temple where a sign proclaims freedom of belief and voluntary donations. M. Svensson photo.

as well as belong to different translocal networks. The Ciyun Temple is a religious space that links up with other Buddhist temples and is part of a translocal network of lay people and monks, and the women can and do easily move between different temples. By contrast the Xiuzhen Temple, albeit sharing some features and spatial practices with other Daoist temples, is part of a tourist itinerary that links tourists with different spatial practices and sites in Wuzhen and beyond, rather than with Daoist temples or Daoist religious practices per se. The majority of those visiting the temple are furthermore tourists that do not know much about, and are not primarily interested in, Daoism.

One thing the two temples have in common, however, is that both sites were physically damaged and their religious practices suppressed after 1949. None of the sites today offers much information about this immediate past, and a casual visitor may therefore remain unaware of these hidden and suppressed narratives and the recent re-creation and reconstruction of religious practices. The reform period has seen a revival of sorts in both places. But whereas the revival of the Ciyun Temple has been a bottom-up process involving and depending upon a religious community led by a religious leader, the revival and rebuilding of the Xiuzhen Temple has been initiated by the tourist company with the aim of attracting tourists and making money. The Daoist priests working in the temple are in fact hired and employed by the tourism company.

The aim of this chapter is to analyze the construction, marketing, and development of different religious sites in Wuzhen, and the role different actors play in this process.[1] Since rebuilding the Xiuzhen Temple in 2000, the tourism company has discovered and re-created new religious sites at the same time as religious communities and local businessmen develop other religious sites. Visitors to Wuzhen come into contact with and interact with these different religious sites, but they do so in different ways and also seem to move in somewhat parallel universes. Wuzhen offers some fascinating insights into how religious spaces in China today are (re-)created and used by different actors and for different purposes, and the contestations that these processes give rise to. Many interesting questions arise regarding the links between religion, the state, and tourism in a locality such as Wuzhen and in the PRC more generally. Why and how do tourism companies promote religious spaces, and what role do local governments play in this context? What kinds of religious spaces are put on the tourist map, and how do they link up with other sites promoted by the tourism company and with more "authentic" religious spaces? What forms do negotiations between religious and tourist spaces and experiences take in China, and what role do religious sites play in the overall tourist experience? How are local and translocal religious communities affected by the attempts by local governments and tourism companies to market religious spaces for economic development?

THE CREATION OF A TOURIST ATTRACTION:
PRESERVING AND MARKETING A WATER TOWN

Wuzhen has, since it was opened for tourism in 2001, rapidly become a very successful tourist destination with some two million visitors annually.[2] This rapid development is due to very ambitious work and active promotion, as well as some fortunate geographical factors. Wuzhen is a so-called water town (*shuixiang*) made up of and crisscrossed by numerous canals and rivers west of the Grand Canal in northern Zhejiang Province. In the past Wuzhen was a central market town of the Grand Canal with many shops, teahouses, and temples. The silk industry was very important for the local economy as described by the author Mao Dun in his early work *Spring Silkworms* (2001). Whereas transportation once was slow and by boat, the town is today easily accessible by highway from Hangzhou and Shanghai, which has helped boost tourism.

The traditional town was made up of four main streets, the South, North, West, and East streets, with the East and West streets being the more commercial streets with numerous shops, some sixty-four teahouses, and more than 120 bridges. Before renovation began on first the East Street in 1998 and then on the West Street in 2004, some of the old houses had been replaced with new houses or neglected as those with money had moved into new modern buildings at the outskirts of the town. The remaining old buildings were mainly inhabited by old people without the financial means to move but with a strong attachment to the old ways of living. After initially turning a deaf ear to preservationists' pleas to protect the town, the Wuzhen authorities in 1998 decided to preserve and rebuild the town after seeing the huge success of neighboring water towns such as Tongli and Zhouzhuang (Ruan 2002). The city adopted a master plan and set up a special committee for the protection and development of Wuzhen, as well as established a tourism company, the Tongxiang City Wuzhen Town Tourism Development Company. The tourist company is a semiofficial entity with strong backing from and links to the local government. Chen Xianghong, originally the vice head of the township, is today its party secretary as well as the head of the tourism company.[3] This official backing has helped the tourism company secure bank loans, land rentals, and building permissions to ensure the takeover of private residential buildings and eviction of residents on the West Street.

The tourism company's policy has been to restore and market Wuzhen as a late Qing town. The restoration work and careful planning of the tourist itinerary has resulted in a town that is considerably neater, cleaner, and more regulated than it originally was. It is mainly the quaint architectural features of the water town, such as its wooden traditional houses, winding alleys, flowing canals, and graceful bridges, that are celebrated. The Wuzhen tourist company has spent much effort in marketing the town. Its advertisements are highly visible at tourist fairs, on TV, in magazines and newspapers, and on billboards all over China. There has been a massive output of publications on Wuzhen, some initiated by the tourism company itself, including both photo books and more in-depth works about history, local traditions, and cultural life (for example, Ruan 2002; Ruan 2004; Chen 2001; Zhang 2002; Wang 2003; Xu 2003). The Wuzhen tourist company's website (www.wuzhen.com. cn) is very attractive and contains a lot of information on the town and its attractions, including history and sights, entertainment, restaurants, accommodations, and shopping facilities. In fact, a prospective tourist can get such a rich and visual experience of Wuzhen through merely visiting the website that a visit to the actual physical place may be unnecessary, or could undermine the cyberspace experience. The Wuzhen that the tourists encounter in cyberspace, in any of the many photo books on sale, or on DVD and film, is a tranquil rural place where local residents live a peaceful life untouched by modernity, although the real Wuzhen is full of tourists and local residents who busy themselves with commercial activities. The tourism company's use of the Internet to promote its picture of Wuzhen is not uncontested, however, as visitors through blogs and other discussion forums can discuss and share their experiences and impressions of Wuzhen, which may undermine or challenge the official representation.

The marketing of Wuzhen has entailed the (re-)construction and careful selection of sites and narratives. This has led to, if not a completely new version of local history, at least a much improved version that has required the rediscovery of many aspects of local history and traditions that had previously been neglected and forgotten (cf. Bellocq 2006 on similar developments in Tongli). When the tourism company began to renovate and promote the East Street, it started with some of the existing and more obvious sights. Foremost among them was the old family home of the author Mao Dun (1896–1981), the pen name of Shen Yanbing, his old school, and the already existing memorial hall.[4] Mao Dun's family house had been recovered by the Chinese state already in 1977. In 1985 the house was opened to the public, and in 1988 the State Council listed the building as a national protected site (*guojia wenwu baohu danwei*). In 1990, a memorial hall was built beside the family home and later designated as a patriotic education base (*aiguo jiaoyu jidi*). Before the days of mass tourism, these sites were mainly visited by political leaders and officials, and by schoolchildren for whom the visit was part of their ideological and political education. In 2006, half of Mao Dun's ashes were on the request of his son and in cooperation with the tourism company moved from the Baobashan Cemetery in Beijing to Wuzhen where the company built a new memorial hall in the recently opened West Street tourist area.

Mao Dun's house and the memorial halls are part of a revolutionary heritage narrative that is now being commodified and coexist with other competing heritage narratives (compare developments in Jinggangshan discussed by Yu Luo Rioux in this volume). Most visitors to Wuzhen would be familiar with Mao Dun's short stories, including *Family Lin Shop*. By an ironical twist of history the name Family Lin Shop has now been appropriated for a souvenir shop. The shop and other sites don't narrate the hardships of life in old Wuzhen as described in Mao Dun's short stories but simply add to the quaint townscape. Even the restored pawnshop is more picturesque than sinister since it doesn't really narrate exploitation and suffering. Wuzhen has not made so much of Mao Dun and his fictional landscape as Shaoxing has done with respect to Lu Xun. Whereas an older generation might recognize the water town landscape from the film version of the *Family Lin Shop* from 1959, a younger generation is more likely to associate Wuzhen with the soap opera *As Life Goes By* from 2003. In the soap opera, which features two of China's most popular young actors, Wuzhen forms the backdrop to a bittersweet love story that never was meant to be.[5] Wuzhen can almost be said to be the third main character in the drama as it plays such a central role, and as the camera again and again lovingly sweeps over each old bridge, canal, house, and lane. The tourism company is heavily exploiting the soap opera as it fits better with its marketing strategy than Mao Dun's slightly outmoded social realism.

The East Street area houses several small museums with exhibitions of folk traditions and collections of different handicraft. Apart from the Xiuzhen Temple, there are also two small shrines to the God of Wealth and to Guanyin on the East Street but it is easy for tourists to oversee them amid the other sights. Tourists can also watch a puppet show and local opera on the centrally placed old opera stage close to the Xiuzhen Temple. But the visitors' experience is mostly about gazing and consuming rather than participating in the town's cultural and religious life. The visual experience is central for tourists and Wuzhen has been heavily marketed for both amateur and professional photo enthusiasts.[6] Tourists are not only engaged in taking their own photos or videos but can also purchase photo books and DVDs of the town. The consumption of food and buying of different kinds of souvenirs and local products, including tea, candy, cakes, rice wine, and batik is also a very important aspect of the tourist experience and souvenir shops dominate the streets of the old center (cf. Oakes 1999).

Restoration of the West Street took several years and included the resettlement of all of its residents and the re-creation of lost buildings and the adding of new buildings. The West Street area also houses several exhibitions and museums, including an exhibition of the making of silk and an exhibition of the making of bean paste. There is also a museum with "lotus foot shoes," that

Figure 8.2.   Small Guanyin shrine off East Street. M. Svensson photo.

focuses more on the aesthetics and fashion of the shoes up until the Republican period than on the issue of the suppression of women in traditional China. But another museum is dedicated to Wang Huiwu, a writer and socialist married to Li Da, one of the founders of the CCP. Wang was an active promoter of women's rights who established and ran schools for women in Wuzhen and Shanghai. This museum gives a different and more in-depth overview of the situation of women in China but few tourists seem to find their way to this museum. Several religious sites have also been rebuilt or re-created in the West Street area, including the Wu Jiangjun Temple, a small Guandi Temple, a shrine dedicated to an official who drowned himself in order to warn local residents of a poisonous well, as well as a shrine to the Silkworm Goddess. Apart from the Guandi Temple, none of these temples and shrines was originally found in this area. The tourism company is not yet pushing or promoting religious practices in any of them on a scale similar to that of Xiuzhen Temple and these temples are therefore more like sites in a theme park than living religious spaces.

The tourism company has obviously tried to base its creation of Wuzhen on historic records and dug up historic figures, sites, and temples to embellish the historic ambience of the town but the effect is more of a theme park than a living old town. The heritage narratives that are told and enacted in Wuzhen mostly reflect a romantic rural gaze combined with vestiges of a more state-oriented revolutionary and patriotic heritage narrative as manifested in the memorial halls dedicated to Mao Dun, long celebrated in the PRC, and less known historic figures such as Wang Huiwu.

SPATIAL MANAGEMENT AND STRUGGLES: THE PRICE OF PRESERVATION

Tourism development in Wuzhen has not been without problems and resentment, although to the author's knowledge there exists no in-depth study of the social and economic impact on people's life or their attitudes toward tourism.[7] People's bodily movements and spatial practices in Wuzhen, whether they are residents or tourists, are heavily controlled and managed by the tourist company. This control of visitors and restriction of access are very common in China where tourists have to buy an entrance ticket in order to visit villages and small towns open for tourism. This controlled and restricted access is even more striking in the newly (2007) opened West Street that is completely cordoned off from the rest of the town, something that is accentuated by the fact that it is at some distance from other residential areas and inaccessible to Wuzhen residents who don't work there. Although the tourism company is a powerful player and an important employer, employing some 1,100 people, local residents in Wuzhen are not passive to the tourism company's efforts to control their spatial practices but engage in different forms of resistance and spatial struggles (cf.Yang 2004). Residents actively try to negotiate or challenge the boundaries and spatial practices laid down by the tourism company. In some cases they simply bypass the tourism company and engage in their own celebrations of local heritage and communal identity, as for example when they go to worship at the two remaining Buddhist temples in the town, but in other cases they engage in open resistance to the tourism company's attempts to control their own and the tourists' movements and spatial practices.

The East Street is clearly defined and divided into a residential area, a handicraft and exhibition area, and a shopping and dining area. The local residents' activities are closely regulated so as to not disturb the carefully planned tourist itinerary and atmosphere. This means that some local residents had to move and that their ability to open shops is severely restricted. Many residents complain about the fact that they are not allowed to set up small stalls in front of their home or open shops in their homes. They can only sell goods and foodstuff before 7:30 in the morning and after 5:00 in the afternoon when most tourists have already left the area. The residents are also hampered in their daily life because guards control and check the entrance to the area, which means that their visitors cannot enter without being met and escorted. The shops and businesses in the area furthermore cater to tourists rather than to local residents. This became particularly obvious during this author's visit to Wuzhen during the SARS crisis in 2003 when the whole area was deserted and the majority of shops and restaurants closed because of the dramatic drop in tourists.

Because there have been constant quarrels and disputes between guards/ tourist company and residents over access, visits, and unapproved commercial activities at the East Street, the tourist company decided to solve the problem by simply moving the more than eight hundred households that lived in the West Street area to a new residential area. There was reportedly a lot of resentment over this resettlement as some people didn't want to move from their old homes and others were dissatisfied with the compensation.[8] Many residents are quick to point out that the West Street today is dead and lacks any kind of human atmosphere (*renqing wen'r*) as nobody lives there anymore and the area only caters to tourists. Since there are not all that many visitors, and exhibitions, shops, and restaurants are rather few in the vast area, the West Street has a deserted ghost town feeling about it.[9] What was once a living community has now become a staged and contrived bounded tourist space. In comparison, East Street is much more natural and alive as many residents still live there. One can see residents move about their houses, wash their laundry in the canal, and water their plants, and in the late afternoons and early evenings, when most tourists have left the town, gather on the many bridges to chat with their neighbors. The East Street rather faces the opposite problem of overcrowding, especially during holidays and weekends, when tourists throng the narrow alleys.

People's access to many important historical and cultural sites in Wuzhen, including religious sites, is now restricted as they are found within the closed and bounded tourist areas. The only open and accessible religious sites are the two Buddhist temples, Ciyun Temple and Shifo Temple, which are found at the outskirts of Wuzhen but within sight from the West Street. Many other public spaces in the East Street have also been lost to the local community. The many simple and small teahouses where men in the past gathered to drink tea and chat have now been replaced with refurbished and upscale teahouses that cater to tourists and are prohibitively expensive for local residents. The major square in front of the Xiuzhen Temple is, however, still a place where local residents more naturally mingle with tourists to watch opera. When nightfall comes the square is reappropriated by the local community who gather there for ballroom dancing and other Western dances.[10]

The tourism company also controls the bodily movements and spatial practices of tourists as it guides them through the town and defines the sites worth

Figure 8.3.   The West Street area is quiet and almost deserted as no local residents live there anymore. M. Svensson photo.

visiting. When tourists arrive in Wuzhen they need to buy an entrance ticket before actually entering the historic town. They are then directed toward the approved sites in a certain order. But rickshaw pullers offer alternative rides to places in Wuzhen that the tourism company considers out of bounds as they undermine the official narrative. The rickshaw pullers for example offer rides to the shabby and dilapidated South Street where they point out some old houses whose former grandeur is still partly visible in the ornaments and physical structures. The ride to South Street reminds the visitor of the huge efforts that the tourist company has put into renovations of the West and East streets and also clearly reveals their planned and staged qualities. The rickshaw pullers also usually take one to the huge old Gingko tree where the temple in honor of Wu Jiangjun, the patron of Wuzhen, originally stood. The tourism company has now rebuilt the temple on a new location in the West Street district, one of the rebuilt religious sites in that area that local residents cannot visit. Sometimes the rickshaw pullers may also suggest a trip to one of the Buddhist temples. Before the West Street was redeveloped and cordoned off, they would also take you to that street. The tourism company is not happy about these enterprising rickshaw pullers and has put up a sign warning tourists of these "unauthorized" tourist guides. They accuse them of swindling tourists of both their money and experience of the "real Wuzhen."

THE HISTORY AND DEVELOPMENT OF TEMPLES AND SHRINES IN WUZHEN: A TALE OF DESTRUCTION AND REVIVAL

Like other Chinese villages and towns, Wuzhen in the past had many temples, ranging from Buddhist and Daoist temples, to those dedicated to local deities of various kinds. The larger Buddhist and Daoist temples belonged to different schools and linked up with temples elsewhere, whereas the many small religious sites and shrines served the local community and were dedicated to local gods and deities, including the City God and the Earth God. It is estimated that Wuzhen in the past had some fifty-three temples and shrines of different sizes, and that at the time of the founding of the PRC some ten temples still existed (Wang 2001, 378). The temples fared differently under different historic periods, and many had already been deserted and become ruins during the late Qing. The nationalists' attacks on religion and what they regarded as superstition during the Republican period (Poon 2008) also led to the disappearance and closure of many temples. The Baoge Temple was for example taken over by the Wuzhen Chamber of Commerce, only to later be converted into a school.

Wuzhen had some ten Daoist temples in the past, of which the Xiuzhen Temple was the largest. Many of these temples were destroyed during the nationalist regime, and in 1949 only five remained, including the Xiuzhen Temple, the Yousheng Gong, Chongfu Gong, and the Guandi Temple. The Yousheng Gong was later used as a granary, whereas the Chongfu Gong after 1911 was used as a school. The Xiuzhen Temple, which originates from 998 and was renovated as late as 1933, was converted into a dormitory and also used as a granary, and during the 1970s the remaining buildings were demolished to make way for a department store.

There were many more Buddhist temples in Wuzhen. The Shifo Temple, or Futian Temple, as it was also known, dating from around the fifth century, was one of the biggest and more famous temples with three beautiful carved stone Buddha; only half of one of the statues still remains. The Pujing Temple was also quite grand to judge by a map from the Republican period but it was destroyed after 1949. Other temples, such as the Ciyun Temple, which together with Shifo Temple are the only existing Buddhist temples in Wuzhen today, were fairly small. In China local cults often developed around historic persons that later came to serve as patrons for the village or area in question. In Wuzhen the local patron was Wu Jiangjun, who was worshiped in a special temple, also known as the Earth God Temple, dedicated to him. The temple is long since gone but the huge Gingko tree on the former temple ground still exists. Another historical figure that served as a patron of the town was Marshal Wen (Katz 1995). His statue was found both in the Xiuzhen Temple and in the City God Temple and paraded in the town during a special religious festival to his honor.

The temples were important places where residents came together to celebrate and manifest their local identity. Many of the festivals were very local in character but some also linked the local religious community with religious communities and temples elsewhere (Wang 2001, 372–76; Xu 2003, 177–84). The Incense Fair (*Xiangshi*) took place during the first twenty days of the third lunar month and involved the City God Temple and the Pujing Temple. Peasants from the surrounding areas would also come to pray and burn incense as well as partake in games, operas, and other festivities during the temple fair. Women from Wuzhen would also travel to other temples, including to Hangzhou, where they offered incense and prayed for protection of the silkworms, so central for the local economy (see also Wang 2000). The Wuzhen City God Festival took place in the seventh month of the lunar calendar and during this festival several deities were paraded around the town. Temple fairs were also arranged at other temples, including a Spring Temple Fair held at the Xiuzhen Daoist Temple.

With the new regime after 1949, religious life was attacked and temples and monasteries were closed, which meant that religious festivals and temple fairs also came to a halt. There was a visible change to the physical landscape of Wuzhen as many religious buildings were either demolished, or taken over and transformed into what Yang (2004) calls "socialist spaces," or simply neglected and left to gradually fall apart. In Wuzhen the Miyin Temple was for example first used as a granary and later taken over by the Wuzhen tax office. Several other temples, like the Guandi Temple, were also used as granaries, whereas some smaller ones were converted into residential uses, and others, such as the Baoge Temple, continued to be used as a school for some time.

With the more relaxed atmosphere in the early 1980s, many temples in China were returned to the official Buddhist and Daoist organizations that now resumed their activities. During this period many local communities also began to reclaim and rebuild shrines and temples. At the village level, where this revival was more prominent, people painstakingly collected money and invested their own labor in this renovation and construction work. In some cases, money was also collected from religious followers living in other villages. Today there is a growing network of lay people based in cities who are willing and eager to help struggling temples (so-called *kumiao*) in rural areas (see Fisher 2008).

It is likely that religious activity continued for some time after 1949 at the remaining major temples in Wuzhen but that the final blow to the temples came in the late 1950s and during the Cultural Revolution. The Ciyun Temple and the Shifo Temple both lost their land during the land reform period in the early 1950s, and the buildings saw much destruction in the years that followed.[11] The efforts to reclaim and rebuild temples in Wuzhen have centered on these two temples and there have been some rather spectacular developments in the past few years. Local residents, mainly women it seems, at first took care of the temples and they continue to come to the temples to worship on the first and fifteenth days of the lunar calendar, during the Chinese New Year, and other significant religious days. What is striking, however, is that local residents today are outnumbered by pilgrims and laypeople from other places, mainly Hangzhou and Shanghai, whose support is the main reason why the temples have prospered in recent years. According to the abbot at the Ciyun Temple, who came to the temple in 1997, it was a woman from Wuzhen who sought him out when he was based at the Shangtianzhu Temple in Hangzhou and convinced him to come to Wuzhen. The abbot has now gathered some twelve to thirteen monks in the temple, many from his hometown in Jiangxi. The temple got official permission from the Tongxiang religious bureau in 1999.[12] There is a close connection between the Shangtianzhu Temple, the Gaoming Temple in Tiantai, and the Ciyun Temple, with links between both abbots and laypeople. The abbot depends on donations from the local community, and increasingly a translocal community of followers, for his work to rebuild the temple. When he first arrived only one building was still standing that he later had replaced. He has since built two new halls that were almost finished during my last visit in April 2008, some office buildings, and a dormitory for visiting laypeople that can accommodate up to one hundred people. The abbot now has a devoted following, consisting mainly of people from the Hangzhou and Shanghai areas. These lay practitioners mainly consist of elderly women, and many tend to come several times every year. One elderly couple from Hangzhou for example take turns in visiting the temple, as one of them has to stay behind and take care of the grandchildren. The couple also often visits the Gaoming Temple but they have never visited the nearby Shifo Temple, or the tourist sites in Wuzhen. People come either individually but more often in larger groups, organized by one of the more active laypeople who serve as the leader and help collect donations.

The Shifo Temple has had a similar development as the Ciyun Temple. In the 1990s, local residents started to rebuild the temple, and in 2003 the current abbot, who is from Jiangsu but graduated from a Buddhist college in Sichuan, came to the temple from the nearby Foyan Temple to which the Shifo Temple historically is linked. The temple got its official permission from the Tongxiang religious bureau in 1999 and currently has twelve to thirteen monks. When the abbot first arrived there was only one hall but since then they have built another hall and a larger dormitory with the donations that they have raised. The abbot has recently been able to buy more land from peasants living in the vicinity, so that the temple now has 40 mu, compared to 8–9 mu in the late 1990s. To the celebration of Guanyin's birthday in 2005 several hundred people came to the Shifo Temple, mainly from Hangzhou and Shanghai, and some stayed for several days. They were mostly retired women seeking spiritual comfort as well as wanting to busy themselves and do something useful. One woman from Shanghai explained that she felt more needed and motivated to help a local temple in the countryside since even small donations mattered and practical work was appreciated. She complained that the big and rich temples in Shanghai did not appreciate her donations and work to the same extent as a poor and struggling temple such as the Shifo Temple.[13]

RELIGIOUS COMMUNITIES, THE STATE, AND TOURISM: CONTESTATIONS OR A MODUS VIVENDI?

In recent years local governments and tourist companies have come to take an active part in the building and rebuilding of shrines and temples. One example of such an active involvement in Zhejiang is the building of temples dedicated to the famous Huang Daxian in the Jinhua area (see Lang, Chan, and Ragvald 2005; Chan and Lang 2007). The local government has consciously supported and promoted the building of several temples in the hope that they would attract tourists and investment from Hong Kong where the deity is hugely popular. Famous temples are usually among the must-see scenic spots and a natural stop on many tourist tours. Religious sites furthermore serve to add *renao* (spectacle) and help diversify tourist attractions.

For the local governments there is an inherent and latent problem with religious tourism as they are hardly interested in promoting religious beliefs per se, and a too active religious community would be something of a liability. Religious practices and religious sites are clearly controlled by the Chinese state (see Oakes and Sutton's introduction in this volume). In Wuzhen, shrines dedicated to popular and local gods have been re-created for tourist consumption but are not intended as living religious spaces as their theme park qualities testify. Their revival is top-down and artificial and has not involved the local community, who doesn't even have access to these shrines since they are within a gated tourist space.

It is more surprising that the "superstitious" practices in the Xiuzhen Temple are not only condoned but seem to be actively promoted (cf. Yu Luo Rioux in this volume). Although fortune telling is officially seen as a form of super-

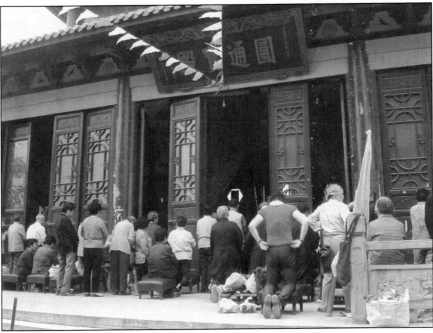

Figure 8.4.   Pilgrims at the Shifo Temple during the celebration of Guanyin's birthday, 2005. M. Svensson photo.

stitious activities, it nonetheless often constitutes an important attraction at religious sites. It is worth noting that the Xiuzhen Temple was rebuilt and is managed by the tourism company. The temple has not been approved or registered by the Daoist Association, and would in fact, strictly speaking, be illegal as it houses at least one ordained Daoist priest and conducts certain Daoist practices. The fact that the temple is run as a tourist enterprise may explain its somewhat unorthodox practices and pushy guides. The only ordained Daoist priest in the temple came to Wuzhen from Jiangxi some five years ago on the invitation of the tourist company.[14] The priest belongs to the school of Total Perfection (*Quanzhen*) and maintains close contacts with his local community in Jiangxi and the local Daoist associations there; there is no Daoist association in Wuzhen. There are a number of other men, some dressed as Daoists, in the temple, and there seems to exist some division of labor between them and the Daoist priest. He is responsible for the more "serious" fortune telling and consultations that requires knowledge of Daoism, whereas the others are engaged in the more "tacky" fortune telling that involves selling the *bagua* amulet and takes place behind closed doors in the smaller side halls in the inner courtyard. The Daoist priest sits at a small table in the first, main hall, where a statue of

Dongyue Dadi holds pride of place with the twelve birth animals at the side-walls. He engages in fortune telling, such as reading people's hands and faces, for a fee, and now and then is also asked to officiate and consecrate (*kaiguang*) statues that some tourists buy. The Daoist priest is aware that the tourists are not interested or knowledgeable about Daoism but regard the temple as a "scenic spot" (*jingdian*) and as something "fun" (*hao wan'r*). The majority of the tourists don't seem to be regular visitors to Daoist temples in their hometowns. One man from Shanghai visiting the temple thus said that he had never visited the Baiyun Daoist temple in downtown Shanghai.

There have been several complaints on the Web and in blogs about pushy guides who persuade tourists to buy incense and amulets in the Xiuzhen Temple. In May 2007, one blogger, a young man living in Beijing, wrote an account of his recent visit to Wuzhen that mainly focused on his experience in the Xiuzhen Temple (Su n.d.). He describes how they were offered so-called birth animal cards for free and instructed to carry this card in their hands to the inner hall where a "Daoist priest" waited to read their fortune. Since he was a bit skeptical he just followed along and observed how two young girls were told that their future would be bright if they only would offer some incense. The girls were then led to the courtyard where they bought incense, which cost between 60 and 130 yuan. Then they were given another round of fortune telling before being prompted to buy a *bagua* amulet. One of the girls refrained to do so but the other girl ended up buying an amulet for 500 yuan. When the blogger later asked the girl why she had gone along, she replied that she had felt "embarrassed" (*bu hao yisi*) to refuse the "Daoist" and that the guide also had said that if one were not polite toward the Daoists it would be "harmful to her" (*dui ziji bu li*). After returning from his trip, the blogger searched the Web and found many other similar accounts of the hoax (*pianju*) carried out at the temple. Other bloggers who had visited Wuzhen and themselves either been tricked or seen others being tricked posted similar descriptions and reactions on baidu.com.[15] They described how they step by step have been led and persuaded to buy first incense and then amulets, and how they were made to feel that they couldn't easily withdraw once they had met with the Daoist and received their first fortune reading. They also said that they had worried that a refusal would bring bad luck. Most of them reacted against the collusion between the guides and what they described as "fake" Daoists, and blamed the tourist management for this hoax. It is perhaps as a response to critique like this that the tourist company has put up a sign that proclaims freedom of belief and tells the tourists that donations are voluntary, although the selling of incense and amulets continued unabated during my latest trip in April 2008.

Local residents in Wuzhen do not have access to the Xiuzhen Temple as all visitors need a ticket to enter the temple. Whereas before 1949, the temple was a central part of the cultural and religious life in Wuzhen, it has today lost this function. This is no doubt a result of the fact that the local community has not been actively involved in rebuilding the temple or attempted to reappropriate it. Local residents would say that the only "real" temples in Wuzhen are the Ciyun and Shifo temples, and the more devoted of them would visit one or the other of them. One old woman, who regularly visited the Ciyun Temple, emphasized that these temples were built by ordinary people (*laobaixing*), whereas the Xiuzhen Temple was built and managed by the tourism company. The Buddhist temples furthermore follow and celebrate different Buddhist anniversaries, whereas the Xiuzhen Temple doesn't seem to celebrate Daoist anniversaries or deities that official Daoist temples do, which also shows that the latter is more of a tourist space than a religious space. However, the fact that local residents don't visit the temple or engage in any religious practices there doesn't preclude other forms of religious contacts. The ordained Daoist priest has some contacts with the local community outside of the temple as they ask for his services, including choosing auspicious days for the opening of a new shop, or in connection with funerals, and so on.

The tourism company has during recent years on several occasions reportedly approached the Ciyun and Shifo temples with offers to incorporate the temples in the tourist itinerary. The temples are situated very close to the newly opened West Street, and the Ciyun Temple is in fact surrounded on three sides by the tourist area (there is a road in front of the temple), so one can understand why the tourist company would want to add the temples to its itinerary. The temples have, however, refused the tourist company's offer. Other temples elsewhere in China have made other considerations and been tempted by the financial benefits or else themselves take a more proactive stance with respect to tourism (cf. for example Fisher 2008 and Sutton and Kang in this volume). The abbots argue that it is against the principles of a temple to engage in commercial activities and charge entrance fees. They also believe that the tourism company is not interested in religion but just wants to add more attractions and the spectacle that a temple would bring to the tourist experience. The abbot at the Ciyun Temple referred in discussions with the tourism company to the principle of freedom of religion as stipulated in national laws, and to the fact that the temple is officially registered with the religious bureau. He is thus able to protect the temple and refuse a proposal coming from a much stronger part (as the resettlement of the whole West Street so clearly illustrated) by basing himself on state-sanctioned legal rights. The financial strength of the tourist company and its recent redevelopment of the West Street have, however, meant that the surrounding land, some of which before 1949 belonged to the temple, has been bought up by the tourist company and that the temple has no possibilities to expand any further.

It is obvious that those managing or constructing religious spaces in Wu-zhen have different motives and engage in different spatial practices. The Buddhist monks in the Ciyun and Shifo temples thus engage and interact with their visitors as part of their own normal daily routine, whereas tour-ist staff and the Daoist priests at the Xiuzhen Temple are more consciously interacting with people without any religious motives and understanding, and also engage in very different spatial practices, checking entrance tickets, managing people's behavior in the temple, and selling souvenirs. The abbots are trying to promote their temples and get more donations but this is part of the "merit making" that constitutes the core of Buddhist religious practices.[16] By contrast, the prime motive of the tourist company and the local authori-ties supporting this endeavor is to make use of religious spaces in order to promote tourism and economic growth. A local businessman in Wuzhen has also entered into the religious market and built a new City God Temple close to the East Street. Hardly anybody seems to visit the temple as it is slightly off the tourist path, and the temple now serves more as an embellishment to the restaurant that he also operates on the premises.

Although religious devotion cuts across gender and socioeconomic status, and leisure travel has become more accessible for broader groups of people, religious pilgrimage is very much dominated by older women and by lower income groups (cf. Dott in this volume). The laypeople who visit the Ciyun and Shifo temples are mostly elderly women who are not interested in visiting Wuzhen's tourist sites and are shocked at the high entrance fee to Wuzhen. One woman from Tongxiang City mentioned that she had visited the Mao Dun fam-ily home long before tourism took off and when the entrance ticket was only 2 yuan. She had not been back since and had no interest to do so. Other pilgrims likewise explained that they had no interest in visiting tourist sites and generally preferred pilgrimage above leisure travel and clearly differentiate between the two. They were more likely and willing to spend their money on merit making than on personal consumption and leisure. The tourists, for their part, would have difficulties in even finding the Buddhist temples since they are not on the tourist itinerary. Their tight schedule controlled by tourism companies further-more makes it impossible to take time for any side trips.

CONCLUSION: RELIGION, TRANSLOCAL COMMUNITIES, AND THE MARKET

In Wuzhen there is hardly any interaction between the temples managed by the local Buddhist association and visited by devotees and pilgrims, and those managed by the tourism company and primarily visited by tourists. In many other places, however, the same religious spaces often both host devotees, pilgrims, and tourists (see other contributions to this volume). In such an event the different groups need to negotiate a shared space, or, as one could also put it, the same space gives rise to different spatial practices and religious activities. This sharing of space can lead to conflicts and to the religious community becoming resentful when their religious space is appropriated for secular use. In China today, tourists often outnumber religious believers and pilgrims at many of the more famous temples. It is not only difficult for practitioners to congregate and pray, but different understandings and uses of religious space can also lead to conflicts. In order to educate tourists to behave in an appropriate and correct way, the Lingyin Temple in Hangzhou has for example put up placards with pictures and written instructions on how to pray, as well as signs warning visitors, who may not be experienced, of fake monks. Tourism appropriation of religious spaces may also give rise to conflicts between religious and secular managers of these sites. In Wuzhen, the Buddhist temples have however successfully, as it seems for now, managed to withstand the tourist company's proposal to include them in the tourist itinerary. Since the Xiuzhen Temple is more of a tourist space than a space for religious activities, and the newly built shrines and temples in the West Street so obviously target tourists, the local religious community and the tourism company is currently able to exist under a modus vivendi.

The struggling religious communities in Wuzhen exist off the tourist path. In Xitang, a water town not far away from Wuzhen, work to rebuild a Buddhist temple is also taking place at the outskirts of the village and outside of the control of the tourist company that manages several other temples. These struggling local temples are driven by bottom-up forces and supported by a growing translocal religious community. Although they operate under quite different conditions and attract different groups of people than tourism-controlled temples do, abbots and laypeople are not immune to or isolated from market forces but partake and compete in the new religious economy (see for example Sutton and Kang, and McCarthy in this volume). In order to secure donations and attract a strong following, temples also need to market themselves and prove that they are efficient and answer people's prayers, in other words show that they are *ling*. Many temples set up their own websites and produce glossy brochures in order to solicit contributions. The growing quest for spirituality among Chinese people under the influence of individualism and the market economy has, however, also resulted in the commodification of religion and in the appearance of fake monks.[17] The commercial activities in the Xiuzhen Temple show the extent to which religion has become another commodity in market-reform China. However, if this causes strong and more open critique among visitors, whether tourists or devout pilgrims, who find the "superstitious" activities offensive, it may backfire and the tourism company could easily find itself in confrontation with the religious bureau, state officials at higher levels, as well as religious organizations. The tourism company could likewise risk being criticized if the Buddhist temples are pressured to open up to tourism.

In contrast with the rebuilding of some of the Huang Daxian temples in Jinhua (which in most cases were initiated by local officials for tourism purposes but later attracted an interest from the local community who began to worship in the temples or built their own competing temples) or the temples in Sichuan discussed by Sutton and Kang in this volume, the official rebuilding of the Xiuzhen Temple has not created any sense of self-identification or support among the local community. The local residents are excluded from the temple and haven't attempted to reappropriate it. The local community's identification and interaction with the two Buddhist temples are much stronger but not unproblematic since they are increasingly marginalized by a translocal network of laypeople who also have claims on the temples. Nonlocal lay practitioners and abbots may not be so embedded in local realities but bring with them a vision of a translocal Buddhism that influences the local community's relations to and uses of the temples and may also revitalize religion (cf. McCarthy's discussion of Buddhism in Xishuangbanna and the importance of transnational networks in this volume).

NOTES

1. I made my first trip to Wuzhen in 2001. I revisited the town in 2003 during the SARS crisis, twice in 2005, once as a member of a Chinese tourist group from Shanghai, twice in 2007, and most recently in April 2008.

2. General information about Wuzhen can be found in Wang (2001) and on the Wuzhen tourism company home page (www.wuzhen.com.cn).

3. For information about Chen Xianghong, who has been hailed as the new Wu Jiangjun, the town's old patron deity, see articles and interviews at www.wuzhen.com.cn.

4. Many works on Mao Dun's relation with his hometown can be bought in Wuzhen, see for example Zhong (1991), Xu (1999), Tongxiang City Mao Dun Memorial Hall (2001), and Zhong (2004).

5. Information on and extracts from the soap opera can be viewed at the tourism company's homepage, see www.wuzhen.com.cn/zxxs/zxxs_ssnh.htm. The female character has become a poster girl for the town, see www.wuzhen.com.cn/xwdt/xwdt_news_jt.asp?mainid=1321&kind=5&nextmainid=&prevmainid.

6. In June 2009, the Hangzhou Buddhist Association's Photographer Group visited Wuzhen. There is no mention of them visiting any of the temples in Wuzhen.

See www.wuzhen.com.cn/xwdt/xwdt_news_jt.asp?mainid=1306&kind=5&nextmain id=&prevmainid.

7. What follows are observations based on several visits and informal interviews. For studies based on surveys and larger interview materials on how tourism has affected residents in two other water towns, see Huang, Wall, and Mitchell (2007) and Fan, Wall, and Mitchell (2008).

8. Forced evictions and complaints over violent methods and poor financial compensation have been common in China in recent years as a result of dramatic city redevelopments. Information on the protests and resentment in Wuzhen can be found in Cui (2005). There were not many other reports in the Chinese media but I have heard similar complaints in many of my informal interviews with residents in Wuzhen and when discussing the development of Wuzhen with cultural heritage officials in Hangzhou. However, Cui's article obviously led to some heated debate and critique against the author for having exaggerated the forceful evictions and for giving inaccurate information. It is difficult to assess either the critique or the accuracy of the original report. Some of those debating the issue seem to allege that preservation concerns would trump people's right to continue to live in their old houses and thus regard preservation as being more about physical structures than about preserving a way of life or a living culture. For the debate, and what is allegedly an apology from Cui, see beloving.bokee.com/568457.html (accessed 9 August 2009).

9. The tourism company has begun to offer to return families to their former homes but information about the scope and form of this resettlement differs and is scarce.

10. Compare the appropriation and reappropriation of space in Lijiang and the interaction between local residents and tourists discussed in Su and Teo (2008).

11. I base the following account on interviews with the two abbots, individual monks, local residents in Wuzhen, and pilgrims from other places, as well as some written information about the temples.

12. In order to engage in religious activities, temples need official permission and have to be registered as a religious activity site (*zongjiao huodong changsuo*). For a thorough discussion of the role of and power struggles among local religious bureaus, Buddhist associations, and temples, see Ashiwa and Wank (2006).

13. Fisher (2008) describes how abbots in big temples do not have time or cannot be bothered to meet laypeople who do not provide big donations.

14. The priest showed the author his various membership and registration cards that prove that he is ordained. On the background, recruitment, and role of Daoist priests at the different Huang Daxian temples in Jinhua, see Lang, Chan, and Ragvald (2005).

15. See tieba.baidu.com/f?kz=257342893; tieba.baidu.com/f?kz=203627551; and tieba.baidu.com/f?kz=178311341 (accessed 9 August 2009).

16. For the struggles and ambitions of individual abbots to build and expand their temples, see also Fisher (2008).

17. For a fascinating account of the marketing and consumption of Tibetan Buddhism, including the appearance of fake lamas, through the Web and other modern marketing techniques, see Yü (2008).

REFERENCES

Ashiwa, Yoshiko, and David L. Wank. 2006. "The Politics of a Reviving Buddhist Temple: State, Association, and Religion in Southeast China." *Journal of Asian Studies* 65(2): 337–50.

Bellocq, Maylis. 2006. "The Cultural Heritage Industry in the PRC: What Memories Are Being Passed On? A Case Study of Tongli, a Protected Township in Jiangsu Province." *China Perspectives* 67: 22–32.

Chan, Selina Ching, and Graeme Lang. 2007. "Temple Construction and the Revival of Popular Religion in Jinhua." *China Information* 21(1): 43–69.

Chen, Xianghong, ed. 2001. *Xu Xiaobing, Hou Bo he sheyingjiamen yan zhong de Wuzhen* (Wuzhen in the eyes of Xu Xiaobing, Hou Bo and their photographer friends). Beijing: Shijie zhishi chubanshe.

Cui, Xiaolin. 2005. "Wuzhen chaiqian: Shui de yanlei zai liushang? (Demolitions and evictions in Wuzhen: Whose tears are flowing?). *Shidai chao* 1, www.people.com. cn/GB/paper83/13869/1238601.html (accessed 9 August 2009).

Fan, Chennan (Nancy), Geoffrey Wall, and Clare J. A. Mitchell. 2008. "Creative Destruction and the Water Town of Luzhi, China." *Tourism Management* 29: 648–60.

Fisher, Gareth. 2008. "The Spiritual Land Rush: Merit and Morality in New Chinese Buddhist Temple Construction." *Journal of Asian Studies* 67(1): 143–70.

Huang, Helen Yi Bei, Geoffrey Wall, and Clare J. A. Mitchell. 2007. "Creative Destruction, Zhu Jia Jiao, China." *Annals of Tourism Research* 34(4): 1033–55.

Katz, Paul. 1995. *Demon Hordes and Burning Boats: The Cult of Marshal Wen in Late Imperial Chekiang*. Albany: State University of New York Press.

Lang, Graeme, Selina Ching Chan, and Lars Ragvald. 2005. "Temples and the Religious Economy." *Interdisciplinary Journal of Research on Religion* 1(1).

Mao, Dun. 2001. *The Shop of the Lin Family, Spring Silkworms*, trans. S. Shapiro. Beijing: Foreign Languages Press.

Oakes, Tim. 1999. "Eating The Food of the Ancestors: Place, Tradition, and Tourism in a Chinese Frontier River Town." *Ecumene* 6(2): 123–45.

Poon, Shuk-wah. 2008. "Religion, Modernity, and Urban Space: The City God Temple in Republican Guangzhou." *Modern China* 34(2): 247–75.

Ruan, Yisan. 2002. *Wuzhen: Jiangnan shuixiang guzhen* (Wuzhen: An old water-town in the Jiangnan area). Hangzhou: Zhejiang zheying chubanshe.

——. 2004. *Zhongguo jiangnan shuixiang guzhen* (Water towns south of the Yangtze River). Hangzhou: Zhejiang shying chubanshe.

Su, Xiaobo, and Peggy Teo. 2008. "Tourism Politics in Lijiang, China: An Analysis of State and Local Interactions in Tourism Development." *Tourism Geographies* 10(2): 150–68.

Su, Zhong. n.d. Blog on sohu.com, suzhong5.blog.sohu.com/45212959.html (accessed 9 August 2009).

Tongxiang City Mao Dun Memorial Hall, eds. 2001. *Wuzhen zhi zi Mao Dun* (Wuzhen's son Mao Dun). Tongxiang: Tongxiang City Mao Dun Memorial Hall.

Wang, Jiarong, ed. 2001. *Wuzhen zhi* (Wuzhen Gazetter). Shanghai: Shiji chuban jituan and Shanghai shudian chubanshe.

Wang, Liping. 2000. "Tourism and Spatial Change in Hangzhou, 1911–1927." In *Remaking the Chinese City: Modernity and National Identity, 1900–1950*, ed. J. Esherick. Honolulu: University of Hawai'i Press.

Wang, Xufeng. 2003. *Shu xiang Wuzhen* (Literary Wuzhen). Nanjing: Jiangsu jiaoyu chubanshe.

Xu, Chunlei. 1999. *Mao Dun guxiang mingsheng fengqing* (Sites and scenic spots in Mao Dun's hometown). Baotou: Neimenggu renmin chubanshe.

Xu, Jiadi, ed. 2003. *Wuzhen zhanggu* (Wuzhen anecdotes). Shanghai: Shanghai shehui kexueyuan chubanshe, 2003.

Yang, Mayfair Mei-Hui. 2004. "Spatial Struggles: Postcolonial Complex, State Disenchantment, and Popular Reappropriation of Space in Rural Southeast China." *Journal of Asian Studies* 63(3): 719–55.

Yü, Dan Smyer. 2008. "Living Buddhas, Netizens, and the Price of Religious Freedom." In *Privatizing China: Socialism from Afar*, ed. L. Zhang and A. Ong. Ithaca, NY: Cornell University Press, 197–213.

Zhang, Jiaqiang. 2002. *Wuzhen yijiu* (Wuzhen unchanged). Nanjing: Jiangsu meishu chubanshe.

Zhong, Guisong. 1991. *Mao Dun yu guxiang* (Mao Dun and his hometown). Chengdu: Sichuan wenyi chubanshe.

———. 2004. *Yu Mao Dun yang chunchong* (Cultivating silkworms with Mao Dun). Hangzhou: Zhejiang wenyi chubanshe.

9

The Return Visits of Overseas Chinese to Ancestral Villages in Putian, Fujian

Kenneth Dean

Several intertwined networks connect the villages and ritual alliances of Putian and Xianyou counties in Fujian Province, historically known as Xinghua Prefecture, across national boundaries with emigrant Xinghua temples and communities in Singapore, Indonesia, Malaysia, Brunei, and the Philippines. These phenomena provide an alternative perspective on the sources of local cultural and ritual change in China. They also raise questions about the nature of return visits by overseas Xinghua emigrants. Can these visits, which are often linked to ritual events, as will be shown below, be described as a form of tourism, or are these return flows best understood as part of an ongoing exploration of an expanding transnational spatial imaginary? What is it about the participatory ritual events performed throughout these networks that enables the ongoing negotiation of the forces of modernity?

This chapter first outlines the historical background to the overseas Chinese transnational networks linking Putian, Fujian, to multiple points in Southeast Asia. Next, two of these overlapping networks are introduced: the network the Huang lineage of Shiting in Southeast Asia and the network of Jiulidong (Nine Carp Cavern) temples that practice the collective training of spirit mediums. The chapter then explores the return visits of overseas Chinese to their ancestral villages to participate in ritual training sessions for new generations of spirit mediums back in Putian beginning in the late 1980s. The touristic aspects of these return visits are discussed, as well as the nature of transnational space within the ancestral villages and their multiple overseas networks. A final section looks into the powers of ritual events occurring throughout these networks to generate new spaces, subjectivities, and experiences.

HISTORICAL BACKGROUND TO FLOATING FRONTIERS

A vast overseas Minnan commercial and cultural "empire" stretches down the coast of China and around the coastal ports of Southeast Asia.[1] In addition to the over 20 million Minnan speakers in Taiwan (which was settled in the seventeenth century onward primarily by immigrants from the Minnan region), there are nearly 8 million Hokkien speakers living in Southeast Asia. They are distributed as follows: Malaysia (1.68 million), Indonesia (1.54 million), the Philippines (1.24 million), Singapore (860,000), Thailand (260,000), Burma (175,000), Vietnam (100,000), Brunei (31,000), Cambodia (30,000), and Japan (3,000). All are descendants of immigrants and sojourners from Fujian, or more recent visitors in the latest round of circulation within this vast network.[2]

When Marco Polo (1254–1324) visited the Quanzhou port of Zaiton (Zitong gang), he described it as the greatest in the world after Hangzhou. Around this time, the Quanzhou customs office was run by Pu Shougeng (1205–1290), the descendant of Arab merchants. In the fifteenth century, following in the wake of the great naval expeditions of Admiral Zheng He (1371–1433), a Hokkien commercial network replaced the earlier established Arab trading networks that had extended all the way from the Gulf of Arabia to the port of Quanzhou. The new Minnan coastal empire was built up through the export of several institutions that had originated in local society in the Minnan region: extended (and mutated) lineages, division of incense temple networks, native place associations, and pooled capital *gongsi* corporations and brotherhoods (usually also under the protection of local gods). Innumerable Minnan "family business" empires were built up out of all these elements. Over time, many of these institutions would transform in reaction to many different local circumstances. The long process of cultural experimentation and flexible forms of organization developed overseas also fed back into the social and cultural history of the local cultures of the southeast Chinese coast.

Many scholars, including G. W. Skinner (1985), E. Vermeer (1990), and Wang Mingming (1999), have erroneously concluded that the greater Minnan region (Quanzhou, Zhangzhou, and the Xinghua region of Putian and Xianyou) declined precipitously during the Ming and Qing dynasties. They attribute this decline to the ban on overseas trade established in the early Ming, later restrictions on coastal and international trade in response to the rise of piracy and later in response to incursions by Western powers, the devastating impact of major pirate raids along the Fujian coast and deep inland, and the effects of the early Qing coastal evacuation and continuing restrictions on long-distance trade. They point to a decline in the overall population of the Quanzhou region, the silting in of the Quanzhou harbor, and the establishment of strict state control over the population through various institutions of local control such as the *lijia* (household registration and taxation), the *xiangyue* (community compacts), the *Baojia* (mutual defense/policing), and the *shengyue* (recitation of the sacred edicts) systems, presumably further limiting local creativity.

But the boundaries of the Minnan region were flexible, and kept expanding, or floating, with the maritime travels of Minnan sojourners across Southeast Asia. Any account of the historical change of the overall population of the Minnan people should take into consideration their growing numbers overseas, not just the declining numbers at home.[3] The harbors of the Minnan area moved over time away from the Quanzhou port to the Anhai port, and then to the ports of Jinjiang, and finally to Xiamen Island. Coastal and even international trade does not appear to have declined during the long period of the official restrictions on overseas trade. Instead, armed merchant fleets arose which could instantly switch from legal to pirate or to intermediate smuggler status.

Close study of local documents reveals that the state was unable to achieve effective social control over local society in late imperial times. Efforts to build forts along the coast to contain piracy and smuggling foundered as the military households of these forts ended up having to join the pirates and smugglers in order to survive. Local control via institutions such as the *lijia* (division into subcanton with tenfold household registration, taxation, and policing system) had the unintended effect of furthering the development of local temple alliances, which later feuded over control of local resources and access to coastal trading ports.

Minnan lineage formations, which ostensibly were modeled on state-sanctioned models, soon mutated into contractually based transnational corporations, or into joint stock companies designed for smuggling and the transnational flows of people, ideas, goods, and images (Zheng 2001). The earliest Minnan *gongsi* (corporations) were groups of investors who pooled capital (divided into shares) in order to sponsor oceangoing boats built and operated by the group of owners (Chen 2006). Later, local institutions such as the temple alliances, the contractual lineages, and the overseas gongsi (corporations often based in same-dialect brotherhoods and temples) spread to the Minnan communities of Southeast Asia, where they interacted with local institutions and changing polities.

There are records of Chinese sojourners in Southeast Asia dating to the Tang and the Song.[4] These communities continued to expand over time. Villages settled by Chinese in Vietnam in the Ming are still referred to as Ming villages. There were large populations of Minnan people already active in Manila in the early 1600s (when twenty thousand were massacred by Spanish authorities) and in Batavia (where up to ten thousand were massacred in 1740 by Dutch authorities). These were, however, temporary setbacks, as colonial authorities soon realized how indispensable Chinese merchants were to the exchange of goods (Chinese silk, porcelain, and iron goods in exchange for Mexican silver and local products in Manila, and in exchange for spices and local products in Indonesia). In Malaysia, Chinese from Minnan had even greater success—the leading mercantile families of Malacca were Baba families of mixed Chinese and Malay ancestry. The Thai leadership included mixed Chinese families, mainly from Chaozhou (Teochow). Each region and culture presented different opportunities and restrictions to the Minnan and other Chinese sojourners. As these regions passed into the hands of Western colonial powers, and later became independent postcolonial nation-states, conditions changed dramatically for the Minnan sojourners living in different ecological and economic niches within them. Nonetheless, they continued to adapt creatively to changing conditions, and preserved corridors of movement of people and capital linking them to their ancestral villages. Over several centuries, there was a continuous coming and going of overseas sojourners back and forth within these corridors.[5] This constant cycling of bodies and experiences meant the many lives were lived in between places within the extended space of the Minnan coastal commercial empire.

The Minnan communities overseas went from being merchant middlemen (sixteenth to eighteenth centuries) handling retail sales of all kinds of goods (including increasingly opium) to becoming suppliers of goods to Western markets by organizing the mining of tin and by helping to manage plantations of tobacco, pepper, gambor, and spices in the nineteenth and twentieth centuries. To handle this major change, they also became after 1840 middlemen in the supply and control of cheap Chinese labor to these production facilities. In the nineteenth century, the Minnan control of the trading ports of Southeast Asia was challenged by the arrival of other dialect groups including the Chaozhou (who ultimately outnumbered the Hokkien speakers, although they too speak a variant of Hokkien), the Cantonese, the Hakka, the Hainanese, and at the end of the century, the Fuzhou and the Xinghua (Henghwa) sojourners. Under increasing control from colonial governments, the Minnan merchants transformed their earlier informal organizations, and developed a plethora of legalized local associations, including *huiguan*, temples, cemeteries, hospitals, chambers of commerce, schools, and so forth.

In the late nineteenth century, the imperial government of China actively sought the assistance and support of the overseas Chinese communities of Southeast Asia, as did various revolutionaries at the turn of the century. Overseas Chinese played a very active role in local society within China in the 1911 Revolution and in the 1920s and 1930s. During the 1920s and 1930s, many overseas Chinese sojourners returned to Fujian or sent funds back to pay for local infrastructure, including ancestral halls and temples, but also to build magnificent homes in their home villages. This was the period in which Jiangkou in northeast Putian saw the construction of dozens of palatial homes built in red brick, with courtyards and gardens and pavilions. Many overseas Chinese returned after the founding of the People's Republic as well. But due to the Cultural Revolution, and the export of Maoist movements, as well as the rise of ethnic nationalism in the postcolonial states of Southeast Asia, Chinese sojourners were largely cut off from their home villages for over twenty-five years (1965–1990). In certain places they were subject to violent attack. Many began to formulate alternative identities as *huaren* (Chinese citizens of X), rather than as *huaqiao* (Chinese sojourner in X). Finally, in the 1990s, large numbers of overseas Chinese began returning to visit their ancestral villages in Fujian and Guangzhou.

The 1980s and 1990s were also marked by a fundamental shift in global capitalism as it developed systems of flexible accumulation, characterized by rapid flows of financial capital, outsourcing of factories to areas with cheap labor, and the development of a cadre of technical midlevel office workers and technicians, along with an elite of high-flying capitalist business leaders and financiers. These economic changes profoundly affected the Hokkien coastal commercial empire. Business leaders became flexible citizens and harbingers of an alternative Asian modernity (as analyzed in Ong and Nonini 1997). But as they also point out, laborers were also forced into new patterns of mobility, as were midlevel office workers. These changes occurred simultaneously with political overtures that opened the blocked networks of the extended Minnan transnational spaces. The overall trend of economic control and comparative prosperity for Chinese in Southeast Asia, now a five-hundred-year tradition, continued under new circumstances, despite various government restrictions. This five-hundred-year background is important for understanding the significance of the revival of temple networks linking Fujian to local nodes across Southeast Asia since the 1980s.

THE XINGHUA OVERSEAS CHINESE NETWORK

Within this epic story of great significance to world history, the sojourners from the Xinghua region (Putian and Xianyou counties, and bordering villages of Fuqing County) entered rather late into the narrative. They first began emigrating in large numbers in the late nineteenth century, mainly to Singapore and Malaysia, where they worked as coolies pulling rickshaws. They quickly monopolized control over the transportation sector, taking over

[handwritten annotations in top margin: "modernity and trades Chinese immigrated in then took control."]

bicycle stores and repairs, and thus they were paradoxically well positioned to ride the technological innovations of the transportation industry in the twentieth century to a position of remarkable prosperity. From rickshaws and bicycles they moved to cars and public buses, and then to spare parts and automobile dealerships, and on to ethanol plants and palm oil plantations. Over 600,000 Putian *huaqiao* (overseas Chinese) now live in over forty countries around the world, with 95 percent in Southeast Asia, primarily in Malaysia (230,795), Indonesia (220,000), Singapore (136,000), Thailand (4,000), and the Philippines (2,500). Some left as early as the 1567 lifting of the Ming ban on overseas trade. A second wave left during the Ming-Qing transition, emigrating to Nagasaki, the Ryuku Islands, and also to Southeast Asia. A third wave was made up mainly of contract laborers shipped to Southeast Asia, the United States, and to Macao in the late nineteenth century. Conditions in the Putian area in the late nineteenth century and early twentieth century deteriorated rapidly. The growth in population and the decline of the complex local irrigation system led to the formation of feuding multivillage alliances. Conditions only worsened in the Republican period, when armies moved through the region, sometimes burning villages in their wake. All these factors led to considerable emigration to Southeast Asia, primarily to Singapore, Malaysia, and Indonesia.

The first Xinghua *Huiguan* (native-place association) was established in Singapore in 1920.[6] In 1921 1,651 Xinghua emigrants were living in Singapore. By 1931 their numbers had increased to over 30,000. A number of branch temples from the Xinghua region were established in Southeast Asia in the first half the twentieth century, some by spirit mediums who carried a statue of the god and incense from their home temple with them on their travels. Some of these temples flourished, and branched off again into temples scattered around Southeast Asia. The earliest of these temples were Tianhou temples linked to the Xinghua native-place associations.

[handwritten annotation in left margin: "native place assoc."]

Another important group of early temples were those of the Jiulidong (Nine Carp Cavern) spirit medium cult. This temple is one of the main sites for a form of collective spirit medium training unique to the northern part of the Putian cultural region. Young boys are taken into the temple for extended periods of training in spirit possession, chanting of invocations of the gods, and collective exorcistic dance (see Dean and Zheng 1993 for a description of these rituals, referred to locally as *guanjie* [lit. to be locked inside the temple in order to receive the prohibitions]). This extremely localized ritual tradition has spread and flourished in the Xinghua communities of Southeast Asia.

A small number of lineage halls were founded in Southeast Asia by Xinghua emigrants from the villages of Jiuliyang irrigated plain of northeast Putian County. Among these emigrants were members of the Huang lineage

Figure 9.1.   At the conclusion of a *guanjie* ceremony, a spirit medium in trance is dressed as a god. K. Dean photo, Liangcuo village, Putian, 1993.

of Shiting, from the Jiangkou region of northeast Putian district. There are ten thousand Huang lineage members currently living in the fourteen villages of the greater Shiting area. But there are over twenty thousand Huang descendants claiming direct links to this lineage living in Southeast Asia. The examination of certain Huang lineage branch genealogies reveals that this lineage was a transnational contractual super-lineage (Zheng 2001) that allowed nonrelated members to buy shares in the lineage. Families within this lineage frequently adopted in unrelated boys who were then sent to Southeast Asia to sink or swim. The lineage pursued multiple strategies of survival and expansion simultaneously. The Huang lineage in Shiting and in Southeast Asia is an example of a transnational lineage.

The back hall of the Tongtiangong Temple in Seremban, Malaysia, houses a shrine dedicated to the ancestors of the Huang lineage. Ancestral worship is conducted in the shrine.[7] However, the Xinghua community, being latecomers to Southeast Asia in comparison to Hokkien, Hakka, Guangdong, and Hainan communities, have not yet developed *tongxinghui* (common surname associations) to link the far-flung descendants of a shared surname together. Other modes of tying the Xinghua community together have developed instead, including the spread of the *guanjie*[8] ceremonies (spirit medium training in collective spirit mediumistic practices). Indeed, the Tongtiangong temple, which primarily serves the extended Huang lineage community, maintains two side halls for two different spirit medium temples from the Jiangkou area, the Mingandian and the Jiulidong (Nine Carp Cavern) temples. The central hall of the temple is devoted to local gods worshiped in the Shiting region. In many respects, the cults of the gods and the powers of the spirit mediums are the main vehicle for the expression of lineage identity.

THE NINE CARP CAVERN TEMPLE NETWORK

The main gods of the Jiulidong (Nine Carp Cavern) Temple are the Four Immortals: Lu Shiyuan, Wang Chengguang, Chen Shande, and Xie Yuanhui. The cult was founded in the 1920s, and was at first based in a side altar adjoining a temple in Shiting. During the Japanese invasion, the gods of this temple were moved inland and kept safe in an ancestral hall. Some of the god statues also appear to have been carried to Singapore around this time, where they became the basis for the first Jiulidong (Nine Carp Cavern) Temple in Southeast Asia, established in 1938. In 1946 a branch temple was established in Tibing Tingyi; in 1955 a third temple was established in Kisaran, Sumatra; and in 1963 a fourth branch temple was established in Jakarta as well.[9] Other related temples include the Dongyueguan founded in 1965 in Medan, Sumatra, which includes altars to the gods of the different sects of the *tanban* (altar association) ritual tradition, along with many other gods (sixty-seven in all). A Jiulidong side altar was set up in the aforementioned Tongtiangong in Seramban, Malaysia, in 1951. Other temples linked loosely to the network can be found in Ipoh in eastern Malaysia, and in Kuching in western Malaysia as well. All of these temples were cut off from developments in Putian from the 1950s onward. Moreover, each of the four main Jiulidong temples (Singapore, Tibing Tingyi, Kisaran, and Jakarta) declared itself to be a *fenzhen* (an independent temple within a loose network, rather than a hierarchical grouping of temples). All of them acknowledge the Jiulidong in Shiting, Putian, to be their founding temple. That temple has been rebuilt or significantly expanded three times since 1980, and has become a site of symbolic struggle between different overseas temple associations. In the 1990s, temple leaders from this network divined the original location of Immortal Lu Shiyuan's temple on a mountaintop in Pinghai, near the ferry to Meizhou Island, and built a new temple there.

Each of the independent Southeast Asian Jiulidong temples have held numerous and regular spirit medium training sessions (guanjie) over the past several decades. In addition, a number of ritual innovations have occurred in these Southeast Asian temples over the course of their independent evolutions, each in a unique political and multiethnic environment. These innovations include the development, starting in Sumatra in the 1970s, of a new set of ritual initiations in the cult of the Goddess Ou Xiangu and in techniques of spirit writing and ritual dance for women's groups. These women participate in the collective dances of the spirit mediums and the tanban (altar association) held at the conclusion of guanjie initiations in the courtyard outside the temple. The women weave in and out and crisscross counterclockwise through the male tanban dancers while following their own banners inscribed with the name of the Goddess Ou Xiangu and her spirit-writing implements. Similar spirit writing training sessions for women spread to Jakarta in the 1990s and some sessions were held recently in Singapore as well. The first female spirit medium training session ever held in Putian, Fujian, was organized in the summer of 2007 at the Jiulidong Temple in Shiting, Putian, by female adherents of Goddess Ou Xiangu from the branch Jiulidong temple in Tibing Tingyi in Sumatra. This is an example of ritual innovation with the transnational network returning from Southeast Asia to effect developments within Putian.

RETURN FLOWS OF OVERSEAS CHINESE TO CHINA

In the 1980s and 1990s, large numbers of overseas Chinese began returning to visit their ancestral villages in Fujian. Many of the Xinghua overseas

Chinese contributed to the repair or rebuilding of local village temples in the mid-1980s. They continued to return regularly to help sponsor and often to participate in guanjie spirit medium training sessions in the newly rebuilt temples. As the economy expanded within China, more and more young men left these villages to seek employment in the cities of China, Southeast Asia, Europe, and North and South America. This meant that guanjie spirit medium trainings had to be held more frequently, as often as once every five years (rather than once a generation). The overseas Chinese spirit medium businessmen found that they had to return repeatedly to their ancestral villages as the pace of ritual activity accelerated (see Dean and Zheng 2010 for a survey of village temples and ritual activities in the Putian area).

TOURISTIC DIMENSIONS TO THE RETURN VISITS OF OVERSEAS CHINESE TO PUTIAN

As return visits to ancestral home villages became possible in the late 1980s and early 1990s, attention was given by Chinese authorities to the development of tourist facilities. Numbers of tourists rose from around five thousand annually in the early 1980s to over thirty-three thousand in the early 1990s, but the overwhelming majority of these visitors were Taiwanese pilgrims to the Tianhou (Empress of Heaven) Temple dedicated to the goddess Mazu on Meizhou Island.[9] Tourist facilities in Putian prior to the early 1990s were quite rudimentary. In the early 1990s the first of what are now several business hotels were built in the city and on Meizhou Island, by the Tourism Bureau of the Putian City Government. Prior to that time, foreign visitors in theory could only stay at the Huaqiao Hotel (Overseas Chinese Hotel). The local bureau of the Overseas Chinese Connection Agency was founded in 1953, temporarily closed in 1966, and reopened in 1979. An Overseas Chinese Service unit was formally established in November 1983.

High-speed highways were also built into the region only in the late 1980s, for the first time linking Putian to airports in Fuzhou and Xiamen. However, informal visits by overseas relatives from Southeast Asia had been going on since the early 1980s. Putian's main tourist attractions are its ancient Buddhist monasteries such as the Guanghuasi and the temple to local gods and goddesses such as the Tianhougong on Meizhou Island. Unfortunately, these sites had undergone extensive destruction. The entire temple complex on Meizhou had been razed in the Cultural Revolution, and the Guanghuasi had been turned into a plastics factory after its monks were forced to recant Buddhism by eating meat, after which they were forced to return to secular life. The Buddhist networks linking Putian to Southeast Asia were crucial to

[handwritten margin top: in the affections that bridge ideologies related to nation, and power + religion and Han Ci]

[handwritten margin right: Han Ci flow money religion and Chinese Ci]

the reconstruction of these sites, as monks who had trained in these temples before traveling overseas returned in the early 1980s with substantial reconstruction funds gathered in Southeast Asia.[10]

The rapid growth of global tourism in the past few decades has led scholars to describe the contemporary scene as a "runaway world" (Giddens 2000).[11] Tourist studies have for the most part been dominated by industry and policy analyses, often turning tourism into a fetishized object of study, and treating tourism almost exclusively in economic terms. More broadly conceived, "tourism is not just an aggregate of commercial activities; it is also an ideological framing of history, nature and tradition: a framing that has the power to reshape culture and nature to its own needs" (Jane Desmond 1999, xiv, cited in Franklin and Crang 2001, 17). Clearly, tourism must be seen as a social phenomenon, filled with significant mobilities and sensibilities and performative dimensions. Tourism forms "a significant modality for the organization of contemporary social life" (exploring the boundaries of leisure, the holiday, and the everyday). This is true for the overseas Chinese on their return visits to their ancestral villages in Putian. Even if we conclude that their actions and movements are best understood in terms of the reinvention, reenactment, and reembodiment of historic transnational spatial imaginaries, aspects of their movements and experiences can be analyzed in terms of cultural tourism. It would however be an exaggeration to say that this kind of cultural tourism, if that is the right term for it, has generated a tourist culture in Putian. Instead, the visits of the overseas Chinese are absorbed into a far more powerful ritual nexus, one which has been at the heart of the transnational network for centuries.

This kind of tourism can be seen as a "mode of experimentation with identities, memories, fantasies, social relations, and to some degree with 'nature'" (Franklin and Crang 2001, 14). As bearers of ritual knowledge, supposedly better preserved overseas (although in fact often substantially modified), the visits back home by the Xinghua huaqiao are instances of knowledge production of power relations. It is difficult to assess whether their visits engage with any sense of the exotic, since they are more strongly motivated by nostalgia and desire for continuation of an intensive ritual tradition, although the visitors clearly act with the conviction that the gods of the ancestral temples are especially powerful and capable of rather exotic forms of spirit possession. But of course, there is a banal aspect to their visits as well, as all modern travel involves long delays in the "nonplaces" of modern tourism, such as airports and visa offices and travel agencies. A few overseas huaqiao visitors prefer to stay in hotels and maintain a distance from their country cousins, while most others prefer to immerse themselves in the sights and sounds of their ancestral village.

[handwritten bottom: ideology too / – good feelings – affective regimes / money religion]

Issues of power, conflict, and control can arise in these interactions—control over desires of many kinds. In some extreme cases, certain villages in Putian are effectively under the complete domination of wealthy overseas Chinese visitors—although in recent years, most ritual events have come to be primarily locally funded in a self-sustaining ritual ecology, thereby diminishing huaqiao control. Other villages are in effect the battleground of rival overseas huaqiao factions. This rivalry can take the form of extravagant, even wasteful outlays of funds, as in the case of the Jiulidong Temple in Shiting, which has been rebuilt three times in the last twenty years by competing groups of overseas devotees.

There are of course many local people who ardently desire to travel overseas to Southeast Asia and beyond, and family relations are no doubt mobilized in every possible way to pressure the visitors to provide opportunities for increased mobilization of members of the network. These kinds of demands (along with demands for funding and investment) ensure that only wealthy or very old overseas Chinese dare to return to their ancestral villages. This complex field of competing desires has also led to the emergence of a new form of middlemen, who attempt to flatter overseas Chinese visitors while inserting themselves into their decision-making process.

The acceleration of the circulation of people, money, cultural and ritual artifacts, and symbolic capital has resulted in a blurring of the boundaries of the everyday and the holiday. The reverse flow of *xinqiao* (new overseas Chinese emigrant laborers or short-term salespeople), along with other flows of ritual specialists (Daoist ritual masters and spirit mediums) and related cultural artists (marionette performers, opera troupes, singers, and entertainers), probably exceeds the numbers of visitors to Putian from abroad. These are instances of a discrepant cosmopolitanism (Clifford 1996)—with an enhanced flow of tourists, increased flow of migrant labor, and more and more shifting personnel of multinational corporations, along with surges of refugees—defining the global system of tourism. While some claim that as migration flows have increased the very notion of migration has been normalized, it is clear that self-control over mobility still is a privilege.[12]

As for the impact of the visiting overseas Chinese on the local villagers of Putian, or tourism in reverse, it is certain that local villagers are strongly impacted by a new cosmopolitan imaginary fed by television and other media, along with their actual encounters with overseas Chinese visitors. They are also subject to both national and local government propaganda on proper modes of identity formation and proper understandings of local culture and history in relation to the national historical narrative. Here the interests of the overseas Chinese visitors clash in interesting ways with official narratives, as the former are deeply interested in rituals dedicated to the local gods, and in participatory rituals in which these gods actually possess young people from the community. While government narratives of modernization can mesh with overseas Chinese investment and support for infrastructure, roads, schools, hospitals, and village reconstruction, they tend to part ways at the door of the temple to the local gods. At one point in the late 1980s, overseas Chinese were only allowed to invest in the temples *after* investments had been made in public works. This was in effect a form of ritual tax.

Despite the clash of narratives, there is little doubt that the acceleration of the spirit medium training sessions has resulted in a considerable increase in local knowledge and pride in the stories and powers of the local gods. This growing sense of local knowledge has political ramifications. These practices have led to new forms of "construction of local identity, of senses of belonging, with a shared past, a renewed sense of place, and membership in a very specific and local culture, along with ownership of this heritage" (Franklin and Crang 2001, 16). Thus we do not find "authentic places" destroyed by tourism, but rather a complex kind of cultural involution wherein "tourism" of a very special kind (participation in ritual) promotes local awareness.[13] The role of the overseas Chinese in the ritual training of young spirit mediums can be seen as a collaborative performative creation of place, one which demonstrates considerable reflexive awareness.

But the enhanced spatial flows of members of the Henghwa (Xinghua) transnational network/spaces have not by any means led to a wholesale change from cultural tourism to a tourist culture. The local ritual traditions are too specific to allow for such a change. While the majority of visitors are male, visits often include extended family members, and thus the familiar metaphor of the male tourist gaze is not entirely apposite in this case. In fact, women from Indonesia and Singapore branches of one of the temple networks have introduced major ritual innovations back into the local ritual arena in Putian. After all, the overseas Chinese have for centuries characterized themselves as sojourners, in effect as resident tourists overseas. In such a complex case, "neither the category of tourist nor that of home can remain unchanged by these practices" (Franklin and Crang 2001, 17). Clearly, the renewed flows within the long-standing transnational networks are creating novel transnational communities under new conditions. New mobilities generate new social relations, new ways of living, new ties to space, new places, new forms of consumption and leisure, and new aesthetic sensibilities.

Some of the sensual, embodied, and performative dimensions of tourism culture can be seen in the foods prepared at the huaqiao hotels in Quanzhou and elsewhere in the Minnan region. Rice porridge with pieces of sweet potato is now served at these hotels. This kind of humble peasant fare was impossible to find in the early 1980s in the newly built hotels, but these institutions adapted quickly to the nostalgic desires for comfort food tied to an earlier, remembered or rumored home village lifestyle in the ancestral villages of the overseas Chinese visitors. At ritual events, all the senses are heightened in an intensification of everyday life with exploding fireworks, music, the cooking of celebratory feasts, the press of crowds, and the descent of the gods. There is no denying the importance of the senses within tourism, and the pleasures of the everyday that sustain such travel.

Objects related to ritual worship and performance, for example the god statues carried on airplanes from Southeast Asia or Taiwan to Fujian, or the new god statues carried back to Southeast Asia, are all examples of the social life of things that play a critical role (as *actants*) in the unfolding of cultural events and processes.[14] These ritual artifacts are "hybrids of the human and the non-human." They are images and objects that are not just symbols but "material practices that serve to organize and support specific ways of experiencing the world" (Franklin and Crang 2001, 17). As Urry points out, "such artifacts will themselves exhibit some of the characteristics of unpredictable agency" (2000, 71). These hybrids function as "unruly connectors of present and past times and distant and homely places." These gods statues and other ritual artifacts, once back in Southeast Asia, work to decenter tourism, which can no longer be composed of a series of presences, but instead becomes permeated by the virtual presence in absence of the entire transnational network, including all its cosmological dimensions and powers.

Several theorists have pointed out the performative aspect of tourism, in which "places become stages for action." This is emphatically the case for overseas Xinghua huaqiao returning to sponsor and participate in ritual training of spirit mediums in their home villages. The "heterogeneous orders of things, performances and places fracture and disjoint ideas of single or stable representations" (Fullagar 2000, cited in Franklin and Crang 2001). Seen in this way, tourism is "the dispersal of action rather than of coherent self-present, self-knowing individuals—an account of becomings rather than beings" (18). This approach to tourism as performance fits the efforts of the Xinghua overseas huaqiao who return to participate in training sessions that lead to sudden and unpredictable events of spirit possession. In these rites, boys become gods, and elders, including those returning from abroad, help to channel the powers of the gods into ritually prescribed forms.

But performativity understood as a mode of copresence and transformative becoming can obscure important aspects of the global systems of tourism, and the power relations under conditions of flexible capitalism that allow certain wealthy overseas Chinese to return to help sponsor and participate in ritual events in their ancestral villages, while other overseas Chinese are forced to remain behind, or are moved into factory labor. These wealthy and mobile visitors are the same patrons who help sponsor return visits by ritual specialists to Southeast Asia (although the latter can achieve a much broader range of patronage within socioeconomically diverse overseas Chinese communities once they have regularized their visits to Southeast Asia).

The contrast between the ritual events of the spirit medium trainings and the far more spectacular, yet highly orchestrated, staged "ritual" performances held at the Tianhou Temple on Meizhou Island are very instructive. On Meizhou these enormous spectacles are held to commemorate the birthday of the goddess on the twenty-third day of the third lunar month. The so-called Song dynasty style rites are performed by hired actors and dancers in a newly built sports stadium adjoining the temple complex. In these cases, the "ritual" has been entirely invented by the tourism bureau, and it is performed for an audience of tourist pilgrims made up of overseas Chinese members of Mazu temples primarily from Taiwan but also from Southeast Asia. In such public spectacles, tourism becomes "a productive system that fuses discourse, materiality and practice." There is some space within these events for "ethnomimesis, where these performances pick up previously circulating representations, and work them through in a poetics stringing together images, visitors, performers and the history of their relations" (Franklin and Crang 2001, 17). Some scholars have argued that such self-aware performances potentially lead to an "emergent authenticity," but this is exceptionally difficult under such strongly staged circumstances.

What *is* interesting is the continuation of local pilgrimages by temples dedicated to Mazu (often called Tianshang shengmu in Putian) and communities on Meizhou Island, as well as from distant points stretching to the opposite side of the Xinghua region, such as the Duwei Longjinggong (Dragon Well Temple) triannual procession (Zheng 2010). The many temples dedicated to Tianhou in Putian and Xianyou are sites for the production of miracles, or tales of miracles. This discourse of efficacy, of miraculous events or visions, centers on specific individuals, communities, or local temples. This discourse and these individualistic practices undermine any attempt at the imposition of orthodoxy or orthopraxy on the cult of Mazu as a whole.[15]

RENEWED FLOWS BACK AND FORTH WITHIN THE TRANSNATIONAL NETWORK IN THE 1990s

In the 1990s, Southeast Asian–based Xinghua business and community leaders began inviting a return flow of local Putian ritual specialists and cultural performers to visit Southeast Asia. These included opera performers, marionettists, Daoist ritual masters, Buddhist monks, spirit mediums, and others.

Part of the demand had to do with the decline within the Xinghua community abroad. For example, every ten years since 1954 the Xinghua community has held a *fengjia pudu* (decennial rite of deliverance of the hungry ghosts) to commemorate the end of the Japanese war. In 1994, for the first time in forty years, there were not enough young people available locally to perform the Puxian opera version of the great Mulian ritual opera (featuring the salvation of the monk Mulian's mother from the underworld). So temple leaders brought in a troupe from Putian, along with Daoist ritual masters and Buddhist monks. Some of the opera singers were in fact marionettists, and they were subsequently taken on tour of Xinghua temples in Malaysia.

Since 1994, a number of Putian Daoist troupes have established regular ritual ties with temples across Southeast Asia, as there is only one active Puxian Daoist ritual master currently living in Singapore, and he is not able to handle all the ritual work of so many scattered Xinghua communities and temples.

THE POWERS OF RITUAL

Clearly, many of the return visits by overseas Chinese are related to the acceleration of the cycle of guanjie rituals within the temples of the Jiulidong

Figure 9.2. Daoist priests from Shiting, Putian, perform in the Singapore Jiulidong 1994 Fengjia Pudu ritual. K. Dean photo.

cult of the Immortals. What demands attention is the ability of ritual-events within these networks to absorb flows of capital or ethnic nationalism or overseas Chinese involvement without losing the power to generate meaningful worlds for participants (Dean and Lamarre 2003, 2007). As Tim Oakes points out in his chapter in this volume, ritual both reestablishes society and allows participants to experiment with it, thus allowing for some ability to negotiate the powers of the state and the forces of capitalism. This is an observation that stands generally for many kinds of ritual performances, from spirit medium trainings to displays of ritual dance for tourists in Guizhou or Yunnan. However, it may be possible to point out additional specific features of the syncretic ritual field in Putian that have enabled participants, whether overseas Chinese visitors, or local inhabitants, to achieve a stronger sense of control and engagement in local cultural expression and self-definition.

As I have described elsewhere (Dean 1998; Dean and Zheng 2010), these ritual-events fold in many disparate cultural elements, historical layers, and ritual traditions, while avoiding any seeming contradiction between different representations of the gods. These deities are themselves multifaceted, protective, and destructive. There are over a thousand deities in the local pantheon, worshiped on the altars of thousands of village temples. These deities are in a metastable state, in a virtual realm of potency, which is dephased into a particular vector of power by the invocations of the ritual specialists. When the gods are moved off their altars into sedan chairs, or even more impressively into the bodies of spirit mediums, the virtual power of the gods is channeled into a powerful flow of movements—what are at first twitching, leaping, uncontrolled movements are gradually channeled into elaborate exorcistic group line dances led by specially trained altar associates or Daoist ritual masters. These dances of the spirit mediums are called by an ancient Chinese term, *xingnuo* (to carry out the Nuo exorcism). The Nuo exorcism has been described by Feuchtwang (2001) as an annual apocalypse. Bodde (1975) analyzed the classical descriptions of the Great Nuo held at New Year's in the imperial palace by a *fangziangshi* exorcist in a four-sided golden mask, wearing a bearskin and brandishing a lance, escorted by twelve demons of the months bearing torches.

Further aspects of the ritual-events of the guanjie ceremonies of Putian should be pointed out. Multiple liturgical frameworks coexist in these ceremonies, as can be seen in the parallel performance of rites by different troupes of ritual specialists. These include the master of the Altar Association and the elder generation of spirit mediums who train the children in chants, invocations, collective dances, legends of the gods, throughout the week to ten-day training sessions. They also regularly record messages from the gods using spirit writing planchettes (forked branches that are used to write in sand on an altar). Meanwhile Confucian masters of ceremony (*lisheng*, locally called *yanshi*) set out the altars and the offerings, and instruct people outside the temple (which is closed off for the training) on how to bow and present offerings, burn incense and spirit money, and pray to the gods. Daoist ritual masters also attend the conclusion of the rites, and welcome the new spirit mediums and altar associates onto the opera stage set facing the temple. There they invoke the gods of the Great Ritual Court of Lu Shan, the holy mountain where the Goddess Chen Jinggu received her training in the magic arts (Baptendier 2008). Then they guide the new spirit mediums and altar associates to place their heads under two crossed swords and to drink from a bowl said to contain sulphur or blood or both (the exact contents are one of many secrets of the initiation process). After this, the Daoist ritual master sprays the mediums with purifying mist, which instantly sends them into trance. They are then dressed as the god who has possessed them. Along with the other altar associates, they are issued Daoist diplomas conferring on them the status of divine officials (*gongcao*). These documents are kept in small wooden boxes in the temple, and are carried to the grave by the altar associates. Subsequent levels of initiation include the *Yuxiu* (Preparatory Cultivation) rites, in which the altar associates are given in effect a preemptive funeral, and are transformed into temporarily earthbound immortals. After this, they can take part in village annual exorcisms as well as funerals without fear of contamination by demonic forces.

Rituals are also sites of chaotic activity with multiple nodes of attraction. For example, several different musical and operatic troupes can be found performing simultaneously in the same public space before the temple. The consciousness and attention of participants at the ritual event are pulled in many different directions at once, contributing to a noticeable dispersal of subjectivity throughout the ritual-event. The movement of forces (affective, libidinal, presubjective) passes at an intracorporeal level through the crowd, as for example when spontaneous possession occurs, sending ripples of *ekstasis* (the presence within of the outside of thought) through the assemblage. In these contexts, ritual artifacts, such as god statues in sedan chairs, can take on qualities of quasi-subjectivity or agency, transforming sedan chair bearers and participating clouds as they pass by.

These rituals fold in more and more frames and features of the contemporary situation, surviving and even thriving in the twenty-first century despite state efforts to cast such activities as national folk customs, or the potential impact of capitalism to turn the events into public spectacles with little significance to local communities. Part of the success of these rituals has to do with their intrinsically local nature as most are at the village level, although as we have seen many of these villages and temples are simultaneously part of a transnational network (yet another source of their resilience). Temple committee leaders (who rotate into positions of authority from throughout the village community and reach decision mainly by consensus) work to forestall confrontation with state authorities. They also reach out to wealthy villagers and overseas Chinese huaqiao to donate some of their capital back into the village ritual celebrations. The participation within some of these rites of overseas spirit medium businessmen also folds in additional realms of experience, management skills, and connective capital, on top of the symbolic capital these wealthy huaqiao can muster in the face of confrontation with local authorities. These rites have something of a self-enclosed, self-sustaining, and self-modifying quality, rather like auto- poetic systems.[16] Nonetheless, they renew the community, merging into a continuum with everyday life. Further research will need to examine class stratification and the reassertion of social and gender hierarchy within these rituals, while also exploring innovations in social roles and transformative moments within ritual-events (including spirit possession and the setting in motion of cosmological forces).

The ritual traditions of collective training of spirit mediums are crucial to the maintenance of the transnational network itself, including the far-flung Huang lineage reaching from Putian to Southeast Asia. While many different dialect groups of China have common surname associations in Southeast Asia, few such groups can match the intensity and ritual complexity of the spirit medium and altar associate guanjie performances of the Huang emigrants from Putian. In recent years, many other Xinghua temples in Southeast Asia have held their own spirit medium training sessions, imitating the success of this highly effective mode of generating bonds within an immigrant community, even if they did not have such ritual traditions in their home villages in Putian. The combination of local god cults, lineage ties, and spirit medium ritual traditions generates a more active, involved, performative, and energetic network. On the one hand, leadership within overseas Chinese communities is closely tied to wealth and personal connections. The ability of these businessmen to send remittances back to their home villages has in a few cases led to their becoming the puppet masters of local village life, breeding a culture of dependency. On the other hand, spirit mediumism appears to partially flatten network hierarchies, and open up leadership to horizontal, more open processes. Moreover, local ritual centers still have privileged access to cosmological powers, which can be claimed through ritual performances, and affect the flow of authority within the network. This openness can be seen as well in the ritual innovations introduced by the female devotees of the Goddess Ou Xiangu in Tibing Tingyi, Jakarta, and now in Shiting as well.

CONCLUSION: THE ROLE OF TRANSNATIONAL
FLOWS IN THE REINVENTION OF LOCAL CULTURE

The reinvention of tradition is highly advanced in coastal Southeast China, and the funding and fervor and ritual knowledge of overseas Chinese spirit medium businessmen has played a key role in this process. Several works in Chinese and Southeast Asian studies have recently explored various theoretical approaches to transnational networks and to translocal spaces (Ong and Nonini 1997, Oakes and Schein 2006, Wang 2005, Feuchtwang 2004; for comparative studies, see also Barnes and Reilly 2007, and Lefebvre 1991). While Ong and Nonini outline certain features of transnational networks of huaqiao capitalists and migrant workers, Oakes and Schein are interested in migration and networks within China, especially all such translocal networks that exceed the boundaries of the natural village. They define the translocal broadly as "being identified with more than one place at a time." They further argue that the translocal creates new identities, subjectivities, and networks that link places together. These new mobilities and multiple localities, often involving leaps across scale, include translocal imaginaries, including the imagined community of the nation-state. Feuchtwang in contrast argues that there are still many specific processes of place-making under way across China, particularly in the area of local territorial cult celebrations, despite the deterritorializing effects of capitalism (and earlier of Maoist nationalism).

These commentators all note the effects of the massive migration of floating populations of workers from the villages to the cities. Some villages in Putian can appear to be empty shells at certain times, with only the elderly and young children left to watch over newly built multistory homes. Nonetheless, these villages become animated and crowded on the feast days of the gods, as factory workers and successful businessmen return from their far-flung networks all over China.[17] Clearly translocal flows are affected by uneven development all across the different regions of China. Oakes and Schein also emphasize embodiment in relation to the creation of space/place/networked space. Domestic spaces, the preparation and consumption of food, memory, and nostalgia, are all experiences deeply rooted in the body (of the overseas Chinese abroad and returning home, as well as in the village women thinking of their children in Southeast Asia while preparing holiday ritual meals).

Peggy Levitt (2001) provides one way to think about the embodied nature of participating in a transnational network through her notion of the "transnational village." Levitt has defined various aspects of the "transnational village," which have considerable relevance for rethinking villages in coastal Southeast and South China. These include (1) actual migration is not required to be a member; (2) the transnational villages emerge and endure partially because of *social* remittances (which include the ideas, behavior, and social capital that flow from receiving to sending communities); (3) the transnational villages create and are created by organizations that themselves come to act across borders (which include political, religious, and social movement organizations); and (4) the development of individuals within transnational villages is diverse (Levitt 2001, 11–12). Levitt describes and analyzes details of transnational villagers' daily life. She points out that members of transnational communities "develop several fluid, sometimes conflicting identities" (202): "How individuals distribute their loyalty and energy between sending and receiving countries depends upon how political, religious, and social life is organized across space" (203).

These concepts fit well with the experiences of the members of the Xinghua transnational network—for many years it was impossible for political reasons for villagers in Putian to move abroad within their potential transnational space. Once the network became reactivated in the early 1980s, many villagers with close huaqiao relations obtained visas for Hong Kong or Southeast Asia. But in recent years, as economic conditions have improved dramatically in coastal Southeast China, many villagers are rethinking their desire to emigrate. Other, older villagers have little desire to uproot themselves now, but are pleased by the renewed activity within the network and in their village temples and in the village economy. The social remittances or cultural exchanges and mutual participation in ritual events are now as significant if not more so than the *qiaopi* (huaqiao remittances) that used to flow in from the overseas networks. This is because local ritual events are now largely self-funded, thanks to the improved economy and the power of local ritual traditions. The return visits of huaqiao to support and participate in these traditions are a powerful boost to their continuing power and appeal. Clearly, the far-flung temple networks have provided the basis for this extended transnational space.

Levitt's emphasis throughout is on concepts of community and social field rather than on individual activities of transnational entrepreneurs or migrant laborers, as tends to be the case in the studies published by Ong and Nonini (1997). In her more recent work, *God Needs No Passport* (2007), Levitt emphasizes the ability of religion to move beyond national borders in creating the spaces of the transnational village. By extending the analysis away from charismatic network founders and networkers, or from a quantitative analysis of the monetary remittances or investments flowing back to the village, but instead looking at the entire village community affected by these agents, we can expand our understanding of the spaces created by these networks, whether these be spaces of melancholy memory, longing, imaginary identifications, actual communication of local cultural knowledge or of innovations in the ritual order (which can flow back and forth as well).

While it is important to look beyond individual charismatic leaders to the larger structure and processes of the transnational networks, another theoretical resource that may help understand the function within transnational space and network process of the returning huaqiao is the concept of "connective capital." This is defined by Ichniowski and Shaw (2005) as the ability of individuals to actively seek to share information to solve problems through reciprocity, which has the effect of a multiplication of human or social capital throughout the entire network. These processes depend on great communicative skills, and result in more efficient problem solving within the network. The spirit medium businessmen of the Xinghua networks frequently embody these qualities and abilities; having succeeded in their businesses in highly complex multicultural contexts, they are especially adept at sharing and exchanging information in the ritual realm, with spillover effects on the network at large. This is not to say that they completely dominate local ritual traditions—there is still a great deal of give and take in these interactions, and local conditions can and often do trump the overseas visitors' prescriptions. Nonetheless, their training and ability to connect with the gods appears to provide these businessmen even more skill in forming and fostering their earthly connections.

These transnational networks bring together successful overseas Chinese businessmen, local Putian boys training to become spirit mediums, and women from Southeast Asia and Putian innovating with new ritual practices. None of these localized ritual practices could be characterized as being orthodox or standardized or mainstream (Sutton 2007). Nonetheless, these "heterodox" local ritual traditions are at the center of a transnational network featuring considerable flows of people, money, ideas, images, and transformative ritual practices.

Besides underlining the economic effects of tourism in a variety of Chinese sites, other chapters in this book uncover new imaginaries, new rituals, and new ritual paraphernalia that are produced there, and demonstrate the active role of both tourists and locals in such cultural innovation. The local/diasporic interactions described in this chapter describe a similar process, though not in the conventional tourist mode. These are not the cursory arm's-length relationships common in the usual one-off tourist visit. For one thing, "tourists" visiting Xinghua are already locals able to play on economic and cultural ties there, and "locals" they meet (including some who visit diasporic communities in Southeast Asia as a species of tourist themselves) are long embedded in these relationships too. These ramifying ties, and the long history of established cultural hybridity in the Xinghua diaspora, increase the possibility of productive interactions, facilitating the remarkable creativity and ongoing cultural change described in this chapter.

Figure 9.3.   A spirit medium in Putian "gathers the flowers of fire" by standing in the shooting flames of a roman candle. K. Dean photo.

NOTES

1. The Minnan region historically included Putian and Xianyou counties (the Xinghua region) as well as the much larger Quanzhou and Zhangzhou regions. The Hokkien speakers of Quanzhou and Zhangzhou regions greatly outnumber the over three million Xinghua people of Putian and Xianyou counties who speak the very different Puxian dialect.

2. If one includes the Xinghua (Henghwa in local dialect) people overseas with the Hokkien speakers, the total in Southeast Asia would rise to 8.5 million people from the greater Minnan region. This represents about a fourth of the estimated 37 million overseas Chinese living in 160 countries around the globe in late 1990s.

3.   The largest numbers of Minnan people moved to Taiwan, where Minnan immigrants numbered approximately 250,000 in 1661–1683. The numbers rose to 1 million by 1782, and to 3.7 million by 1926 (at which time over 85 percent, or 3,192,600, were from the Minnan region).

4. A Song inscription from Putian records the success of a local merchant in his voyage to Sanfoqi in Sumatra (Dean and Zheng 1995, 11–13). In the Yuan, in the twenty-seventh year of the Zhizheng reign period (1367), a Xianyou man from Fengting named Yu Liangu escaped trouble by moving to Japan, where he carved woodblocks for book printing. Members of the Cai lineage, which produced Song prime minister Cai Xiang, also immigrated to the Ryuku Islands of Japan, as is shown in their respective genealogies. According to the Japanese descendants, this first occurred in 1392. From the founding of the Ming to the start of the Yongle period (1368–1401) members of the Chen, Huang, Ke, Cai, Xu, Li, Wang, and Lin lineages moved from Putian and Xianyou to Southeast Asia. In 1405, a Xinghua officer, Weiyousuo Liu Xing, followed Admiral Zheng He on his expeditions to the South Seas and to Africa, as did other Xinghua sailors on the 1421 expedition. In 1567, the Fujian prefect Xu Zemin requested that the court lift the ban on overseas trade. During this period (the Zhengde reign period), a Wang lineage gazetteer from Xianyou records that one Wang Shiqi, of the eighteenth generation of the lineage, went to the South Seas to make his living (*Putianshi zhi* [Putian City gazetteer] 2001, vol 3: 2431–33). For more concrete examples drawn from 176 lineage gazetteers from the Quanzhou and Jinjiang region, see Zhuang Weiji and Zheng Shanyu, eds. *Quanzhou pudie huaqiao shiliao yu yanjiu* (Research on historical materials from Quanzhou genealogies concerning overseas Chinese), 2 vols. Beijing: Zhongguo huaqiao chubanshe, 1998.

5. Philip Kuhn (2008, 5–6) cites the research of Sugihara on the cumulative flows of people through the ports of Xiamen, Shantou, and Hong Kong from 1869 to 1939 as showing an outflow of 14.7 million people and an inflow, or return flow, of 11.6 million people over this period.

6. Xinghua sojourners also established thirty-eight native-place associations in Malaysia beginning with one in Taiping in 1898. They went on to establish five associations in Singapore, beginning in 1921, and fourteen in Indonesia, beginning in 1953.

7. Further research is needed to determine the scope of these rites.

8. See further discussion of these ceremonies in Dean and Zheng 2010.

9. Salmon and Lombard 1980, 208–13. The Fu Pu Xian Zongyici (Fuqing, Putian, and Xianyou collective ancestral temple) had been built in Jakarta in 1950, around the grounds of a Buddhist monastery called the Yuliantang, founded in 1927, which in 1951 changed its name to the Guanghuasi, at the instigation of the abbot, Buddhist monk Benqing, who had been ordained at the Guanghuasi in Putian (191–97).

10. Buddhist monk Yuanchan brought 1.5 million yuan back from the Southeast Asian branch temples of the Guanghuasi to rebuild it in 1983. The Meizhou Tianhougong was initially rebuilt by local islanders under the leadership of a woman named Ahmei, who had received commands from the goddess in a series of dreams to lead the reconstruction. She has remained a force to be reckoned with in the leadership of the temple, even as most of the funding for the complete makeover of the temple has come from Taiwanese temple members. Taiwan has over five hundred temples dedicated to Mazu, and leaders of the main temples vied to contribute funds and build temples and towers at the Meizhou Tianhougong throughout the 1980s and 1990s.

11. The following paragraphs respond to the prolegomena to tourist studies outlined by Adrian Franklin and Mike Crang (2001), "The Trouble with Tourism and Travel Theory?" published in *Tourist Studies* 1(1): 5–22, by drawing on the terms and concepts introduced in that essay.

12. In Putian, as elsewhere along the southeast Chinese coast, migration has become a big business, handled by human smuggling companies run by "snakeheads." These companies openly advertise their services, and their fees, and they have certainly overtaken the role of overseas Chinese in accelerating the movement of local populations overseas.

13. Deleuze and Guattari (1987, 238) discuss favorably various forms of cultural involution, although they are less interested in issues of identity formation or self-awareness than in unexpected, transversal connections between material processes and cultural processes that tend to be disruptive of fixed identities.

14. I have often had the privilege of sitting next to a god statue occupying a seat on a flight from Hong Kong to Xiamen.

15. I have visited the Tianhougong on Meizhou on several occasions, and twice witnessed spirit mediums being carried on sedan chairs up the steps of the temple complex, leading pilgrims in a great procession from local Putian or Xianyou temples dedicated to Mazu. The mediums then took over the central temple and led their worshipers in rituals of offering and prayer to the goddess.

16. See Dean 2001; Dean and Lamarre 2003, 2007; and Dean and Zheng 2010, ch. 10, for further discussion of the construction of spaces of relative autonomy in the ritual-events of this area of Southeast China.

17. These include major enclaves such as "Little Putian" outside of Beijing. In general, Putian businessmen have concentrated on the transportation industry and electronics in their business networks around China.

REFERENCES

Baptandier, Brigitte. 2008. *The Lady of Linshui: A Chinese Female Cult.* Trans. Kristin Ingrid Fryklund. Stanford: Stanford University Press.

Barnes, Nielan, and Reilly, Katherine. 2007. "Conceptualizations of Transnational Networks: A Selective Literature Review." Paper presented at the annual meeting of the International Studies Association 48th Annual Convention, Chicago, 28 February 2007, www.allacademic.com/meta/p180461_index.html.

Bodde, Derk. 1975. *Festivals in Classical China: New Year and Other Annual Observances during the Han Dynasty, 206 B.C.–A.D 220.* Princeton: Princeton University Press.

Cheah, Pheng. 2006. *Inhuman Conditions: On Cosmopolitanism and Human Rights.* Cambridge, MA: Harvard University Press.

Chen, Zongren. 2006. "'Gongsi' yuanliu chutan: jianlun Ming qing shidai shangchuan de renyuan jisegou ji qi sushu guanxi (Preliminary discussion of the origins of the term 'Gongsi' [corporation], together with a discussion of structure and hierarchical relations of the crews of merchant ships in the Ming and Qing). In *Qingshi lunji* (Collected essays on Qing history), ed. Chen Jianxian, Cheng Chongde, and Li Jixiang, vol. 1. Beijing: Renmin chubanshe.

Chun, Allen. 2001. "Diasporas of Mind, or Why There Ain't No Black Atlantic in Cultural China." *Communal/Plural: Journal of Transnational and Cross-cultural Studies* 9(1): 95–110.

Clifford, James. 1996. *Routes: Travel and Translation in the Late Twentieth Century.* Cambridge, MA: Harvard University Press.

Dean, Kenneth. 1993. *Taoist Ritual and Popular Cults of Southeast China.* Princeton: Princeton University Press.

———. 1998. *Lord of the Three in One: The Spread of a Cult in Southeast China.* Princeton: Princeton University Press.

———. 2001. "China's Second Government: Regional Ritual Systems in Southeast China." In *Shehui, minzu yu wenhua zhanyan guoji yantaohui lunwenji* (Collected papers from the International Conference on Social, Ethnic and Cultural Transformation). Taipei: Center for Chinese Studies, 77–109.

———. 2010. "Spirit Mediums as Global Citizens: Tracing Trans-national Ritual Networks from the Village Temples of Shiting, Putian to Southeast Asia." In *Selected Papers from the International Conference on Study of Local Ritual Traditions,* ed. Tam Wai-lun. Hong Kong: CUHK Center for the Study of Religion and Society (forthcoming).

Dean, Kenneth, and Thomas Lamarre. 2003. "Ritual Matters." In *Traces 3: Impacts of Modernities,* ed. Thomas Lamarre and Kang Nai-hae. Hong Kong: Hong Kong University Press, 257–84.

———. 2007. "Microsociology and the Ritual-Event." In *Deleuzian Encounters: Studies in Contemporary Social Issues,* ed. Anna Hickey-Moody and Peta Malins. London: Palgrave Macmillan, 181–97.

Dean, Kenneth, and Zheng Zhenman. 1993. "Group Initiation and Exorcistic Dance in the Xinghua Region." In *Min-su ch'ü-i* (Chinese ritual and drama) 85(2): *Zhongguo Nuoxi, Nuo wenhua guojiyantaohui lunwenli* (Proceedings of the International Conference on Nuo Theater and Nuo Culture), ed. Wang Ch'iu-kuei, 105–95.

———. 1995. *Epigraphical Materials on the History of Religion in Fujian. Volume 1: The Xinghua Region.* Fuzhou: Fujian Peoples Publishing House.

———. 2010. *Ritual Alliances of the Putian Plain.* 2 vols. Leiden: E.J. Brill

DeBernardi, Jean. 2004. *Rites of Belonging: Memory, Modernity, and Identity in a Malaysian Chinese Community.* Stanford: Stanford University Press.

———. 2006. *The Way That Lives in the Heart: Chinese Popular Religion and Spirit Mediums in Penang, Malaysia.* Stanford: Stanford University Press.

Deleuze, Gilles, and Felix Guattari. 1987. *A Thousand Plateaus: Capitalism and Schizophrenia.* Trans. Brian Massumi. Minneapolis: University of Minnesota Press.

Faure, David, and Helen F. Siu. 2006. "The Original Translocal Society and Its Modern Fate: Historical and Post-Reform South China." In Oakes and Schein, 36–55.

Feuchtwang, Stephen. 2001. *Popular Religion in China: The Imperial Metaphor.* Richmond, Surrey: Curzon.

————, ed. 2004. *Making Place: State Projects, Globalization and Local Responses in China*. London: UCL Press.

Franke, Wolfgang, and Chen Tie Fan, ed. 1980–1985. *Chinese Epigraphic Materials in Malaysia*. 3 vols. Kuala Lumpur: University of Malaysia Press.

————. 1988–1997. *Chinese Epigraphic Materials in Indonesia*. With the collaboration of Claudine Salmon and Anthony Siu, and with the assistance of Hu Juyun and Teo Lee Kheng. 4 vols. Singapore: Nanyang Xuehui.

Franklin, Adrian, and Mike Crang. 2001. "The Trouble with Tourism and Travel Theory?" *Tourist Studies* 1(1): 5–22.

Fujiansheng Putianshi difangzhi bian zhuan weiyuanhui, ed. 2001. "Huaqiao" (Overseas Chinese), and "Lüyou" (Tourism). In *Putianshi zhi* (Putian City gazetteer). Bejing: Fangzhi chubanshe, 2430–63, 2526–68.

Fullagar, Simone. 2000. "Desiring Nature: Identity and Becoming in Narratives of Travel." *Cultural Values* 4(1): 58–76.

Giddens, Anthony. 2000. *Runaway World: How Globalization Is Reshaping Our Lives*. New York: Routledge.

Ichniowski, Casey, and Kathyrn Shaw. 2005. "Connective Capital: Building Problem-Solving Networks within Firms." Working Paper, October 2005. faculty-gsb/stanford.edu/shaw/personal_page/research.html (accessed 9 August 2008).

Jiang Weiji, and Zheng Shanyu, ed. 1998. *Quanzhou pudie huaqiao shiliao yu yanjiu* (Research on historical materials from Quanzhou genealogies concerning Overseas Chinese). 2 vols. Beijing: Zhongguo huaqiao chubanshe.

Kuah, Khun Eng. 2000. *Rebuilding the Ancestral Village: Singaporeans in China*. Aldershot: Ashgate.

Kuhn, Philip. 2008. *Chinese amongst Others: Emigration in Modern Times*. Lanham, MD: Rowman and Littlefield.

Latour, Bruno. 2005. *Reassembling the Social: An Introduction to Actor-Network-Theory*. Oxford: Oxford University Press.

Lefebvre, Henri. 1991. *The Production of Space*. Trans. D. Nicholson-Smith. Oxford: Blackwell.

Levitt, Peggy. 2001. *Transnational Villagers*. Berkeley: University of California Press.

————. 2007. *God Needs No Passport: Immigrants and the Changing American Religious Landscape*. New York: New Press.

Oakes, Tim, and Louisa Schein. 2006. "Translocal China: An Introduction." In Oakes and Schein, 1–36.

————, eds. 2006. *Translocal China: Linkages, Identities, and the Reimagining of Space*. London: Routledge.

Ong, Aihwa, and Donald Nonini, eds. 1997. *Ungrounded Empires: The Cultural Politics of Modern Chinese Transnationalism*. London: Routledge.

Putianshi zhi (Putian City gazetteer). 2001.

Sahlins, Marshall. 1988. "Cosmologies of Capitalism: The Trans-Pacific Sector of 'The World System.'" *Proceedings of the British Academy* 74: 1–51.

————. 1993. "Goodbye to Tristes Tropes: Ethnography in the Context of Modern World History." *Journal of Modern History* 65: 1–25.

Salmon, Claudine, and Denys Lombard. 1980. *Les chinois de Jakarta: temples et vie collective.* 2nd ed. Paris: Editions de la Maison des Sciences de l'Homme.

Sangren, P. Steven. 1984. "Traditional Chinese Corporations: Beyond Kinship." *Journal of Asian Studies* 43(3): 391–415.

Shiting Fuli jijinhui and Huangshi zupu bianweihui. 1990. *Chongxiu Shiting Huangshi zupu* (Rev. Shiting Huang lineage genealogy).

Skinner, G. W. 1957. *Chinese Society in Thailand: An Analytical History.* Ithaca, NY: Cornell University Press.

———. 1958. *Leadership and Power in the Chinese Community of Thailand.* Ithaca, NY: Cornell University Press (Monographs of the Association for Asian Studies, III).

———. 1964–1965. "Marketing and Social Structure in Rural China. Parts I, II, and III." *Journal of Asian Studies* 24(1, Nov. 1964): 3–44; 24(2, Feb. 1965): 195–228; 24(3, May 1965): 363–99.

———. 1971. "Chinese Peasants and the Closed Community: An Open and Shut Case." *Comparative Studies in Society and History* 13(3): 270–81.

———. 1985. "Presidential Address: The Structure of Chinese History." *Journal of Asian Studies* 44(2) February: 271–92.

———. 1996. "Creolized Chinese Societies in Southeast Asia." In *Sojourners and Settlers: Histories of Southeast Asia and the Chinese,* ed. Anthony Reid. Sydney: Allen and Unwin, 50–93.

Sutton, Donald S. 2007. "Ritual, Cultural Standardization, and Orthopraxy in China: Reconsidering James L. Watson's Ideas." *Modern China* 33(1): 3–21.

Tu, Weiming. 1991. "Cultural China: The Periphery as Center." *Daedelus* 120(2): 1–32.

Urry, John. 2000. *Sociology beyond Societies: Mobilities for the Twenty-first century.* London: Routledge.

Van der Veer, Peter. 2001. "Transnational Religions." Paper presented to the Conference on Transnational Migration: Comparative Perspectives at Princeton University.

Vermeer, E. B. 1990. "The Decline of Hsing-hua Prefecture in the Early Ch'ing." In *The Development and Decline of Fukien Province in the 17th and 18th Centuries,* ed. E. Vermeer. Leiden: E.J. Brill, 101–61.

Wang, Jing, 2005. "Introduction: The Politics and Production of Scales in China: How Does Geography Matter to Studies of Local, Popular Culture?" In *Locating China: Space, Place, and Popular Culture,* ed. J. Wang. London: Routledge, 1–30.

Wang, Mingming. 1999. *Shichu de guangrong* (Lost splendor). Hangzhou: Zhejiang renmin chubanshe.

Watson, James L. 1985. "Standardizing the Gods: The Promotion of T'ien-hou ('Empress of Heaven') Along the South China Coast, 960–1960." In *Popular Culture in Late Imperial China*, ed. D. Johnson, E. Rawski, and A. Nathan. Berkeley: University of California Press, 292–324.

Yang, Mei-hui Mayfair. 2000. "Putting Global Capitalism in Its Place." With responses by Gene Cooper, Michael Dutton, Stephan Feuchtwang, J. K. Gibson-Graham, Richard Perry, Bill Maurer, Lisa Rofel, P. Steven Sangren, Mingming Wang, Yao Souchou, and Zhou Yongming. *Current Anthropology* 41: 477–509.

Zheng, Zhenman. 2001. *Family Lineage Organization and Social Change in Ming and Qing Fujian.* Trans. Michael Szonyi with the assistance of David Wakefield and Kenneth Dean. Honolulu: University of Hawai'i Press.

———. 2010. "Meizhou zumiao yu Duwei Longjinggong: Xinghua minjian Mazu chongbai de jiangou" (The Meizhou founding temple and the Dragon Well Temple of Duwei: The construction of the popular cult of Mazu in the Xinghua region). *Min-su ch'ü-i* (Studies in Chinese ritual and drama), 167: 123–50.

Afterword

Rubie Watson

Focused on the intersection of religious practice, economic development, heritage tourism, and state power in China, *Faiths on Display* is very timely and most welcome. The subject matter is wide-ranging with authors moving from the "homecoming tourism" of overseas Chinese, who have revitalized ruined temples throughout Southeastern China, to the plight of Tibetan monks struggling to maintain a precinct of religious meaning in one of China's largest national minority theme parks.

As the Chinese Communist Party and its local agents rebuild temples, employ monks, appoint abbots, support pilgrimages, and ingratiate themselves to Singapore cult members, one might expect, with considerable justification, that the tensions between an official ideology of radical secularism and a dizzying array of religious practices would escalate into open hostility and conflict. Yet, the fabric spun out of the threads of mutual benefit and compartmentalization appears to hold. Perhaps it holds because the players—national party apparatchik, local party baron, ordained priest, religious pilgrim, and curious tourist—share a geographic space but not a mental one. One could argue that ideology has so overwhelmed empirical evidence that a resurgence of religion is unthinkable. (Many in present-day China might reason: "Maoist education has triumphed and has so marginalized feudal superstition [i.e., religious practice] that it no longer plays any important role in Chinese society.") Or, perhaps, officials and religious adherents go along to get along as the space for both religion and commerce expands in China. One would be justified for taking any one of these perspectives. The actions of party officials keen to secure funding sources for their town or county or province are clearly dominated more by pragmatism than by the kind of ideological purity that so characterized Maoist China.

Since 1949 when Mao Zedong stood atop Tiananmen Gate to declare the formation of the People's Republic of China, the Communist Party has struggled with China's religious and cultural traditions. In 1949, the Chinese landscape was littered with the physical remains—the palaces, temples, pilgrimage sites, tombs, and graves—of long dead emperors and religious communities of all kinds. As any good revolutionary will tell you, there are three choices for dealing with the past, including the visual past: rejection, transformation, or invention. At any given moment, Mao and his followers have tried all three.

The chapters in this book trace the recent history of Chinese attitudes toward religion. By attending to the complicated terrain of international, indeed global, flows of people, ideas, and money, these studies move the reader beyond state-society dichotomies to take account of the complex interactions of party cadre, pilgrims, religious professionals, devotees, tourists, national minorities, and diaspora tourists. China is the geographic focus of these studies, but the complex interactions they explore can be found well beyond the confines of the Chinese state.

Using a variety of ethnographic and archival research methods (often in creative combination), the authors of *Faiths on Display* address the ways in which the current Chinese state has converted popular religion, and especially its many physical expressions, into heritage as they seek on the one hand economic development and on the other avenues for patriotic education. For centuries, Chinese states have tried to suppress, or domesticate, or appropriate the kinds of religious practices that have long been the mainstay of rural villagers, urban workers, and ethnic minorities. Qing emperors encouraged sinification of non-Han populations, Kuomintang officials tried to rein in "extravagant festivals" and, of course, Maoists infamously stamped out feudal superstitions (which included religious practices of all kinds) wherever they were found. In recent years, however, we learn in rich detail and vibrant language that China's religious terrain has not only been energized but made extraordinarily complex. The state-sponsored looting and destruction of the Cultural Revolution is a far cry from the comparative (and apparent) religious tolerance one finds today. This tolerance, it must be said, has its strict limits, especially when unauthorized religious groups are deemed dangerous to the status quo. Nevertheless, under the rubric of heritage and profit, local officials tolerate and even promote many forms of religious expression.

In this volume, we meet monks in theme parks, ritual performers in "authentic minority villages" and hotel restaurants, as well as contemporary missionaries who are reintroducing spirit medium cults to their "homeland" at the same time that they themselves are reenergized by the reflected charisma of "mother temples."

Today's Communist Party boss may see the economic potential of the old, the religious, the culture and rituals of national minorities as a meal ticket, but a meal ticket whose existence must be closely tied to nationalist discourse. China's cultural industry and the lure of tourists' dollars may well lead a local party establishment to recover and support important pilgrimage sites under the framework of cultural heritage, and in doing so, as we learn here, rewrite regional ethnic histories. Apparently, these "recoveries" are acceptable, so long as they contribute to the celebration of Chinese cultural achievement and national values as the Communist Party defines these.

The detailed accounts of minority reactions to tourist interest and state-sponsored attempts to folklorize and commodify "their" religious practices provide fascinating reading. In many respects, these experiences are duplicated among many indigenous populations throughout the world. From the Native American communities of the American Southwest to the islands of the Pacific, one finds people performing their rituals for tourists. The degree to which tourists are cast in the role of consumer, or supplicant, or novice learner varies. The timing and place of performances also vary, as does the commercial exchange between performer and "guest." In the 1920s, tourists were made to feel like privileged guests allowed to see the authentic rites of Navajo healers, whose sand paintings, created in the context of healing ceremonies, were available (for a fee) to non-Navajo onlookers. What the tourists who attended these rituals did not appreciate were the ritual elements that the healer withheld. The sand paintings produced in these rituals were alive to the tourist but not to the Navajo. Commercial paintings were not enlivened by powerful spirits, who in a complete rite would inhabit the painting and whose presence was essential for the renewal and healing that were the sole purpose of the original rite.

Issues of authenticity are important. In *Faiths on Display,* the link between ritual, tourism, performance, and performer is fascinating. To what degree do tourists and tourist dollars keep rituals alive, to what degree are rituals changed by commercial performances, and to what degree does tourist performance provide a precious space for religious practice among members of the performing community? These are the kinds of important questions that preoccupy the contributors to this volume, and they are to be congratulated for the sophistication and precision with which they are addressed.

In Hong Kong's New Territories where some villages date to the Song and Ming dynasties, government and foundation funds are available for local temple and ancestral hall renovations, if they are deemed to be Declared Monuments—part of Hong Kong's officially recognized cultural heritage. Not surprisingly, government funds do carry stipulations, which restrict how renovation work is done and by whom. The relevant government agency (the Antiquities and Monuments Office) oversees the standards by which stone and wood carvings, support beams, and wall hangings are produced; and, once renovation is complete, the monument must be open to the public. Some villagers balk at this last requirement and decide to go it alone, which may mean no repairs or "inappropriate repairs" as far as conservationists are concerned. In Hong Kong's old villages, as well as in China, one must ask what results from situations in which *my* festival—*my* temple—*my* music becomes *your* heritage and/or commercial product. We cannot assume that tourism and religious practice, heritage and history, commercial performance and community ritual are necessarily incompatible. Rather, *Faiths on Display* opens our thinking to ideas and to situations that are far more complex than any standard set of dichotomies can provide.

In the museum world, discussions of decontextualization and the power to re-present are common. The removal of an object from its original setting (or any setting for that matter) inevitably involves a process of decontextualization. A ceremonial mask is removed from its place of use (and, therefore, can no longer be danced); it is packed and transported to a museum (local, national, international, it makes little difference), to a dealer in primitive art, or to a collector. No matter how many images, video files, field notes, and interviews accompany the mask, it has become, in the process of decontextualization, something different from what it was. It has become an artifact, a representative of similar masks, and may come to stand for a ritual complex (perhaps even a whole social complex). It may be re-presented as art, or artifact, or specimen, or commodity, or all four.

The success of a revolution might be judged in part by how and to what effect the materials of the old order—its art and artifacts—are decontextualized and re-presented (or reinscribed with new significance). During the French Revolution sacred objects began the long-term process of becoming art or artifacts—a process that any visitor to an old village church or ancient cathedral will notice is still under way. The interesting thing about objects is that they rarely stop being altogether what they were. Communities of interest do not suddenly accept a totally new and different understanding of a treasured object. In fact, many icons, temples, monuments take on greater significance because neither their decontextualization nor their recontextualization is ever completely successful. Groups of people and their descendants may well retain some purchase on the object itself even if it has been physically removed from their grasp. Dueling discourses of context (what is this statue, where and to whom does it belong) often provide the match that ignites ethnic and international conflict. We have but to look to yesterday's newspaper to find examples of this phenomenon.

Sometimes different contextualizing communities easily coexist. In a French cathedral, the bishop, the supplicant, the art historian, the day tourist, touring school child, and the janitor may all happily rub shoulders on any given day; each aware of the other but largely intent on his own interests and objectives. And, of course, one must always be open to the possibility that the art historian may be a believer or the "secular tourist" may light a candle at the altar of the Virgin Mary. The authors of this volume are right to point out the dangers of assuming clear demarcations where they do not exist. In China, religious heritage tourism has created spaces for a wealth of behaviors that may foster ethnic difference and pride and religious revivals. Such variety—perhaps even heterodoxy—remains acceptable if it promotes economic development and does not directly threaten party control. China's current powerbrokers seem secure in their ability to contain serious deviation. Or perhaps they are oblivious to the possibilities.

Throughout the world, heritage tourism has emerged as a primary tool for disseminating national values and patriotic sentiments. But it is also true that heritage provides an arena of contestation for those who seek alternative histories, or yearn for less pollution, or press for more secure property rights. David Lowenthal, who has written extensively on the conservation phenomena in Europe and North America, argues that conflict is endemic to heritage. In China, the Communist Party has made heritage tourism serve many approved masters: rural development, patriotic education, and nationalist pride. Whether it also serves religious practitioners is the focus of this volume; and the responses to that question are fascinating.

Index

Note: Page numbers in *italics* designate illustrations.

271

About the Contributors

Kenneth Dean is James McGill Professor and Lee Chair of Chinese Cultural Studies in the Department of East Asian Studies at McGill University. He is the author of *First and Last Emperors: The Absolute State and the Body of the Despot* (with Brian Massumi; 1992), *Taoist Ritual and Popular Cults of Southeast China* (1993), *Lord of the Three in One: The Spread of a Cult in Southeast China* (1998), and with Zheng Zhenman, *Epigraphical Materials on the History of Religion in Fujian* (3 vols.): *The Xinghua Region* (1995), and *The Quanzhou Region* (2004), and *Ritual Alliances of the Putian Plain*, 2 vols. (2010).

Brian R. Dott is associate professor of history, Whitman College. He received his Ph.D. in Chinese history from the University of Pittsburgh in 1998. He is the author of *Identity Reflections: Pilgrimages to Mount Tai in Late Imperial China* (2004). His current research examines the emergence of Mount Tai as a national symbol for China, and the cultural impacts of the introduction of the chili pepper into East Asia.

Xiaofei Kang was educated at Beijing and Columbia universities. She has taught at St. Mary's College of Maryland and Carnegie Mellon University and in fall 2010 joins the Religious Studies Department at George Washington University. She is the author of *Power on the Margins: The Cult of the Fox in Late Imperial and Modern North China* (2005) and coauthor of a forthcoming book, *Contesting the Yellow Dragon*, with Donald Sutton. Her current research examines elderly women in Chinese religion.

Charlene Makley received her Ph.D. in anthropology at the University of Michigan (1999). An associate professor of anthropology at Reed College in Portland, Oregon, she is the author of *The Violence of Liberation: Gender and Tibetan Buddhist Revival in Post-Mao China* published in 2007. Her current book project has the working title *Development and State Violence Among Tibetans in China: An Olympic Year*.

Susan K. McCarthy is an associate professor of political science at Providence College in Rhode Island. She received her Ph.D. in political science from the University of California at Berkeley in 2001. She is the author of *Communist Multiculturalism: Ethnic Revival in Southwest China* (2009). Her latest project examines faith-based civil society organizations in contemporary China.

Charles F. McKhann (Ph.D., University of Chicago) is professor of anthropology and director of Asian studies at Whitman College. He has been studying religion, art, social organization, ethnicity, history, and tourism in southwest China for twenty-five years. His most recent article is "Taming the Dragon: The Search for Sustainable Tourism in Southwest China" in *International Journal of Environmental, Cultural, Economic and Social Sustainability* (2005/2006). He is currently writing about the life of David C. Graham, American anthropologist, missionary, museum curator, and collector in Sichuan (1911–1948).

Tim Oakes teaches cultural geography at the University of Colorado, Boulder. He is the author of *Tourism and Modernity in China* (1998), and coeditor of *Translocal China* (2006), *Travels in Paradox* (2006), *Reinventing Tunpu* (in Chinese, 2007), and *The Cultural Geography Reader* (2008). His research focuses on cultural development, tourism, and culture industries in China.

Yu Luo Rioux received her Ph.D. in human geography from the University of Colorado at Boulder in 2008. Her primary research interests are in China's tourism development and landscape. Her most recent publication is "Green with Red: Environment and Jiangxi's Tourism Development" in *Asian Geographer* (2006, published 2009). She presented a paper on museums in China at the 2009 New England Regional Conference of the Association for Asian Studies at Brown University.

Donald S. Sutton, professor of history and anthropology at Carnegie Mellon University, recently wrote *Steps of Perfection: Exorcistic Performance and Chinese Religion in 20th Century Taiwan* (2003) and coedited *Empire at the*

Margins: Culture, Ethnicity and Frontier in Early Modern China (2006). Other projects nearing completion are a collaborative book with Xiaofei Kang on pilgrimage and tourism in northern Sichuan and a volume of his articles on ritual in Chinese societies.

Marina Svensson is an associate professor at the Centre for East and Southeast Asia Studies, Lund University, Sweden. Her research focuses on legal and social developments, as well as media and cultural heritage issues in China. She wrote *Debating Human Rights in China: A Conceptual and Political History* (Rowman and Littlefield, 2002), and coedited *The Chinese Human Rights Reader* (2001) with Stephen C. Angle. Recent coedited works are *Gender Equality, Citizenship and Human Rights in China and the Nordic Countries* (2010) and *Making Law Work: Chinese Laws in Context* (2010).

Rubie Watson recently retired as curator of comparative ethnology at the Peabody Museum and senior lecturer in anthropology, Harvard University. She was the director of the Peabody Museum, Harvard University, from 1997 to 2004. She is the author, among other works, of *Inequality Among Brothers: Class and Kinship in South China* (1985), the editor of *Memory, History and Opposition under State Socialism* (1994), and the coauthor (with James L. Watson) of *Village Life in Hong Kong* (2003).